CHRONICLING HISTORY

CHRONICLING HISTORY

CHRONICLERS AND HISTORIANS IN MEDIEVAL AND RENAISSANCE ITALY

EDITED BY

Sharon Dale,
Alison Williams Lewin,
and
Duane J. Osheim

THE PENNSYLVANIA STATE UNIVERSITY PRESS
UNIVERSITY PARK, PENNSYLVANIA

Library of Congress Cataloging-in-Publication Data

Chronicling history : chroniclers and historians in medieval and Renaissance Italy /
edited by Sharon Dale, Alison Williams Lewin, and Duane J. Osheim.
p.   cm.
Includes bibliographical references and index.
ISBN 978-0-271-03226-9 (pbk. : alk. paper)
1. Italy—History—476–1268—Sources.
2. Italy—History—1268–1492—Sources.
3. Historiography—Italy—History—To 1500.
I. Dale, Sharon, 1951– .
II. Lewin, Alison Williams, 1957– .
III. Osheim, Duane J.

DG501.C48 2007
945.0072'02—dc22
2007019547

CONTENTS

PREFACE

This collection of essays began with papers at a number of conferences prompted by a perceived need to boost recognition of the interest and vitality of the local historians of the towns and regions of Italy. The editors would like to thank our collaborators for their patience with what has turned out to be a long process. We also would like to thank Gregory Hays, Alessandro Vettori, Ben Kohl, and Samuel Edwards for advice about some of the translations, and Keith Monley, who saved us from many gaffes. Finally, we would like to thank Peter Potter for his encouragement of this project from our first discussions.

INTRODUCTION

Literally thousands of annals, chronicles, and histories were produced in Italy during the Middle Ages, ranging from fragments to polished humanist treatises. This book offers eleven case studies exploring the kinds of historical writing most characteristic of the late Middle Ages and Renaissance. It is meant to serve as an introduction to this largely unappreciated historical resource.[1]

The volume and diversity of Italian historical literature reflect a complex society that evolved from the creation of the Lombard kingdom through the forging of a political order based on communes and finally into a system of regional Renaissance states. While waves of conquest maintained monarchic rule in the south of Italy, the papacy claimed temporal control of a broad swath of central Italy. Thus, the historical circumstances that created strong centralized monarchies in northern Europe did not exist in Italy. Instead, its history is a fractured mosaic of local and regional stories. As Italians displayed their extraordinary capacity for evolving new and contrasting types of communities and forms of government, they explained their experiences in an equally creative chronicle tradition.

Chroniclers were not modern detached historians. They were opinionated, often deeply partisan, and intensely personal. Idiosyncrasy and anecdote pervade their accounts. Yet their value to historians is inestimable. Often our only sources of information about momentous events,[2] they have shaped the historiography of Italy. Moreover, it is precisely this mix of the anecdotal and the historic, of portents and politics, that makes these writers so engaging to read.

We might expect a typical medieval chronicler to be a monk or cleric, but the chroniclers of communal and Renaissance Italy were overwhelmingly secular. Many were jurists or notaries, whose professions granted them access

---

1. An exception and the indispensable starting point for any study of Italian chronicles is the classic study by Louis Green, *Chronicle into History: An Essay on the Interpretation of History in Florentine Fourteenth-Century Chronicles* (Cambridge: Cambridge University Press, 1972). See as well Gary Ianziti, *Humanistic Historiography Under the Sforzas: Politics and Propaganda in Fifteenth-Century Milan* (Oxford: Oxford University Press, 1988), and Eric Cochrane, *Historians and Historiography in the Italian Renaissance* (Chicago: University of Chicago Press, 1981).
2. For example, Giovanni Villani's account of the crowning of the antipope Nicholas V in 1328.

to political institutions and public debate. Others were merchants, reflecting the importance of trade, banking, and business in the history of Italian cities. But most of all they were townsmen, and it is in the city that their accounts are situated. Although a past framed by Rome or an evocative *Italia* often provided chroniclers with some variant of a foundation myth, it was the promotion of the greatness of one's own city that inspired most chroniclers. Even the chroniclers of important families such as the Carrara or the Visconti were shaped by a sense of place, be it Padua or Milan.

Paul the Deacon, who wrote in the eighth century, established a much imitated precedent with his *History of the Lombards.* Portraying the Lombards' evolution from a primitive and rustic conquering tribe to a sophisticated and complex dynasty that dominated Italy, Paul's *History* became the narrative touchstone for numerous early writers, particularly in southern Italy, where Norman and Hohenstaufen conquerors replaced Arab and Lombard rulers. An alternative, short on narrative but often endowed with bursts of eyewitness description, was the annalist tradition, whose emergence coincided with the flowering of the northern Italian communes in the twelfth century. Perhaps the greatest stimulus for the production of chronicles was Italian cities' emerging maritime dominance. Rivalry between cities and sometimes between families was keen and stoked a desire to justify current status with a propitious past. The chronicle form provided the right blend of past and present.

This book approaches the diversity and creativity of the Italian historical tradition through a series of introductory essays and extensive translations from a number of Italian chronicles composed between the twelfth and the fifteenth centuries. The chronicles vary greatly by time and place; they also differ from the spare annals and chronicles generally composed in northern Europe during the same period. In northern Europe it was clerics, bishops, monks, and secular clergy who were inspired to write. And not surprisingly their concerns revolved about the royal court, the episcopal palace, and the monastic house.[3]

In medieval Italy concerns were different. The annalists with whom we begin mark a transformation in Italian historical writing. The older tradition of the ninth and tenth centuries that followed on the work of Paul the Deacon had largely disappeared along with any sense of the early medieval Italian state. As described by Edward Coleman, the annalists recorded the wars

---

3. Bernard Guenée, *Histoire et culture historique dans l'Occident médiéval* (Paris: Aubier Montaigne, 1980), 44–73, is an outline of the people in northern Europe who most often wrote histories in the High Middle Ages.

and exploits of the twelfth-century Lombard towns, the immediate events that dramatically affected life in their cities. They paid scant attention to the distant past and had little sense of how their own experiences were connected to the wider world. In the Genoese chronicle tradition, as John Dotson makes clear, that narrow understanding of what should be recorded expanded over the course of the twelfth and thirteenth centuries. Genoese annalists began to include internal political and institutional information in addition to the wars and lists of officials that were the traditional fare of annalists.

The essays by Graham Loud and Alison Williams Lewin offer an important counterpoint to the Lombard and Genoese annalist traditions. Loud introduces readers to "the other Norman Conquest," the one less remembered in the Anglophone world. The migration of Norman adventurers to the south of Italy and their eventual creation of a Norman kingdom greatly altered the political dynamics of the Italian peninsula, and, significantly for our studies, the Norman histories of Italy more resembled their English counterparts than the communal annals of Lombardy. The central issue for these historians was the expansion and the power of the Norman kingdom.

Alison Williams Lewin's essay analyzes Salimbene de Adam's vision of Italian history. Salimbene spent most of his life traveling among the cities of northern and central Italy. But he was uninterested in communal government or political life, unless, of course, either influenced his beloved Franciscan religious order or his understanding of God's plan for history. In some respects Salimbene's chronicle resembles northern religious writing. Its first chapters, now lost, began with creation and maintained a fairly traditional Christian frame of sin and salvation. Nonetheless, Salimbene was describing life in an Italian cultural world. He was profoundly influenced by the prophecies of Joachim of Fiore and the common belief that Italy and the world would shortly enter Joachim's "Third Age of the Spirit" and that Final Judgment must soon follow. It was in this context that Salimbene recorded religious life in Italy and the history of Emperor Frederick II, the medieval emperor who attempted to unite northern and southern Italy into the largely German medieval empire.

The fourteenth century was the great age of chronicle writing. Our essays outline a far-ranging and discontinuous transformation of such writing until we reach the historians of the fifteenth century, who intended to place Italy in a broad historical context.[4] Essays on Florence, Lucca, Milan, and Venice

---

4. The bibliography on Italian historical writings is immense. The following works in English are especially useful. On the precommunal historical tradition, see the essays collected in Chris J. Wickham, *Land and Power: Studies in Italian and European Social History*,

demonstrate the range of complexity and purpose that can be found in fourteenth-century chronicles. Paula Clarke introduces us to Giovanni and Matteo Villani of Florence. Giovanni Villani may well be the most famous chronicler of medieval Italy, and his work certainly represents the most sophisticated of the four fourteenth-century traditions represented here. More than the compilers of the Lombard and Genoese annals, the Villani chroniclers place their Florentine hometown, and indeed all of Tuscany, in a broader, more historical frame. Giovanni Villani famously announces that he resolved to write his history after a pilgrimage to Rome, which revealed to him that Florence was in no way inferior to that historic city. As Clarke makes clear, the resulting *New Chronicle* was composed in the context of Florence's Roman heritage, its growing importance in Tuscany, and its tumultuous social and political life. For Villani, Florence's ancient history was a key to understanding its present dilemmas.

Giovanni Sercambi's Lucca was a very different sort of Tuscan town, and the history Sercambi produced was much less sophisticated—more narrowly focused and less ambitious—than Villani's meditation on history, morality, and politics. As Duane Osheim indicates, Sercambi's emphasis is liberty. He explains how Lucca lost its political liberty early in the fourteenth century, regained it in 1369, and struggled to retain its liberty in the late fourteenth and early fifteenth centuries. In many respects his concentration on contemporary local events recalls the earlier Lombard annalists, insofar as he viewed most events from the limited perspective of their immediate significance for his own city. Like many of our historians, Sercambi feared the divisive effects of faction and assumed that discord, violence, and lack of communal feeling were a direct result of human moral failings and the insidious workings of the devil. Ironically, as Osheim shows, Sercambi began by describing the restoration of liberty through republican government. But as a result of factional struggles in Lucca, he ends up advocating one-man rule in the hands of Paolo Guinigi. Sercambi always saw himself as a defender of Lucchese liberty, but to his mind the means of protecting that liberty had radically changed between 1369 and 1400.

Whereas Sercambi viewed the events of the late fourteenth century from behind the beleaguered walls of his provincial town, Galvano Fiamma and Pietro Azario, the Lombard chroniclers Sharon Dale introduces, recorded

---

400–1200 (London: British School at Rome, 1994), esp. "The Sense of the Past in Twelfth-Century City Chronicles," 295–312; Green, *Chronicle into History*; and Cochrane, *Historians and Historiography*.

the events of the tumultuous rise of the Visconti family first in Milan and later throughout Lombardy. Especially in Azario's telling, it is the Visconti and not the communal governments that offer hope. And the prize they offer is not the liberty that Sercambi and other Tuscans celebrated, but peace. It was a twofold peace, an end to factional divisions within cities and also an end to the endemic warfare between towns and regions. Unlike the earlier Lombard annalists of the twelfth century, Dale's Lombard chroniclers had a clear concept of Lombardy and Italy, a perspective that differs significantly from the Tuscan view of the Italian world found in Giovanni Sercambi and the Villani.

Venetian historical writing in general and *The Morosini Codex* in particular present a quite different historiographical situation, as John Melville Jones elucidates, for Venice lacked ancient religious or cultural roots. It was a new city, made wealthy through trade with the eastern Mediterranean. Many of the stories that Venetians recalled about themselves and their world reflect a strong imperative to justify their prominence in the Italian world. *The Morosini Codex* itself is what one scholar has called a "social chronicle."[5] In Venice the production of historical works by members of the Venetian patriciate was a sign of family nobility and an opportunity to celebrate the accomplishments of ancestors while simultaneously recounting important events in the city's history. Unlike the Villani chroniclers of Florence or the chroniclers of Visconti Lombardy, who worked in a limited historical tradition, Venetians read and copied from each other to the point that it is nearly impossible to follow various historical tales to their origin.

The Morosini Codex marks a notable transition in the Italian chronicle tradition. The last three essays in our book reflect the more complex world of the late fourteenth and fifteenth centuries. It is a world of courts, emerging regional states, and renewed humanistic interest in the past. Benjamin Kohl's discussion of the historians of Carrara Padua reveals the transformation of historical writing in a courtly milieu. As his title indicates, the experience at Padua, an ancient republican commune now firmly under the control of the Carrara dynasty, illustrates how civic chronicles were reformulated into legends that celebrated the noble rulers of the city. Giovanni Conversini da Ravenna was a courtier in the fullest Renaissance sense. He lived at the feet of Francesco il Vecchio Carrara, and he tells the favorite Carrara myth that the family was descended from Carolingian and imperial origins and thus had a natural right to rule in Padua as well as claims to

5. John Kenneth Hyde, "Italian Social Chronicles in the Middle Ages," *Bulletin of the John Rylands Library* 49 (1966): 107–32.

many other parts of the Veneto. His was a history, or perhaps a myth, with obvious social and political utility. At virtually the same time, as Kohl shows, Pier Paolo Vergerio wrote a history of the family using the available historical sources. His work was innovative because he consciously followed the models for historical biography in the classical works of Suetonius and Plutarch. His was, in short, a humanist work that subtly investigated the interests and motivations of the Carrara lords.

In his use of classical models and in his consciousness of classical historical traditions, Vergerio was similar to the last two historians considered in this book. Gary Ianziti's introduction to Leonardo Bruni's *History of the Florentine People* makes a telling comparison with Paula Clarke's study of the Villani. Bruni and the Villani studied the same subject, Florence and its state, and Bruni knew the work of the Villani; but written in the fifteenth century, his work challenges and transforms the chronicle tradition. As Ianziti explains, Bruni provides a fresh paradigm for Florentine history, one that recognizes the newly important oligarchic domination of Florentine public life, the concomitant promotion of professional government, and the value of prudence as the supreme attribute of that government.

As Nicoletta Pellegrino shows, Flavio Biondo also creates a new paradigm. But Biondo, a papal secretary, writes from an Italian perspective and not from a regional or communal one. Like Vergerio and Bruni, Biondo was conscious of the connection between papal Rome, and indeed Italy as a whole, and the political and intellectual heritage of classical Rome. In his *Decades* he is acutely aware of Roman language and traditions. The Roman heritage provides the context in which Biondo understands the history of the Italian cities that are at the heart of our chronicles.

Flavio Biondo's history marks a convenient stopping point for this book. The French invasion of 1494 and the wars that followed in its wake destabilized and transformed Italy, its regions and its cities. And the histories of Niccolò Machiavelli and Francesco Guicciardini reflect that new reality. Both writers discarded the classical and humanistic aims of Bruni and Biondo, but they appreciated and used the Florentine tradition represented by the Villani. They shared a political realism found in the vernacular historians, but they wrote about factions and the wealthy optimates in a different context. Guicciardini ultimately wrote about Italy, not Florence, and the context of his history was Europe.[6]

6. On Machiavelli, Guicciardini, and the Florentine historical tradition, see Mark S. Phillips, "Machiavelli, Guicciardini, and the Tradition of Vernacular Historiography in Florence," *American Historical Review* 84 (1979): 86–105.

Hans-Werner Goetz has observed that historical writings are a complex of present concerns and knowledge of the past.[7] In that sense, Italian chronicles must first be seen as a subset of the medieval tradition of historical writing. Italian chronicles shared religious ideas, imperial symbols, and, in some cases, the chivalric ethos of northern writers. In a series of lectures before the Royal Historical Society, Richard Southern outlined three distinct themes that seemed to characterize much of medieval European historiography.[8] The first was royal history, largely based on classical Roman images of both secular and divine rulership. This was a tradition that continued strongly until the religious reforms of the late eleventh century made ideas of divine kingship highly controversial. A second theme was divine direction of universal history. Hugh of St. Victor, for example, saw God's covenant with Abraham and later the New Covenant of the birth and sacrifice of Christ as marking two of the three ages of human history. Finally, building in many respects on ideas of universal history, writers influenced by Joachim of Fiore and various prophetic texts wrote history as eschatology, a way to mark the progression to the *eschaton*, the End Days before Final Judgment.

In northern Europe the chronicles that dealt with these themes were usually written by clerics, in the context of a monastery or a royal or noble court. The narrative was most easily organized around the lives of succeeding abbots or kings. Whether the focus was monastic or royal, the narrative often justified rights and privileges. Writers occasionally even inserted copies or descriptions of charters. Some writers, especially those at court, described chivalric traditions at the local or regional level. Chronicles charted the rise of elite families and established their claims to local and even national preeminence. Their tales were often military. Jean Froissart explained that his history of what would be called the Hundred Years' War was written "in order that the great deeds of arms . . . should be prominently recorded and committed to perpetual memory . . . and credited to those who, by their prowess, have performed them."[9]

7. Hans-Werner Goetz, *Geschichtsschreibung und Geschichtsbewusstsein im hohen Mittelalter* (Berlin: Akademie Verlag, 1999), is especially concerned with the historians who wrote in the context of the great eleventh-century church-reform movements.

8. Richard Southern, "Aspects of the European Tradition of Historical Writing," *Transactions of the Royal Historical Society*, 5th ser., 20 (1970): 173–96; 21 (1971): 159–79; 22 (1972): 159–79.

9. Quoted in Chris Given-Wilson, *Chronicles: The Writing of History in Medieval England* (London and New York: Hambledon, 2004), 99. On historical writing, see also Guenée, *Histoire;* Goetz, *Geschichtsschreibung;* and Donald R. Kelley, *Faces of History: Historical Inquiry from Herodotus to Herder* (New Haven and London: Yale University Press, 1998), 99–129.

Whether focused on noble families, religious figures, or heroic kings, historical works lend themselves to various forms of reading and analysis. Historians approach a text in one of three general ways: as a self-contained unit, as the product of an author, or as the product of an interpretative community.

The first approach emphasizes the text and the reader's response to it. Strongly influenced by modern critical and ideological movements, this "linguistic turn" in historiography is perhaps most closely identified with Hayden V. White and Dominick LaCapra.[10] In this view, texts are always contemporaneous with the person reading them. Each text is assumed to be complete and self-referential; thus meaning and understanding come from the literary, ideological, and cultural background of the reader. Moreover, texts do not depend on historical context for meaning, since it is already provided by the narrative pattern of the text itself. Patterns of symbols provide the social and cultural process by which the reader engages the text in a form of dialogue.[11]

Were one to apply Hayden White's analysis to the annals and chronicles in our book, one might profitably examine the early Lombard annals, with their spare prose entries, as a form of "narrativity" in which the plot exists as a "structure of relationships by which the events contained in the account are endowed with a meaning by being identified as parts of an integrated whole."[12] In this reading the context of the Cremona annals reveals itself as structured by Christian mission, war, violence, and contested authority. Likewise, one might examine any of our fourteenth-century chroniclers as participants in historical discourse in which events are judged real not because they occurred but rather because they are both remembered and then judged important enough to be included in a chronological sequence.

These theorists find medieval chronicles, in their often idiosyncratic inclusions, distortions, and omissions, to be excellent examples of the tension between the historical account that claims authority from reality itself and the narrative process that gives form, coherence, and authority to the text.[13] Theorists find earlier historical constructs to be "destructively oversimplified";

10. Hayden V. White, *Metahistory: The Historical Imagination in Nineteenth-Century Europe* (Baltimore: Johns Hopkins University Press, 1973), and idem, *The Content of the Form: Narrative Discourse and Historical Representation* (Baltimore: Johns Hopkins University Press, 1987). Dominick LaCapra, "Rethinking Intellectual History and Reading Texts," *History and Theory* 19 (1980): 245–76.

11. A useful reflection on these issues is Anthony Pagden, "Rethinking the Linguistic Turn: Current Anxieties in Intellectual History," *Journal of the History of Ideas* 49 (1988): 519–29.

12. White, *Content of the Form*, 9.

13. Ibid., 20.

newer linguistic approaches, on the other hand, can be "refreshing in their speculative intricacy."[14]

The second approach to historic texts emphasizes the interests, culture, and experiences of the author or compiler of a text. Chroniclers were often inspired to write by their own sense of living in important times or by witnessing significant events. Exemplified by Chris Given-Wilson's recent book on English chronicles,[15] this approach emphasizes the formation of the historian and the quality of source materials available. The chronicler is portrayed, in most cases, as a writer who is part of a complex intellectual tradition. The textual studies in this volume, treating the chronicles of Salimbene, Giovanni and Matteo Villani, Pietro Azario, and Giovanni Sercambi, reveal a range of autobiographical influences.

The third approach to historical texts emphasizes the community in which the text has been produced, the "social memory" of writers and readers, as James Fentress and Chris Wickham have termed it.[16] Here, chronicles are construed to operate like oral traditions. They are homeostatic; that is, they are written to reflect the issues and concerns of the people at the time they are composed. In effect, they include the materials necessary to explain how the ancient past is connected to the world in which the writer lived. This approach emphasizes the materials available to the author, as well as the language, values, and cultural milieu of the intended readers of the text. In this view, chronicles are not merely a collection of facts to be mined. Rather, facts, symbols, and images derive meaning from context. Thus detail can be added or subtracted, forgotten or invented, as necessary in order to create a history that makes sense at the point it is being written.

This is basically the technique used by Gabrielle Spiegel, who, in a series of essays, has investigated a number of medieval French historical works, seeking "to locate texts within specific social sites" in order then to examine the "situated uses of language" inherent in those texts and to understand how linguistic and social realities are interwoven.[17]

The intention of our essays is more modest. We hope to accomplish the essential first step of her project, returning a text "to its social and political

14. Nancy S. Struever, "The Study of Language and the Study of History," *Journal of Interdisciplinary History* 4 (1974): 413.

15. Given-Wilson, *Chronicles;* see also idem, *The Chronicle of Adam Usk, 1377–1421* (Oxford: Clarendon Press, 1997).

16. James Fentress and Chris Wickham, *Social Memory* (Oxford and Cambridge, Mass.: Blackwell, 1992).

17. Gabrielle Spiegel, *The Past as Text: The Theory and Practice of Medieval Historiography* (Baltimore: Johns Hopkins University Press, 1997), 27, 24.

context." And having accomplished that first step, a number of themes and historiographical concerns emerge from diverse worlds of our chroniclers. It is essential to note, for example, that the readily available frame for the twelfth-century annalist was the list of communal officials, or that Giovanni Sercambi had little more than folk memories and popular songs and poems available as a basis for parts of his chronicle. On the other hand, Morosini's Venetian codex was one of hundreds of fragmentary patrician historical tracts. And if chroniclers were partial to portents and signs of astrological or divine involvement in the affairs of the world, they were equally convinced that momentous events were frequently effected by the smallest precipitate. Thus the rebuke of a nobleman's servant by another lord could cause major warfare and complex political realignments. Similarly, larger patterns of diplomacy are explained by simple expedients: Matteo Villani, for example, dismissed a Visconti truce with the papacy as a ploy to gain approval for a pending marriage.

Yet, these texts are products of their times and places. Beginning with the annals of Lombardy, Italian texts reveal a keen sense of civic identity and rivalry with other cities, reflecting the reality of late medieval and Renaissance Italian political and economic life. Good governance and wise leadership are praised, if often laconically. Perhaps their rarity is the reason that corruption, duplicity, and cruelty by kings, lords, magistrates, and prelates are condemned even as wrongs are graphically and even salaciously examined. Scandal is more riveting than virtue, then as now. But the very act of writing about government and discerning good and bad in political life signals a sophisticated awareness of the possibilities inherent in government.

Chroniclers strove to place the events they saw unfolding around them in a scheme that made political and even ethical sense to them. Giovanni Villani's strongly Guelf vision stands in contrast to Matteo's more sophisticated and nuanced civic ideology formed in reaction against the factionalism and oligarchic ideas that came to dominate Florence. Giovanni Sercambi's definition of liberty mutates with the political transformation of Lucca. In war-ravaged Lombardy, Pietro Azario defines peace, not liberty, as the overarching goal of sound government. And in an emerging humanist world, chronicle will become legend in Padua, rationalize sovereignty in Florence, and revive a classical ideology in Rome.

While chroniclers may have had different reasons to write and often very different points of view, they shared a belief that the past might explain the present. Moreover, their audiences usually shared the worldviews and civic identities of the chroniclers, so that these texts are glimpses into deeper cultural and intellectual contexts. Seen more broadly, therefore, chronicles are far more than entertaining and informative narratives. They become part of the very history they are describing.

Yet chronicles are not static or frozen in time. Our introductory essays generally locate these chronicles in a social, historical, or biographical context. But these approaches do not preclude subjecting the chronicles, and perhaps the introductory essays as well, to a more "performative" reading. As LaCapra has suggestively observed, "We as interpreters [of text] are situated in a sedimented layering of readings that demand excavation."[18] Readers of the chapters that follow are invited to dig in the various and exciting products left by these creative and exciting communities.

18. LaCapra, "Rethinking Intellectual History," 261.

1

Lombard City Annals and the Social and Cultural History of Northern Italy

Edward Coleman

The Lombard chronicle-writing tradition is a product of the precocious wealth, power, and educational level of its cities.[1] Beginning early in the eleventh century, Milan, the largest Lombard city, produced no fewer than three important accounts of the conflict over ecclesiastical reform between 1050 and 1130. Further Milanese prose and verse material survives from the twelfth century, particularly the years during which the city led Lombard opposition to the German emperor Frederick I Barbarossa (1150s–1180s).[2] Smaller centers, such as Bergamo, Como, and Lodi, also produced significant texts. Thirteenth-century narrative sources from Lombard cities are still more abundant and varied and include works by such well-known and much studied authors as Bonvesin de la Riva and Salimbene.[3]

---

1. In this discussion Lombardy is understood as comprising the western half of the Po plain and the western foothills of the Alps. Confusingly, though, the entire north of the Italian peninsula was also commonly known as Lombardy and its inhabitants as Lombards; See Giancarlo Andenna, "Il concetto geografico-politico di Lombardia nel Medioevo," in *Comuni e signorie nell'Italia settentrionale: La Lombardia*, ed. Giancarlo Andenna et al., UTET: Storia d'Italia, 6 (Turin: UTET, 1998), 3–20, reprinted in idem, *Storia della Lombardia medievale* (Turin: UTET, 1999).

2. For general orientation on Milanese historiography in the medieval period, see Paolo Chiesa, ed., *Le cronache medievali di Milano* (Milan: Vita e pensiero, 2001).

3. Bonvesin de la Riva, "De magnalibus urbis Mediolani," ed. Francesco Novati, *Bullettino dell'Istituto storico italiano per il Medio Evo* 20 (1898): 61–176; Italian translation by Giuseppe Pontiggia, *Le meraviglie di Milano* (Milan: Bompiani, 1974). Salimbene de Adam, *Cronica a. 1168-1287*, ed. Giuseppe Scalia, Corpus Christianorum, Continuatio Mediaevalis, 75, 2 vols. (Turnhout: Brepols, 1998–99); English translation by Joseph L. Baird, Giuseppe Baglivi, and John Robert Kane, *The Chronicle of Salimbene de Adam*, Medieval and Renaissance Texts and Studies, 40 (Binghamton, N.Y.: Medieval and Renaissance Texts and Studies, 1986).

Importantly, not only were all of these chronicles written in cities, they were also about cities. Even Salimbene's religiously charged chronicle about popes and emperors frequently recounted events in his native Parma and other Lombard cities.[4] In other words, Lombard chroniclers, like their contemporaries in the neighboring Trevisan March and in the maritime republics of Genoa, Pisa, and Venice, viewed the world primarily through the prism of their cities. The history of Lombardy in the twelfth and thirteenth centuries is therefore composed of the histories of individual cities.[5] The communes achieved unprecedented economic expansion and political independence in these years, and they celebrated and commemorated their success in a variety of ways, including the commissioning of official city histories. Thus, as Eric Cochrane has correctly observed: "communal patriotism was the principal ingredient of north Italian chronicles."[6]

Despite their number and significance, these histories, representing a substantial and homogeneous body of source material, are not well understood. Virtually every narrative history of a major Lombard city during this period was composed in the form of year-by-year records of events, usually known as annals. Although numerous examples of city annals have been preserved, scant attention has been paid to them. Indeed, the first critical analysis of them as texts was undertaken by their late-nineteenth-century editors, who largely concerned themselves with sorting out manuscript traditions.[7] Historians of the Italian communes, on the other hand, have tended to regard annals simply as mines of factual data, sources for narrative history. Little serious attempt has been made to place them in a sociopolitical context, still less a cultural one.

Yet, on closer inspection it is apparent that many city annals provide more than the mere lists of consuls and "scattered notes" to which some historians

---

4. Ludovico Gatto, "Il sentimento cittadino nella 'Cronica' di Salimbene," in *La coscienza cittadina nei comuni italiani del Duecento,* Convegno del Centro di studi sulla spiritualità medievale, 11 (Todi: Accademia Tudertina, 1972), 365–94.

5. A survey of the communal period can be found in Edward Coleman, "Cities and Communes," in *Italy in the Central Middle Ages: 1000–1300,* ed. David Abulafia, The Shorter Oxford History of Italy, 2 (Oxford: Oxford University Press, 2003), 27–57.

6. Eric Cochrane, *Historians and Historiography in the Italian Renaissance* (Chicago: University of Chicago Press, 1981), 94.

7. The majority of city annals are to be found in volumes 18 (Hanover: Hahn, 1863) and 19 (Hanover: Hahn, 1866) of the *MGH: Scriptores* series, both edited by Georg Heinrich Pertz et al.: *Annales Bergomates,* 18:809–10; *Annales Brixienses,* 18:811–20; *Annales et Notae Parmenses et Ferrarienses,* 18:660–799; *Annales Mantuani,* 19:19–31; *Annales Mediolanenses,* 18:383–402; *Annales Placentini (Annales Gibellini),* 18:457–581. See also *Annales Cremonenses,* in *MGH: Scriptores,* 31, ed. Oswald Holder-Egger (Hanover: Hahn, 1903), 1–21.

have rather dismissively assumed them to be limited.[8] This is particularly so if one considers them as a group of related texts rather than in isolation. Given they are structurally analogous, focus on the same relatively restricted geographical and chronological space (the Po plain ca. 1100–1300), and exhibit many other similarities with regard to authorship, aims, and audience, they can easily and fruitfully be compared with one another. Accounts of the same events as recorded in annals of neighboring cities, or indeed in the annals of a single city for which more than one set of annals survives, provide historians with alternative, and often conflicting, views of the past. In other words, city annals may be used as a sort of controlled sample of the kaleidoscopic Lombard civic memory that was forged from the diverse experiences of different cities.

Annals and Chronicles: Some Terminological Issues

Annals and chronicles have different origins. Annals are generally thought to derive from the marginal and interlinear historical notes entered in Easter Tables, records compiled in monasteries in the seventh and eighth centuries and used to calculate the correct date for Easter. Chronicles, on the other hand, evolved ultimately out of the two great historiographical traditions— namely the Greco-Roman and the Judeo-Christian—which mingled and cross-fertilized in the early medieval West.[9] Through time, however, the distinctions between annals and chronicles became blurred, as medieval writers noted. Gervase of Canterbury, writing in the late twelfth century, for example, states that the purpose of *both* chronicles *and* annals was to record events, portents, miracles, and the deeds of princes within an accurate chronological framework.[10] But in the nineteenth and twentieth centuries, when scholars were assembling compendia of medieval sources, they tended once again to separate annals and chronicles into distinct generic categories.[11]

8. Cochrane, *Historians and Historiography*, 90.

9. Beryl Smalley, *Historians in the Middle Ages* (London: Thames & Hudson, 1974), and Denys Hay, *Annalists and Historians: Western Historiography from the Eighth to the Fifteenth Century* (London: Methuen, 1977), provide accessible introductions to the topic.

10. Janet Coleman, *Ancient and Medieval Memories* (Cambridge: Cambridge University Press, 1992), 298–300.

11. See *Repertorium Fontium Historiae Medii Aevi*, vol. 2 (Rome: Istituto storico italiano per il Medio Evo, 1967), where annals are listed separately (243–53) from chronicles. A similar distinction is made in R. C. van Caenegem, *Guide to the Sources of Medieval History* (Amsterdam: North-Holland Publishing Company, 1978), 18–25, 30–34.

Various criteria were formulated to differentiate annals from chronicles, and these are still broadly accepted today. Structural and stylistic considerations carry particular weight. The structure of annals derives from the discrete year-by-year entries, the content of which is not necessarily linked, while chronicles present a flowing and uninterrupted narrative. Stylistically, annals are usually more repetitive and less accomplished than chronicles; they make greater use of literary clichés and lesser use of classical, biblical, and patristic allusion. There are also differences of spatial and temporal perspective: annals are generally more narrow and local in their coverage than chronicles; chronicle history moves toward a predetermined end within an eschatological framework, whereas annal history appears more random in its beginning and end. The two genres of chronicle and annal are also distinguished by authorship: most chronicles are written by a single individual whose identity and background are known; annals are by their nature the work of more than one author, most of whom remain anonymous.[12]

While such criteria are generally valid, they tend to denigrate any source classified as an annal, creating the impression that chronicles are *per se* more useful and more interesting than annals. Even the common statement that chronicles are "written," while annals are merely "compiled," carries the inherent implication that the chronicler is a literary figure, whereas the annalist is simply a collector and synthesizer of factual data.

The creation of a kind of hierarchy in modern source criticism in which chronicles rank above annals may have contributed to the neglect of Lombard city annals. If so, this is particularly unfortunate, since it is arguable that in the specific case of Lombardy the issue is more terminological than substantive. In the first place, the nineteenth-century editorial practice of grouping together and classifying various twelfth- and thirteenth-century Lombard city histories as annals does not always respect their designation in earlier editions, or indeed in manuscripts.[13] Furthermore, the typological

---

12. A basic introduction can be found in Michael McCormick, *Les annales du haut Moyen Âge*, Typologie des sources du Moyen Âge occidental, 14 (Turnhout: Brepols, 1975); for Italy, see Girolamo Arnaldi, "Annali, cronache, storie," in *Lo spazio letterario del Medioevo*, sect. 1, *Il Medioevo latino*, ed. Guglielmo Cavallo, Claudio Leonardi, and Enrico Menestò, vol. 1, *La produzione del testo* (Rome: Salerno, 1993), pt. 2, 463–513, esp. 473–75, 484.

13. For example, although in the original manuscript of Giovanni Codagnello's "Annals of Piacenza" the text is indeed entitled *Annales Placentini*, it was given the title *Chronicum Placentinum* in the first edition, published in 1856; then, seven years later, the *MGH: Scriptores* edition reverted to *Annales Placentini*. See Bruno Andreolli et al., eds., *Repertorio della cronachistica emiliano-romagnola (secc. IX–XV)*, Nuovi studi storici, 11 (Rome: Istituto storico italiano per il Medio Evo, 1991), 269.

categorization of annals and chronicles commonly found in modern guides to medieval sources is based almost exclusively on north European examples; in the case of annals this means texts produced in an episcopal or, above all, monastic environment.[14]

Lombard city annals do not conform to this type. Their origins are far from clear, but it is indisputable that they are highly secular works. Therefore no reason exists to suppose that they are based on ecclesiastical models or in any way linked to them. Indeed, the sharp distinction that has been drawn between annals and chronicles seems inappropriate for northern Italy generally, where the similarities between the two types of narrative are more apparent than the differences. In Lombardy both chronicles and annals are civic in tone and content, and their authors are, as often as not, educated laymen, frequently members of the urban notariate or communal officeholders. Both display a strong preference for recording local, as opposed to general, history, and both concentrate their attention heavily on recent and contemporary events. Stylistically, city annals are generally more terse and less polished than city chronicles; but even so, some Lombard texts that have been classed as annals go well beyond the simple and brief recording of events normally associated with the annal form. Moreover, particularly if one reads parallel extracts from more than one annal, with an eye to the selection and omission of material on the part of their authors, it can be seen not only that they contain bias, which is in itself hardly surprising, but also that they communicate subtle, one might even say subliminal, messages, which probably would have been well understood by their readership. In sum, the characteristics of Lombard city chronicles and city annals are not so very different; although for the sake of convenience the terminological distinction between chronicle and annal will be retained in the following discussion when citing sources, the reader should not interpret this rigidly.

The Making of City Annals

One of the characteristics of the annal genre is the arrangement of the text in year-by-year entries, although every year may not receive an entry, and the entries themselves may vary in length. In common with other European annals, it is likely that Lombard city annals were compiled either synchronically or diachronically, by which I mean that texts were either composed to

---

14. In *Les annales*, Michael McCormick mentions city annals only very briefly in passing.

reflect a single point in time or composed after the passage of a number of years to narrate the changes that had taken place. In each the narrative is arranged by year, but information would have been entered either for each year, at its end, or for a bloc of several years at one time. Some entries would also have been revised at a later date. The precise process of compilation of an annal can only be determined on paleographic grounds, and it is thus unfortunate that the majority of Lombard annals only survive in later copies. Nevertheless, the techniques of compilation employed by the various annalists at work on the same text can often be discerned through careful analysis of its content.

Although at first sight the year-by-year format of annals suggests they were normally compiled synchronically, closer inspection often reveals evidence for diachronic compilation and revision. This point may be illustrated by considering a series of entries from the annals of the city of Cremona, which refer to a war between Cremona and its smaller neighbor Crema:[15]

> 1098. There was the first war with Crema. . . .
> 1130. There was the second war with Crema. Ribald and Anselm were consuls in the kalends of June. . . .
> 1157. There was the third war with Crema, on the eighth day before the end of May. . . .[16]

Here the Cremonese annalist was apparently aware when noting the "first war" with Crema in 1098 that a second war would erupt in 1130 and third war in 1157. It would seem likely, therefore, either that all three entries were written after 1157 or that the earlier entries were revised at some point. In either scenario the entries for 1098 and 1130, in the form we have them now, could not have been written in or immediately after the year to which they refer, or synchronically. Another example of a diachronic entry or revision occurs in the same annals, under the year 1218: "In the same year [1218], peace was made between the Milanesi and Piacentini and their party, and the Cremonesi and Parmigiani and their party, by Hugh, bishop of Ostia and Velleteri, cardinal of the apostolic see, who later became pope and took the name Gregory IX."[17] The key word in this extract is obviously "later." As it stands, although the entry refers to the year 1218, it must have been written or revised in or after 1227, the year Gregory IX became pope.

---

15. More extensive extracts from this text are translated in the appendix to this article.
16. *Annales Cremonenses*, 3–5.
17. Ibid., 14.

Obviously, annals that are kept up over a long period of time (even allow-ing for a mixture of synchronic and diachronic compilation) cannot be the work of a single author. Annals are thus always multiauthor works, compiled by successive authors, each one taking up his pen where his predecessor left off, when death or some other circumstance intervened. The voluminous annals of Genoa, discussed in Chapter 3 by John Dotson, are the best-known example of this process.[18] Successive authorship doubtless occurred in the annal production of smaller cities where we have little or no information on the annalists. In the Cremona annals, for example, a clear break occurs at the year 1182, after which the entries are written in a different style and are much fuller. It would seem very likely that this represents a change in authorship.

Although most Lombard annalists are anonymous, it is widely agreed that, like the authors of many city chronicles, they were often notaries. This mingling of the notarial profession and the practice of history writing is of fundamental importance. It imparted a particular character and style to the annals, which are strikingly similar from city to city. It also helped to embed notaries as a group at the heart of the political life of their city. The key role of the notary/chronicler was first highlighted by Girolamo Arnaldi and has recently been reassessed by Gabriele Zabbia.[19] They concentrate on later-thirteenth- and fourteenth-century authors, and on areas outside Lom-bardy, but many of their observations are relevant to Lombard sources.

The main function of the notary was the redaction of legal documents. Notaries enjoyed *publica fides* (public trust)—in recognition of their pro-fessional status—which meant that their act of writing a document in itself authenticated it.[20] The same status may also apply to histories written by

18. Luigi Tommaso Belgrano and Cesare Imperiale di Sant'Angelo, eds., *Annali gen-ovesi di Caffaro e de' suoi continuatori dal MXCIX al MCCXCIII,* Fonti per la storia d'Italia, 11–14bis, 5 vols. (Rome: Tipografia del Regio istituto sordo-muti, 1890–1929).

19. Girolamo Arnaldi, "Il notai-cronista e le cronache cittadine in Italia," in *La storia del diritto nel quadro delle scienze storiche* (Florence: Leo S. Olschki, 1966), 293–309; idem, "Cronache con documenti, cronache 'autentiche' e pubblica storiografia," in *Fonti medioevali e problematica storiografica* (Rome: Istituto storico italiano per il Medio Evo, 1976), 1:351–74, reprinted in *Storici e storiografia del Medioevo italiano,* ed. Gabriele Zanella (Bologna: Pàtron editore, 1984), 111–37. Arnaldi's classic work, *Studi sui cronisti della Marca trevigiana nell'età di Ezzelino da Romano,* Istituto storico italiano per il Medio Evo: Studi storici, 48–50 (Rome: Istituto Palazzo Borromini, 1963), was republished with a postscript by Marino Zabbia in 1998. Marino Zabbia, *I notai e la cronachistica cittadina italiana nel trecento,* Istituto storico italiano per il Medio Evo: Nuovi studi storici, 49 (Rome: Istituto Palazzo Borromini, 1999).

20. Gian Giacomo Fissore, "Alle origini del documento comunale: Rapporti fra i notai e l'istituzione," in *Civiltà comunale: Libro, scrittura, documento,* Atti della Società ligure di storia patria, n.s., 29 (103), fasc. 2 (Genoa: Società ligure di storia patria, 1989), 99–128.

notaries, thus giving these a public or official character—making them *croniche authentiche,* as Arnaldi has put it.[21] Certainly many of the better-known city annals and chronicles written by men with a notarial background were adopted as official city histories: Caffaro's annals of Genoa, Rolandino of Padua's chronicle of the cities of the Trevisan March (extracts of which were read at meetings of the ruling council of Padua), Martino da Canal's chronicle of Venice, Ogerio Alfieri's history of Asti.[22] It seems reasonable to think that the anonymous annals of the Lombard cities, so similar in other ways to these more celebrated works, shared this official character.

Other functions fulfilled by notaries amply qualified them to be civic historians. They were charged with the compilation of *libri iurium,* literally "books of rights," which a number of city communes ordered to be drawn up in the thirteenth century as a handy reference to the nature, location, and antiquity of their rights and privileges.[23] Later they were involved in the production of the first city statutes and maintained the minute books of the commune's council meetings. They also served as custodians of the archives of the commune. Notaries thus had access to and familiarity with all the relevant documentation that a historian would require. Moreover, they were intimately acquainted with how city government worked and with the men who ran it. In this sense the writing of city history was a natural extension of their activities, and a task that they appear to have readily embraced. Crucially, their close association with the commune, which provided them with employment and a certain social status in the urban community, would almost inevitably have predisposed them to hold a positive and patriotic view of city history, particularly in the period since the establishment of the communal regime.

Concepts of Space and Time

To a considerable degree, the interests of Lombard city annalists were spatially and temporally circumscribed. The spatial limits of the annals' coverage corresponded fairly closely to the area of the Po plain. But even within this relatively restricted area each city annal had its own smaller zone of interest—namely the city, the city territory, and the territories of its immediate

---

21. Arnaldi, "Cronache con documenti," 360–61, 368–69.
22. Cochrane, *Historians and Historiography,* 63, 67, 93–94.
23. Antonella Rovere, "I 'libri iurium' dell'Italia comunale," in *Civiltà comunale: Libro, scrittura, documento,* 157–99.

neighbors. The only exceptions to this rule were events that affected the region as a whole, such as the relatively rare occurrence of large-scale warfare involving many cities, as opposed to the more common local skirmishing between just one or two protagonists. The most obvious examples of the former are the military campaigns conducted by the emperor Frederick I Barbarossa against the Lombard League in the years 1158–76, which are mentioned in virtually all city annals. However, the annal structure dictated that these wars not be treated as a continuous and coherent story; instead, they appeared episodically under annual entries. Furthermore, the tendency on the part of each annalist to concentrate on events that occurred within his particular local zone of interest and to give little attention to—or even omit—other developments means that an overall view of Barbarossa's wars is conspicuously absent in the annal accounts.[24] The inward-looking attitude of the city annals perfectly reflects the self-centeredness of the city communes with regard to their political and military alignments, whether pro- or anti-imperial. But it is also indicative of a general parochialism that pervades the annalists' selection, organization, and recording of data.

Apart from the parallel notices of Frederick I's wars, a number of annals also have entries in common relating to weather conditions and natural phenomena, the effects of which were felt across the whole region at roughly the same time. This is particularly true of earthquakes. Lombardy was struck by major earthquakes in 1117 and in 1222. The epicenter of the latter appears to have been in or around the city of Brescia, and its devastating effects are widely recorded, as, for example, in the following entries in the annals of the nearby cities of Parma, Bergamo, and Milan:

> [*Parma*] 1222. In that year there was a great earthquake throughout all of Italy, and it was on Christmas Day between the sixth and the ninth hour; and men fled out of the city believing they would soon die; and a large part of Brescia was destroyed.[25]

> [*Bergamo*] 1222. In the same year, on the day of the Lord's Nativity, around the sixth hour, there was a great earthquake; and chiefly in Brescia and its district numerous buildings collapsed and many men and women died.[26]

24. The most coherent accounts are to be found in the Lodi annals of Otto and Acerbo Morena and in the major annals of Milan.
25. *Annales et Notae Parmenses et Ferrarienses*, 667.
26. *Annales Bergomates*, 809.

[*Milan*] 1223. On the eighth day before the kalends of January (25 December), Sunday, around the sixth hour, there was a great earthquake in the whole of Italy; and it brought about the total destruction of the city of Brescia and devastation in the same bishopric; and many men, women, and children were killed in that city.[27]

Drought and famine were also frequently recorded in the annals, though the scatter of entries relating to different years suggests that the effects of these, unlike earthquakes, were often quite localized. Annalists usually recorded the price of grain in times of shortage and were occasionally moved to describe the hardship endured by the population, as in this passage in the major annals of Parma relating to the years 1180–81:

> The lord Ugo Arpinio and Guido Rogerio and Guido Barato and Alberto Gilio and Alberto Tebaldo of Parma were consuls in 1181. And in the following time there was a famine because a *sextarius* of corn was being sold for four or five imperial *solidi*, and a *sextarius* of spelt for two imperial *solidi*. And there was an immense mortality among men in these two years in the city of Parma and in many other places, such that four or five bodies were brought every day to the cathedral church of Holy Mary for the greater part of the said two years, and in many another church of Parma five, eight, ten, or more were brought daily for burial in the one church.[28]

Rivers, especially the Po, the main artery of transport across the plain for people and merchandise, were closely monitored by the annalists. Rivers were important for irrigation but could be dangerous in extreme weather conditions. Consequently city annals recorded when they burst their banks (1180, 1194)[29] or froze over (1116, 1216).[30] Other natural phenomena—exceptionally heavy rainfalls or snowfalls, for example—are noted when they happened to catch the attention of the particular annalist.[31] Among the more unusual reports are a gold rush in the hills around Brescia[32] and the appearance of "a certain monster" in the church of San Vincenzo, Milan.[33] The

27. *Annales Mediolanenses* (*Notae Sanctae Mariae Mediolanenses*), 389.
28. *Annales et Notae Parmenses et Ferrarienses*, 664.
29. Ibid.; *Annales Cremonenses*, 9
30. *Annales Cremonenses*, 13.
31. E.g., *Annales Mediolanenses* (*Annales Mediolanenses Minores*), 395–96 (1167).
32. *Annales Brixienses*, 815 (C).
33. *Annales Mediolanenses*, 386 (*Notae Sanctae Mariae Mediolanenses*).

annalists also display a general curiosity about celestial movements, particularly comets and eclipses of the sun and moon. One such event, which occurred in 1222, is picturesquely described in the Milanese annals: "On the feast of Mary a star appeared in the sky with a large tail at which men marveled greatly. And afterward the moon seemed almost dead [as] it did not shine and was like a star itself."[34]

Celestial phenomena were commonly interpreted as signs or portents in the medieval imagination, and some annals explicitly link them to terrestrial events.[35]

The annals record the coronations and deaths of kings and emperors, the elections of popes, and any other political events that struck the annalists as noteworthy. But their coverage of such topics is unsystematic and usually intermixed with local news. Only occasionally, and then in exceptional circumstances, do nonlocal occurrences command particular attention. A case in point is the death of the emperor Frederick I on crusade in 1190—a major event by any standard, concerning a ruler who was very well known in northern Italy. The so-called Ghibelline annals of Piacenza provide a detailed narrative of the emperor's journey to the East, his clashes with Muslim forces, and his untimely death by drowning in the river Saleph.[36] But the notices given in the majority of annals, even in this instance, are much more condensed and incidental. The following entries in the annals of Brescia, Cremona, and Mantua are typically terse:

[Brescia] 1189. Around the Feast of Saint George (23 April) the emperor Frederick went overseas with his son the duke, and with princes and an innumerable following, and after another year he drowned in the river Saleph. And Pietro Vilano and his associates were made consuls [under] the portico of the assembly place.[37]

[Cremona] 1189. Gaferio Isembardo, citizen of Pavia, was elected podestà in the city of Cremona, and at this time the city and its district were peacefully governed. And in the same time the emperor

34. Ibid., 389 (*Notae Sancti Georgii Mediolanenses*); the event was also noted in nearby Bergamo, *Annales Bergomates*, 809.

35. For example, *Annales Mediolanenses*, 386 (*Notae Sancti Georgii Mediolanenses*). Implicit linkage is more common, however, by way of simple juxtaposition of portentous occurrences and political events. For an example, see the entry for the year 1174 in the annals of Cremona, translated in the appendix.

36. *Annales Placentini (Annales Gibellini)*, 466–67.

37. *Annales Brixienses*, 814 (A).

Frederick [I] went over the sea against Saladin and died on the journey.[38]

[*Mantua*] 1190. Ottobono Malevicio was consul with his associates; and in that time the emperor Frederick [I] died.[39]

In all of these annals the emperor Frederick's death is deemed worthy of notice, but not so important as to displace other news, such as the appointment of communal officials.

Increasingly from the late twelfth century, the terms of civic office appear to function as the chronological basis for the annalists' narratives and perhaps also as a sort of aide-mémoire for organizing their material. The standard thirteenth-century annal entry begins by listing the individuals who held the principal positions of podestà and consuls of the commune—offices usually held for between one and three years—followed by notes on the events that occurred while they were in office. History was therefore not reckoned principally in years but as a series of terms of civic office. Frequently entries also contain information about building projects carried out in the city during the terms of particular officials. The annalists may have had access to lists of communal officeholders, which survive as separate documents in a number of cities from the second half of the twelfth century; perhaps the information about buildings also came from these sources. For example:

1185–87. Alberto de Sale, citizen of Brescia, was podestà of Cremona for two years, and he had the gates of the city wall built.[40]

1206. Iacopo de Bernardo, citizen of Bologna, was podestà of Cremona for one year. He built the communal palace in front of the cathedral.[41]

The frantic pace of building work in Lombard cities—of walls, gates, churches, baptisteries, communal palaces—can thus be traced through the numerous entries in various city annals, as can the vulnerability of the urban fabric to fire, flood, and earthquake.

Within the year-by-year framework of annals the passage of time is measured in further detail in terms of months, weeks, and days. Days are

38. *Annales Cremonenses*, 7–8.
39. *Annales Mantuani*, 19.
40. *Annales Cremonenses*, 7.
41. Ibid., 11.

identified by name or, commonly, by reference to a saint's day. Precise references to the time of day are also frequently recorded, usually to the hour, though sometimes according to the ecclesiastical time (Nones, Vespers, etc.). Given the probable involvement of notaries in the composition of annals, it is worth mentioning that dates are often fixed in relation to the beginning or end of a month (*intrante, exeunte*), which is precisely the way notarial documents were dated. Overall it would seem that the Lombard city annalists paid close attention to the measurement of time, as was characteristic of the European annal genre in general. It does not necessarily follow, however, that time was accurately measured. Many annals contain obvious mistakes in the dating of well-known events, and they quite often contradict one other in matters of chronology where the issues in question are too local or obscure to determine correct dating.

Annals are essentially a contemporary record of events, the temporal limitations of which are partly a consequence of the organic structure of the genre: entries begin and end at apparently arbitrary points in time; they were compiled shortly after the events they describe had occurred; and they were revised only occasionally, if at all. But more fundamentally, the annals betray no awareness even of the *existence* of a past prior to the contemporary reality of city and commune, still less of any teleological or eschatological scheme of "Ages," as one might find in more sophisticated works of history in the twelfth and thirteenth centuries.

This last point is best illustrated by considering dates at which a selection of annals begin; it is striking that these are very rarely earlier than the mid–twelfth century. The major annals of Parma, which start in 1165, and the annals of Mantua, which start in 1184, provide fairly typical opening entries:

> [*Parma*] Lord Maladobato de Maladobato and his associates were consuls of Parma in 1165. Lord Nigerio Grasso of Milan was podestà of Parma in 1165. And during his office the first *carroccio* [communal war chariot] was made. And he was podestà for three full years.[42]

> [*Mantua*] In the years 1184, 1185, 1186, Bishop Grascivino was podestà of Mantua; and in the first year Pope Lucius [III] came

---

42. *Annales et Notae Parmenses et Ferrarienses*, 664. On the *carroccio* see Ernst Voltmer, *Il carroccio* (Turin: Einaudi, 1994).

to Verona; and in the second year of the podesterate the same pope
died; and in the third year the treaty with Luzzara was made, and
he [the bishop] died and was buried there.[43]

It is noticeable that these annals lack any preamble. Composed from
their beginning of brief factual statements, they are structured chronologically around terms of civic office with no further explanation. Even annals
that open with a more detailed entry (as do the Lodi annals and Giovanni
Codagnello's annals of Piacenza) or that report an external event, such as
the calling of a Crusade (as in the Cremona annals and the minor annals of
Parma), are still firmly anchored in the recent past. In rare cases where
annals open with pre-1100 entries, these are very sparse and schematic; for
example, the minor annals of Milan: "A.D. 397. The blessed Ambrose died
on the eighth day of April, and lived as archbishop twenty-five years, four
months, and five days."

The stature of Saint Ambrose in Milan was such that mention of him in
the opening line of a historical text relating to that city is not very surprising. But after Ambrose, the Milanese annalist does not find anything worthy of record until 1104, the date of the next entry in the text.[44]

The annals of Brescia appear at first sight to be an exception to this rule:
"The first age, from Adam to Noah, was 2,242 years; the second, from Noah
to Abraham, 965 years; the third, Abraham to David, 940 years; the fourth,
David to the transmigration of the sons of Israel to Babylon, 86 years; the
fifth, from the transmigration to the Coming of Our Lord, 614 years, which
altogether totals 5,196 years. The sixth age lasts from the First Coming of
Our Lord to the Second Coming [the date of which] is unknown to us."[45]

But after its portentous opening, this text too moves rapidly forward to
the twelfth century: the next entries record an earthquake in 1117 and a visit
of Pope Innocent II to Brescia in 1132.

There would seem to be two possible ways of interpreting these twelfth-
century start dates: either the annalists lacked information, or for some
reason they chose deliberately to exclude it. It is worth considering the possibility that even had annalists known about the early Middle Ages, the period
would not have constituted a very relevant or usable past for them. None of

---

43. *Annales Mantuani*, 19.

44. *Annales Mediolanenses*, 389 (*Annales Mediolanenses Breves*).

45. *Annales Brixienses*, 812 (A); the B version of the Brescia annals begins in 1014, but
the eleventh-century entries are few and extremely brief; the C version of the annals begins
in 1139.

the few early medieval texts that survive from Lombardy before 1100 covers city history in the sustained way that the annals do for the twelfth and thirteenth centuries.[46] In this sense annals are entirely a product of the communal age: their chronologies, based on consular terms of office, their late start dates, and their nearly exclusive concentration on contemporary history show that, although never explicitly stated, they are intended as histories of communes rather than as histories of cities.

Civic Identity and Civic Pride

A single theme, warfare, dominates the narratives in all city annals. The vast majority of the so-called wars were in fact low-level raids, ambushes, and skirmishes involving neighbors, rather than the eye-catching exploits enacted on a grand scale across the entire Po plain by the emperor Frederick I. Though minor, these clashes were incessant and of paramount importance for each city. In the view of its annalist, the city's security, prestige, and economic well-being were at stake.[47] Naturally each annal celebrates victories won by the city and laments defeats. But, interestingly, comparison of different annal accounts of the same wars can reveal attempts by annalists to manipulate the historical record by emphasizing, downplaying, or omitting information. Since each annal was probably a quasi-official city history, written from a strongly patriotic standpoint, the passages concerning war are particularly relevant in gaining insight into the mentality of the annalists, and indeed that of their intended audience. Consider, from the Cremona and Brescia annals, two related entries describing the siege and capture of the town of Crema in 1159–60:[48]

> [*Cremona*] 1159. The emperor Frederick [I] captured Crema on the [feast of] the conversion of Saint Paul [recte 25 January 1160] and remained there for seven months.[49]

46. Chris J. Wickham, *Land and Power: Studies in Italian and European Social History, 400–1200* (London: British School at Rome, 1994), esp. "The Sense of the Past in Italian Communal Narratives," 310–11; and the discussion in "Lawyers' Time: History and Memory in Tenth- and Eleventh-Century Italy," 275–93, is also relevant.

47. See Aldo A. Settia, *Comuni in guerra: Armi ed eserciti nell'Italia delle città* (Bologna: CLUEB, 1993).

48. Ibid., 261–76.

49. *Annales Cremonenses*, 5.

[*Brescia*] Crema was besieged and captured, not without very great suffering during the capture. And King Frederick [I] was defeated in battle by the Milanesi and Bresciani at Carchanum.[50]

Although the basic fact of the capture of Crema is common to both of these entries, its presentation differs noticeably. The annals of Cremona simply record that the Cremonesi remained at Crema seven months with Frederick I, though the entry fails to specify whether the stay occurred before or after the town fell. The Brescian annals, by contrast, completely omit Cremona's role in the capture of Crema, ascribing it to imperial forces alone. The Brescian version of events, moreover, states that the siege was protracted and difficult and that Frederick's moment of triumph was short-lived because his army was defeated soon after by the Bresciani themselves and the Milanesi, a development the Cremona annals omit. Therefore it does not take much reading between the lines of these entries to surmise that Cremona and Brescia were enemies at this time and that the former was pro- and the latter anti-imperial.

Not surprisingly, enemies report wars differently, but sometimes the accounts of allies also differ, as in the case of the Parma and Cremona annals for the year 1216. The Cremonese version of events runs as follows:

> Count Enrico of Sospiro or Roversella, citizen of Pavia, was elected podestà of Cremona. In his time he laid waste to the entire territory of Milan and Crema around the [*river*] Adda, and the entire territory of Piacenza between the Monti del Po and the lower Piacentino; and he took Pontenure and destroyed it; and he defeated the Piacentine militia near Montile, between Pontenure and Piacenza, and carried off many noble captives to Cremona.[51]

The account of the same campaign at Pontenure reads rather differently in the major annals of Parma:

> Lord Isaaco of Dovara was podestà of Parma in 1216. And in that year the Parmigiani went to Pontenure in Piacentine territory . . . and there was a battle there, and the enemy was put to flight with great suffering; and this took place from Vespers up until evening.

---

50. *Annales Brixienses*, 813.
51. *Annales Cremonenses*, 13.

And then the Parmigiani rode to Montale as far as the hospice, and this was on the feast of the beheading of Saint John the Baptist. The next day the knights of Parma fought there against the Piacentini, Lodigiani, Cremaschi, and Milanesi and captured many of them; and a few Cremonese knights fought [there].[52]

Clearly, both the Cremona and Parma annals seek to emphasize the contribution of their own forces in this campaign and downplay that of their allies: the Cremonese annals give the entire credit for the operation to the podestà of Cremona; the Parma annalist does the same for his man, while admitting—almost as an afterthought—that a few Cremonese knights did also participate.

The reports of war in the annals are a vital guide to the ever-changing patterns of alliances among cities and the disposition and strength of their forces. References to war are not only very frequent but sometimes quite detailed, even evocative. Indeed, perhaps the most striking aspect of the treatment of war in the annals is the language of the reports, which often differs from the dispassionate matter-of-fact tone adopted in the entries dealing with other matters. Exemplary of this difference are, once again, contemporaneous entries from the Cremona and Brescia annals, this time concerning a war fought between the two cities in 1191:

> [*Cremona*] Ughino de Boxio, citizen of Mantua, was elected podestà in Cremona. In his time a large [Cremonese] army [marched] in the service of Bergamo against Brescia. Near Civitale, a Bergamasco castle, at an ill-starred crossing of the river Oglio, a terrible death befell us. And many of the Cremonesi died by divine will without the enemy being present, and many were captured by the Bresciani.[53]

> [*Brescia*] 1191. In this year, on the feast of Saint Appollinarus, around Vespers, the Cremonesi and Bergamaschi, with a great multitude and with great frenzy, broke into Brescian territory at Ponte Oglio. But their frenzy was changed into sadness: while the Brescians remained safe and sound, some twelve thousand [Cremonesi and Bergamaschi] perished there, and in time their bodies were

---

52. *Annales et Notae Parmenses et Ferrarienses*, 666 (*Annales Parmenses Maiores*).
53. *Annales Cremonenses*, 8.

picked clean by beasts, and some of them floated in the river, horribly swollen.[54]

A Milanese annalist, recording the same event, pointedly suggested that it had been the intervention of the Milanese saint Ambrose that had thrown the Cremonese forces into confusion and disarray: "The Bresciani overcame the Cremonesi on the banks of the river Oglio with a banner of a cross invoking Saint Ambrose. The Cremonesi began to flee on hearing the name of Saint Ambrose, and many of them were drowned in the Oglio and many were captured."[55] Apart from the blatant inflation of the casualty figures on the part of the Brescian annalist,[56] it is interesting to note here how each annal puts a decidedly different spin on the same events.

As annal accounts of war become fuller in the course of the thirteenth century, annalists give freer rein to their intense civic patriotism. They often abandon the use of the neutral third-person singular or plural, "he" or "they," in favor of the more partisan "we" and "us" (*nos*), as in the annals of Cremona quoted above. This practice lends both force and immediacy to their prose.

The physical focus of civic loyalties was the *carroccio,* a war chariot, used as a standard and rallying point by armies on the battlefield and as a focal point of civic ceremonies. The *carroccio* was closely associated with the city's patron saint—it often carried holy relics as well as banners and insignia—and was thus seen as a tangible embodiment of civic spirit.[57] These powerful and passionate sentiments are apparent in the following entries in the Cremonese and Parmense annals:

[*Cremona*] 1150. The Milanesi fought with the Cremonesi at Castelnuovo, and many men and horses were killed there, and the Milanesi shamefully abandoned their *carroccio* on the fifth day of the month of July.[58]

[*Parma*] Lord Cavalcabo of Cremona was podestà of Parma in 1229. And in that year on the feast day of Saint Odelric there was

---

54. *Annales Brixienses,* 814–15 (C).

55. *Annales Mediolanenses,* 387 (*Notae Sancti Georgii Mediolanenses*).

56. Another Milanese source (*Annales Mediolanenses,* 400 [*Memoriae Mediolanenses*]), puts the Cremonese dead at five thousand, along with two thousand Bergamaschi, still an impossibly high figure.

57. Voltmer, *Il carroccio.*

58. *Annales Cremonenses,* 4.

a clash of arms and great battle between the Bolognesi and Romagnoli and other knights of Lombardy, with their men, on one side and Parmigiani and Modenesi and their followers and others; and this occurred at San Cesario in the territory of Bologna; it began before Vespers and lasted until midnight. At length the Bolognesi and their men were defeated, and most of them were captured and led into captivity in Parma and Modena. And the Bolognese *carroccio* was captured, turned over and thrown into a ditch and covered with branches. The Modenesi wanted to take it to Modena, but the Parmigiani refused, nay, forbade this. They took "Maganellus" [the name of the Bolognese *carroccio*] to Parma and guarded it inside the cathedral.[59]

It is evident that the *carroccio* was seen as a war trophy whose capture brought glory to the victors—the Parmigiani displayed the captured Bolognese *carroccio* in their cathedral. By the same token its loss was a humiliation—the Cremonese annalist reviles the Milanesi for abandoning their *carroccio* on the field of battle. In general these entries reveal the annalists as not merely faceless compilers but living authors animated by strong emotions and deep-rooted prejudices; far from simply recording war, they describe it with feeling, and their prose is infused in equal measure with intense pride in their city and intense hatred of its enemies.

Conclusion

At first sight it may appear that Lombard city annals conform very well to Ambrose Bierce's satirical definition of history as "an account mostly false, of events, mostly unimportant, which are brought about by rulers, mostly knaves, and soldiers, mostly fools."[60] Yet closer examination shows them to be more than simple recitation of facts. Although not unknown to historians of the period, their potentiality has yet to be fully exploited. Given that so many different annals cover a relatively small geographical area and time span, they offer the possibility of comparing and contrasting various accounts of the same events. The extent to which the past was remembered and presented differently in the histories of different cities may shed light on the

---

59. *Annales et Notae Parmenses et Ferrarienses,* 668 (*Annales Parmenses Maiores*).
60. *The Collected Works of Ambrose Bierce,* vol. 7 (New York and Washington, D.C.: Neale Publishing Company, 1911), 138.

civic ethos of the early communes.[61] In cities where more than one set of annals survives, for example in Milan or Piacenza, alternative *internal* views of the past can also be examined. A systematic contextualized study along the lines of the present discussion would undoubtedly yield interesting results. Being products of a lay urban environment, and often accorded official or semiofficial status as civic histories, city annals not only provide essential factual narratives but also reveal the attitudes, concerns, and collective self-image of the ruling elites of north Italian society during the communal period.

APPENDIX: THE ANNALS OF CREMONA, 1096–1270[62]

The annals of Cremona exhibit many of the typical characteristics of city annals. Their start date coincides with the establishment of the city commune. The entries are short and factual. There are sometimes gaps of several years between entries. Chronology is imprecise, though events are often dated with reference to saints' days and other festivals of the liturgical year; from 1180 podestarial and consular terms of office become the principal dating tool. Local information predominates, but events of wider import—for example, the deaths of popes and emperors and major events in their reigns, the prog-ress of the Crusade in the East—are interspersed in the text. There is an over-whelming concern with war among Lombard cities and a marked tendency to emphasize victories won by the city and to omit or downplay defeats. Civic

---

61. Renato Bordone, *Memoria del tempo e comportamento cittadino nel Medioevo italiano* (Turin: Scriptorium, 1997).

62. The earliest surviving manuscript of the *Annales Cremonenses* dates from the fifteenth century, but it is safe to assume the text was written at some point during the twelfth or early thirteenth century. The standard modern edition is that in *MGH: Scriptores*, 31, edited by Oswald Holder-Egger. Earlier editions (covering only the years 1096–1232) were edited by Philipp Jaffé, in *MGH: Scriptores*, 18 (Hanover: Hahn, 1863), 800–807, and by Ludovico Antonio Muratori, *RIS*, 7 (Milan, 1725), cols. 629–44. A version of *Annales Cremonenses* fuller than that which has come down to us is known to have existed in the fourteenth century, when Albertus de Bezanis, abbot of the monastery of San Lorenzo, Cremona, incorporated parts of it into his universal chronicle of popes and emperors, written ca. 1370 (*Alberti de Bezanis abbatis S. Laurentii Cremonensis Cronica pontificum et imperatorum*, in *MGH: Scriptores rerum Germanicarum in usum scholarum separatim editi*, [3,] ed. Oswald Holder-Egger (Hanover and Leipzig: Hahn, 1908). The additional entries were edited by Holder-Egger under the title *Supplementum Annalium Cremonensium* (in *MGH: Scriptores*, 31, 184–88 [hereafter *Supp. AC*]). Together with the chronicle of Bishop Sicard of Cremona, probably written ca. 1212 (*Sicardi Episcopi Cremonensi Cronica*, in *MGH: Scriptores*, 31, 22–183 [hereafter *Sicardi Cron.*]), the *Annales Cremonenses* forms the basis for the narrative history of Cremona for the medieval centuries contained in local antiquarian literature beginning with Antonio Campi, *Cremona fedelissima città* (Cremona, 1585).

building projects are deemed worthy of record, and extreme or unusual mete-orological conditions and natural phenomena are also periodically noted. The section of the annals translated here (1096–1182) covers the first phase of the history of the commune, from the establishment of consuls to the election of the first podestà, the early skirmishes (ca. 1090s–1130s) between Milan and Cremona in the territories of Lodi and Crema, which lay between the two larger cities, and the wars between the emperor Frederick I Barbarossa and the Lombards (ca. 1150s–70s).

In the name of Our Lord Jesus Christ.

1096.[63] The pilgrims captured Jerusalem and Antioch. They departed in October, and at that time they were at Cremona.[64]

1098. There was the first war with Crema in the month of May.[65]

1107. The Cremonesi, Lodigiani, and Pavesi burned Tortona on the vigil of Saint Bartholomew['s Day, 23 August].[66]

1110. There was a battle at Bressanoro in June,[67] on the vigil of Saint Imerius['s Day, 16 June].[68]

63. All entries in the *Annales Cremonenses* for the years 1096–1177 begin with the word "when" (*Quando*), as, for example, in this entry: "Quando peregrini ceperunt Hyerusalem et Antiochiam." For ease of reading in English, "when" has been omitted in the translation.

64. Preparations for the First Crusade (1095–99). The annalist's chronology is vague here. Antioch was captured in 1098, Jerusalem in 1099. If crusaders were indeed gathering at Cremona in the autumn of 1096, they were somewhat early, since the main Lombard force did not leave for the East until 1100. For a recent analysis, see Giancarlo Andenna and Renata Salvarani, eds., *Deus non voluit: I lombardi alla prima crociata, 1100–1101; Dal mito alla ricostruzione della realtà* (Milan: Vita e pensiero università, 2003).

65. This was the first in a series of wars between Cremona and her smaller neighbor. Cf. the entries for the years 1110, 1130, and 1157, and for the background, see *Crema 1185: Una contrasta autonomia politica e territoriale* (Crema: Biblioteca comunale di Crema, 1988).

66. On the broad geopolitical canvas of Lombardy, Cremona, Lodi, and Pavia were generally opposed to Milan, Piacenza, Brescia, and Bergamo, though these alliances were never totally rigid. Here the first group were launching an attack on a minor ally of Milan. Three years later the Milanesi mounted a successful counteroffensive (see the entry for 1110). In the middle decades of the century, on account of the interventionist Italian policy pursued by the emperor Frederick I, the two sides divided into pro- and anti-imperial camps. See Renato Bordone, "L'età dei comuni," in *Comuni e signorie nell'Italia settentrionale: La Lombardia*, ed. Giancarlo Andenna et al., UTET: Storia d'Italia, 7 (Turin: UTET, 1998), 327–84.

67. The protagonists in this battle are not identified in the *Annales Cremonenses* but are known from other sources. Bishop Sicard states in his chronicle that it was fought between the Cremonesi and the Milanesi (*Sicardi Cron.*, 162). Given the location of Bressanoro (modern Santa Maria di Bressanoro) on the lower reaches of the river Serio a few kilometers

And in the same year [recte 1111] King Henry [V, emperor, 1106–25] was in Rome and captured [Pope] Paschal [1099–1118].

1111. The city of Lodi was captured on the last Wednesday of May [24 May].[69]

And in this year the countess Matilda died [recte 1115].[70]

1113. Cremona was burnt on the feast of Saint Lawrence [10 August].[71]

1116 [recte 1117]. There was an earthquake on the octave of Saint John the Evangelist [3 January] at the time of Vespers.[72]

1116 [recte 1127]. The city of Como was captured on Saint Alexander[’s Day, 26 August].[73] In the same year, the Po froze in December.[74]

---

east of Crema and the hostile relations between Cremona and Crema, it would seem likely that the Cremaschi were also involved in this battle, on the side of the Milanesi. The annalist does not indicate the outcome, probably because it was not favorable to Cremona. Bishop Sicard's entry on the events—"fuit bellum inter Mediolanenses et Cremonsensibus aput Brixianorum, Cremonsensibus pernitiosum"—is more candid. The defeat thwarted Cremona's attempt to prevent the capture of her ally Lodi by the Milanesi, which occurred the following spring (see the entry for 1111).

68. Saint Imerius (4th–6th century) was a Calabrian hermit and bishop of Amelia (Terni) whose relics were brought to Cremona in 965 by Bishop Liutprand (the chronicler). The relics were lost when the cathedral collapsed in an earthquake in 1117. However, they were rediscovered during excavations connected with the building of the new cathedral and reinterred in 1128 or 1129. Saint Imerius was adopted as a civic saint, and his cult remained strong in Cremona throughout the Middle Ages. See the entries for the years 1116 and 1128.

69. Bishop Sicard states that Lodi was destroyed by the Milanesi (*Sicardi Cron.*, 162).

70. The death of Countess Matilda of Canossa (1046–1115) is mentioned in numerous north Italian sources. The way in which it is recorded here suggests the notice may have been inserted in the *Annales Cremonenses* after the main entries had been compiled. Matilda played an important part in the history of Cremona around this time, investing the city with possession of Crema and its surrounding territory in 1098, an act that gave rise to the subsequent conflict between the two cities, as recorded in the *Annales Cremonenses* (*Die Urkunden und Briefe der Markgräfin Mathilde von Tuszien*, in *MGH: Laienfürsten- und Dynastenurkunden der Kaiserzeit*, 2, ed. Elke Goetz and Werner Goetz [Hanover: Hahnsche, 1998], 150 n. 48). The investiture is also important, since it is the earliest record of the commune of Cremona.

71. The effects of this fire were devastating: the *Supplementum* lists no fewer than twenty-nine churches and monasteries that were destroyed. This source also gives notice of a second fire in the city, in 1118 (*Supp. AC*, 85), which is not recorded in the *Annales Cremonenses*.

72. This earthquake is mentioned in many other Lombard sources. Bishop Sicard adds that the cathedral collapsed and the body of Saint Imerius was buried under the ruins (*Sicardi Cron.*, 162; also *Supp. AC*, 185).

73. The capture of Como by the Milanesi (*Sicardi Cron.*, 163) brought to an end a war between the two cities that had begun in 1118.

74. Horses and carts were able to cross the ice (*Sicardi Cron.*, 163).

1120. There was the first war with Parma, and this conflict was fought . . . around Saint John['s Day; i.e., near the end of June].

1129 [recte 1128]. The Milanese made Conrad [III, emperor, 1138–52] king [of Italy]. And in the same year the body of Saint Imerius was discovered in the month of May.[75]

1130. There was the second war with Crema. Ribald and Anselm were consuls in the kalends of June [1 June].[76] And in the same year the Cremonesi went [on campaign?] in Busseto, and the greater part of them perished in the river Po, and this was in the month of October.[77]

1132. King Lothar [emperor, 1125–37] was at Crema when it was being besieged by Cremona, and he stayed there for a month around the feast of All Saints [1 November].[78]

1133. Pizzighettone was constructed around the feast of Saint Michael [29 September].[79]

1136. King Lothar was in Rome, then at Roncaglia, where he issued laws in June. And in the same year he captured San Bassano and Soncino, and this was in the month of October.[80]

75. According to Sicard, Saint Imerius's body was found a year later, in 1129 (*Sicardi Cron.*, 164).

76. This is the first mention of consuls of the commune of Cremona in a narrative source. Consuls are not explicitly mentioned in the documentary records of the city until 1150 (*Le carte cremonesi dei secoli VIII–XII*, ed. Ettore Falconi, vol. 2 [Cremona: Biblioteca statale di Cremona, 1984], no. 349). However, it is probable that representatives of the commune recorded in various documents from 1098 onward effectively filled this role.

77. These events are also noted in the *Supplementum* (*Supp. AC*, 185), but under the year 1131, where it is stated that the Cremonesi went not to Busseto but to Bersellum (Brescello?). Holder-Egger considered the latter locality more plausible because it is on the Po. The entry in the *Supplementum* also leaves no doubt about the military context of the occurrence, noting that in addition to the many who perished in the Po, the greater part of the Cremonesi were captured.

78. A continuation of the hostilities begun in 1130 (also in *Sicardi Cron.*, 164). Unusually, it would appear that a winter campaign was in progress.

79. Pizzighettone, on the lower course of the river Adda, is called a *castrum* in the corresponding entry in the *Supplementum* (*Supp. AC*, 185), where an implicit connection is made between its construction and a Cremonese offense to imperial majesty, recorded in same year. This is also noted by Bishop Sicard (*Sicardi Cron.*, 164) and can presumably be linked to the invasion of Cremonese territory by imperial forces and the capture of San Bassano and Soncino, which is recorded in all three Cremonese sources under the year 1136. At the Diet of Roncaglia, Lothar had been persuaded by the Milanesi to intervene in support of Crema.

80. San Bassano and Soncino were Cremonese strongholds located respectively on the banks of the rivers Serio and Oglio. The former was intended as a bulwark to the west of the

1138 [recte 1139]. The greater part of the Cremonese people were captured at Crema on the fifth day of June, and the Milanesi were there.[81]

1147. There was a [plague of locusts?].[82]

1149. The Cremonesi and Parmigiani captured the Piacentini at Tabiano [near Borgo San Donnino] the day of Sunday [12 June], in the evening.[83]

1150. The Milanesi fought with the Cremonesi at Castelnuovo, and many men and horses were killed there, and the Milanesi shamefully abandoned their *carroccio* on the fifth day of the month of July.[84]

1151 [recte 1150]. The Cremonesi restored Castelnuovo to the Piacentini in the month of December.[85]

1152. Medesano was captured by the Cremonesi on a Monday, the thirteenth day of July [recte 14 July], and they remained there for seven weeks.[86]

---

city against Crema and Milan, while the latter looked eastward toward Brescian territory. Bishop Sicard (*Sicardi Cron.*, 164) states that the laws issued by Lothar at Roncaglia concerned fiefs.

81. The annalist is (intentionally?) vague here, merely stating that "the Milanesi were there" when the Cremonesi were captured at Crema. Bishop Sicard, on the other hand, informs us explicitly that the Cremonesi were captured and imprisoned by the Milanesi (*Sicardi Cron.*, 165). The event is also mentioned in a number of other Lombard annals under the years 1138 or 1139. The "second war with Crema," as the annalist calls it, had thus clearly ended in defeat and humiliation for Cremona. It is notable that apart from a very brief nature notice in 1147 there are no further entries in the *Annales Cremonenses* for a decade. They pick up again in 1149, when there was better news to report, from a Cremonese point of view.

82. "Tempus rugarum fuit"; also *Sicardi Cron.*, 165: "pestis erucarum invaluit super terram et bona terre consumpsit. unde sequenti anno famis nonnullos macervit egentes."

83. Cremona and Parma, at war in 1120, were now allies.

84. For Castelnuovo (modern Castelnuovo Bocca d'Adda), see the following note. The *carroccio*, or war chariot, was a symbolic standard and rallying point on the field of battle for all communal armies. It was considered a humiliation to abandon it. On its origins and role in warfare, see Voltmer, *Il carroccio*.

85. Castelnuovo Bocca d'Adda was a settlement on the west bank of the river Adda, near the confluence between the Adda and the river Po (hence the modern name). Two documents dated 9 and 11 December 1150 (the first enacted in Piacenza, the second in Castelnuovo Bocca d'Adda) reveal the terms of a complex deal between Cremona and Piacenza with regard to their dispute over this locality (*Le carte cremonesi*, vol. 2, no. 349)—far more complex, it might be added, than the annalist's brief notice implies. In effect the Piacentini handed Castelnuovo over to Cremona, a move that probably resulted from Cremona's resounding military victory over Piacenza's ally Milan earlier in the year. However, the dispute over the locality, which also involved the Piacentine monastery of San Sisto, was set to continue throughout the twelfth and thirteenth centuries.

86. Medesano, in the modern province of Parma, was completely destroyed, according to Bishop Sicardo (*Sicardi Cron.*, 165).

1153. The city of Ascalon was captured in the month of August.[87]

1155. Tortona was captured by the emperor Frederick [I, 1152–90]. And in the same year coins were minted at Cremona for the first time.[88] And on a Monday in November, when the aforementioned emperor returned, he burnt Senigola.[89]

1157. There was the third war with Crema, on the eighth day before the end of May [24 May]. They [the Cremonesi?] went first into the Lodigiano.

The Milanesi and Bresciani captured Vigevano, thirteen days from the end of June [18 June]. And at the same time, Tortona was rebuilt by the Lombards.[90]

1158. The emperor Frederick made peace with the Bresciani in the month of July. In the same year, he besieged Milan with Cremona and remained there for five weeks. And in the month of August he made peace [with Milan].[91] And on his return he captured Trezzo.

1159. The emperor Frederick [I] captured Crema on the [feast of] the conversion of Saint Paul [recte 25 January 1160] and remained there for

87. By King Baldwin III of Jerusalem (1152–63).

88. The original imperial diploma conceding this important privilege survives and is conserved in Cremona (for a transcription, see *Die Urkunden Friedrichs I.*, in *MGH: Die Urkunden der deutschen Könige und Kaiser*, 10, ed. Heinrich Appelt [Hanover: Hahn, 1975], pt. 1, no. 120).

89. The corresponding entry in Bishop Sicard's chronicle (*Sicardi Cron.*, 165–66) suggests the emperor's "return" refers to his return to Germany, following a period spent in Rome.

90. Bishop Sicard states that the Milanesi and the Bresciani destroyed Vigevano, a *castrum* of pro-imperial Pavia (*Sicardi Cron.*, 166), and also that it was specifically the men of these two cities who rebuilt Tortona; the annalist, on the other hand, uses the more generic term "Lombards." This interesting linguistic nuance suggests that the annalist may here consciously be using the term "Lombards" in the pejorative sense with which it came frequently to be used in imperial diplomas and pro-imperial chronicles, that is, with the meaning "enemies of the emperor." Pro- and anti-imperial camps were already forming among the Lombard cities ahead of the Diet of Roncaglia (1158), which marked the watershed in relations between Frederick I and his allies, on the one hand, and Milan and its allies, on the other. Despite its age, Cesare Vignati's *Storia diplomatica della lega lombarda* (Milan: P. Agnelli, 1866) remains an excellent "blow-by-blow" narrative account of Frederick's wars in Lombardy. Among many modern accounts of the unfolding events of these years, see Franco Cardini, *Il Barbarossa: Vita, trionfi e illusioni di Federico imperatore* (Milan: A. Mondadori, 1985), and Bordone, "L'età dei comuni."

91. Cremonese support of Frederick at the first siege of Milan demonstrates that Cremona hoped to exploit Milanese difficulties with the empire to build on the military success it had achieved in 1150. This policy was consistently pursued by the commune over the next twenty-five years, making Cremona the foremost pro-imperial city in Lombardy and a frequent recipient of imperial favor.

seven months.[92] And during that time the queen [Beatrice] remained at San Bassano.

1162. The emperor Frederick captured Milan in the kalends of March, on the day of Thursday [1 March].[93]

1167. The baptistery of Cremona was begun in the month of March. And in the same year, on the fifth day of April, Milan was rebuilt by the Lombards. And in the same year, the emperor Frederick went to Rome, and the greater part of his army died there.[94] And in the same year, the Lombards made an agreement together in the month of April.[95]

1168. The city of Alessandria was built by the Lombards on the feast of Saint George [23 April].[96]

1174. The Po turned black.[97] And in the same year [recte 1176], the Lombards defeated the emperor Frederick at Legnano.[98] And in the same year, a market was established at Mosa.[99]

1175 [recte 1177]. The emperor Frederick made peace with the Lombards. And in the same year, Pope Alexander [III, 1159–81] made peace with Frederick.[100]

---

92. The capture of Crema effectively ended its independent existence.

93. It is notable here that the annalist omits to mention that after Milan was taken, Frederick ordered it to be razed to the ground, a fact noted in numerous other sources. Yet it is clear from the next entry that he was well aware that the city had been destroyed. Bishop Sicard too is somewhat oblique on the matter (*Sicardi Cron.*, 166).

94. The army was struck by an outbreak of malaria.

95. This led to the formation of the Lombard League.

96. For numerous angles on the role of Alessandria in the wars between Frederick I and the Lombard League, see *Popolo e stato in Italia nell'età di Federico Barbarossa: Alessandria e la lega lombarda* (Turin: Deputazione subalpina di storia patria, 1970).

97. Also in the *Supplementum*, under the year 1178 (*Supp. AC*, 186). Since we can assume that the annalist would have viewed the defeat of Barbarossa as a setback for pro-imperial Cremona, the juxtaposition of the notice of the battle of Legnano and that of the Po's turning portentously black may not be coincidental.

98. Bishop Sicard gives much more space than the *Annales Cremonenses* to the events of the years 1167–76, especially Frederick's retreat in disarray from Italy in 1167, his return there in 1174, his failed siege of Alessandria the following year, and his ultimate defeat at Legnano in May 1176 (*Sicardi Cron.*, 167).

99. A district of Cremona, to the south of the medieval city center, probably near the north bank of the river Po at the time.

100. Not for the first time, the annalist's chronology is vague. Peace negotiations between Frederick and the Lombards were opened after Legnano, but no peace was settled until 1183. It is possible, however, that he is referring to the negotiations at Montebello, which took place in April 1175 and in which the Cremonesi took a prominent role.

1180 [recte 1182]. Gerard of Carpeneta became the first podestà of Cremona. He died of natural causes and was buried in a stone tomb in the cathedral on the feast of Saint Donninus(?) [9 October].[101]

1181 [recte 1183]. After him Manfred Fantus, son of Manfred of Modena and son-in-law of Gerard [of Carpeneta], was elected podestà, and he completed the term of Gerard and remained for one more year. During his term he built Castel Manfredo and named it after himself.[102]

1182 [recte 1184]. Afterward Guazo de Albrigone de Guazonibus and Gerard of Dovara were elected as podestà for two years. Gerard was stabbed to death by his squire, and Guazo held office [by] himself one year.[103] In his time [the emperor] Frederick came to Cremona and sat in majesty on a dais set up in the cathedral square.

101. From this year onward the entries in the *Annales Cremonenses* generally begin with the word "post" and become more expansive than hitherto. It seems likely that they are the work of a new annalist. The position of podestà, or chief magistrate, became the principal civic office in most Lombard city communes in the last quarter of the twelfth century. For a comprehensive analysis and discussion of the office of podestà in northern Italy, including Cremona, see Jean Claude Maire-Vigueur, ed., *I podestà dell'Italia comunale*, pt. 1, *Reclutamento e circolazione degli ufficiali forestieri (fine xii secolo–metà xiv secolo)* (Rome: Istituto storico italiano per il Medio Evo, 2000). If the *Annales Cremonenses* can be considered an "official" history of Cremona—which, on the basis of what we know about other cities, such as Genoa, would seem a reasonable assumption—the change of annalist and the passage from a consular to a podestarial regime may possibly be connected. However, in Cremona, as in other Lombard cities, there were periodic returns to rule by a college of consuls, as subsequent entries in the *Annales Cremonenses* make clear.

102. It was common practice to elect a podestà who was not a native of the city. Castel Manfredo, modern Castelleone, is situated on the lower reaches of the river Serio, a tributary of the Adda. It was to have an eventful history in the years following its foundation.

103. The election of two podestà is suggestive of the kind of discord and factionalism that also occurred in other Lombard cities. This may provide a context for the murder of Gerard of Dovara who came from a powerful local family. A relative of his, Osbert, had been bishop of Cremona (1117–62), and many other members of the family held important offices in the church and commune during the twelfth and thirteenth centuries, including the famous Buoso of Dovara, who ruled Cremona as *signore* in 1266–67.

2

History Writing in the Twelfth-Century Kingdom of Sicily

Graham A. Loud

Count Roger II of Sicily created the kingdom of Sicily in the years 1127–30. Following the death of his childless cousin Duke William of Apulia, in 1127, he extended his rule over most of mainland southern Italy. In doing so, he reunited the various lands that had once been governed by his uncle, the leader of the Norman invaders of the region during the eleventh century, Robert Guiscard, "the cunning" (d. 1085).[1] Subsequently, in 1129, Roger secured recognition of his overlordship from Prince Robert II of Capua, the ruler of the one independent Norman state in the south that Guiscard had never conquered. Having united the whole of southern Italy, Roger then secured the agreement of Pope Anacletus II to his coronation as the first king of Sicily, a ceremony that took place on Christmas Day 1130. The new king, however, still faced both internal revolt and external threats. A number of the most powerful mainland nobles and some of the south Italian towns were reluctant to accept his authority, while several external powers refused to recognize the validity of his royal title, not least because Anacletus was one of two rival contenders for the See of Saint Peter and, as it turned out, the one who ultimately lost the contest. Roger spent nearly ten years suppressing rebellion, and although his regime was internally secure after 1140, he still faced a problematic relationship with the papacy and the outright hostility of both the Western (German) and Eastern (Byzantine)

---

1. For the Norman conquest, see Graham A. Loud, *The Age of Robert Guiscard: Southern Italy and the Norman Conquest* (Harlow, Essex, and New York: Longman, 2000). Guiscard, the first Norman duke of Apulia, ruled from 1059 to 1085. His youngest brother, Count Roger I of Sicily (d. 1101), was the father of Roger II.

Empires.[2] Under his son William I (king, 1154–66) internal dissent recurred, complicated by factional dispute at the royal court, which continued into the minority of his son William II, who came to the throne in May 1166, just before his thirteenth birthday.

Despite the drama of such events, and indeed of the conquest of southern Italy by the Normans in the previous century, the scale of contemporary historical writing in southern Italy was limited compared with the extensive range of such literature produced, for example, in Anglo-Norman England or Salian and Staufen Germany. We do possess, however, three significant, but very different, contemporary accounts of the first forty years of the new kingdom of Sicily: *The History of King Roger*, written by Abbot Alexander of Telese around 1136; the chronicle of Falco of Benevento, which takes the form of detailed yearly annals, compiled over a long period and now surviving incomplete for the years 1102–40;[3] and the *History of the Tyrants of Sicily*, attributed to the so-called Hugo Falcandus, a sophisticated history on the classical model, describing events in Sicily, particularly those at the royal court, from 1154 until 1169.[4]

Alexander of Telese's work is a continuous narrative, divided into four books, ostensibly in the form of a biography. King Roger's childhood and early years as count of Sicily are passed over in a couple of anecdotal paragraphs, however, and the real narrative commences with the death of Duke William and Roger's successful attempt, in the face of fierce opposition, to vindicate his claim to the ducal title and to rule over Apulia. His struggles with the duchy's nominal overlord, Pope Honorius II, and with his domestic opponents on the mainland in the years 1127–29 take up book I of the *History*. Book II, appreciably the longest of the four, commences with his elevation to the kingship, with a vivid description of the splendor of his

2. See Hubert Houben, *Roger II of Sicily: A Ruler Between East and West*, trans. Graham A. Loud and Diane B. Milburn (Cambridge: Cambridge University Press, 2002).

3. *Alexandri Telesini Abbatis Ystoria Rogerii Regis Sicilie Calabrie atque Apulie*, ed. Ludovica de Nava, commentary by Dione Clementi, Fonti per la storia d'Italia, 112 (Rome: Istituto storico italiano per il Medio Evo, 1991) (hereafter *Al. Tel.*); Falcone di Benevento, *Chronicon Beneventanum*, ed. Edoardo D'Angelo (Florence: SISMEL edizioni del Galluzzo, 1998) (henceforth *Falco*).

4. *La historia o Liber de Regno Sicilie e la Epistola ad Petrum Panormitane Ecclesie Thesaurarium di Ugo Falcando*, ed. Giovanni Battista Siragusa, Fonti per la storia d'Italia, 22 (Rome: Istituto storico italiano per il Medio Evo, 1897) (henceforth *Falcandus*), English translation by Graham A. Loud and Thomas E. J. Wiedemann, *The History of the Tyrants of Sicily by "Hugo Falcandus," 1154–69* (Manchester: Manchester University Press, 1998) (hereafter *Tyrants*). References below will normally be to the translation, except where the actual wording of the Latin text is significant.

coronation, which Alexander himself may have attended (see Appendix A), and then recounts Roger's campaigns against the repeated rebellions on the mainland during the years 1131–34, which ended with the king seemingly victorious and his enemies either once more obedient, in prison, or fled into exile. Most of the remainder of the text is devoted to the king's travails ruling Apulia.

Alexander's work is not properly a biography, but rather an account of how, over the years 1127–35, the king imposed his rule on mainland southern Italy. It is primarily propaganda, justifying King Roger's actions as divinely inspired and condemning those who opposed him. Indeed, Alexander makes his theme clear right from the start, when in his short preface he writes:

> So that the iniquity that greatly overflowed in many people might be brought to an end, it had to be ground down by the whip of this man, according to the secret judgment of God. For just as the great sin of the Lombards was once overcome by the violence of the Normans when they arrived [here], according to God's plan or at least with God's permission, in the same way today it is also certain that it was given, or at least permitted, to Roger by Heaven to coerce the immense malice of these regions by means of his sword. . . . God, greatly offended by these crimes, drew Roger from the sheath of the province of Sicily, so that, holding him in His hand as though a sharp sword, He might repress those who had committed these evil deeds.[5]

The first chapter develops this theme. The death of Duke William had unleashed anarchy on the mainland. "If God had not preserved a scion of the Guiscard's lineage through whom the ducal power might quickly be revived, almost the whole country, burdened by unbelievably horrible crimes, would have rushed headlong to destruction."[6] This refrain continues throughout the work. The young Roger "showed such activity and demonstrated such admirable firmness, ruling the whole province of Sicily so well and strongly and exercising such terrible authority over all, that no robber, thief, plunderer, or other malefactor dared to stir out of his lair."[7] After describing

5. *Al. Tel.*, prologue, 3.
6. Ibid., 1.1, 6. Citations to Telesini will normally be to book, chapter, and then page of the 1991 edition. Thus book 1, chapter 1, page 6.
7. Ibid., 1.4, 8.

Roger's peace edict proclaimed at Melfi in 1129, the abbot concludes: "it is no wonder that he was able with the aid of God to bring all these lands under his power, since everywhere he ruled he promulgated such mighty and thorough justice that continuous power was seen to endure. As the Psalmist says, 'His place is made in peace.'"[8] The king's own personal qualities were manifest: "He was a lover and defender of justice and a most stern judge of evildoers. He had above all a great dislike for liars, and if somebody who ought to have spoken the truth instead produced a lie, then ever after he could scarcely if ever bring himself to believe them. . . . In doing things he was not headlong, but before he did anything he was careful to study it with the eye of prudence. Nor did he seek to punish anybody or to exact any due without proper hearing."[9] By contrast, those who opposed him were enemies of one who had been chosen by God to bring peace to southern Italy. Furthermore, they were not just rebels but perjurers, for by violating the oaths of fealty that they had sworn to Roger, some of them more than once, they not only incurred Roger's justifiable wrath but had also breached God's law. Hence Alexander had little sympathy with the harsh fates inflicted upon those who opposed the king. He recounts with some glee how Count Alexander of Conversano fled across the Adriatic, intending to travel on to the court of the Byzantine emperor, and was then robbed and left stranded and in penury in Albania. Yet he was lucky compared with some others, notably Roger of Plenco (or Pleuto), "a very fierce knight who was most hostile to the king," hanged at Montepeloso in 1133, and Count Alexander's brother Tancred, captured at the same time as this Roger, who was sent to Sicily in chains.[10] Falco of Benevento denounces the execution of Roger of Pleuto as an example of the king's cruelty (see Appendix B); but to Alexander both this execution, horrible as it was, and the subsequent destruction of the rebellious town of Montepeloso were appropriate punishments for perjury.

The prophetic dreams, or visions, that conclude the work are an important and integral part of the whole, for they foretell the inevitability of Roger's triumph and the divine sanction accorded to his rule.[11] "If therefore

8. Ibid., i.21, 19: Psalm 76:2.
9. Ibid., iv.3, 82.
10. Ibid., ii.38, 41–42; also ii.45–46, 44–45. Alexander gives the surname as "de Plenco." This may be scribal error. Falco calls him "de Pleuto," the most probable derivation of which is from Chieuti, on the Gargano peninsula in northern Apulia; see *Falco*, 261.
11. The dreams were omitted from the first printed edition, of 1578, and all subsequent editions (most of which were simply reprints of Zurita's one of 1578) until the most recent. They were first printed by M. Reichenmiller, "Bisher unbekannte Traumerzählungen Alexanders von Telese," *Deutsches Archiv für Erforschung des Mittelalters* 19 (1963): 339–52,

it is a sin to resist the ordinance of God, it is equally one to fight against him. Indeed if Roger had not received his power from above, he could not have done anything." Alexander concludes that "it should be known by all that Roger undertook the royal dignity not by chance but by the grace of Divine election."[12] The work ends with an *alloquium* (exhortation) to the king, in which Alexander commends to him the virtues of piety and humility and also appeals for reward for himself, "not however so much for this little work [*libellus*]" as for praying to God for the king's soul and prosperity.[13]

The work of Alexander of Telese is more subtle than might at first be assumed of such a piece of royalist propaganda, one liberally laced with flattery toward the king. The account of Roger's elevation to the monarchy is notable for the complete omission of Anacletus II, who in fact sanctioned this new royal title in a bull of 27 September 1130.[14] By contrast, Alexander's account (Appendix B) attributed this promotion first to the suggestion of Roger's counselors and then to the sanction of an assembly of notables held at Salerno, the principal city and de facto capital of the duchy of Apulia. He also justified it on historical grounds, that Sicily had once possessed kings in the distant pre-Roman period, lost in the mists of antiquity. This last claim was undoubtedly part of the official ideology of the new kingdom; it was, for example, repeated in the foundation charter of Roger's new palace chapel in 1140 and has been taken (though probably wrongly) to indicate a claim to royal status independent of papal sanction.[15] But the concern in Alexander's *History* was not necessarily to deny that the pope was the traditional overlord of southern Italy. Alexander had earlier described in some detail how Roger had attempted to obtain investiture as duke of Apulia from Pope Honorius II (1124–30) and eventually forced the reluctant pontiff to grant this. Honorius was indeed criticized for his stubbornness in opposing Roger, the legitimate heir to the duchy, but Alexander did not deny the pope's

and Dione R. Clementi, "Alexandrini Telesini 'Ystoria Serenissimi Rogerii Primi Regis Siciliae,' Lib. iv.6–10 (Twelfth-Century Political Propaganda)," *Bullettino dell'Istituto storico italiano per il Medioevo* 77 (1965): 105–26, which contains a useful discussion.

12. *Al. Tel.*, iv.9–10, 87–88.

13. Ibid., 89–90.

14. Edited most recently by Hartmut Hoffmann, "Langobarden, Normannen, Päpste: Zur Legitimationsproblem in Unteritalien," *Quellen und Forschungen aus italienischen Archiven und Bibliotheken* 58 (1978): 173–75.

15. *Rogerii II Regis Diplomata Latina*, ed. Carl-Richard Brühl, Codex Diplomaticus Regni Sicilae, 2:1 (Cologne: Böhlau, 1987), 133–37, esp. 136, no. 48. The historiography here is extensive; for a useful recent discussion, in English, see Thomas S. Brown, "The Political Use of the Past in Norman Sicily," in *The Perception of the Past in Twelfth-Century Europe*, ed. Paul Magdalino (London and Rio Grande, Ohio: Hambledon Press, 1992), 191–210.

right to invest him or to receive his homage. Indeed, he only called Roger by the ducal title once he had received this investiture, in August 1128.[16] The problem with the kingship was rather the legitimacy of Anacletus as pope and hence of any sanction that he may have given to the creation of the new kingdom. The omission of Anacletus reflects the time when Alexander was writing, in 1135–36. By then, the position of Anacletus was very different from what it had been in 1130, when Roger had, in effect, recognized him as pope in return for Anacletus's agreement to his royal title. Although neither of the rival popes elected in February 1130 had a strictly canonical title, Anacletus was the choice of a majority of the cardinals, albeit a narrow majority, and he was in possession of Rome, while his rival Innocent II had fled into exile.[17] But by 1135–36 the rulers of northern Europe had all recognized Innocent as the legitimate pope; the monastic orders were firmly, indeed vociferously, on his side; and with Milan transferring its allegiance in 1135, so too was almost all of northern Italy. It was surely clear by now that the cause of Anacletus was doomed, and hence there was good reason to omit any mention of his sanction in a work that was intended to promote the king's cause and to glorify his name.

Another area where Alexander had to tread carefully was in his attitude toward Roger's principal south Italian opponent, Count Rainulf of Caiazzo. His problem here was not just that Rainulf was the lord of the region where Alexander's monastery was situated, nor even that Rainulf's grandfather had probably founded that monastery.[18] It was rather that his work had been commissioned by Count Rainulf's wife, Matilda, who was also the king's sister. Alexander did admittedly provide some detail about the quarrel between Matilda and Rainulf, which had precipitated the latter's breach with the king in 1131. The mention by Falco of Benevento of "the many insults and injuries" that Matilda had received from her husband, however, may suggest that there was more to this issue than, as Alexander states, simply a dispute about her dower lands.[19] Nonetheless, although Matilda appears to have taken her brother's side in the conflict, she and her husband were for a time reconciled after the latter's submission to the king in 1134, and in

16. *Al. Tel.*, i.15, 14–15.

17. On the 1130 schism, see Ian S. Robinson, *The Papacy, 1073–1198: Continuity and Innovation* (Cambridge: Cambridge University Press, 1990), 69–77, summarizing a vast foreign-language literature, and (more controversially) Mary Stroll, *The Jewish Pope: Ideology and Politics in the Papal Schism of 1130* (Leiden: E. J. Brill, 1987).

18. Luigi R. Cielo, *L'abbaziale normanna di S. Salvatore de Telesia* (Naples: Edizioni scientifiche italiane, 1995), 4–8.

19. *Al. Tel.*, prologue, 2; ii.14–16, 29–31; *Falco*, 120.

deference to her feelings Alexander had to exercise some discretion in his treatment of her husband's repeated revolts. In contrast to the other nobles who opposed the king, whom the abbot repeatedly denounces for their perjury, Rainulf is, until a late stage in the narrative, spared such condemnation. When he first opposes the king, in 1128, it is because he is "badly advised."[20] Only in 1135, after Rainulf has rebelled for a third time, is he openly accused of perjury. Alexander then attributes to the king a long and bitter speech, in which Roger nonetheless shows great magnanimity:

> How can Count Rainulf in the future be received and believed by me, for he has always done me harm, and neither blood relationship nor, after I received his homage, the oath of fealty has restrained him? How can his good faith be trusted any more after he has violated his oath? That love by which I was united and bound to him as a relation, because of his marriage to my sister, shall be wholly sundered. But even now, if he should return to my fealty and seek my glory and honor, I shall forget all those injuries which he has done me.[21]

Alexander himself may well have been no great admirer of the count, for he goes on to contrast King Roger's generosity toward his monastery, of which he and his son Anfusus became *confratres*, with Rainulf's removal of its altar's precious ornaments: "By doing this he offended God, and hindered by his sin he was unable to prevail over Roger." But until a late stage in his narrative, he handles the count with kid gloves, and he is also careful to be tactful and to praise his (and Matilda's) son for his courage, even though that son was fighting against King Roger.[22]

Alexander had to be cautious about one further issue. Although by 1136 Roger's victory seemed certain, the process had been neither smooth nor easy, and at times the king had suffered reverses. How could this be reconciled with divine approval of his mission to bring peace and order to the south Italian mainland? Most difficult to explain was the major defeat the king had suffered in open battle with Count Rainulf and Prince Robert of Capua at Nocera in July 1132. Alexander suggests that God had interrupted what had hitherto been an unbroken chain of successes in order to remind Roger of the need for humility. He returns to this theme in his concluding

20. *Al. Tel.*, I.8, 10; for the battle, II.31, 37.
21. Ibid., III.10, 64–65.
22. Ibid., III.27, 29–30, 73, 75–76.

remarks, contrasting the disaster that had overtaken a proud ruler such as Nebuchadnezzar with the success attained by those such as David and Constantine, who behaved humbly and remembered the source of their good fortune.[23]

Alexander's work is a clearly constructed narrative with overarching themes that infuse and bind the work as a whole. By contrast, the work of his contemporary, Falco, notary and later judge of Benevento, is much less ambitious in concept: a set of annals, albeit often very detailed, recording events on a year-by-year basis. These works in fact present the classic contrast between the two distinct subgenres of "history" and "chronicle," although such a division was less rigid in the twelfth century than it was to be in the later Middle Ages. No medieval manuscript of Falco's work survives, but evidence suggests that the text spanned the years 1101–44.[24]

The first third of Falco's chronicle, covering the years up to Roger II's entry into Apulia, is a patchwork, incorporating fragments of several different earlier sources. The focus is very largely on Benevento itself and its immediate surroundings, with some excursus on papal history. (The papacy had been the overlord of Benevento since 1073, and from 1101 onward had been energetically strengthening its direct rule over the town.) The early part of the chronicle is a compilation, most likely put together in the 1120s. Parts of it *were* undoubtedly written by Falco himself; in vivid descriptions of religious ceremonies, involving the translation (reburial) of holy relics, in both 1119 and in 1124, he draws attention to his own participation: "I indeed, though unworthy, kissed the bones."[25] But the inconsistencies in this section of the work, both in coverage and style, suggest that he also reworked existing material written by others.

---

23. Ibid., II.32, 38; cf. also 91–92.

24. The original scope of Falco's *Chronicle* can be reconstructed from a later thirteenth-century text whose author used it. This later work was the *Chronicle of Sta. Maria di Ferraria*, which concerned a Cistercian house in the diocese of Teano, north of Capua; and the Beneventan material therein suggests that Falco's full text spanned the years 1101–44. (*Chronicon Ignoti Monachi Cisterciensis S. Mariae de Ferraria*, ed. Augusto Gaudenzi [Naples: F. Giannini, 1888], 15, 37.) This dovetails with what we know from surviving charters from Benevento about the author's life. The last charter in which his name is mentioned is dated September 1143. It is probable, therefore, that only the first and last folios of the original work have been lost and that Falco died soon after 1144. For a fuller discussion, see Graham A. Loud, "The Genesis and Context of the *Chronicle* of Falco of Benevento," in *Anglo-Norman Studies, XV: Proceedings of the Battle Conference, 1992*, ed. Marjorie Chibnall (Woodbridge: Boydell Press, 1993), 177–98, reprinted in idem, *Montecassino and Benevento in the Middle Ages: Essays in South Italian Church History* (Aldershot: Ashgate, 2000).

25. *Falco*, 46–52, 74–78, esp. 46 n. 1.

From 1127 onward, however, not only does the scale of the coverage for individual years increase, but its scope is extended. While events in Benevento remain at the heart of the work, the focus spreads to include both the principality of Capua and the region of Apulia. The bulk of the narrative is devoted to Roger II's attempts to impose his rule on these provinces, a struggle into which the hapless citizens of Benevento were unwillingly drawn. What we have here is undoubtedly the original work of Falco himself, and his authorship is identified in the entry for 1133.

Falco's viewpoints, and indeed his obvious bias, are explicable primarily by his concern for the well-being and independence of his native town, and secondarily by the bitter factional disputes that convulsed Benevento for much of this period. Falco recorded with some amazement that in May 1119, at the *inventio* (reburial) of the relics of various saints "that had formerly lain for a long time in unworthy tombs," the rejoicing was such that "you would have seen a most unusual procession, and something unheard of for many years, the city of Benevento moved only by honor and love for the saints." The implication is that such domestic concord was most unusual.[26]

Although the first half of the 1120s appears to have been relatively peaceful, problems, both internal and external, recurred from 1128 onward. First Count Roger's partisans threatened the town and its *contado* (countryside under a town's jurisdiction) as a means of pressuring Pope Honorius to grant him investiture as duke of Apulia. Then, on 29 September 1128, during an uprising within the town, the unpopular papal rector, William, was murdered as he cowered behind an altar in the chapel of the princely palace. A commune was organized, and various members of the existing civic regime were exiled. Even a personal plea by the pope, delivered when he visited the town in August 1129, could not secure their recall.[27] The papal schism of 1130 sharpened these domestic divisions, not least because in his bull creating the kingdom of Sicily in September 1130 Anacletus II granted the new monarch "the aid of the men of Benevento against your enemies." This concession was extremely unpopular in the town. When Roger invoked this clause in 1132, the rector who had negotiated with the king was driven from the city by another popular uprising. Falco recorded the citizens' complaint: "We are unwilling to be bound to the king and to be forced by oaths to wear ourselves out on his expeditions and to pant under the burning sun along with the Sicilians, Calabrians, and Apulians. We are used to an easy life and have

26. Ibid., 48.
27. Ibid., 88–90, 102–4.

never been accustomed to military dangers; we will have nothing to do with this agreement with such a king."[28]

Roger's opponents, Robert II of Capua and Count Rainulf, shrewdly took advantage of this feeling by promising to respect Benevento's neutrality, provided that the townsmen agreed not to assist the king. The Beneventans thus greeted the news of their victory at Nocera in July with rejoicing. Subsequently, toward the end of 1132, a faction within the town invited a cardinal loyal to Innocent II to be its rector, in place of the Anacletan cardinal Crescentius. Falco himself was a partisan in these events and was recommended for promotion to be one of the city judges by Innocent's rector, Cardinal Gerard.[29] Not surprisingly, therefore, his involvement is reflected in his chronicle. When Crescentius and his supporters tried to seize Benevento in November 1133, Falco exclaimed: "What a terrible thing to record! In the alleged name of the Roman See they planned to make the city of Benevento, which had for a long time flourished in freedom and in fealty to Saint Peter, submit to the cruelty of this king, the memory [of which] ought, or so I consider, to be execrated."[30] He went on to denounce those who were killing the townsmen "but cried out that they wanted peace. . . . How, by killing or mortally wounding people, was the cause of peace advanced?" But Count Rainulf's surrender to the king, and in the summer of 1134 the virtually complete collapse of the coalition that opposed Roger, led to the restoration of the Anacletan regime at Benevento. Falco and other supporters of the pro-Innocent party were exiled, although we only learn of this by a retrospective mention in the chronicle.[31]

Falco's hostility to King Roger clearly stemmed from his belief that the king was threatening the independence of Benevento, whereas the king's opponents were prepared to respect it. Falco's attitude toward Anacletus and his rector became increasingly hostile as well. The papal schism did not create the factional dispute at Benevento, however—it was already present in 1130—nor was Anacletus unpopular because of any illegitimacy in his title as pope. Falco and others opposed him because he did his best to suppress the commune.

In the chronicle Falco's growing antipathy is evident in the change from

28. Ibid., 130.
29. Ibid., 144, 148.
30. Ibid., 164. The translation of this last sentence is problematic. I have here followed the suggestion of Edoardo d'Angelo, in *Falco*, viii, that the phrase *execrandae memoriae* refers rather to the cruelty than to the king himself. There would therefore be no need to translate *memoria* as "reputation," as I suggested in "Genesis and Context," 183.
31. *Falco*, 184.

"Pope Anacletus" in passages concerning 1130–31 to "the pope masquerading as Anacletus" [pontifex sub nomine Anacleti coloratus] in 1134.[32] One can also contrast his attitude toward Count Rainulf before 1130, which was by no means particularly flattering, with his very positive view of him once he had emerged as the most forceful leader of the opposition to King Roger. Thus, when Falco describes the conflict between Rainulf and his local rival Count Jordan of Ariano in 1119, his sympathies appear to lie with the latter: "Count Jordan, who was careful and of great wisdom, knew the impudence of Count Rainulf and that audacity of this sort did not come from the treasures of prudence."[33] In 1132, however, he describes how Rainulf "sallied forth with a joyous and intrepid heart, desiring to suffer death before disinheritance and exile in foreign and unknown parts." The count "was a man of good sense and greatly grieved the loss of his cherished wife."[34] When Rainulf was chosen as the new duke of Apulia by Pope Innocent and the emperor Lothar in 1137, Falco praised him as "a man both prudent and discreet" and claimed that his promotion was greeted by unparalleled rejoicing.[35] When he died from a sudden fever at Troia, in April 1139, Falco claimed that

> [t]he people of Bari, Trani, Melfi, Canosa, and all the other towns under his rule and trusting in his protection abandoned consolation, tore their hair, beat their breasts, and wore out their knees, with far more than the customary mourning, for they lamented a most pious duke and father of all, who laying aside vindictiveness had ruled over his duchy with sweetness and humanity. What more? Even the fiercest of his enemies had compassion for his death and lamenting his [lost] prudence they were moved to tears.[36]

If Rainulf is increasingly one of the heroes of Falco's chronicle, King Roger is of course the principal villain. Yet here too the emphasis changes. Though Falco is never very enthusiastic about Roger, his treatment of him is at first relatively balanced. When Roger makes his first appearance in the narrative, at Salerno in 1127, Falco inserts into his mouth a speech to the citizens in which he makes a reasoned plea for his hereditary claim to succeed Duke

32. Ibid., 172.
33. Ibid., 46.
34. Ibid., 122, 136.
35. Ibid., 190.
36. Ibid., 216.

William as lord of the city, even though Falco later accuses him of "pride" (*animus elatus*) in seeking the ducal title. In 1133, however, Falco's attitude changed abruptly with Roger's campaign in Apulia, which was marked by extensive use of his Muslim troops from Sicily and savage reprisals against rebel towns (see Appendix B). From then on, Falco denounced the king as a tyrant, whose brutal measures fell upon not merely those who actually opposed him, but women, children, and the clergy. "Who at any time, hearing of the deadly fury of such an evil king, would not be terrified to submit to his lordship? We testify to the Eternal King and Judge of all that according to what we have read even Nero, the cruelest emperor of the pagans, did not inflict such slaughter among Christians."[37]

A prime example of Roger's vindictiveness was, according to Falco, shown in his reaction to the death of his staunchest opponent, his brother-in-law Rainulf. While the people of Apulia lamented, "King Roger was filled with vanity and pride, and rejoiced more than seemed humanly possible." The sequel was much more chilling. When Roger led his army to Troia in the summer of 1139, he refused to enter the city, and by implication to grant the citizens pardon for resisting him, so long as Rainulf lay buried in the cathedral. One of the latter's own men was forced to disinter the corpse, which was then dragged ignominiously through the streets and eventually flung into a ditch in some charcoal workings outside the town. Falco works himself up to a fine rhetorical frenzy here: "I testify to the Eternal King, Judge of the Centuries, that we have never read of such a ghastly thing having happened in previous generations or [even] among pagans. How could such cruelty as this profit the king's authority? What victory or royal glory could it lead to? But desiring to satisfy his rage against one whom he could not exercise it while he was alive, he did it when he was dead."[38] It was only after Roger's own son had reproached him for his action that Rainulf's corpse was once again granted a Christian burial. Falco's reaction could reflect genuine outrage at the king's behavior, but the denunciation of Roger here is part of a much more extended critique of his actions, one among a number of examples cited of his tyranny. Falco does not just suggest that Roger was cruel; he also portrays him as deceitful. When Bari surrendered in 1139 on terms that guaranteed the safety of its defenders, terms ratified on oath, the king then found a pretext to renege and had the prince of Bari and his counselors hanged and other prominent men mutilated or imprisoned. "Such

37. Ibid., 158.
38. Ibid., 216, 224–26; quotation on 226.

fear and horror invaded the city that neither man nor woman dared to go out into its squares and streets."[39] By the last stages of his chronicle, Falco criticizes almost every action of the king. The royal order to issue new silver and copper coinage, introduced in 1140, and probably much needed given the shortage of lower-denomination coins in the region up to that time, Falco denounces as "a terrible edict, hated throughout Italy and leading to death and poverty. . . . All the people of Italy suffered and were reduced to poverty and misery by this horrible money and as a result of these oppressive actions hoped for the king's death or deposition."[40] Yet this is rhetoric, not reality. The new "ducat" that was introduced in 1140, far from being "much more copper than silver," as Falco alleges, actually had a 60 percent silver content, which was much the same as that of the *miliaresia* that had circulated in the previous century, gradually disappearing after the end of Byzantine rule in Apulia, in 1071.[41]

Falco's view of the king in the later stages of his chronicle is almost uniformly hostile. Yet this bias often tells us more about the author than about the king. Certainly the story had another side, and although Alexander's narrative ends in 1135 and is of course equally and more artfully slanted in the opposite direction, the comparison can be illuminating. Roger's treatment of Count (Duke) Rainulf's remains, assuming (as I think we must) that it occurred as Falco describes, was explicable given Rainulf's history of perjury and disloyalty. He had submitted to the king three times, sworn fealty to him, and then broken his word. Roger's behavior in 1139 suggests the essential truth underlying the denunciation of the count that Alexander attributes to him in 1135. Kings could not allow disloyalty to go unpunished; *fidelitas* (loyalty) was the fragile glue that held society together, and especially in a new entity such as the kingdom of Sicily, an amalgam of different provinces, peoples, and traditions. Nor could King Roger allow Rainulf's tomb to become a shrine and a focus for dissent.[42] That Roger was generally considered a severe ruler is undoubted, but the verdict of the last of the

39. Ibid., 230.

40. Ibid., 234.

41. Lucia Travaini, *La monetazione nell'Italia normanna* (Rome: Istituto italiano per il Medio Evo, 1995), 55–60.

42. As had, for example, the tomb of the antipope Clement III at Civita Castellana, where a miracle cult had developed, much to the annoyance of the reform papacy, and would (much later) the tomb of Simon de Montfort (d. 1265) at Evesham abbey. On the former, see Jürgen Ziese, *Wibert von Ravenna: Der Gegenpapst Clemens III. (1084–1100)* (Stuttgart: A. Hiersemann, 1982), 270–74; on the latter, Ronald C. Finucane, *Miracles and Pilgrims: Popular Beliefs in Medieval England* (London: J. M. Dent, 1977), 131–35.

three south Italian historians assessed here, the so-called Hugo Falcandus, who was no uncritical sycophant of rulers, is interesting in this context: "[S]ome writers categorize many of his actions as tyrannical and call him inhuman because he imposed on many men penalties that were severe and not prescribed by the laws. It is my opinion that as a prudent man he intentionally behaved in this way when his monarchy was only recently established . . . if perhaps he seemed to have acted somewhat harshly against some, I suppose that he was forced to it by some necessity."[43]

One further aspect of the chronicle of Falco merits consideration. Benevento had, albeit with great difficulty, maintained its independence from the Norman warlords who had conquered almost all of southern Italy during the eleventh century, although its submission to papal overlordship was the price that had had to be paid for this. Benevento remained a stronghold of the indigenous south Italians, who still called themselves "Lombards" (Latin *longobardi*, differentiated from *lombardi*, which was the twelfth-century term for north Italians). At a few points in the early sections of the chronicle Falco, or possibly the source he was using, refers to the Lombard-Norman antithesis. Thus, in 1113, seeing the success of Constable Landulf de Graeca in defending the territory of Benevento, Falco says that the prince of Capua and the counts of Caiazzo and Ariano "were convulsed with envy and hatred of the Lombards . . . they plotted with all the Normans of the neighboring areas, declaring that they would levy war and rapine against the Beneventans as long as Landulf remained their constable."[44]

Yet after 1114 mention of Normans all but disappears from the chronicle. There are but two further references, both during the 1130s, and they concern the dues the Beneventans were accustomed to pay to the Norman lords whose lands bordered the city's *contado*. Such "servitude and tribute" was clearly a matter of great concern to the Beneventans; hence, in 1137 they obtained privileges from both the emperor Lothar and Roger freeing them from these payments.[45] But after 1114 the chronicle conveys no sense of Lombard-Norman hostility. Indeed, even at this earlier period, one of the "Normans" who was harassing the town in 1113 was a certain Landulfus Burrell, whose name strongly suggests that he was actually of Lombard descent.[46]

43. *Tyrants*, 58.
44. *Falco*, 10.
45. Ibid., 128, 192.
46. Landulfus was a generic Lombard name, and although Normans might use Lombard names for their daughters, they never did for their sons, although Lombards often used French names for *their* sons. The Borrel/Burelli were an indigenous family of Lombardo-Frankish descent who dominated the Sangro Valley and northern Molise in the eleventh

Furthermore, Count Rainulf and Robert II of Capua, whose fortitude in resisting Roger's "tyranny" Falco so praises, were both Normans, and indeed cousins. The Norman conquest had not been forgotten in the 1130s—Alexander of Telese wrote (as we have seen) of how it had been part of God's plan, and a precursor to Roger's conquest, because of the sins of the Lombards.[47] But the Lombard-Norman division was no longer important, not least because of intermarriage. Only in the earliest parts of the chronicle, compiled no later than the early 1120s, does the author display any consciousness that being Norman or Lombard mattered. Admittedly "Hugo Falcandus" suggests that King Roger extended warm welcome to people from north of the Alps because he remembered his own Norman descent.[48] But it is clear from his *History* that the real division in the higher social ranks of mid-twelfth-century Sicily was between *regnicoli* (inhabitants of the south Italian kingdom), whatever their descent, and newly arrived *transmontani* (ultramontanes), not between descendants of conquerors and conquered.

Falco's prose style, despite the frequent repetition of banalities such as "O reader, if you had been there!" is not as simple as it might at first sight appear, for as a notary he had mastered the rhyming prose of the *cursus* (a convention of writing that arose in the eleventh-century papal Curia). But though clearly familiar with the Bible—for example, comparing the king's opponents with the Maccabees—his intellectual background was, as one might expect of a layman, severely restricted, his reading limited to local annals and hagiography.[49] Alexander, as a monk, was familiar not just with the Bible but with at least some of the standard texts of monastic libraries such as Gregory of Tours and Cassian. But though his Latin was sufficiently classical to suggest acquaintance with the standard schoolbooks, the only classical text with which he seems to show familiarity is Seneca's *Naturales Quaestiones.*[50] The author of the third south Italian text, on the other hand, was steeped in the Latin classics; his work displays a sophisticated Latin style that puts him at the forefront of the intellectual revival often known as the twelfth-century Renaissance.

---

and twelfth centuries. Was this Landulf a relation of theirs? He was probably an ancestor of the Landulfus Burrellus who had a fief at Strangogallo (Caserta) in the mid–twelfth century. *Catalogus Baronum*, ed. Evelyn M. Jamison (Rome: British School at Rome, 1972), 153 art. 844.

47. *Al. Tel.*, 3.
48. *Tyrants*, 58.
49. *Falco*, cxxix–clxiv; Maccabees, e.g., ibid., 126.
50. *Al. Tel.*, xxii–iv.

The *History of the Tyrants of Sicily* is the principal narrative source for the history of the kingdom of Sicily from the death of King Roger to the minority of King William II. The last events mentioned therein are the earthquake that devastated Catania in eastern Sicily and the recall from exile of Count Robert of Loritello (February–March 1169). The work ends quite abruptly and has sometimes been taken to be unfinished, although such a conjecture is by no means certain. The *History* falls into two distinct sections, of roughly equal length. The first discusses the reign of King William I from 1154 until 1162. The reign was a troubled one, with a serious revolt on the mainland and external attack by the Byzantine Empire (1155–56), the repulse of which is described. Most of the rest of this section is devoted to the murder of the king's unpopular chief minister, Maio of Bari (November 1160), and the subsequent attempted coup against the king (March 1161). This coup coincided with another widespread rebellion, both on the island of Sicily and on the mainland, which was suppressed with considerable difficulty. The last four years of the king's reign are then passed over in a few sentences about the king's palace building, and the second half of the work begins with his sudden death (May 1166). There follows a detailed account of the factional strife at court during the minority of William II, who succeeded to the throne a month short of his thirteenth birthday. Eventually the direction of the government was taken over by the new archbishop of Palermo, Walter.[51]

The text was conceived as one continuous narrative on the classical model. Dates are rarely, if ever, mentioned—these have to be derived from other sources, especially the contemporary chronicle, in annalistic format, attributed to Romuald II, archbishop of Salerno, 1153–81, a work that is far inferior in scale, style, and interest but serves as a useful check on the account given by Falcandus.[52] Like classical historians, the author prefers to use vague phrases to indicate the passage of time, such as "after a little while" or "a few days later." But while steeped in the Latin classics, he hardly ever quotes them directly, although many of his phrases adapt those of the classical authors whom he had read, above all Sallust, who is his principal

51. William II did not even formally assume the reins of government until early in 1172, when he was eighteen, but in practice day-to-day rule continued to be exercised throughout his reign by a group of three or four *familiares*, of whom Walter, archbishop of Palermo 1169–90, was always one. See Hiroshi Takayama, *The Administration of the Norman Kingdom of Sicily* (Leiden: E. J. Brill, 1993), 119–25.

52. *Romualdi Salernitani Chronicon*, ed. Carlo Alberto Garufi, *RIS*, n.s., 7, pt. 1 (Città di Castello: Stamperia S. Lapi, 1935). The section covering the same period as *Falcandus* is translated in *Tyrants*, 219–43.

model as a historian. Again like classical historians, Falcandus is interested in the motivation of individuals, and he sketches (often uncharitably) the characters of the main protagonists in a few pithy sentences. Here, for example, is Archbishop Roger of Reggio: "He thought that no labor was too hard if there was any hope of gain thereby. He put up with hunger and thirst beyond human capacity, if it could cut down his expenses. He was never cheerful when he dined at home, never sad at anyone else's dinner-party. He frequently spent whole days in fasting, waiting for someone to send him an invitation."[53]

Although far superior as a work of literature to the historical writings of King Roger's reign, and also to those earlier works describing the eleventh-century conquest, the *History of the Tyrants* poses many problems, not the least of which is the question of authorship. The attribution to the otherwise unknown "Hugo Falcandus" comes only in the first printed edition of 1550, which was made from a manuscript now lost. None of the four extant manuscripts mentions this name. Various ingenious attempts have been made to identify a possible author; none has been convincing. The most recent revives an old theory attributing the work to Hugues Foucaud, abbot of Saint-Denis, the royal abbey just outside Paris, from 1186 to 1197.[54] This theory is superficially attractive, not least because one can see how scribal error could corrupt the author's name to "Hugo Falcandus," but also because it explains how the text was known (as it was) at Saint-Denis by the late thirteenth century.[55] Yet, the evidence to suggest that Hugues Foucaud had any connection with Sicily is tenuous in the extreme.[56]

53. *Tyrants*, 143. The phrase about hunger and thirst is drawn from Sallust's description of Catiline.

54. Gwenyth E. Hood, "Falcandus and Fulcaudus, 'Epistola ad Petrum, Liber de Regno Sicilie': Literary Form and Author's Identity," *Studia medievali*, 3rd ser., 49 (1999): 1–41. The principal evidence comes from a letter Peter of Blois wrote to Abbot H. of Saint-Denis in which Peter requests a copy of "the tract you have written about the state of Sicily." Peter, *Ep.* 116, in *PL*, 207, cols. 345–46. For other attempts to identify the author, and for the date of the text, see *Tyrants*, 28–42.

55. This theory is flawed not least in that it does not address the problem of dating the text. Most discussions of the authorship have argued, as does this most recent one, that the text was written after the death of William II in 1189. But other sound arguments suggest that it was in fact composed during that king's lifetime, and perhaps that the two sections were written at different times in the reign. See Hartmut Hoffmann, "Hugo Falcandus und Romuald von Salerno," *Deutsches Archiv für Erforschung des Mittelalters* 23 (1967): 133–38, but compare *Tyrants*, 39–42, for some cautionary remarks.

56. "Falcandus" saw Sicily as his *nutrix* (nurse), and hence was a native (*Falcandus*, 170 [*Tyrants*, 252]). Hood speculates that therefore Foucauld could originally have hailed from there, an eventuality made all the more possible because nothing is known of his background or career before appearing as prior of Saint-Denis in 1183 (Hood, "Falcandus and

Whoever the author was, he was undoubtedly an insider with a close personal knowledge of the personalities of the court and of the workings of the royal administration. Nonetheless, the extraordinary bias he displays and the vituperation he heaps on all but a very few of the people mentioned dictate that despite the detailed knowledge and first-hand nature of the text, its opinions be treated with care. The tone is overwhelmingly bitter. The author begins his account by saying, "[I]n Sicily there is nothing amazing about the performance of deeds of extreme wickedness," and he goes on amply to document this proposition. William I was an idle and cruel tyrant, his minister Maio worse, a power-hungry intriguer and sexual predator who was, Falcandus claims, conspiring to murder his own master when he himself fell victim to assassination by the man he had chosen as his son-in-law. The courtiers under William II plotted against and slandered each other. Even when the author (henceforth Pseudo-Hugo) included some element of charity or praise in his verdicts, he found it hard to be entirely complimentary. Thus, although his comments on Caid Peter, the convert from Islam who was the trusted minister of Queen Margaret in the early days of the regency, were in some respects favorable, the barbs show through:

> Although Peter was not a very shrewd man and tended to keep changing his mind, he was, however, gentle, pleasant and likeable, and his actions gave no grounds for criticism. He practiced liberality above all the other virtues, and thought that giving gave more satisfaction than receiving. Because of this his knights loved him dearly . . . and if the vice of his race had not cancelled out his innate peaceableness, preventing him from genuinely abandoning his hatred of Christianity, the kingdom of Sicily would have enjoyed much peace under his administration.[57]

Yet one should note that Peter had since childhood been brought up at the Sicilian court, presumably therefore as a Christian, and that his eventual

---

Fulcaudus," 5). But Hugues Foucaud was actually a nephew of the famous Abbot Suger (Abbot of Saint-Denis, 1122–51) and presumably therefore brought up in France; see Lindy Grant, *Abbot Suger of St. Denis: Church and State in Early Twelfth-Century France* (London and New York: Longman 1998), 76, 292. Nor can Hugues have been one of those who accompanied Stephen of Perche to Sicily in 1167, for Peter wrote later that of the thirty-seven people who came to Sicily with Stephen, only he and Master Roger the Norman were then (ca. 1174) still alive (*Ep. 46*, in *PL*, 207, cols. 133–34).

57. *Tyrants*, 139.

flight to North Africa was caused, by Pseudo-Hugo's own account, not by any hatred of Christianity but by the threats made against him by the queen's cousin, Count Gilbert of Gravina.[58] Here Pseudo-Hugo's dislike of the Arabic Christians who staffed the royal administration shows through.

The supreme villain of the *History* is Maio of Bari, whom Pseudo-Hugo loathed: "a beast [*monstrum*] than whom no more repellent pest could be found, none more effective in achieving the destruction and overthrow of the realm." Maio, we are told, was intelligent but utterly unscrupulous, able "to pretend and dissemble whatever he pleased," "keen on sexual gratification," especially with respectable women, always scheming, "yet he managed to hide the tempest within his seething mind behind a calm appearance."[59] All this, repeated and elaborated at length, is a damning indictment. Yet what other evidence we have suggests that Maio was neither quite the upstart portrayed by Pseudo-Hugo nor the villain; indeed, he appears to have been a man of some piety.[60] Furthermore, the picture presented of Maio is very largely a literary one, based upon classical prototypes. The use of the word "monstrum" to describe him was taken from Cicero's descriptions of his Roman enemies, the archconspirator Catiline and the aristocratic political gangster Clodius. The phrase about his ability to dissimulate came from Sallust's *Catiline;* those about his keenness for sexual gratification and his seething mind were reworked from the same author's *Jugurtha.* Indeed, the very idea of sexual depravity as the sign of the tyrant was a classical topos— think, for example, of the emperors Caligula and Nero. Pseudo-Hugo's *History* contains a number of specific incidents whose accounts are based on classical prototypes, for example the charge that William I caused the death of his eldest son. More generally it is suffused with the language and concepts of the Roman classics.[61] The most important of these concepts is the role of Fortune, which is deployed on the very first page of the *History:* "nowhere else [than Sicily] does Fortune give her wheel a more sudden twist, or sport more hazardously with mortal men."[62] Fortune reoccurs over and over in the *History:* for example, "Fortune did not desert his preparations . . . she began to bring the top of her revolving wheel down against

58. Ibid., 147. For Peter's origins, see Ibn Khaldun, in Michele Amari, ed. and trans., *Bibliotheca Arabo-Sicula* (Turin: E. Loescher, 1881), 2:187.

59. *Falcandus,* 8 (*Tyrants,* 60).

60. Donald J. A. Matthew, "Maio of Bari's Commentary on the Lord's Prayer," in *Intellectual Life in the Middle Ages: Essays Presented to Margaret Gibson,* ed. Lesley Smith and Benedicta Ward (London and Rio Grande, Ohio: Hambledon, 1992), 119–44.

61. See *Tyrants,* 42–50, for discussion; ibid., 114, for the death of Prince Roger.

62. Ibid., 55.

him ⌈Maio⌉"; "Fortune had exhausted Sicily with great unrest"; and "while Fortune was arranging the development of this conspiracy."[63] Again, the theme is taken from Sallust, who wrote that "there can be no question that Fortune is supreme in all human affairs" (*Catiline*, 8.1). The figure who is entirely absent from Pseudo-Hugo's account is God, and in this respect his work is a complete contrast to that of Alexander and Falco. The omission of the deity is surely also a strong argument against the authorship by a Benedictine abbot.

The overall theme of the work is Sallustian. In the introduction to his history of the conspiracy of Catiline, Sallust compares the public morality that had motivated the early Romans with "the gradual degeneration of its noble character into vice and corruption" (*Catiline*, 6.1). Similarly, Pseudo-Hugo compares the power and repute of the kingdom of Sicily under King Roger with the way that "all this tranquility slipped away"—here the author reworks a phrase from the *Jugurtha*—because of the bad character of William I and Maio. The same theme, the inferiority of the present age with respect to the past, reappears in the narrative after the death of William I, when "private enmities were taking precedence over the business of the realm." Here Pseudo-Hugo quotes Lucan, purporting to give the words of Cato Uticensis on the death of Pompey.[64] Hence history was to Pseudo-Hugo very much Gibbon's "register of the crimes, follies, and misfortunes of mankind."

What therefore is the value of this text to the historian of the kingdom of Sicily, as opposed to the historian of the twelfth-century classical revival? What other evidence we have, Romuald's chronicle, the (admittedly generally much later) Arabic sources, and the documentary evidence—charters, papal letters, a few letters from Peter of Blois—indicates that the *History* was for the most part factually accurate, albeit hardly complete, for the wider international context of the Sicilian kingdom is almost entirely ignored. The reliability of the author's viewpoint is quite another story. Indeed, the continuing tensions within Sicilian society that Pseudo-Hugo reveals suggest, quite contrary to his interpretation, that King Roger's state building was far from complete and had left many problems with which his successors had to grapple.[65] Clearly this text must be used with extreme caution, for it is a manifesto rather than a history in our sense—although admittedly

63. Ibid., 94, 126, 175.
64. Ibid., 59–60, 151.
65. Graham A. Loud, "William the Bad or William the Unlucky? Kingship in Sicily, 1154–1166," *Haskins Society Journal* 8 (1999, for 1996): 99–113.

not a party manifesto, for Pseudo-Hugo has so little good to say that he can hardly be said to support anyone. One could, of course, equally criticize Alexander or Falco, the one writing a manifesto for King Roger, the other attacking the king as a tyrant, but such criticism ignores *why* history was written in the Middle Ages. With these two authors, at least, one can always compare and contrast the one against the other. However, the brevity of Romuald's annals leaves Pseudo-Hugo very much in isolation for the period after 1154. All three historians were products of troubled and contentious times; it would be naïve, therefore, to expect fairness or neutrality from them. Yet the bias and complexities of these texts only add to their interest, and the contrasting viewpoints of monastic panegyrist, lay civic patriot, and classical moralist reveal how varied historical writing in the twelfth century could be. What is, however, both surprising and disappointing, given the interest of these texts, is that for half a century or more after the time of Pseudo-Hugo the tradition of historical writing in southern Italy was so thin.[66]

APPENDIX A: ROGER OF SICILY BECOMES KING, FROM THE HISTORY OF ALEXANDER OF TELESE, BOOK II, CHAPTERS 1–6[67]

(1) With so many successes achieved, all the lands of Bohemond[68] and the whole duchy seemingly in his power, the prince of the Capuans, the *magister militum* of Naples and all the land up to the borders of the city of Ancona subject to him, and his opponents in war subdued, those close to Duke Roger, and particularly his uncle Count Henry, by whom he was loved more than anyone,[69] began very frequently to suggest to him the plan that he, who with the help of God ruled so many provinces, Sicily, Calabria, Apulia, and other regions stretching almost to Rome, ought not to have just the ducal title but ought to be distinguished by the honor of kingship. They added

66. Romuald's chronicle concluded in 1178, and the Casauria Chronicle of John Berard was completed in 1182; thereafter we have only Peter of Eboli's poem on Henry VI's conquest, the Carpineto chronicle (the scope of which is strictly local), and two or three very thin sets of annals (from Cava, Montecassino, and Fossanova, the last of which was just outside the kingdom) until Richard of San Germano's chronicle in the 1240s.

67. *Al. Tel.*, 23–26.

68. Bohemond II, prince of Taranto and Antioch, another cousin of Roger II. He had left his south Italian lordship in 1126 to go to Syria, where he was killed fighting the Muslims in 1130.

69. Henry, count of Butera, the king's maternal uncle (died after 1136).

that the center and capital of this kingdom ought to be Palermo, the chief city of Sicily, which once, in ancient times, was believed to have had kings [who ruled] over this province but now, many years later, was by God's secret judgment without them.

(2) After turning over in his own mind their well-intentioned and praise-worthy suggestion, he wanted to have sure and certain counsel. He jour-neyed back to Salerno, and just outside it he convoked some learned churchmen and most competent persons, as well as certain princes, counts, barons, and others whom he thought trustworthy to examine this secret and unsought matter. Examining the issue carefully, they unanimously, as if with one voice, praised [this proposal] and conceded, decided, and insisted with mighty prayers that Duke Roger ought to be promoted at Palermo, the chief city of Sicily, to the royal dignity, since he held not only Sicily, his hereditary patrimony, but also Calabria, Apulia, and other lands—not just obtained by military prowess but devolved to him by right of his close rela-tionship to the preceding dukes. For it was certain that kingship had once existed in that city, governing all Sicily; it seemed to have been in abeyance for a long time, but now it was right and proper that the crown should be placed on Roger's head and that this kingdom should not only be restored but should be spread wide to include those other regions where he was now recognized as ruler.

(3) Once the duke had taken counsel with them and had been strength-ened by their sincere approval, he went back to Sicily, ordering that all the men of dignity, power, and honor from his lands and provinces should gather together at Palermo for his coronation, which would take place on Christmas Day. On the constituted day all they and a numberless populace both great and small flocked together. All were once again solemnly asked the same question and answered in the same way as above; to the glory of God and the advantage of his Church all in the royal city of Palermo ap-proved the promotion to the kingship for him to whom so much power had been given by God and who had already greatly extended the lands of his family, that he might exercise it to punish the evil and to preserve justice.

(4) When, therefore, the duke was led to the archiepiscopal church in royal manner and there through unction with the holy oil assumed the royal dig-nity, one cannot write down or indeed even imagine quite how glorious he was, how regal in his dignity, how splendid in his richly adorned apparel. For it seemed to the onlookers that all the riches and honors of this world

were present. The whole city was decorated in a stupendous manner, and nowhere was there anything but rejoicing and light.

(5) The royal palace was on its interior walls gloriously draped through-out. The pavement was bestrewed with multicolored carpets and offered a flowing softness to the feet of those who trod there. When the king went to the church for the ceremony, he was surrounded by dignitaries, and the huge number of horses that accompanied them had saddles and bridles deco-rated with gold and silver.

(6) Copious amounts of the choicest food and drink were served to the din-ers at the royal table, and nothing was served except in dishes or cups of gold or silver. No servant wore aught but a silver tunic—the very waiters were clad in silk clothes! What more is there to say? The glory and wealth of the royal abode was so spectacular that it caused great wonder and deep stupefaction—so great indeed that it instilled not a little fear in all those who had come from so far away. For many saw there more things even than they had heard rumored of previously.

APPENDIX B: THE HORRORS OF KING ROGER'S CAMPAIGN IN APULIA IN 1133, FROM THE CHRONICLE OF FALCO OF BENEVENTO[70]

Meanwhile the prince and the count had gone to Rome, albeit unwillingly, followed by the emperor. While they were there, King Roger of the Sicilians gathered an army of Saracens and unexpectedly crossed the Straits of Mes-sina; he then marched speedily into Apulia and stormed the city of Venosa (which Tancred had captured)[71] and other towns and gave them over to fire and the sword. In them he killed men, women, and children; indeed, some of them he burned. We testify to the Eternal King that he demonstrated such cruelty toward Christian people as has scarcely or ever been heard of in our century. The prince and count were immediately informed of this while they were staying in Rome, and [were told] that they should return as fast as possible to resist this great tyrant and to protect their property from the appetite of such a robber. They did indeed return as soon as the message reached them, and had their heralds rouse the whole principality

70. *Falco*, 150–56.
71. Tancred, brother of Count Alexander of Conversano and formerly lord of Brindisi. Their grandmother was a sister of Duke Robert Guiscard.

of Capua and the city of Benevento, to take up arms and manfully resist this perfidy and tyranny, which indeed was done and everything put in readiness. Count Rainulf, accompanied by nearly a thousand knights, marched toward the borders of Troia. He sent messengers to the city of Troia requesting that the citizens fulfill the oaths they had sworn to him and to the prince. However, the people of Troia were influenced by their fear of the king and put their trust in his deceitful words of peace. They refused to accede to the count's wish, principally because the bishop of the city persuaded all the people not to abandon their fealty to the king. Hearing this, the count remained in the area for forty days and then returned to Benevento.

While these and other events were occurring, the king besieged a city called Matera. Attacking it fiercely, he captured it through the treachery of its people, and there he took prisoner Godfrey, son of Count Godfrey, the lord of the city. After doing this, he obtained power over another city, called Anzi, where he found the gold and silver treasure of Count Alexander. What more? All Alexander's cities and towns submitted to his will. The count, like a shipwrecked sailor, went, poor man, to Count Rainulf and died there. The king then devastated the city of Trani and all Apulia with fire and sword. What shall I say? The king behaved toward Christians in a way that had never been heard of in this century. Moving his army on, King Roger, still not satiated by human blood, besieged Montepeloso, where were those warlike and energetic men Tancred of Conversano and Roger de Pleuto. He remained there fifteen days. Tancred and Roger manfully and bravely resisted the king and his army. However, seeing their constancy, King Roger ordered wooden machines and [other] war engines to be built [for use] against Montepeloso. As a result, a group of the ordinary people of the city who were aware of the king's harshness and of the horrors of battle refused to fight him—they claimed that they were unable to defend themselves. What further? With war engines all round the walls, trumpets sounding, and shouts rising to Heaven on every side, he attacked Montepeloso. Seeing this assault, Tancred of Conversano and the aforesaid Roger mounted their horses and with their knights fought back to the limit of their powers. Finally, however, by the intervention of Divine Judgment and to their awful misfortune, the city of Montepeloso was captured. Tancred and the unfortunate Roger threw down their arms and took refuge in dark and hidden parts of the city. However, they were found by their pursuers and brought before King Roger. O what grief and horror hitherto unknown! If you had been there, reader, how dreadfully you would have grieved! The king immediately ordered Roger to be hanged. He also ordered that Tancred should pull on the rope attached to the noose with his own hand. What a wicked thing and how terrible to record! Tancred himself unwillingly obeyed the king's command. The whole army was amazed and horrified by this deed of the king's, praying the King of Heaven to see fit to resist such a cruel tyrant. After doing this, he ordered this splendid man Tancred of Conversano to be imprisoned. As we have heard it, he was led off captive to Sicily. Without further delay the king sacked the city of Montepeloso and its monasteries and slew all its inhabitants, men, women, and children, by the sword or in the fire.

He then set his army in motion once again and made a forced march to the city of Troia. The citizens, who believed his deceitful assurances of peace, awaited him without foreboding. Bishop William[72] summoned all the clergy and monks of the city, clad in white, and went out in procession to meet the king with the *laudes*, thinking as we have heard to soothe his ferocious spirit by carrying before him the bodies of the saints. However, the furious king entered the city and seeing this glorious procession forgot his promise of security and, being unmindful of the Catholic faith and the enemy of the Christian religion, with burning eyes put an end to that procession. "I do not want," he said, "honors of this sort, but if life is granted to me, I shall destroy everything and exile everyone." The clergy and people who had gone out to meet him were put to flight, and everybody fled as best they could. He immediately arrested many of the Troian citizens and put the women and children in chains. He ordered a judge named Robert and four other distinguished men to be hanged. Many Troians abandoned their property and fled with their wives and children to Benevento. He then ordered that the houses and property of the Troians be given over to the sword and consumed by fire. O what a wailing of women and children arose over the whole city of Troia! If my tongue had a hundred voices to narrate everything that happened, then I would still fail to do it justice in writing them down! A few days later the king gathered together his army and marched on the city of Melfi, which, so we heard, he stormed and placed under his power.

In this same year, seeing the ferocity of King Roger and the death and destruction menacing the whole of Apulia, and fearing that the king would then invade his principality, Prince Robert took counsel, went on board ship, and hastened to the city of Pisa. He was honorably received there and was asked why he had made such a journey. The prince then described in detail King Roger's ferocity and threats and the resulting dangers. He humbly

---

72. William II, bishop of Troia, 1106–41, one of the most prominent bishops of northern Apulia.

begged that the city of Pisa grant him help and advice, and they agreed between them a treaty, as will be described below in this work. On 24 June the prince put to sea and sailed from Pisa. How he dealt with the Pisans has not yet come in any detail to our notice, so let us return to our story.

After the king had devastated Troia and Melfi, he divided his mighty army into sections, or so we have heard, and returned to the city of Bari. Meanwhile Count Rainulf raised the whole principality of Capua and mobilized the help of all his lands and of Rolpoto, the constable of Benevento, and every section and street of Benevento, that everyone should bear arms and resist the tyrant king. All unanimously and devotedly obeyed Count Rainulf's wish. They cried out that they would rather suffer death than bow their heads to the rule of such a wicked king.

3

The Genoese Civic Annals:
Caffaro and His Continuators

John Dotson

Caffaro di Rustico reports that in 1152 he presented a copy of the annals he had been compiling to the consuls of Genoa. They ordered that it be copied into the city's public records. This was the beginning of an almost two-century tradition of Genoese government-sponsored civic history written by educated laymen, a tradition unique in Italy and Europe. The Genoese tradition was an expansion and continuation of the Lombard annalist tradition considered previously. But more than those of Lombardy, the Genoese annals must be seen as "authentic communal documents" in and of themselves.[1] Each of the annals I consider was either approved by the government for inclusion in civic records or specifically commissioned as an official document, and thus was part of the city's "official memory." The first and last annalists, Caffaro di Rustico and Jacopo Doria,[2] were from distinguished and powerful families; their writings were independently written and approved by the commune only after the two had composed all or most of their work. The intervening annalists were scribes, notaries, and other government functionaries. Their work was rarely as independently produced as that of Caffaro and Doria. The resulting annals are secular, patriotic, and often biased in favor of the party in power at the time. Nonetheless, they are

1. Giovanna Petti Balbi, *Caffaro e la chronachista genovese* (Genoa: Tilgher, 1982), 143. She is basing her observations on the work of Girolamo Arnaldi, especially "Cronache con documenti, cronache 'autentiche' e pubblica storiografia," in *Fonti medioevali e problematica storiografica* (Rome: Istituto storico italiano per il Medio Evo, 1976), 1:351–74.
2. See Giovanna Petti Balbi, "Caffaro," in *Dizionario biografico degli italiani*, 16:256–60 (Rome: Istituto dell'enciclopedia italiana, 1973), and Giovanni Nuti, "Iacopo Doria," in ibid., vol. 41 (1992), 391–96.

distinctive, valuable, and often overlooked sources for the history of Italy and Europe as well as Genoa.[3]

This remarkable tradition began with the reminiscences of a prominent and brilliant Genoese patrician who participated in some of the greatest undertakings of his age. Caffaro di Rustico, lord of Caschifellone, was born around 1080 into one branch of a prominent family that claimed descent from the tenth-century viscounts of Genoa.[4] During his long life—he lived to be more than eighty-five years old—the city underwent tumultuous and momentous developments. A commune was established, and it soon sent a fleet to support the First Crusade, waged war with Genoa's Tuscan neighbor Pisa, and crusaded in Spain. Caffaro witnessed many of these events. Indeed, he played an important part in many of the great events of his age. He served six terms as consul (one of four chief magistrates on a board of the commune), two terms as judge, and intermittently as an ambassador, with a number of important and delicate missions. He was an admiral in command of fleets in wars against the Pisans and the Spanish Muslims. As a very prominent figure in the early commune, he was for two-thirds of a century a knowledgeable first-hand observer or well-placed participant in most of the important events in the history of the early Genoese commune.[5]

Caffaro was too young to take part in the first Genoese expedition to Syria, in 1097, but was certainly old enough to be aware of the undertaking and its importance for his city. Three years later, at the end of the summer of 1100, he joined another, larger fleet as it sailed for the Holy Land. This would prove to be a life-shaping experience for the young aristocrat. Caffaro saw crusades and expeditions to the eastern Mediterranean as part of a period of glorious accomplishment for Genoa, and they became the main focus of his writings. In addition to the annals that became the foundation of a Genoese tradition, Caffaro produced two other works dealing with the crusading movement. *De liberatione civitatum Orientis* is an account of the First Crusade and the period immediately following. The *Ystoria captionis Almarie et Turtuose* is an account of campaigns against the Muslims in Spain. He might also have written or had some part in composing *Notitia*

3. A good overview, in English, of Genoese history may be found in Steven A. Epstein, *Genoa and the Genoese, 958–1528* (Chapel Hill and London: University of North Carolina Press, 1996). The preface surveys the historiography of the city, xiii–xviii.

4. Luigi Tommaso Belgrano, ed., *Annali genovesi di Caffaro e de' suoi continuatori dal MXCIX al MCCXCIII*, Fonti per la storia d'Italia, 11 (Rome: Tipografia del Regio istituto sordo-muti, 1890), 1:70.

5. Richard D. Face, "Secular History in Twelfth-Century Italy: Caffaro of Genoa," *Journal of Medieval History* 6, no. 2 (1980): 169–84.

Episcoporum Ianuensium and *Breve historia regni Iherosolymitani.* All of these works turn on the themes of crusade and civic pride.[6]

In the spring of 1101, Caffaro was among the Genoese who, having landed in the Holy Land the previous autumn, made a pilgrimage to Jerusalem for Easter. They then took part in the capture of Arsuf and, later, of Caesarea. He returned to Genoa with the triumphant and booty-laden fleet in October 1101. After that, not much is known of his activities until 1121, when he participated in an embassy to the papal court in Rome. He and his fellow ambassador won for the archbishop of Genoa the right to consecrate and thereby effectively to choose the bishops of Corsica.[7] In 1122 he was chosen consul of the commune for the first of many times. In 1125 he commanded a flotilla of seven galleys in the war against Pisa. He was consul again in 1127 and in that same year went to Barcelona with a colleague to negotiate with Count Berengar III a treaty that would end hostilities between the count and the commune. By the age of forty or so, Caffaro had become an important member of Genoa's elite, entrusted with very sensitive diplomatic missions, high office, and military command.

Over the next decades, Caffaro continued his active participation in the affairs of the commune. In 1144, while in his mid-sixties, he commanded an expedition that captured the island of Minorca, laid siege to the Muslim city of Almería, and negotiated a treaty with Alfonso VII of Castile. He served as consul for the last time in 1149, although he continued to be active in public life well after that.[8] As a senior statesman of the commune, he was chosen in 1154 and again in 1158 to represent Genoa in negotiations with the formidable German emperor, Frederick I Barbarossa.

When Caffaro presented his account of the city's history to Genoa's consuls, he was a preeminent figure in Genoese public life. The annals were read in *parlemento,* that is, in a public assembly of all the citizens of the city gathered before the consuls of the commune.[9] In essence, Caffaro's annals became an authentic public record not unlike the Lombard annals and notarial chronicles discussed by Edward Coleman.[10] This public presentation was the

6. In translation, the titles of the works are *The Liberation of the Cities of the East, A History of the Capture of Almería and Tortosa, Notes on the Bishops of Genoa,* and *A Brief History of the Kingdom of Jerusalem.*

7. Epstein, *Genoa,* 40–41; Belgrano, *Annali genovesi,* 1:75–76.

8. The two offices of consul of the commune and consul of pleas were initially combined, so that he sometimes served as both.

9. Petti Balbi, *Caffaro,* 104; Face, "Caffaro of Genoa," 171. Also Belgrano, *Annali genovesi,* 1:85.

10. See pages 1–27 above.

first step in a process that granted Caffaro's account a privileged status unique to Genoa. The consuls directed that his history be transcribed by the consular secretary and then be placed among the government's official documents, in effect making his annals the city's authorized version of a crucial period in its history.[11] This action was probably a tribute to Caffaro's immense prestige and long public service as well as a favorable response to the patriotism and civic pride that colored his account of the city's recent history.[12] Caffaro continued to record Genoa's story for the next eleven years. In his old age, he was assisted in his work by Macobrio, a scribe, to whom Caffaro dictated and who probably also acted as a kind of collaborator. The more formal and consciously elaborate tone of the entries for these later years probably reflects the impact of Macobrio.[13]

Caffaro's conception of history is patriotic, moral, and didactic. Unlike many medieval chroniclers, he does not begin with the Creation or the Incarnation or any account of classical origins. Instead, he begins with Genoa's participation in the First Crusade, an event within both living memory and his own life experience. The Crusade and Genoa's seafaring tradition thus permeate his concept of civic identity. Caffaro establishes the authority of his account by asserting that he had taken part in and witnessed events or had heard of them from witnesses or had consulted official records to establish the facts.[14] Though he never (at least as far as can be determined) engages in outright falsehood, he is not above weighting interpretations to favor his compatriots through emphasis, anachronism, or omission.[15] We know, for example, that Caffaro's trip to Rome to protest Pisan ecclesiastical claims on Corsica involved liberal bribes (fifteen hundred marks of silver and fifty ounces of gold) to the pope and Curia. In the annals, however, he reports that the Curia decided the Pisan claims were unjustified, but says nothing of the private negotiations.[16] He adds that the Pisans left Rome in a rage, while he and the other Genoese ambassadors brought back a papal privilege to public acclaim. Caffaro's account is a patriotic and communal version of the event that celebrates the evident justice of Genoa's claim.

11. On "authentic chronicles," see Arnaldi, "Cronache con documenti," and his classic work, *Studi sui cronisti della Marca trevigiana nell'età di Ezzelino da Romano*, Istituto storico italiano per il Medio Evo: Studi storici, 48–50 (Rome: Istituto Palazzo Borromini, 1963).

12. Petti Balbi, *Caffaro*, 104, suggests that one should not discount Caffaro's own wishes and influence in achieving this response.

13. Ibid., 107.

14. Belgrano, *Annali genovesi*, 1:81.

15. Petti Balbi, *Caffaro*, 106.

16. On the affair, see Face, "Caffaro of Genoa," 176–77.

The chronological framework of his annals is also communal, based on the secular consular year, the term of office of Genoa's governing executive board.[17] The year 1099 was a pivotal time for Caffaro's annals to commence. It was the year Genoa emerged as an independent commune with named consuls and the year in which it took part in a great communal enterprise, sending its fleet in support of the First Crusade.[18] These events set the tone for Caffaro's work, which has been described as "civil-service history,"[19] for it unabashedly celebrates the accomplishments of Genoa and its citizens. The narrative arc then follows the emergence and actions of the annual consulate, ending with what even Caffaro seems to perceive as the senescence of that institution as a period of internal strife began in 1163. And it is in this time of strife that Caffaro explains why he believes his history is important. It is conceived, he says, to instruct those citizens in the successes that they have achieved while working together and to warn them of the dangers of internal division or indifference. His last entry, for example, is an entreaty to avoid hate and favoritism: "Consuls of cities and villages must avoid hate and the desire [for individual advantage], since they will drive out love of truth, which is required for just decisions. . . . It should be clear to all who have listened [to Caffaro's annals] that by promoting the common good and waging vendettas against thieves, criminals, and every sort of lawbreaker, the consuls can provide that neither within the city nor outside it will there be riots or strife."[20]

This decline in civic feeling marks the end of Caffaro's annals. Steven Epstein argues that laws allowing Genoese to go armed in the streets for self-defense are evidence of the increasing political violence.[21] But Caffaro is largely silent on the most contentious issues, as if he feared exacerbating ill feelings by pointing to specific problems. Certainly there were stresses abroad. The war with Venice had reached a stalemate but could not be brought to an end. The Byzantine emperor had regained control of Constantinople without direct help from the Genoese, though they were still useful to him as a bulwark against a Latin countercoup. As the restored Greek

17. See note 69 below.

18. Whether, in fact, 1099 marks the establishment of the Genoese commune is debatable. What is not in question is that Caffaro presents these two momentous events as linked. His account is laconic but informative: see the translated text below. See also Petti Balbi, *Caffaro*, 108–12.

19. Beryl Smalley, *Historians in the Middle Ages* (New York: Charles Scribner's Sons, 1974), 107.

20. Belgrano, *Annali genovesi*, 1:73–74.

21. Epstein, *Genoa*, 67–68.

government became increasingly stable, their attitude toward the Genoese became more dismissive. At roughly the same time, Frederick Barbarossa was pressuring the Italian cities, including Genoa, to accept the active overlordship of the German king. Immediately after his brief mention of civic disturbances, Caffaro describes how the commune had sent a flotilla of five galleys as escort to protect from Muslim attacks Genoese ships sailing between Corsica, Sardinia, and Denìa in Spain.[22] The ruling noble families seem to have become factionalized, perhaps over differences in approach to the challenges of foreign affairs, perhaps simply because of clashing ambitions.[23] In any case, during the 1160s and 1170s threats to peace, both internal and external, were many.

In 1169, six years after Caffaro's last entry and three years after his death, the government of the commune decided to resume a state-sponsored authentic narrative of the city's deeds. It must have seemed an opportune time to take up the story of Genoa once again. Perhaps the consuls even thought that the kind of history that Caffaro advocated, with Genoa itself, rather than individuals, as the central subject, would help heal some of the rifts in the city's political fabric. But the annalists and their annals were significantly different. Unlike Caffaro, they usually were middling functionaries and not aristocratic leaders. They tended to lack the political vision of active leaders. And given the often tense political situation and the multitude of popular and aristocratic factions in the city, they were much more sensitive to the political interests of those in power than was Caffaro or, in the late thirteenth century, Jacopo Doria.

The first person selected to take up Caffaro's task was Oberto Nasello, better known as Oberto Cancelliere ("the Chancellor"). Oberto served as chancellor of the commune for some twenty years.[24] He was a man of considerable importance, though not of Caffaro's stature. Caffaro's son, Ottone, who was one of the consuls at the time of Oberto's appointment, might well have played a part in seeing that his father's work was continued and that the prominent chancellor, judge, and diplomat was chosen to carry out the task.[25] Oberto took up the story in 1164, where Caffaro had left off, and continued it for exactly a decade, until 1173. In continuing Caffaro's work, Oberto consciously modeled his style on the spare, economical prose of his

22. See Appendix A.
23. Epstein, *Genoa*, 75–76.
24. Petti Balbi, *Caffaro*, 31.
25. Belgrano, *Annali genovesi*, 1:100.

Table 1. Genoese Chroniclers, 1099–1293

		Period Covered	
Chronicler	Began to Write	From	To
Caffaro	ca. 1100	1099	1163
Oberto Cancelliere	ca. 1169	1164	1173
Ottobono Scriba	ca. 1195	1174	1196
Ogerio Pane	1197	1197	1219
Marchisio Scriba	1220	1220	1223
Anonymous Scribes of the Chancery	ca.1229	1225	1264
Lanfranco Pignolo Guglielmo di Multedo Marino Usodimare Enrico di Gavi	1264	1264	1265
Marino dei Marini Guglielmo di Multedo Marino Usodimare Giovanni Suzobono	1265	1265	1266
Nicoló Guercio Guglielmo di Multedo Enrico Drogo Buonvassallo Usodimare	1267	1267	1269
Oberto Stancone Jacopo Doria Marchisino di Cassino Bertolino di Bonifazio	some years after 1270	1270	1279
Jacopo Doria		1280	1298

predecessor.[26] but unlike Caffaro, Oberto was often more a spokesman for the regime that employed him than a recorder of the great deeds of the Genoese people as a whole.[27]

The new annalist prefaces his work with a preamble in prose and verse praising Caffaro's work and noting that he was chosen by the consuls to continue it. He also provides a discussion of the importance of the work of the annalist, who provides guidance for the future in his accounts of the past.[28] The major themes of the decade from 1164 to 1173 were Genoa's internal

26. Petti Balbi, *Caffaro*, 31.
27. Ibid., 32.
28. Belgrano, *Annali genovesi*, 1:107; Petti Balbi, *Caffaro*, 32.

conflicts, the ongoing war with Pisa over domination of Sardinia, and the larger struggle between the Lombard communes and Frederick Barbarossa. Oberto Cancelliere was often close to the center of Genoese policy and diplomacy, though, unlike Caffaro, he was no warrior. He also differed from his predecessor in his emphasis on great men. Where Caffaro sees cities, especially Genoa and Pisa, in military and diplomatic conflict, Oberto tends to see specific personalities at the roots of conflict.[29] Oberto regularly names the consuls in command of fleets. He also includes descriptions of Pisan and imperial opponents.

Oberto Cancelliere probably died early in 1175.[30] Again, with the death of the annalist, the record was allowed to lapse. But this time, and for a generation, no effort was made to continue the civic annals. When, after some twenty years, the communal government decided to renew the project, they chose Ottobono Scriba, a relatively anonymous government employee, to write it.[31] With his appointment, the Genoese civic annals truly become a government record, written by employees of the regime with the purpose of justifying the actions and policies of those in power.[32] Hereafter, the record is continuously maintained. Caffaro's idea that a record of the past had value in preserving the memory of the virtues and achievements of the commune and its citizens, and in providing instruction for the future, seems to have been accepted by the leading citizens of Genoa. The annals are institutionalized as a way for regimes both to immortalize and to vindicate their actions.

But as the records become regular and governmental, they lose the moral sense that Caffaro thought was at the heart of the tradition. There is little talk of avoiding favoritism and hate. Ogerio Pane's entries are a case in point. He began to write in 1197, taking up events just where Ottobono's account leaves off. For the first time the record becomes completely contemporary; no intervening period had to be covered retrospectively.[33] In some respects Ogerio's

---

29. Petti Balbi, *Caffaro*, 35.

30. The last evidence indicating that he was still alive dates from December 1174; Belgrano, *Annali genovesi*, 1:105.

31. Luigi Tommaso Belgrano and Cesare Imperiale di Sant'Angelo, eds., *Annali genovesi*, Fonti per la storia d'Italia, 12 (1901), 2:22; Petti Balbi, *Caffaro*, 37f. The evidence indicating that Ottobono Scriba began to write around 1195 or 1196 is indirect and internal. The dating rests largely upon the way certain privileges granted to Genoa by the emperor Henry VI in 1191 were recorded. The entry speaks of the emperor's perfidy, which could not possibly have been known until after his repudiation of the privileges in 1194. Furthermore, Ottobono was in Sicily and did not return to Genoa until 1196. See Petti Balbi, *Caffaro*, 39f., and Belgrano and Imperiale di Sant'Angelo, *Annali genovesi*, 2:19ff.

32. Petti Balbi, *Caffaro*, 37.

33. Ibid., 43.

annals are slipshod. Though he follows the established framework, beginning each year's account with a list of those who held the important offices
of the republic, the words of praise for them become repetitive and formu-
laic. He concludes his entries with praise for the consuls' love of justice: "The
consuls of pleas and consuls of the Court for Foreigners by God's grace have
fulfilled their office in the best manner. They have acted honestly and properly, giving their justice amicably to everyone." He offers virtually the same
praise to the "consuls of the courts for citizens and noncitizens."[34] He repeats
some information, occasionally putting virtually identical accounts in different years. Clearly he viewed the operation of government as largely routine.

Yet, Ogerio faithfully represents the changed environment in Genoa. His
interests are wider than those of the earlier chroniclers. Unlike his precur-
sors, he does not confine his attention to Genoa. In many respects, Ogerio's
annals are almost as much a record of Europe and the Mediterranean world
in the years from 1197 to 1219 as they are a chronicle of his city. That wider
view rescues Ogerio Pane's work from mediocrity.[35] Nonetheless, it exhibits
the chief shortcoming of the annal form—mere recounting of events, following one upon another without interpretation or evaluation. At least this
is true of the politically controversial internal history of the republic. During a period of important constitutional developments for Genoa, as the
form of government changes, consuls giving way to a podestà, the annalist
is mute or neutral. Yet, no such reticence restrains him from passing judgment in external affairs. The competitors or enemies of Genoa are freely
excoriated. He also shows a real enthusiasm for the exploits of the Genoese
on the seas.[36] While these failings and biases are almost certainly a reflection of Ogerio's personality, as well as a by-product of the journalistic style
of recording events as they occurred, they must also reflect the civil servant's natural inclination to protect his position.

In the thirteenth century, Ogerio's reticence became a regular attribute
of the committees of writers commissioned to continue the annals. These
men were for the most part chancery scribes.[37] Giovanna Petti Balbi attributes this development to the increasing instability of Genoese politics in
these years, which saw rapidly changing regimes with alternating and often
conflicting points of view.[38] Although occasional glimpses emerge of named

---

34. Belgrano and Imperiale di Sant'Angelo, *Annali genovesi*, 2:102, 103.
35. Petti Balbi, *Caffaro*, 44f.
36. Ibid., 46f.
37. Ibid., 55.
38. Ibid., 54–55

individuals associated with the annals in the period between 1225 and 1264, it is impossible to assign authorship to any one of them at any particular time.[39]

After a hiatus during the worst of Genoa's internal battles at the end of the 1220s, the annals were resumed, probably in 1229, at the direction of the city's Bolognese podestà, Jacopo di Balduino. This resumption of the public record of the city's history marked a brief return to peace and stability.[40] For two generations the civic annals became the work of a faceless committee that presented the official viewpoint of the moment. As a result, the annals are often contradictory and inconsistent. These were tumultuous years for Genoa. While the Genoese largely avoided the conflict between the Lombard communes and Frederick II, they did not generally favor the emperor. After Frederick's death, in 1250, Genoa became embroiled in the first of a series of wars with Venice that would come to overshadow in scope and ferocity the long-running rivalry with Pisa. The 1250s also saw the first captain of the people, Guglielmo Boccanegra, marking the culmination of a popular revolution.

Genoa's political transformation was not unique. In the mid–thirteenth century many of the communes of northern and central Italy saw the emergence of a broadly based political movement usually identified as *il Popolo* (the People). The leaders of these movements were usually men who had become rich in the expanding economy of the thirteenth century, members of families that had not been prominent when the communes were established and were, therefore, excluded from the consulate. Seeking political power commensurate with their economic worth, they allied with shopkeepers and artisans to form this movement, which they quite deliberately identified as "popular" in order to emphasize its opposition to the magnates (the "great ones"), or nobles, who had, up to that point, dominated communal politics. In some cities, though not in Genoa, the People even organized their own militias. As these movements coalesced into organized parties, they elected "captains of the people" to create a kind of "shadow government" that sometimes succeeded in capturing the actual government of the commune. This, in fact, is what happened in Genoa in the winter of 1257, when, responding to the call "fiat populus! [let there be (a government of the) people]," a large number of citizens gathered in the church of San Siro and chose Boccanegra to head a new government. Shortly after that, a new

---

39. Ibid., 57.
40. Ibid., 55.

governing assembly was created, the council of elders (Anziani), consisting of four men from each of the eight *compagne,* or districts, that made up medieval Genoa. Far from celebrating this event, the official annals record Boccanegra's election in disapproving and pejorative terms.[41] The anonymous scribes, functionaries who were sympathetic to the aristocratic regimes that preceded and followed the five-year government of the People, describe Boccanegra's elevation as having taken place "without discretion but with tumult and shouting."[42]

Genoa's external relations were equally turbulent and dangerous. The first war with Venice, the so-called War of San Saba, was actually a local conflict between the Genoese and Venetian residents in Acre, the most important of the ports of the Crusader States.[43] The metropolises were quickly drawn into the brawl, but fighting remained largely localized in the Levant. Genoese fleets performed miserably, failing to win a single set-piece battle.[44] The Genoese were expelled from Acre and retreated to Tyre, where their friendly relations with the ruler of that city assured them of a continued foothold in the Levant. Shifting their effort to the diplomatic front, the Genoese in 1260 allied with Michael Paleologus, one of several Greek claimants to the throne in Constantinople and the one who seemed most likely to succeed in regaining that city. When the Greeks expelled the Latins from Constantinople in 1261, this alliance bore fruit in the form of the "little Genoa" established in Pera across the Golden Horn from the imperial city. However, the war with Venice continued in a wider form and brought Genoa into conflict with Pope Urban IV and his ally Charles of Anjou.[45] Inevitably, the stresses of these hostilities were felt in the city. The popular revolt that had brought Guglielmo Boccanegra to power was followed by an aristocratic reaction. Even though Boccanegra continued to receive support from the powerful Grimaldi and Doria families, he was driven from the city in 1262, and noble-dominated government by a podestà was restored.[46]

41. Ibid., 61.

42. Cesare Imperiale di Sant'Angelo, ed., *Annali genovesi,* Fonti per la storia d'Italia, 14 (1926), 4:25. "Sine discretione sed cum tumultu et vociferatione."

43. The event that touched off the conflict was supposedly a dispute between Venetian and Genoese residents of Acre over possession of the monastery of San Saba.

44. John E. Dotson, "Naval Strategy in the First Genoese-Venetian War, 1257–1270," *American Neptune* 46 (1986): 84–90.

45. John E. Dotson, "Venice, Genoa, and Control of the Seas in the Thirteenth and Fourteenth Centuries," in *War at Sea in the Middle Ages and the Renaissance,* ed. John B. Hattendorf and Richard Unger (Woodbridge, Suffolk, and Rochester, N.Y.: Boydell Press, 2003), 119–35.

46. Epstein, *Genoa,* 152.

After 1264, the civic annals continued to be produced by committee but not one made up of insignificant clerks.[47] No longer entrusted to chancery scribes, the job of maintaining Genoa's official history was given to a carefully structured and balanced board of two legal experts and two prominent laymen.[48] Two motives seem to have driven this change: First, the return of aristocratic domination of the government brought men of higher social status to the creation of the commune's official memory. However, the chancery clerks had been sympathetic to the government of the nobles all along, so a merely propagandistic motivation does not sufficiently explain the reorganization. But now the carefully balanced structure of the committee, split between legal experts (*giurisperiti*) and men who were socially prominent and politically connected, indicated a concern that the official record of the commune's actions be perceived as accurate and authoritative.

The first committee of four consisted of Lanfranco Pignolo, a jurist from a very important and well-connected family; Guglielmo di Multedo, a judge; Enrico, marquis of Gavi; and Marino Usodimare, from one of Genoa's oldest and most prominent families.[49] The composition of the board of annalists changed in 1265, 1267, and 1270, but there was always some continuity in membership (see Table 1). Guglielmo Multedo was the longest-serving of the first board, remaining with the project until 1269. Perhaps he had a special aptitude for the work; he might have been the most influential of the annalists in these years.[50] Each annalist wrote a prologue to that part of the annals for which he was responsible, a custom that had been abandoned during the period of the anonymous scribes. These prologues reveal a seriousness of purpose that underscores the government's commitment to record everything that happened regarding Genoa, including "both propitious and inauspicious events." The new committee appointed in 1267 extended the scope of their writings to include events in "Lombardy, Tuscany, and other parts of the world."[51]

But whether anonymous or notable, the annalists carefully filtered the

47. The authors of the annals from 1224 to 1264 were probably not literally anonymous in their own day, and even now some of them can still be identified. However, these chancery scribes were not socially or politically significant and did not usually identify themselves individually with their work.

48. Petti Balbi, *Caffaro*, 62ff.

49. Imperiale di Sant'Angelo, *Annali genovesi*, 4:50–56.

50. Ibid., 4:56.

51. Petti Balbi, *Caffaro*, 63. The Latin phrase "tam de prosperis gestis, quam etiam de adversis" was repeated by every committee. In 1267, the language was "in Lombardia, in Tuschia et in aliis diversis mundi partibus."

information they included. In 1265, for example, they reported that "all the Genoese were ousted from the imperial city of Constantinople by order of the Paleologus emperor and his nuncios."[52] They later claimed that this happened only because of a plot to overthrow the emperor in which the Genoese podestà of the Pera district in Constantinople was implicated. The truth was more complex. The Genoese seem to have been expelled because of a broader Greek suspicion of Genoese political and economic influence in the city. It was in truth a defeat for Genoa's rulers. The disgraced podestà that the annalists blamed for the expulsion was, however, a member of an opposing faction. Thus, the annalists were presenting the government's version and blaming political opponents for an uncomfortable defeat.[53]

Later that year the annalists deliberately misrepresented Oberto Spinola's coup against the restored government of the podestà. Even though the Spinola were the largest fief-holders in Liguria, dominating much of the Riviera di Levante,[54] the chroniclers appointed by the regime, including the marquis of Gavi, portrayed the rebels as a violent mob from the underclasses of the city.[55] Spinola was able to consolidate his position, and shortly after this two members of the committee of annalists were replaced. Lanfranco Pignolo and Enrico di Gavi were replaced by Marino dei Marini, who, like Pignolo, was a jurist with a prominent record of office-holding, and Giovanni Suzobono, a man from a little-known family.[56] The Spinola government's choice to replace the marquis of Gavi with the obscure Giovanni Suzobono was, without a doubt, a political move. But the fact that the committee of annalists was reshuffled so quickly after the coup is an indication of the importance attached by Genoese governments of all leanings to the official historical record.

An "authentic" record was deemed essential because Genoa, like many Italian cities, had seen political divisions grow between Guelfs and Ghibellines during the reign of Frederick II.[57] Almost every communal government found itself forced to take sides, making external and internal enemies in

52. Imperiale di Sant'Angelo, *Annali genovesi*, 4:65.

53. Petti Balbi, *Caffaro*, 63–64; Epstein, *Genoa*, 153, generally follows the annals' version of the story.

54. That is, the coast east of Genoa to the border of Tuscany near La Spezia. West of Genoa to the vicinity of Nice lies the Riviera di Ponente.

55. Epstein, *Genoa*, 153–54.

56. Imperiale di Sant'Angelo, *Annali genovesi*, 4:66.

57. Nominally, Guelfs were supporters of the papacy, and Ghibellines were supporters of the imperial position. To some extent, these ideologies had political resonance in city populations, but, on the whole, local rivalries, cloaked in these larger party names, were more important.

the process. When Pope Urban IV negotiated an intervention by Charles of Anjou[58] against Frederick's illegitimate son, Manfred, the leader of the Hohenstaufen cause in Italy, divisions took on a new color. Manfred was killed in battle against Charles's forces at Benevento early in 1266. Later, in 1268, Conradin, Frederick's grandson, was executed by the French. By 1268 Charles had taken control of all of southern Italy. In addition, he held territories in southern France that abutted the western borders of lands claimed by Genoa. After the extermination of the Hohenstaufen, he became king of Sicily, ruler of lands of vital economic importance to the Genoese. The question whether to accommodate or oppose French claims in southern Italy was a major issue of Genoese politics in the late thirteenth century.

Matters were further complicated in 1270, when a coup in Genoa installed a Ghibelline government headed by Oberto Spinola and Oberto Doria as joint captains of the people and podestà. It is about this time that the Ghibellines in Genoa came to be considered more "popular" and Guelfs more "aristocratic," even though leaders of both parties came from the nobility of Liguria. Certainly it is ironic that leaders of two of the oldest and most elite of Genoese families were celebrated as leaders of *il Popolo*. No annals exist from these years. After a considerable hiatus, the Spinola-Doria government appointed an entirely new committee of annalists, including Oberto Doria's brother, Jacopo. It is impossible to determine just how much time elapsed between the coup and the resumption of the annals, for the committee's work was inserted in the annals only upon its completion in 1279.[59] These annalists emphasized the violence, disorder, and death in the months before the October coup that brought Spinola and Doria to power. They also took every opportunity to imply a broad base of support for what was in reality an aristocratic faction. Thus we read, "Doria and Spinola called together and took counsel from their friends, both nobles and of the people," and "the Doria, the Spinola, and their noble and popular followers and friends were victorious." The annalists summed up the coup by saying that they "ruled a city previously terrorized by factional and civic discord, acting to bring tranquillity to the city and district . . . and because of this, the said captains [Spinola and Doria] ruled a peaceful and quiet city and district."[60] Unity seems to have been the most important result.

58. Charles was the younger brother of King Louis IX (Saint Louis) of France.
59. Imperiale di Sant'Angelo, *Annali genovesi*, 4:4; Petti Balbi, *Caffaro*, 67. Petti Balbi notes that the work of this new committee was not inserted into the official record until 1279, the last year of their mandate.
60. Imperiale di Sant'Angelo, *Annali genovesi*, 4:139–41.

After the mandate of the committee of annalists expired in 1279, no official annalists were appointed until, in 1294, Jacopo's account of the period up to 1293 was attached to the annals as the official record of the period, much as Caffaro's had in 1152.[61] He likely maintained some kind of record or draft of the annals in the years between 1279 and 1293 that he presented to the podestà, captain of the people, and council of elders of Genoa. And as with Caffaro, they declared the work to be exemplary and ordered that it be added to the authentic city chronicle.[62] This is merely one of many striking similarities between the first of the Genoese annalists, Caffaro, and the last of the official annalists, Jacopo Doria.[63] Both were patriots from leading families. Both merged a deep commitment to telling the story of their city with a strong belief in the utility of knowing the past. Just as Caffaro had written in a period when Genoa seemed to be accomplishing great things, Doria wrote in a period, the 1280s and 1290s, of power and prosperity for the Ligurian city.[64] Doria's annal is our source for the famous attempt of the Vivaldi brothers in 1291 to sail west into the Atlantic as a route to Asia. More significantly for the Genoese, Doria also carefully describes the Sicilian Vespers, the revolt by which the French were driven off the island and replaced by the Aragonese. Once again, the political and economic interests of the Genoese were threatened by events outside their control. Finally, Doria records the naval battle of Meloria in 1284, which marked the final triumph over Pisa, Genoa's ancient enemy.

But there were also differences. Caffaro began his account in 1099, with the creation of the commune and with no reference to a biblical past or search for classical origins. In contrast, Doria inserted a long digression between the prologue and the annals proper in which he searched for classical references to Genoa.[65] Doria was a genuine historian with an intense interest in the past and a respect for his sources. While his brother was one of the captains, he served as archivist for the city and even traveled as a communal representative. Like Caffaro, he wrote from an aristocratic background, which had allowed him long experience in public life. He expected that he would have successors in the two-century-long tradition of Genoa's official history. Yet, after he died, the Genoese annals came to an end. The writing of the

61. Petti Balbi, *Caffaro*, 68.
62. Cesare Imperiale di Sant'Angelo, ed., *Annali genovesi*, Fonti per la storia d'Italia, 14bis (1929), 5:176.
63. Petti Balbi, *Caffaro*, 17.
64. On Genoese culture in this period and Doria himself, see Epstein, *Genoa*, 160–65.
65. Petti Balbi, *Caffaro*, 72ff.

annals had previously come to a halt for long periods, but this time, for reasons that are impossible to determine, the cessation was permanent.

The Genoese historical tradition did not cease, but it was transformed. Jacopo da Varagine, a Dominican friar and later archbishop of Genoa, wrote a history of Genoa at almost the same time that Doria was writing. Jacopo is better known for his *Legenda Aurea,* or *Golden Legend,* a compendium of saints' lives and one of the most popular books of the late Middle Ages. In his history of Genoa, Jacopo departed from the strict chronological framework of the annalistic style. With a more narrative turn of mind, he structured his work in twelve thematic parts. Since he thought that Genoa lacked a history, he included foundation myths worthy of an illustrious city and inserted sections on Roman Genoa as well as on its Christian conversion. There is little originality in da Varagine's narrative of more recent Genoese history except for the section devoted to Genoa from 1291 to 1297, the year before his death.[66] For the most part he depends on the annals themselves for earlier events. His purpose is generally didactic, and many of the stories he recounts sound like the commonplaces typical of a Dominican's sermon.

After Varagine, the Genoese historical record is silent for almost exactly a hundred years, until Giorgio Stella began, in 1396, again to record the history of this remarkable city. But the "authentic history" Caffaro and his successors hoped to create was transformed. Where Caffaro described a commune and Oberto Cancelliere recounted the role of families and personalities, later historians tried to compose a carefully balanced history respectful of the factions that threatened Genoa's stability. Jacopo and Giorgio Stella did continue the historical tradition, but it never again had the close connection to public life that was the key to Caffaro's great annals.

APPENDIX A: CAFFARO, GENOESE ANNALS[67]

Whoever desires for his own benefit or for the benefit of others news from the time of the expedition to Caesarea to the present should read these writings by Caffaro, and having read them, he will know the truth. For Caffaro, from the time of that expedition until now, either guided and was part of

---

66. Epstein, *Genoa,* 173–74.

67. These translations are based on Belgrano and Imperiale di Sant'Angelo, *Annali genovesi:* Caffaro, 1:3–7, 59–64; Stancone et al., 4:129, 131–32, 133, 134, 135, 138, 140; Doria, 5:3–13.

the consulate of the Genoese city or saw and knew the others who were consuls during those years. And having considered [these matters] in his heart and mind, he himself has dictated their names, their terms of office, the events of their consulate and the districts [*compagni*] from which they came. He includes as well victories achieved and changes in money made during the same consulate, just as you will read below. In the time of the consuls Tanclerio and Rubaldo Bisaccia and Ansaldo Spinola [1152] he presented this writing in full council. The consuls, having taken the advice of the counselors, ordered Guglielmo di Colomba, the public scribe, to transcribe the book composed and written by Caffaro into the communal cartulary, so that from then on for all times the victories of the men of the Genoese city shall be known, those who departed in 1100 and returned in 1101.

> His name is Cafarro whom the present image portrays
> May he live forever and may his progeny be abundant.
> Genoa was certainly safe in the past when he was consul
> And the city undertook this work because he knew how things
>   happened.

At the time of the expedition to Caesarea or shortly before [1099], an association[68] with six consuls was formed for [a term of] three years. The names of the consuls were Amico Brusco, Mauro di Piazzalunga, Guido di Rustico di Reso, Pagano della Volta, Ansaldo di Brasile, Buonmatto di Medolico; and each was consul of the commune and of the court of pleas [court of justice] for three years. After a year and a half, in the kalends of August, twenty-six galleys and six sailing ships departed Genoa for Jerusalem. They came with the army to the port of Latakia [in northern Syria], and there they remained for the entire winter. And since the Genoese discovered that the eastern lands lacked a king in Jerusalem and a prince in Antioch, they held these aforesaid lands for a long time under their control and protection until such time as by direction of the legate of the Roman Curia there should be a king in Jerusalem and a prince in Antioch. And so immediately the Genoese took counsel with the legate of the Roman Curia and sent nuncios to Baldwin in Edessa and Tancred in Tiberias [beside the Sea of Galilee], saying that they should come. And Tancred came without

---

68. The year is 1160. Caffaro writes "Compagnia," or association. He is, in fact, referring to the formation of what would eventually be called the commune, or government, of Genoa. His remark underlines the voluntary and informal nature of early communal government. In fact, he himself later refers to the leaders as "consuls of the commune."

delay and was made prince of Antioch by order of the legate and the Geno-ese. After that Baldwin came to Latakia with two hundred knights and three hundred infantry to confer with the Genoese. There he was advised and urged to accept the kingdom of Jerusalem, and he promised to do so. He said "If you promise to give me your aid for taking two cities of the Sara-cens I wish to capture this summer, I promise to go immediately to take possession of the kingdom. And after three days he began to travel. As he approached Beirut, he was blocked by three thousand Turkish knights who were remaining in the area. Then, since he knew that he would not be able to cross that area, Baldwin armed himself and mounted his horse and pre-tended to retreat. Immediately the multitude of Turks descended onto the plain. Then, knowing that the Turks were in the open field, Baldwin with his all his knights turned forcefully toward the enemies of God. The Turk-ish knights, however, when they saw Baldwin come toward them with such ferocity, dropped their arms and turned their backs and with horses began to flee. But Baldwin, the knight of God, followed and killed them before they reached safety. Almost all of them were left dead on the field. He cap-tured the arms and horses they had with them, which he distributed to his knights and to his infantry according to the customs of warriors. And after this triumph he went to Jerusalem, where he was received with great joy by the patriarch Dambert and all the inhabitants. And he was placed on the royal throne, and he accepted the crown of the kingdom. He ruled the king-dom and held it manfully for seventeen years. . . .

In the fortieth year of the consulate[69] there were four consuls of the com-mune, namely Ruggerone de Ita, Lanfranco di Alberico, Enrico Guercio, Ansaldo d'Oria. . . .

Because it is good and useful to record the past, to meditate on the pres-ent, and to anticipate the future, Caffaro, since he was twenty years old, has undertaken to write and make known the names and endeavors of the

---

69. Caffaro organized his annals according to the consular year. Each commune had its own custom of dating. In Genoa the first consuls had served for four years, but this was reduced to two in 1118 and then to one in 1122. The Genoese civil year began on December 25, *nativitatis Domini* (the Nativity), so that dates in this style anticipated the current cal-endar from that date until December 31. However, the consuls' one-year term began on February 2, *in die purificationis beate Marie* (the day of the Purification of the Blessed Mary), and ran through February 1 (Belgrano, *Annali genovesi*, 1:83). Therefore, the Genoese con-sular year corresponds to the current calendar from February 2 to December 31 but is behind it from January 1 to February 1. Thus, neither the consular year nor the civil year coincides with the current calendar, beginning on January 1.

Genoese consuls past, present, and future and also what occurred each year in the city. Caffaro began to take notice and to write these things, just as they are written in the book, when he was twenty years old. He has composed and recorded the events written in this book right up to the present day, and he promises, God willing, to continue to do so in the future. Just as these above-mentioned consuls have managed Genoese affairs in this year, the year in which Caffaro began and completed his eightieth, so too he will make the truth known by this present writing. Therefore let it be known to all those listening that the present consuls freed the government from the servitude of debt by paying all of the ninety *lire* owed by earlier consuls. Besides that, they paid three hundred *lire* for the work on the towers of the city walls. And having paid the lender one hundred *lire* for the mortgage, the castle of Voltaggio was returned to the possession of the commune and placed under the administration of the new consuls. Furthermore, they had walls built around the town of Portovenere. They dispatched legates on communal business: Enrico Guercio, a consul, to the emperor of Constantinople and Oberto Spinola to Lupo, king of Spain. In addition, they sequestered their greatest enemies among the citizens so that during their consulate there were no serious brawls or assaults. They had consuls elected to succeed them from among the best men of the city. 1160.

In the forty-first year of the consulate there were five consuls of the commune; they were Rodoano, son of Guglielmo Maurone, Filippo da Lamberto, Marchio, son of Ingo della Volta, Guglielmo Cigala, and Oberto Spinola. . . .

At different times many events, both propitious and adverse, often happen in the world, and in this year many even greater and more important than usual occurred in the kingdom of Italy.[70] But since it would be long and burdensome to narrate individually every event that happened, leaving aside the other matters, Caffaro will write down without delay how at that time the aforesaid consuls administered the government and kept the city in good order. Having from the beginning thought a great deal about administration and what seemed the best and most effective way to secure peace and concord, the aforesaid consuls began to negotiate and take action within and without the city. Troublemakers who were in the city were made to

70. Caffaro is correct that the year 1161 was a momentous one in northern Italy. Frederick Barbarossa's war with the Lombard League reached a climax with the siege of Milan. There was also a disputed papal election. The outcome of both these conflicts was still in doubt during the year, and it was probably prudent of Caffaro not to appear publicly to support any particular position. However, he did, tacitly, show Genoa's preference in papal politics in his description of Alexander III's visit to Genoa.

swear in the presence of the consuls that they would not cause or start any of their usual plots or brawls. The others who might take up arms and assault any of the government were warned that their towers and houses would be destroyed and money held as security for their promises would be confiscated. They were required, whether they wanted to or not, to swear a new oath to maintain the peace. Additionally, one of the consuls, Oberto Spinola, a wise and experienced man, was sent with five galleys to protect shipping between Corsica and Sardinia as far as Denìa [on the Spanish coast]. On account of this, the Saracens, in fear and dread, refrained from equipping their galleys and left their sails and oars in their arsenal. And so the Genoese ships, tranquilly going and returning, completed their voyages unharmed. And so long as the Genoese galleys stayed in the vicinity of Denìa, Lupo, the king of Spain, declared he would without any deceit remain at peace and concord with the Genoese at the will of their consuls. After the consul heard the embassy of the king delivered with such humility and patience, he accepted advice from the consuls of pleas, Lamberto, the son of Filippo, and Ansaldo Golia, who were with him, and from the commander of the galleys. He answered that peace could be had upon payment of ten thousand *marabotini*[71] and if he relinquished all the commerce of his kingdom to Genoese merchants. The king, having heard the embassy of the consuls, promised with joyful spirit that everything the consul had ordered would be done without doubt. Then the king without delay sent letters to Genoa asking that a legate be sent to him to receive the *marabotini* and to give and receive security for peace, as was promised. The consuls, seeing the letters and hearing commands of the king, sent Guglielmo Cassizo, son of Ingo della Volta, a wise and illustrious man, as legate to the king to accept those *marabotini,* restore and establish security for peace, and regulate all the commerce of the kingdom.

Furthermore, another legate, Ottone Bono, brother of Nuvolone, a wise and noble man, was sent to the king of the Almohads,[72] and he was received with great honor throughout all their lands. He proceeded to the king of Morocco and was received by him with great honor. The king signed a peace with all the Genoese for a term of fifteen years, so that the Genoese could go safely through all the Almohad lands and possessions with their goods, by land and by sea, with the understanding that they not pay more than 8

---

71. *Marabotini* were gold coins initially minted by the Muslim Almoravid rulers of Spain. By the twelfth century *marabotini* carried both Arabic and Latin inscriptions.

72. The Almohads were Muslim Berbers who replaced the Almoravids in North Africa and Spain.

percent duty except in Bejaïa, where they would pay 10 percent, of which a fifth would be returned to the commune of Genoa. And, furthermore, they directed another legate, the consular nobleman Ansaldo Spinola,[73] to eastern lands, that is, to the holy city of Jerusalem. He went with a legate of the Roman Curia, Giovanni, cardinal priest of San Giovanni e Paolo, to seek justice for the Genoese. Besides these things, the consuls caused strong and beautiful new works to be built, refurbishing the old fortifications of Voltaggio, Falcone, Parodi, Rivarolo, and Portovenere outside the city. They were so admired by everyone who passed by that they could talk of nothing else. Only to hear of these strong new works brought happiness to friends and awe to enemies.

Nor will Caffaro forget how Lord Alexander,[74] the pope, was received by the Genoese archbishop, clergy, consuls, and all the people. Let the whole world know how the whole people, the archbishop with clerics and consuls, and the whole populace of men and women, old men, young men and boys, all were gathered with magnificence and honor, amid acclamations and universal praise, and the bells rang throughout the whole city as they received the pope, praising God and exalting his name as is read in the Book of Psalms: "young men, and maidens, old men and children: Let them praise the name of the Lord for his name alone is excellent."[75] And, in truth, on that day the name of God was exalted when the Genoese received Pope Alexander, the vicar of the Lord, just as the Lord himself says in the Gospels: "he that receiveth you, receiveth me," and elsewhere, "I was a stranger and ye took me in."[76] Then, indeed, they took in the Lord Jesus Christ when on his behalf they devoted their palaces and worthiest lodgings and limitless tribute to the pope and his bishops and cardinals with great love and dancing. Then, the pope himself, since he was mindful of such great honors and benefices, began to discuss with the aforesaid consuls how he might honor the church of the Genoese city. But since these consuls, because of the brevity of the term of their consulate, could not complete the discussions they had begun, they left them to the new consuls to complete. Caffaro—if he lives—God willing, when there is time, will not omit to write what the new consuls will have done regarding this matter and regarding all increases of the government during their term. 1161.

73. Spinola was called "consular" because he had been consul in 1159.

74. Alexander III, who reigned from 1159 to 1181. Early in his reign he faced an antipope, Victor IV, who was backed by Emperor Frederick I Barbarossa. The enthusiasm for Pope Alexander that Caffaro attributes to the Genoese seems to reflect their distaste for Barbarossa.

75. Psalm 148:12–13. The translation is from the Douay-Confraternity English translation, which is based on the Latin Vulgate, which Caffaro used.

76. Caffaro is quoting Matthew 10:40 and 25:35.

APPENDIX B: THE ANNALS OF OBERTO STANCONE, JACOPO DORIA, SON OF THE LATE PIETRO, MARCHISINO DI CASSINO, AND BERTOLINO DI BONIFAZIO

Our historiographer Caffaro began this praiseworthy work. He recorded what happened during his lifetime, based upon the traces that remained, for the memory of future generations. He arranged these events according to the [terms of office of the] priors of his fatherland. For this, his memory must be praised, as should that of those wise men who carried on this work, which was begun so well. For they have taken care to describe in writing what happened at particular times. And it was done this way so that our descendants should know and hear what they have not seen and thus be instructed by our earlier history. However, since 1270 this work has not been carried forward. Nonetheless, many and varied events have happened that are believed to be worthy of memory; therefore the noble lords Oberto Spinola and Oberto Doria, the honorable captains of the commune and People of Genoa, whose rule guards the city and countryside with the consent and will of the Anziani, have charged the following, whose names are included here, with resumption of the work: Oberto Stancone, Jacopo Doria, son of the late Pietro, Marchisino di Cassino, and Bertolino di Bonifazio. They are to carry on this work for ten years, as can be noted in reading what follows, acting faithfully, rejecting falsehood and embracing pure truth. In the current year, that is, 1270, Rolandino Putagio, Parmense citizen, was podestà in the government of the city. In that same year Louis, the illustrious king of the French, intended to make war on the Agarenos [i.e., Saracens, or Arabs], imitators of the Christian faith. He took the sign of the Cross with his three sons, . . . his brother, . . . many other barons and prelates, and a great multitude of men . . . and boarded a ship at Aigues-Mortes. [Instead of sailing to the Holy Land, his army was diverted at the last minute to Tunisia] . . . More than ten thousand Genoese were also in the army. They had fifty-five ships and barques with covered forecastles and a great number of other navigable barques, all prepared to fight. The king's ships and the galleys were also armed by the Genoese. There were so many Genoese in the army that they elected their own consuls, the nobles Ansaldo Doria and Filippo Cavaronco. They presided and rendered justice at that time as rectors of the commune of Genoa. . . . On the day that the army arrived in Tunisia, the Genoese merchants who had previously come to Tunis with merchandise were taken captive and detained by the command of the king of Tunisia, unaware of the impending arrival of the army. Those who had been taken and detained on the king's command were placed and held in a handsome palace, so that they had no complaint about the offense. The king's intention then was not to offend but rather to protect the Genoese merchants who came before the army arrived. He believed and concluded that it was not the Genoese but other counselors who had diverted the army toward Tunisia. . . . Insults and vexations were exchanged between the army of the French blockading Carthage and the army of the king of the Agarenos resisting them. The [Genoese] large barques with forecastles moved about everywhere carrying food, arms, and the things necessary for the army. Their movements made clear to all that the army had been diverted [from the Holy Land] to Tunisia. Later, when this became known in Genoa, the Genoese were pained and all were surprised and violently shocked. It had been the intention of all the wise men of the commune that the army of the king of the French and the crusade should be carried [by the Genoese] for support of the Holy Land and recovery of the Lord's Sepulcher, which, to the shame of Christians to whom it belonged, was irreverently held by the Saracens. And this was the cause of the pain, since not just to the wise, but to almost all, it was apparent that said army could accomplish nothing, or almost nothing, in Tunisia. Nor could any praiseworthy result be achieved, as was clear by the end of these events. . . .

This is how things came to pass. It happened that Tristan, the son of the king of the French, was, unknown to the king, ill with a grave infirmity as he declined and completed his last days. Thus the king likewise caught this serious infirmity. He died from the son's illness, which he had not recognized, and after a few days, his son died as well. . . . [After the death of Saint Louis, the crusade stalled.] Then, however, ransoms were arranged between the two armies, and out of the negotiations between the two sides truces were arranged and an agreement was affirmed in writing: 105,000 ounces of gold were promised to the Christian kings by the king of Tunisia, one half of which would be paid immediately, and the other half was to be paid within two years. The sums were to be divided proportionately. . . . [The king] promised that, within a certain time, quantities of money would be paid to the Genoese, truly that which was owed to them. . . .

In that same year the Genoese city, with all its countryside, lived in bitterness. Such division reigned between citizens and countrymen that poisonous actions proliferated throughout the villages and localities of the commune of Genoa. Homicides and thefts were committed indifferently, because of which banishments from both [city and countryside] were innumerable for those who caused riots in public streets, insulted men, and committed murder and despoiled their enemies and other travelers. Thus it happened that the road to Rapallo could not be traveled with security. And these acts were performed by countrymen supported by some citizens. . . . Everyone defended his own party [faction]. Also, as peace and concord were banished, discord, the opponent of peace, continued and entered the city. . . .

[A factional dispute over who should be podestà of Ventimiglia resulted in a coup that drove the elected podestà from the government.] At that time the factions fought against one another. It happened that those of the Doria and Spinola faction seized the Palace of the Podestà. So Rolandino Putagio, then podestà, retreated to the palace of the Fieschi clan, in the parish of San Lorenzo. And having with him not a small multitude of men, noble as well as popular, and armed and prepared to fight the Doria and Spinola faction and their followers, he prepared to resist them if he could. However, the Doria and Spinola and their noble and common supporters seized the podestà and violently expelled his supporters from the houses of the Fieschi. And that same day the honorable Oberto Spinola and Oberto Doria were made captains, the same title previously given them by their friends and followers. And all power was bestowed [on them] by the people, that is, full jurisdiction in the city and countryside. . . .

APPENDIX C: JACOPO DORIA, ANNALS OF THE GENOESE, INTRODUCTION AND 1280

Since there is great utility in writing of things past and present, not only so that in future times they will not be forgotten, but also so that, through the past, the future may be known, I, Jacopo Doria, son of the late Pietro, son of the late Oberto, shall draft in writing all the things that were done by the commune of Genoa from 1280 through the year 1294. [I will include] what befell the city and the citizens of Genoa, all I have seen and witnessed as well as those things truthfully reported to me by others who saw them. Thus any Genoese, upon reading of these things, will be fully informed of the best deeds of this commune and of his predecessors. By their example and by the welcome rewards that were the worthy results of their labors, he can be, and should be, zealously moved to manage and maintain the honor and well-being of this said commune. However, since in the said times many notable things happened in various parts of the world, I will describe some of them briefly rather than fully. But, before I approach my proposed subject, I will record in writing some things regarding the city of Genoa that may be found in certain ancient histories and legends, and, after that, I will return to attend to my subject.

Since I have not found any writing before Caffaro, noble citizen of Genoa, who began the work of this present chronicle in the year of Our Lord 1097 (as is found in the beginning of this chronicle),[77] nor have I found the building of this city in any book (while the builders of many other cities of Italy and other regions of the world are found written in the works of Isidore and Solinus[78] and other historians), I was moved by wonder to think with a quiet and alert mind how I could find anything from ancient times. But I have not been able thus far to find anything of its builders in any authentic ancient book, perhaps because of its antiquity. Yet popular opinion in Genoa maintains that, after the destruction of Troy, a certain noble Trojan by the name of Janus sailed to this region, to a place now called Sarzano, that is, Janus's Wood.[79] He landed and had a castle built in the place now called Castello, where the archiepiscopal palace is today. The city of Genoa took its name from him, that is, from Janus. It is true that in the book of Titus Livi,[80] who was the great historian of the city of Rome, our city is found several times, which demonstrates, in part, its antiquity. Therefore, I will transcribe his words, word for word, in this present work and after that what is found in other ancient writings.

Consequently, in Titus Livi, in the second part, where he deals with the Second Punic War, between the Romans and the Carthaginians, in the first book in the year after the foundation of the city, 534,[81] which is 218 years before the birth of Christ, the following is found: "Publius Cornelius Scipio, being in Marseilles with his ships and having heard that Hannibal proceeded against Italy, sent his brother, Scipio, into Spain against Hasdrubal with the greater part of the army. He himself boarded his ships and sailed to Genoa with elite troops to oppose Hannibal when he had crossed the Alps, etc." Likewise, in the same, book VIII, near the end, from the foundation of the

---

77. Caffaro's annals begin in 1099, though his *De liberatione civitatum Orientis* begins with the preaching of the crusade in Genoa in 1097. The latter work was incorporated into the civic annals by Jacopo Doria. Giovanni Monleone, trans., *Annali genovesi di Caffaro e dei suoi continuatori*, vol. 8, *Jacopo Doria* (Genoa: Municipio di Genova, 1930), pt. 1, 6 n. 1.

78. Isidore the Younger, seventh-century bishop of Seville, and C. Julius Solinus, third-century Roman author.

79. In Latin, *saltus Iani.*

80. Livy (d. 17 C.E.) wrote a history of Rome called *From the Foundation of the City.*

81. The Romans dated from the founding of the city—*ab urbe condita,* or A.U.C., in Latin. The presumed founding of Rome was in 753 B.C.E., according to our current reckoning. A.U.C. will indicate that the date is a traditional Roman one.

city . . .[82] which is . . . years before the birth of Christ, one learns as follows: "In that same summer, Mago, son of Hamilcar, transported from the lesser island of the Balearics,[83] where he had wintered, to Italy around thirty ships with rams[84] and loaded on many of them twelve thousand infantry and almost two thousand cavalry and suddenly made landfall at Genoa—which no one had foreseen—and where no one was guarding the shore. From there to the Ligurian riviera, etc." Likewise in book VIII, around the third part, one learns as follows: "almost on the same day, the ships that the Carthaginians had sent to Mago arrived between the Liguri Albingauni[85] and Genoa. Perhaps it was in this area that Mago kept his fleet." Likewise, in the same author, book X, around the beginning, in 545 A.U.C., which is 207 years before the birth of Christ, one learns as follows: "Cornelius Servilius being consul in the sixteenth year of the Punic War, Lucretius's command was extended so that the town of Genoa, which had been almost destroyed by Mago, could be rebuilt.

Also, there is found in the legend of the blessed martyrs, Nazarius and Celsus, who were crowned with martyrdom in the time of the emperor Nero, who ruled in the year of the Lord 58, as follows: "and they laid Saint Nazarius to rest in a place about six hundred paces[86] from the Genoese city, where by the merit of their offerings and prayers [their sins] were absolved, and they called that place 'the place of the Pilgrim Saints.' From there they entered into the city of Genoa and then proceeded to Milan, etc." In the legend of the blessed martyr Fructuosus and his associates, who were crowned with martyrdom by the governor Emilianus in the time of the emperor Galienus, who ruled in A.D. 256, one learns as follows: "there is in the region of Italy, within the boundaries of the city of the Genoese, a wilderness near the sea that is called Capo di Monte, where my relics were carried."[87] Likewise, in the *Lombard History,* in the second book, one learns as follows: "Consequently, entering into Liguria, Alboin, who reigned in the year of the Lord

---

82. The manuscript has a blank space at this point.

83. That is, Minorca.

84. *Rostratis navibus.* The ram (*rostrum*) would be found only on rowed warships, generically referred to in modern usage as galleys.

85. The Liguri Albingauni were a Ligurian tribe that lived in the area of the present-day province of Imperia, to the west of Genoa.

86. The Roman pace was measured from the place where the heel of one foot touched the ground to the place where the heel of the same foot touched down again. It was standardized at a little less than 1.5 meters in modern measure. Six hundred paces would be about 0.9 kilometer.

87. The abbey of Capo di Monte in the small village of San Fruttoso sits in the modern nature preserve of Monte Portofino, east of Genoa. It is presently a museum.

568, etc., from there took all of the cities of Liguria except for those on the shore of the sea from Luni to the Gallic lands. And Archbishop Honoratus, abandoning Milan, fled to Genoa, where he remained secure." Likewise, in the *Dialogues* of Pope Gregory, who reigned in the year of the Lord 600, one learns as follows: . . . .[88]

Likewise, in *The Deeds of Charlemagne,* one learns as follows: "In A.D. 770 Charlemagne held a synod in the city of Genoa, and in that assembly he divided the army in two parts; keeping one part, which crossed the mountains of Genoa, he placed his maternal uncle Bernardus at the head of the remaining part, which was commanded to enter Genoa by Monte Giove. Desiderius, king of the Lombards, fled and shut himself up in Pavia." Likewise, in the chronicle of Philibertus[89] one learns as follows: "In A.D. 913[90] a fountain of blood flowed plentifully in the city of the Genoese, perhaps presaging its ruin. Indeed, in that same year, it was taken by the Africans, and all of its citizens, except for the very young and the women, were taken and killed, and it was spoiled of its treasures, etc." The aforesaid fountain of blood came forth in the place that is today called Fontanella, above the place where the arsenal was built behind the breakwater. And there is a popular opinion among the Genoese that at that time almost all the Genoese were away from the city, at sea with the fleet, and when they returned and found the city so desolate, they immediately pursued the Africans and found them in the islands of the Businarie,[91] which are called Iscla-Mortor. They attacked them there, slaughtering them all by the sword, as is shown by the many bones of the slain that are found there even today. The Genoese recovered their youth and women and all of the treasure and returned to Genoa.

Moreover, in many other writings I have found mention made of the city of Genoa, but for the sake of brevity I have said enough. But since in certain histories and legends our city is called Genoa, and in others, Janua, I will write something of the etymology of both of these words. Genoa are the joints between the thigh and the shin, thus called because they are opposite to the cheeks in the womb,[92] where they are found near one another because

88. The manuscript has a blank space of five or six lines at this point.
89. The modern editor, Cesare Imperiale di Sant'Angelo (*Annali genovesi,* 5:6 n. 4), comments that the chronicler is not Philibertus but Sigibertus and that the passage is found in *MGH: Scriptores,* 6:347.
90. Monleone, *Annali genovesi,* 8:16 n. 1, asserts that the correct reading should be 933.
91. According to Imperiale di Sant'Angelo, *Annali genovesi,* 5:6 n. 1, the Isole Businarie are found between Corsica and Sardinia in the Strait of Bonifacio.
92. "Genu" is knee in Latin, the plural is "genua." Cheeks in Latin are "genae." Doria is engaging in some fanciful wordplay at this point. Imperiale di Sant'Angelo, *Annali genovesi,*

in the womb the infant lowers its head between its knees, and this is why, when men drop to their knees, they immediately weep. Nature wants to remind them of the maternal womb, where they made their home in darkness before coming into the light; for, according to the philosophers, the knees are consecrated to mercy. Indeed, Genoa was so called because it is above all other cities in mercy, as is known from many experiences. And just as the infant in its mother's womb holds its face between its knees, almost all the cities of Lombardy hold their head between the knees of Genoa.[93] Indeed, when it turns aside, they must also turn aside, as may be seen manifestly in past times. Janua is so called from Janus. This Janua—that is, "gate"—is the first entry, the first entrance, because Janus was the god of beginnings, to whom the ancients consecrated all exits and entrances. Just as the gate is the entrance and exit to every house, so our city is the entrance and exit to all of Lombardy. Or, indeed, it is called Janua from Janus, the god of beginnings, who is depicted having two faces, that is, before and behind; thus the city of Janua looks out before it on the sea and behind on the land; and it is said to have two views, that is, two gates, east and west, so the city of Janua has two gates, a sea gate and a land gate. This told, I will return to the promised subject.

Therefore, in A.D. 1280 Lord Cavalcabo de Medici, citizen of Pavia, a man skilled in the law, directed the government of the city of Genoa for the aforesaid captains, who ruled with him.[94]

In that said year three Genoese galleys were equipped in Genoa for a voyage to Romania[95] and loaded with merchandise worth more than one hundred thousand *lire*. When they were near Kefalonia, on the Monday after Palm Sunday, going toward Kyllene, there appeared three galleys of the Venetians coming from the direction of Zakynthos. The Venetians were, at that time, at war with the Anconitans, and therefore the aforesaid galleys were patrolling in that area, just as many [Venetian] armed galleys [sailed] in different regions for protection as well as to attack their enemies, the Anconitans. The said galleys of the Venetians unjustly set upon our galleys,

---

5:7 n. 3, points out that this whole passage is taken almost word for word from the *Etymologies* of Isidore of Seville.

93. The Latin wordplay here simply does not translate into English, because, in English, there is no "genua"/"Genua" parallel.

94. Of course, Doria continued where the earlier annals ended, so that the story of the dual captaincy of Oberto Spinola and Oberto Doria (Jacopo's brother) was already established.

95. Romania—"the land of the Romans"—was the name applied by medieval Italians to the lands that are now most frequently referred to as the Byzantine Empire.

attacking them even though they recognized the flags of the Genoese. The Genoese, recognizing and seeing the Venetians arrogance, vigorously drove their galleys forward, entering into battle from one side and another near Kyllene, about three miles distant. The Genoese came out with the victory, so that they captured two of the Venetian galleys, while the third rowed swiftly away. In that battle most of the Venetians were drowned in the sea or perished by the sword. Then, the Genoese, aware that our Lord Jesus Christ had given them the victory, admonished the Venetians they had taken alive against breaking faith and lying, then allowed them to go with their galleys and all their goods. The Genoese then proceeded joyfully to Romania. Also in that same year four merchant galleys were sumptuously equipped in Genoa, and it was ordered that the noble gentleman Manuel di Negro, a messenger for the commune to the Paleologus emperor, would depart in them and would command the aforesaid galleys. On Monday after the feast of the Resurrection of the Lord, in the sea about sixty miles off Cape San Panagia,[96] there appeared another three galleys of the Venetians that were similarly on guard in the war against the Anconitans, as was said before. As they came near, the Genoese recognized that they were Venetians, but their galleys were not concerned to arm themselves, because there was a truce between the Genoese and the Venetians. The Venetians, however, rushed furiously at ours, shouting insultingly that they would be thrown into the sea if they did not await their swords. The Genoese were completely amazed and in an instant took up arms and, only half armed, vigorously and swiftly boarded the galleys of the Venetians, killing almost all of them with the sword. Those who evaded the Genoese swords perished in the sea; the remainder, who escaped death, were taken with their galleys to Cape San Panagia. After they were warned against breaking faith and lying, they were set free, and all their goods were restored to them. However, their admiral and galley commanders and second officers were taken to Messina, where they were turned over to the Venetian resident ambassador in Messina with an official declaration of vendetta for him to transmit to their doge. From there they proceeded quickly on their successful voyage to Romania.

And, in that same year, on the twenty-second day of August, Pope Nicholas was residing safe and unharmed in the castle of Soriano, which had been forcibly seized from its lord,[97] when suddenly catarrh ran down his throat,

---

96. Cape San Panagia is on the eastern coast of Sicily, near Syracuse.

97. Pope Nicholas III (1277–80). The lord of Soriano (near Viterbo) was accused of heresy, and the castle was given to Orso Orsini, a cousin of the pope and podestà of Viterbo. Imperiale di Sant'Angelo, *Annali genovesi*, 5:10 n. 2.

and as a consequence he died without saying a word. The Roman Church remained vacant until 22 February of the following year.

In the same year, the said podestà[98] wisely and with great diligence discovered an iniquitous crime perpetrated by a certain Genoese citizen named Traverino Traverio. This man had been born to a good man of the *popolo* and was comfortably well off. Men considered him trustworthy, and on this account a certain man named Oliverio di Border recommended him to a young man, Guilliermo Alnardo, his cousin-german, who had 2,200 jars[99] of oil to carry from Seville to Tunis. Traverino Traverio set out with the said Guillermo and, selling the oil, had 1,300 *doplas*[100] and returned with Guillermo and the money to Genoa and stayed with him in his house. And, one night, moved by a diabolical instinct, he struck him on the head with a hoe while he slept, killing him. Putting him in a sack on a horse, he sent him to be buried by his foster brother at his villa at Casamavari.[101] This was in the year of the Lord 1278, on the eighth day of October, a night in which, as was told in the entry for that year, there was a great inundation of water. And the said Traverino told it widely about the city that Guillermo had remained with Oliverio. Traverino then took ship for Majorca. But when Oliverio could not find his cousin Guillermo or have any news of him, he sent one of his other cousins to Genoa, setting him up as his agent there. And this agent appeared before the podestà and wisely explained the matter and asked that the said Guillermo and the money together be restored to him. Now, since Traverino was in Majorca, the podestà wrote to him by letter that within a certain period of time he must appear before him in Genoa to answer the aforesaid agent both for the death and for Guillermo's money. Traverino was concerned about nothing because he was surrounded in Genoa by powerful relatives and friends, while the agent was a foreigner. He hurriedly returned to Genoa within the determined period. There he appeared before the podestà several times. The podestà, just as he was about to acquit him, perceptively and carefully discovered the crime. He sent to Casamavari, where he had the body exhumed from the grave. On 14 July, Traverino was

---

98. That is, Cavalcabo de Medici, mentioned at the beginning of this year's entry.

99. In the Latin, "iaris," from the Genoese "giare." These were large earthenware vessels used to store or transport oil or wine.

100. The *dopla*, or "double dinar," was a gold coin in common use in Tunis in the late thirteenth century. John Dotson, ed. and trans., *Merchant Culture in Fourteenth-Century Venice: The Zibaldone da Canal* (Binghamton, N.Y.: Medieval and Renaissance Texts and Studies, 1994), 192–93.

101. A village in the Bisagno valley, near the present site of Genoa's famous Staglieno cemetery. In the thirteenth century it would have been well outside the city walls.

ordered to restore the money and was condemned to death in the same way that he had killed Guillermo, as is contained in the records of the court. Whereupon the king of Castile and the said Oliverio and all who heard of the aforesaid justice rejoiced and admiringly commended the commune and the justice of Genoa. And since the Lord says, "Vengeance is mine, I will repay," after this, our Lord conferred upon the commune and men of Genoa many good and admirable victories, as will be noted, God willing, in the following pages.

4

Salimbene de Adam and the Franciscan Chronicle

Alison Williams Lewin

Salimbene de Adam (ca. 1221–87) created one of the lengthiest and most complex chronicles of thirteenth-century Italy. Born in Parma to prosperous parents, Salimbene, around the age of sixteen, decided to become a Franciscan friar, much to his father's disappointment. He was educated but no scholar, abandoning theological studies in Paris after only a week. Yet his pleasing personality and sophistication made him stand out among his peers; because of his abilities, his order sent him on various missions that introduced him to many places and people, including Pope Innocent IV, King Louis IX of France (Saint Louis), and the Holy Roman Emperor Frederick II.

Like many Italian writers of the late Middle Ages, Salimbene seems at once traditional and innovative. His life was bracketed by Saint Francis at the beginning and Dante at the end.[1] Salimbene reflects the medieval world, since he, like Saint Francis, rejected secular success and wealth to become a friar, bound by vows of strict poverty, chastity, and obedience. And while Franciscans gained a reputation for scientific advances, particularly in the field of optics, Salimbene himself had no interest in such inquiries, but rather dismissed modern experiments conducted by Frederick II as *superstitiones*.

At the same time, Salimbene reveals sensibilities that point to the Renaissance. Although much of his work is in Latin, he often writes in the vernacular. Like many medieval chroniclers, Salimbene uses the works of previous

---

1. A point noted by nearly every commentator on Salimbene. See, for example, G. G. Coulton, *From St. Francis to Dante*, 2nd ed., introduction by Edward Peters (Philadelphia: University of Pennsylvania Press, 1972), xviii.

historians, primarily the chronicle of Sicard of Cremona.[2] Yet he acknowledges his debt and, more importantly, evaluates Sicard's work. He comments
on Sicard's verbosity, faulty grammar, and failure to assess sources critically.
Salimbene assures his reader at one point that "we can report historical
events only with respect to the actual facts as we saw them with our own
eyes in our own time during the time of the empire of Frederick and after
his death during the long period up until the present day in which we are
now writing."[3] When he leaves Sicard aside and begins to record only what
he has seen or heard, beginning with the events of 1212, he promises to do
so carefully. He intends to relate only what he knows to be true, another
sign of the critical historical mentality that was to characterize humanist
writers in later centuries.

When Salimbene began writing, in 1283,[4] he was at the end of a long
career that had taken him from his birthplace of Parma to many important
cities in Italy and France. He had already written a number of historical and
theological works: a book on Roman history, a treatise on Pope Gregory X,
The Book of Pests, a text on the prophet Elijah, a work paralleling the life of
Saint Francis with that of Christ, and *The Book of the Prelate*, written to
denounce Brother Elias, a minister-general of the Franciscan Order.[5] None
of these texts is extant in the original, although portions of several found
their way into his *Chronicle*. The *Chronicle* itself survives in a single manuscript, thought to be autograph, in the Vatican Library. The manuscript is
over seven hundred folios long and is missing about two hundred folios. In
the remaining text, which begins with 1168, Salimbene primarily narrates
the events of his own century. Since he relies heavily on Sicard of Cremona
for historical material, it is possible that Salimbene's original manuscript
began with the Creation, as Sicard's had done.

Salimbene tells us that he began writing for his niece Sister Agnes, a re-
cluse in a convent of Poor Clares. He recounts for her the history of the

2. Sicard of Cremona, *Cronica*, in *MGH: Scriptores*, 31, ed. Oswald Holder-Egger (Hanover: Hahn, 1903), 78–181.

3. Salimbene, *The Chronicle of Salimbene de Adam*, trans. Joseph L. Baird, Giuseppe
Baglivi, and John Robert Kane, Medieval and Renaissance Texts and Studies, 40 (Binghamton, N.Y.: Medieval and Renaissance Texts and Studies, 1986), 176.

4. In the text, Salimbene says that he is writing "in the year of the Lord 1284." Ibid.
However, it is generally agreed that he began the text a year earlier and concluded writing
in 1288, shortly before his death. See Peters, introduction to *From St. Francis to Dante*, xviii,
and Baird, introduction to *Chronicle of Salimbene de Adam*, xi.

5. On Salimbene's life and works, see Lester K. Little, "Salimbene," in *Dictionary of the
Middle Ages*, ed. Joseph R. Strayer (New York: Scribner, 1982–89), s.v.

Adamo family and his own decision to become a Franciscan. As a youth Salimbene had felt a very strong vocation, so strong that it led him to defy his father and contribute to the destruction of his lineage "in both the male and the female line by entering the Religious Order."[6] His strong religious calling is reinforced in the few but vivid accounts of Salimbene's mystical visions that occurred very early in his life as a Franciscan, events of some significance in both his life and in his writing of history.

Soon after Salimbene's entrance into the order, his father came to beg him to return home to his family and position. Salimbene refused, and his father left, cursing him and "troubled beyond measure."[7] The very next night, while praying, Salimbene heard the Blessed Virgin calling him. When he responded, Mary let him hold the Christ child for a long time, until at last she gently asked him to surrender the babe before the friars found him there at Matins. He obeyed, and the vision disappeared. "But," he recalls, "so great a sweetness remained in my heart that I could not tell it. Truly, I confess that never in the world have I ever experienced such great sweetness."[8] He follows with the tale of a dream in which the son of a lord kills a monk; a few days later he finds out that, indeed, the man in question has just committed such a murder. He concludes, "And so we realized that sometimes dreams do come true."[9] The inclusion of the vision, along with a dream whose truth Salimbene asserts, suggests a strong desire to believe, even in his old age, what had been vouchsafed him in youth.

Two other youthful visions concern his vocation as a Franciscan. When still a new friar, Salimbene and his companion were begging bread, as Francis had commanded. Suddenly they found themselves in a strange courtyard with luxuriant vines, leopards and other unusual beasts, handsome young men and women, splendidly dressed, who carried harps, viols, and other instruments, "on which they played sweet melodies. . . . It was a strange and beautiful song that they sang—not only in the words sung but also in the harmonious variety of vocal melody—so much so that joy beyond measure filled our hearts." Salimbene and his companion stood transfixed for a long time, and Salimbene was at a loss to explain it: "I know not—God knows—how such an occasion of so great joy came about, for we had never seen the like before, nor were we likely to ever see it again."[10]

6. *Chronicle of Salimbene*, 33.
7. Ibid., 15.
8. Ibid.
9. Ibid., 16.
10. Ibid., 18–19.

Immediately after this vision, the two friars encountered a man who rebuked Salimbene harshly, saying, "You should be riding through the streets of Parma on your fine horse and engaging in tournaments: in that way you would bring happiness to the sorrowful, cut a fine figure before the ladies, and be a source of comfort to the minstrels. Instead, on your account your father is consumed with grief and your mother almost despairs of God because of her love for you whom she is unable even to see."[11]

Salimbene answered the man with a veritable torrent of biblical authority, and the man departed, "in confusion, not knowing what to reply."[12] Salimbene was tormented by the man's reproaches, however, thinking that the life he had chosen would prove an embarrassing and unbearable trial, beyond his power to endure.[13] He slept fitfully that night until, he says, "it pleased God to send me a most beautiful vision, which brought consolation, happiness, and unbelievable sweetness to my soul." In this vision Salimbene saw the Holy Family begging, and Christ himself explained to the young friar that He wished His servants and friends "to beg with such effort and labor," so that He could reward both parties in the transaction: those "giving for love of me" and those "begging for love of me."[14] After an animated conversation between Salimbene and Christ, during which the latter effusively quoted Scripture, Salimbene concludes, "The vision which I described above is true and contains absolutely nothing false."[15]

Despite the clarity of the visions, from this point on his *Chronicle* includes little of begging and a great deal about important people and the fine foods and wines that Salimbene enjoyed in their company. Perhaps he did eat many meals of cabbage, which he tells us he hated. Maybe he even begged for some, but in contrast to the spiritual joy and certainty he had experienced as a youth, his later spiritual energies seem directed toward other goals. Salimbene may have learned to eat cabbage—and he certainly admired those who could live a life that conformed to that of Francis and the early brothers—but in the account he renders of his own life and the weight he gives his own social position and comfort, Salimbene gives no

---

11. Ibid., 19.

12. Ibid.

13. Ibid.; "verum etiam labor erubescibilis et intolerabilis ultra vires," Salimbene de Adam, *Cronica*, ed. Giuseppe Scalia, Scrittori d'Italia, no. 232 (Bari: Laterza, 1966), 1:65.

14. *Chronicle of Salimbene*, 20–21. From there Salimbene segues into many biblical passages, ranging from God's giving the Jewish people meat and manna to Elisha's multiplying the oil of the widow woman in IV Kings 4 (1–7) to Saint Benedict, Saint Jerome, Psalms, John, and Matthew. This list is by no means complete; ibid., 21–25.

15. Ibid., 29.

indication he truly internalized the lessons Christ himself had deigned to give the young novice.

Salimbene's conflicted state embodied the dilemma of the thirteenth-century Franciscan order, conceived in poverty and simplicity, yet growing rich and powerful. Salimbene's visions, granted early in life, lend a prophetic quality to the *Chronicle.* While he will only write about what he sees with his own eyes, a lingering echo of prophecy survives to give meaning to the events that Salimbene records. His appealing curiosity, the inner tension he reveals between his own mundane desires and his vocation as a Franciscan, his pro-papal, partisan condemnation of Frederick II and simultaneous fascination with him, and his ability to portray vividly personages and events combine to create a work both enticing and challenging.

In his *Chronicle,* Salimbene presents multiple strands of contemporary history, his own life, his particularly Franciscan spirituality, and observations on everything from wine to siege tactics. Throughout his text, Salimbene makes liberal, even profligate use of biblical quotations as a rhetorical device. They are not exegetical, intended to explain either the grand scope of historical time or a deeper spiritual truth. Rather, they are associative and resonant of his own thought processes. Biblical phrases and images were always in his mind and grant his narrative a structure and authority that the mere recitation of events could not provide.

In order to attain some understanding of this extensive text, I shall examine three interwoven themes: Frederick II's impact on Italy, Salimbene's vocation as a Franciscan friar, and his understanding of history.

Salimbene's reflections on the meaning of Frederick's deeds, and his polemical narrative of Franciscan history, are key to his own prophetic view of history. The young friar was an early and fervent adherent of Joachim of Fiore and is in fact one of our best sources for early Joachism. Because of Salimbene's own fascination with temporal history and his confessed belief in the abbot's writings, some knowledge of Joachim's own historical vision is essential for understanding the *Chronicle.*

For Joachim, the Bible was a prophetic, dynamic text that already contained the seeds of all history within it, each of which would sprout and flower in a unique moment in human time.[16] Like many Christian writers, Joachim believed that the Bible contained concordances between the Old and New Testaments. More importantly, history could be divided into three

---

16. Bernard McGinn, *The Calabrian Abbot: Joachim of Fiore in the History of Western Thought* (New York: Macmillan, 1985), 124.

ages corresponding to the Trinitarian Father, Son, and Holy Spirit. The first age, of the Father, is the age of the laws and the patriarchy of the Old Testament. The second age, of the Son, is the age of the New Testament and the medieval Christian Church. The third age, however, yet to come, stands as the central focus of Joachim's thought and of Salimbene's speculation. Both expected the third age, that of the Holy Spirit, to be an age of peace and concord, followed by the coming of the Antichrist and the Final Judgment.

Salimbene's eschatological worldview appears most vividly in his treatment of Frederick II, Holy Roman Emperor, *stupor mundi,* and nemesis of the Roman Church. Frederick ignored any and all spiritual penalties imposed upon him by various prelates, which alone would have irritated the Church. His political ambitions were even more irritating to the papacy, though, for Frederick was heir to both the Holy Roman Empire and the Norman kingdom of Sicily. Seeking to recover imperial lands in northern Italy and rule them actively, he reaped considerable revenues as his reward for careful stewardship. His dynastic claims to both northern and southern Italy threatened the independence and the political influence of the pontiff, whose own holdings in central Italy were by this time substantial.

In Salimbene's view, Frederick's power had been foretold in numerous apocalyptic texts like the prophecies of Merlin, commonly believed to have been written by the magician of Arthurian legend. Here Salimbene articulates the fears of the thirteenth-century Church, which are his own fears as well. Initially Salimbene had supposed that Frederick was the warrior-king, identified by Joachim and other prophetic writers, whose life would mark the beginning of a new age of tumults and wars, leading to the reign of the Antichrist before the Last Judgment. But when Frederick died suddenly, Salimbene concluded that his death and the deaths of his heirs fulfilled another prophecy of Joachim's, that the empire would come to an end. Frederick's deeds were and remained matters of great symbolic importance. For Salimbene, Frederick's life was part of a cosmic design, one more complex than he had initially believed.

How then does Salimbene characterize this most obnoxiously present and active ruler? He begins by casting doubt upon his lineage and legitimacy. Frederick's mother was Constance, the daughter of King William II of Sicily. "On his deathbed, William II commanded his sons—I know not by what spirit—not to give Constance in marriage. The sons obeyed the father's command and kept Constance with them until she was thirty years old. Yet she was a perverse woman who constantly caused trouble among her brothers' wives and the entire family." Here Salimbene cites Ecclesiasticus 25:23, "It will be more agreeable to abide with a lion and a dragon, than to dwell with a wicked woman." Apparently the brothers agreed with this insight, for they stated:

> "Let us marry our sister off and put a great distance between her and us." And so they gave her in marriage to King Henry, who was to become Emperor Henry VI, son of the first and great Frederick. Then in the March of Ancona in the city of Jesi, Constance gave birth to a son, Frederick II. But it was said that Frederick was the son of a certain butcher, and that Constance had merely simulated giving birth to him. Thus Merlin said of the second Frederick, "an unexpected and miraculous birth," either because his mother was very old, or (certainly) because he was a suppositious and fraudulently acquired son.[17]

From this ambiguous beginning, Salimbene, by listing the ten misfortunes, personal and political, of Frederick II, then makes clear both the emperor's political importance and the divine significance of his ultimate defeat. His eldest son, Henry, rebelled against him and committed suicide. Another son was captured by the Bolognese and later died. Frederick could not dominate Lombardy either militarily or politically, for as Salimbene observes, "when he won them on one side he lost them on the other."[18] Ultimately even his own Sicilian princes and barons rebelled against him. Frederick failed most spectacularly, however, in his desire to subjugate the papacy. "But God did not allow him to perform his will," Salimbene observes, because God himself says (Zachariah 2:8), "For he that toucheth you, toucheth the apple of my eye."[19] Salimbene implies quite strongly that Frederick's life, from beginning to end, represented far more than secular history.

Like Frederick, Francis and the Franciscan order had a significant role in the unfolding of apocalyptic temporal history. As a Franciscan in the thirteenth century, Salimbene was uniquely situated to observe and comment on the dramatic growth of his order. Francis had founded an order of twelve humble, begging, lay brothers. By the time Salimbene wrote, the order of the Friars Minor had hundreds of convents and thousands of members. The order's dizzying increase had given rise to many disagreements and crises, however. Salimbene worried that the order's gain in wealth and prestige

---

17. *Chronicle of Salimbene*, 361.
18. Ibid., 343.
19. Ibid.

diminished its spiritual vocation. His concerns find their focus in the person of Brother Elias, minister-general of the Franciscans between 1232 and 1239. An indication of Salimbene's view of Elias is his inclusion of what he terms a "Tuscan rhyme":

There he goes, Old Brother Elias,
Not too good and not too pious.[20]

The themes of overweening pride and misuse of power by those in command concern Salimbene here, as they had with Frederick II. Though Salimbene condemns the latter (and others) for impious or arrogant actions, his real passion against such abuses comes out only toward Brother Elias. Anger and resentment mark this section of the *Chronicle,* but little rancor characterizes Salimbene's condemnation of Frederick, though the author himself and his beloved city of Parma suffered extensively at the hands of the emperor, who disobeyed the Church and got his just desserts.

In *The Book of the Prelate,* included in the *Chronicle,* Salimbene unleashes a long biblically inspired invective against Brother Elias. He enumerates Elias's many faults, which threaten the social and spiritual health of the order. Much of Salimbene's criticism reveals his own original highborn prejudices: Elias does not respect his social superiors; he admits unworthy laymen into the order; he promotes the unworthy to high offices; and he governs the order irresponsibly.

Using Elias as his model, Salimbene then emphasizes the ways in which God can exalt the humble and crush the mighty. He concludes his observations on Elias by quoting Proverbs 16:18, "Pride goeth before destruction: And the spirit is lifted up before a fall."[21] Quick though he is to criticize Elias's arrogance, Salimbene yet reveals his own, being most irritated that a man of such humble origins, one who "used to earn his living by sewing cushions and teaching the children of Assisi to read their psalters,"[22] should ever have risen as high as he did.

Salimbene's harsh view of Elias reflects the thirteenth-century Franciscan dilemma: Can an order of great influence and wealth celebrate humility and poverty?[23] The *Chronicle* contains little about the life of Saint Francis,

20. Ibid., 152.
21. Ibid., 92.
22. Ibid., 75.
23. The Franciscan dilemma has been the subject of several studies by David Burr, most recently and most importantly in *The Spiritual Franciscans: From Protest to Persecution in the Century After Saint Francis* (University Park: Pennsylvania State University Press, 2001).

a tale that dominates the writings of Salimbene's Franciscan contemporaries.[24] His omission of the topic may well reflect his desire to avoid engaging in any of the furious debates about Francis's intentions that had already divided his order into several mutually hostile camps. At the heart of the debates lay the issue of the absolute poverty that Francis insisted upon for himself and his followers, the same poverty he claimed governed the lives of Christ and the apostles. The larger issue, for Salimbene and many in his order, however, was the place of Francis in Christian history.

Joachimite belief and the inevitable strains of growth within the Franciscan order intersect often in Salimbene's *Chronicle*. Many Joachimites, including Salimbene, believed that the third age of history would begin in 1260 and would be foreshadowed by the arrival of two groups of spiritual men whose mission was to reform the Church. Salimbene, like many of his brethren, was convinced that the Franciscans were one of them.[25] Hence, Joachimite ideas were very influential among the Franciscans.

Salimbene liberally cites Joachim in his *Chronicle*. His familiarity with Joachim's works was, in large part, due to his friendship with Brother Hugh of Digne. As he reports:

> Brother Hugh gladly lived in this town [Hyères]. And there were a large number of notaries, judges, physicians, and learned men there who, on solemn feast days, would gather in Brother Hugh's chambers to hear him speak on the doctrine of Joachim, teaching and expounding the mysteries of Holy Scripture and predicting the future. For he was a great Joachite, and he had all the books, in elaborate versions, that Abbot Joachim wrote. And I myself was among the group that gathered there to hear Brother Hugh. For I had heard of this doctrine earlier when I was living in Pisa, where I was taught it by a certain abbot of the Order of Fiore, an old and holy man,

24. In one of the few instances where Salimbene writes something about Saint Francis, he does so with warmth, but with little of the eschatological expectation that marked many other narratives of Francis's life. In 1244, Crescentius was elected minister-general of the order, and directed Thomas of Celano to write another life of Francis. Salimbene seems for the first time to connect emotionally to the saint, writing, "For daily in various parts of the world the Lord continues to work great miracles through his servant Francis." *Chronicle of Salimbene*, 166. Similarly Salimbene writes later, "I believe that just as the Son of God wanted to have one special friend like unto Himself (that is, St. Francis) so the devil had Ezzelino." Ibid., 186.

25. Members of other religious orders had similar beliefs. See, for example, Marjorie Reeves, "Joachimist Expectations in the Order of Augustinian Hermits," *Recherches de théologie ancienne et médiévale* 25 (1958): 111–41.

who had collected and stored in the convent at Pisa all the books
by Joachim that he owned, since he was afraid that the Emperor
Frederick would destroy his own monastery. . . . For he believed
that in Frederick all the mysteries were to be fulfilled at that time,
because Frederick had such great discord with the Church.[26]

John of Parma, elected minister-general in 1247, embraced Joachimite
ideas. He was a noted scholar and preacher, a great lover of poverty and
simplicity who traveled extensively on foot visiting chapters, healing divisions in the order. As harshly as he condemns Brother Elias for his many
spiritual failings, Salimbene praises John of Parma, for he was "a man of
good example and great edification,"[27] of outstanding humility,[28] "generous,
open, courteous, loving, humble, gentle, good, and long-suffering. He was
a fine speaker, and as a man devoted entirely to God, was pious, merciful,
and compassionate."[29] His fervor and eloquence moved men to tears; he
traveled widely, visited all provinces of the order, and healed the rift between
the masters of the University of Paris and the mendicants. He enjoyed such
a reputation for goodness and mercy that even the reprobate Elias, excommunicated for disobedience and for his association with Frederick, said that
"because of the great good I have heard of the venerable John of Parma, I
would not fear to throw myself at his feet and confess my sin, feeling fully
confident of his mercy."[30]

The saintly John was forced to step down at the chapter meeting of 1257,
the victim of a controversy over the expansion of the Franciscan order.[31] In
the century after Francis, the order had increasingly been divided between
those who held strictly to Francis's ideals of humility and poverty, eventually
called Spirituals, and those who argued that the order had to seek a reconciliation between poverty and power to meet Francis's own evangelical and
spiritual goals, the Conventuals. Early in the fourteenth century, Spirituals
wrote that Saint Bonaventure, John's successor as minister-general, and
others forced John to resign because they hated his strict interpretation of
Franciscan ideas of poverty.

Salimbene's *Chronicle*, which offers valuable insight into the circumstances of John's resignation, tells a more complex story. In 1256, Pope

26. *Chronicle of Salimbene*, 228.
27. Ibid., 296.
28. Ibid., 295.
29. Ibid., 297.
30. Ibid., 154.
31. On the debate over John of Parma, see Burr, *Spiritual Franciscans*, 33–39.

Alexander IV officially condemned Joachim of Fiore. The issue was not so much what Joachim had said as what others had taken him to say. Gerard of Borgo San Donnino had gone so far as to claim that in "The Age of the Spirit" Joachim's writings would replace the Bible! In that climate John of Parma's admiration of Joachism elicited criticism from the papacy as well as from some within his own order.[32] The nearly constant turmoil in the order meant that "it would not do to have as Minister General a man who might be accused of heresy. Complaints were made against him, and the pope was obliged to take action."[33] John resigned, and Saint Bonaventure (himself a Joachimite, but a much more subtle one) became the new leader and second founder of the order.

Salimbene felt nothing but admiration for John of Parma.[34] He himself attempted to persuade John to abandon his Joachism, which he terms "frivolous beliefs."[35] Salimbene makes clear that at the time of John's resignation, Joachism, not poverty, was the issue. Perhaps he found it easier to blame a maligned and papally discredited philosophy rather than the contentious and unsettled question at the heart of Franciscan identity.

Joachism itself raised many question for Salimbene, however. In one of his numerous lists, Salimbene presents "three problems which make Joachim's doctrine difficult to believe."[36] Joachim's condemnation of Peter Lombard as a "heretic and a madman" was obviously an error, and yet Salimbene is quick to point out that he himself has identified eight places in the *Sentences* where Peter Lombard erred.[37] Salimbene continues: "The second problem with Joachim that inhibits belief is that he predicted future tribulations. . . . For carnal men do not hear future tribulations gladly; they prefer consolation, as Isaiah 30[:10] says: 'speak unto us pleasant things, see errors for us.' Thus when he spoke of tribulations, Joachim added, 'Those men who have hearts hardened by ambition will not believe this. For those who hate the kingdom of heaven do not want the kingdom of the world to perish.'"[38]

32. John R. H. Moorman, *A History of the Franciscan Order from Its Origins to the Year 1517* (Oxford: Clarendon Press, 1986), 114. Salimbene says, "Because he believed so strongly in the doctrine of Joachim, Brother John was hated by certain Ministers, as well as by Pope Alexander IV and Pope Nicholas III"; *Chronicle of Salimbene*, 301.

33. Moorman, *Franciscan Order*, 115.

34. *Chronicle of Salimbene*, 295–313.

35. Ibid., 303.

36. Ibid., 230.

37. On Joachim and Peter Lombard, see E. Randolph Daniel, "The Double Procession of the Holy Spirit in Joachim of Fiore's Understanding of History," *Speculum* 55 (1980): 469–83.

38. *Chronicle of Salimbene*, 230.

Here, too, Salimbene establishes Joachim's essential validity, since only the carnal and ambitious would seek to discredit him. Finally, though, Salimbene arrives at the central difficulty for Joachism:

> The third problem comes from Joachim's own believers, because they have sought to set precise limits where he set none. . . .
>
> *The Abbot Joachim did not set a definite time period for the coming of the Antichrist nor for the end of the world.* Although it seems so to some men, Abbot Joachim did not set a definite time period whatsoever. But he set a number of terminal points, saying [*sic*] "God is powerful and able to make his mysteries clearer, as those who are then living will see."[39]

Here again, Joachim is not wrong; he is misunderstood. Yet time passes, beliefs change, and Salimbene concludes that those who cannot abandon "frivolous beliefs" have "no resilience of character."[40] In a passage that explicitly links John of Parma's beliefs to Salimbene's own, he writes that he had "fully believed, and even hoped, that Frederick would do even greater wicked deeds in the future than he had yet done, numerous as his past evils had already been"; thus would God signal the approaching end of the world, as Joachim had foretold.

When Frederick died and the portentous year 1260[41] passed without incident, Salimbene "completely abandoned that doctrine," vowing from that point on "to believe only what I can see."[42] Yet Salimbene could not allow the death of Frederick to pass without finding some prophetic significance in it. Even his death date was significant. If he died on the feast day of Saint Lucy, as "some people say, . . . that is not without its hidden meaning. For St. Lucy announced to the people of Syracuse, I bring you the news that peace has returned to the Church: Diocletian is cast down from his reign and Maximian is dead today."[43] Moreover, "the words of Isaiah about

39. Ibid., 230–31.
40. Ibid., 302.
41. This year was not accorded significance directly by Joachim, but by others who made calculations based upon the schema Joachim had outlined. According to some, the last seal would open that year, and the end of the world and sacred history begin.
42. *Chronicle of Salimbene*, 302. He made this statement, however, to Brother Bartholomew Calaroso of Mantua, who had said of Brother John of Parma, a famous Joachimite, "because he believed so strongly the prophecies of fantastic men, he condemned himself and did great harm to his friends."
43. Ibid., 349.

the destruction of Babylon and Lucifer can be adapted to Frederick and his sons."[44] Finally, "'In that man, also, the Empire will come to an end, because even if he has successors they will be deprived of the supreme honor of the imperial name of Roman.' These are the words of one of the Sibyls—or so it is said, although I have not found them among the sayings of the Erythraean or the Tiburtine Sibyl. . . . How true that prophecy is, however, is made clear both by the Imperial and the Church party" [that is, by both Ghibellines and Guelfs].[45]

If the passing of this momentous year without incident destroyed the initial framework in which Salimbene had seen contemporary events, as he himself tells us it did, some of the randomness of his *Chronicle* becomes understandable. Certainly, while writing his *Chronicle* in the 1280s, Salimbene still believed that there was a pattern and purpose to the events he had observed. His regular comments that particular events had been predicted by Joachim, Merlin, or other prophetic texts, and his frequent citations of biblical texts, show his belief in a divine pattern to history. Nonetheless, Salimbene appears as a shrewd observer of human beings, intensely concerned with people's motives and aware of the postures people assume to fit circumstances. He is able, therefore, to see many events as logical and even predictable within a purely earthly, human framework.

Salimbene says that he is now no longer a Joachimite. Yet writing twenty years after the fact, he still speaks warmly of many of Joachim's followers and praises many of Joachim's prophecies as having been correct. Even early in his *Chronicle* Salimbene writes that God could reveal "future events and celestial secrets"[46] to his prophets. And God had granted Salimbene himself visions that suggested a divine involvement in the world. On this score Salimbene's *Chronicle* often seems inconsistent, sometimes embracing a Joachimite or prophetic view of the world and at other times viewing skeptically any vision of human history that presumed to interpret or predict God's plan. This inconsistency reflects Salimbene's own conflicts and those of his age. His own spiritual needs clashed with his critical intelligence, as his admiration for John of Parma (and John's Joachism) collided with his cool appraisal of what would be best for the Franciscan order. Salimbene retained a Joachimite framework for making sense of his world even when he committed himself to telling only what he saw with his own eyes. His

44. Ibid.
45. Ibid., 351.
46. Ibid., 3.

own early visions and certainty about his religious calling invited, almost commanded, him to place these events in the context of divine order and justice. For Salimbene, reading and, more importantly, narrating history could make God's intentions clear.

APPENDIX: SALIMBENE, THE *CHRONICLE*[47]

[12–13; 14; 15] I, Brother Salimbene, was the third son [several generations later], and when I had completed a decade and a half of my life and had arrived at the turning point of the proverbial Pythagorean Y,[48] I entered the Order of the Friars Minor. And I have been in this Order for many years as priest and preacher; I have lived in many provinces, seen many things, and learned much. . . . All his life my father sorrowed over my entrance into the Order of the Friars Minor, and would not be comforted, because he had no son left to him as an heir. And so he complained to the Emperor,[49] who was at that time in Parma, that the Friars Minor had stolen his son away from him. The Emperor then wrote to Brother Elias, Minister General of the Order,[50] enjoining him to return me to my father, if he wished to remain in his good graces. It was, indeed, Brother Elias himself who had received me into the Order in 1238, at the time he was making his way to the

---

47. From *Chronicle of Salimbene*. Page numbers are indicated in brackets beginning each section.

48. According to Isidore of Seville (ca. 560–636 C.E.), *Etym.* I.iii.10–16; trans. in S. K. Heninger, *Touches of Sweet Harmony: Pythagorean Cosmology and Renaissance Poetics* (San Marino, Calif.: Huntington Library, 1974), 269: "Pythagoras of Samos was the first to fashion the letter Y into a pattern of human life. The straight portion at the bottom signifies the first, uncertain age, which at that point has been given over to neither vices nor virtues. The bifurcation at the top, however, begins at adolescence. The path to the right is difficult, but it tends toward a blessed life. The path to the left is easier, but it leads to ruin and destruction."

49. Though crowned Holy Roman Emperor in 1220, Frederick II was deposed in 1245, five years before his death, in 1250.

50. One of Saint Francis's earliest companions, Elias was born near Assisi around 1180 and became vicar-general of the Franciscans in 1221. His zeal in collecting funds for the basilica at Assisi alienated many ascetics in the order, and Giovanni Parenti was elected minister-general in 1227. Some sources suggest that Elias attempted to seize control of the order in 1227, then retreated to live a life of extreme penance when the attempt failed. Regardless, Elias was elected next minister-general in 1232, amid great tumult. After leading the order for nearly seven years, Elias's violations of Francis's own rules regarding money, and his generally arrogant demeanor, led to his deposition by Gregory IX in 1239. Elias made common cause with Frederick II and was subsequently excommunicated and expelled from the order. For more details, see *The New Catholic Encyclopedia* (Farmington Hills, Mich.: Gale, 2003), 5:156–57.

Emperor on a mission from Pope Gregory IX. My father then went to Assisi
to see Elias and handed him the Emperor's letter in person. . . . After reading the Emperor's letter, Brother Elias immediately wrote the friars in the
convent at Fano, where I was then living. And his command was that if I
wished to leave the Order of my own free will, they should return me without the slightest delay to my father, but that if I did not wish to go, they
should retain me and cherish me as they would the very pupils of their eyes.
And so my father came to the convent at Fano, accompanied by a large
number of knights, curious to see how the matter would end. To them, the
whole matter was a mere spectacle; to me, the very root of my salvation. . . .
[The friars] listened behind the door to what was being said, for they trem-
bled like a reed in the water lest my father should change my mind by his
persuasion. They were fearful, after all, not only because the salvation of my
soul was at stake but also because my departure might prevent others from
entering the Order.

Then my father said to me: "My beloved son, don't put any faith in these
piss-in-tunics"—that is, those who urinate in their robes—"who have deceived
you. But come with me, and all that I have I will give to you." And I answered
and said to my father: "Go, go, father! The Wise Man says in Proverbs
3[:27]: 'Do not withhold him from doing good, who is able: if thou art
able, do good thyself also.'" And in tears my father answered: "What, son,
what shall I say to your mother, who suffers unceasingly on your account?"
And I said to him: "Tell her for me: thus says your son: 'my father and
mother have left me: but the Lord hath taken me up'" [Psalms 26:10]. . . .
Hearing all these things and despairing of further attempts to persuade me
to leave, my father prostrated himself on the ground in the presence of the
friars and the laymen who had come with him, and he said: "Accursed son,
I give you to a thousand devils, along with your brother, who is here a friar
with you, assisting in your deception. I lay my everlasting curse upon your
head and bequeath you to the infernal demons."

[74] *The Beginning of the Book of the Prelate which I wrote about Brother
Elias;*

And at the time Gerard of Corigia, who was called *de Dentibus* because
he had huge teeth, was podestà of Parma, and accompanied by a number of
knights, he made a personal visit to the convent to see Brother Elias, the
Minister General. And when the podestà entered and greeted him, Brother
Elias neither stood up nor moved from his place, as I saw with my own eyes,
conduct which was thought most discourteous, since God himself says in

Holy Scripture, Leviticus 19[:32]: "Rise up before the hoary head, and honour the person of the aged man," and also Ecclesiasticus 3[:20]: "The greater thou art, the more humble thyself in all things, and thou shalt find grace before God."

For Elias was of humble parentage—his father was from Castel de' Britti in the bishopric of Bologna and his mother from Assisi—and before he entered the Order he used to earn his living by sewing cushions and teaching the children of Assisi to read their Psalters. In the secular world he was called Bonusbaro,[51] but on entering the Order he took the name Elias. He was elected Minister General twice, and he stood in the good graces of both the Emperor and the Pope.

Yet eventually God humbled Brother Elias, in keeping with the Scripture [Psalm 74:8]: "One he putteth down, and another he lifteth up."

[79] A second fault of Brother Elias was that he accepted many useless men into the Order. I lived in the convent of Siena for two years, for example, and I saw twenty-five lay brothers there. Then I lived in Pisa for four years, and I saw thirty lay brothers living there.

[81] The third fault of Brother Elias was that he promoted unworthy men to offices in the Order. For he placed lay brothers in the positions of guardians, custodians, and ministers, an absurd practice, since there was an abundance of good clerks available in the Order.[52] I myself, for instance, was under the authority of a lay custodian, and, in the course of my life, more than one lay guardian. I was never governed by a lay minister, it is true, but I have seen many of them in other provinces. And there is really no cause to wonder that Elias favored such men, for Ecclesiasticus 13[:19–20] says that "Every beast loveth its like: so also every man him that is nearest to himself. All flesh shall consort with the like to itself, and every man shall associate himself to his like," and also Ecclesiasticus 27[:10]: "Birds resort unto their like: so truth will return to them that practice her," and Ecclesiasticus 10[:2]: "As the judge of the people is himself, so also are his ministers: and what manner of man the ruler of a city is, such also are they that dwell therein."

... The fourth fault of Brother Elias was that during his entire term of office there were no constitutions instituted to govern the Order and thereby

---

51. Salimbene may be joking at Elias's expense; in Latin "Bonusbaro" means "the good blockhead, the good simpleton."

52. On the difficulty of assimilating laity and clerics, see Burr, *Spiritual Franciscans,* 5–6.

to attain the desirable goals of preserving the Rule and regulating the Order and making it uniform.

[83] When I first entered the Order of the Friars Minor, there were many men of extraordinary sanctity and learning. For Brother Elias did have this single good quality: he promoted the study of theology in the Order. On my entry, the Order had been in existence for thirty-one years, and I saw the first Brother admitted by St. Francis himself, as well as other original members of the Order. While I was at Parma I sat under Samson the Englishman, lecturer in theology, and during my novitiate at Fano—then divided into two separate districts under separate ministers—under Brother Humile of Milan. And it is now the year 1283, the feast of St. Gorgon the martyr, and Martin IV is currently Pope.

Therefore, my conclusion is this: that general laws for the Order are a blessing, since they promote unity in the religious life and produce many desirable results. The fact that under Elias' governance there were no such rules is a great defect. In this respect the Lord says in Hosea 8[:12]: "I shall write to him," that is, to the Order of the Friars Minor, "my manifold laws, which have been accounted as foreign." This was fulfilled in the following year when Brother Elias was deposed, and a great many rules were drawn up.

[154–55] The thirteenth fault of Brother Elias was that he never sought to be reconciled to his Order, but persisted in his obstinacy until the day he died. Brother John of Parma,[53] however, sent Gerard of Modena to speak with him, for Gerard was one of the early Brothers of the Order and knew Elias well. But when Gerard besought him for the love of God and of St. Francis to return to the Order, not only for the welfare of his soul but also for the good example this would set for others, he answered, "Because of the great good I have heard of the venerable John of Parma, I would not fear to throw myself at his feet and confess my sin, feeling fully confident of his mercy. But I am concerned that the Provincial Ministers whom I have offended might make sport of me, put me in chains, thrust me in prison,

---

53. The Blessed John of Parma (ca. 1209–89) became minister-general of the Franciscans in 1247 and held the post for ten years. He was a man of great erudition, and his piety and devotion to the ideals of Saint Francis did much to heal divisions within the order. After visiting many provinces of the Franciscans, John went on a mission to the East to attempt reconciliation between the Eastern and Western Christian churches. He also attempted to smooth over tensions between the Franciscan and Dominican orders. His close friendship with Gerard of San Donnino, whose beliefs had been condemned by the professors of Paris and a commission at Anagni, together with his literal observance of the Rule and Joachism, led Pope Alexander IV to urge him to resign. John did so, promoting Saint Bonaventure as his successor. *New Catholic Encyclopedia*, 7: 979–80.

and give me [Isaiah 30:20] 'spare bread, and short water.' Furthermore, since I also offended the Papal Court, I am afraid that the Cardinal-Protector of the Order will take it upon himself to lay penances on me. Besides I do not want to lose the Emperor's favor." Thus did Brother Gerard of Modena spend the entire day in Cella di Cortona talking with Elias and doing his best to persuade him and his entire retinue to return to the Order and submit to its rule, according to the words of Proverbs 21[:12]: . . . Yet Brother Gerard labored in vain, for Elias would not yield for the reasons we have just given, so that the words of the Scripture [Psalm 108:18] might be fulfilled: "he would not have blessing, and it shall be far from him," and the last chapter of Apocalypse [22:11]: "He that hurteth, let him hurt still: and he that is filthy, let him be filthy still." Furthermore, Brother Gerard spent the whole of the following night without sleep, because, as he reported later, it seemed to him that demons were swarming throughout the whole place like bats. He even heard their cries, and, Job 4[:14, 15], "fear seized upon" him, "and trembling," and "the hair of" his "flesh stood up," and all his "bones were affrighted." As soon as morning came, Gerard bade farewell and left that place in haste with his companion, and he reported everything that he had seen and heard to the Minister General.

Finally, Brother Elias died. Earlier, he had been excommunicated by Pope Gregory IX, and whether or not he was ever reconciled to the Church and had put his soul in order, he now knows.

[176–77] The various digressions that we have indulged in throughout this chronicle may be excused for three reasons. First of all, such things came to mind despite ourselves and at times when, in good conscience, we could not avoid them, because "the Spirit breatheth where he will," and it is not "in man's power to stop the spirit," as John 3[:8] and Ecclesiastes 8[:8] report. Second, such digressions have enabled us to say many good and useful things which can best be reported in such a history. Third, we always return to the original subject and never leave out any of the facts of the history on account of the digressions. Some writers produce their works with beautiful, lucid, mellifluous eloquence, like Job, Isaiah, Ecclesiasticus, John Chrysostom, St. Gregory, St. Bernard, and many others. . . . I myself in writing various chronicles have always used a simple, clear style, so that my niece, for whom I wrote, would be able to understand it. And elegance of style was far less important to me than the truth of the history.

[181–82] *The harsh and complex war between the Church and the Empire, or between the Emperor and the Pope.*

So that the complexity of these matters may be understood, it should not be omitted that the imperial party was in control of the city of Modena, with the Church party cast out. The same was true of Reggio, and, later, of Cremona. And thus there was a bitter war in those days which lasted for many years, and men could not plow, not plant, nor reap, nor plant vineyards, nor harvest the grapes, nor even live in villages. And this was especially true in Parma, Reggio, Modena, and Cremona. Indeed, men did their necessary work near the cities under guard by civil troops, divided into four parts according to the gates of the city, and thus armed troops stood guard over the workers the whole day long so that the farmers could attend to the fields. Such procedures were necessary because of the huge number of bandits, thieves, and predators, who would take men captive, imprison them, and hold them for ransom. They would also drive the oxen off and eat them or sell them. And if the ransom were not paid, they would hang their victim up by the feet or hands, pull out his teeth, and put toads or frogs in his mouth to persuade him to pay up. These men were crueler than demons, and their deeds harsher and more abominable than any kind of death. And so it was during that time that a man would far rather meet a devil on the road than another man. . . . [The wild animals] gathered in great numbers around the moats of the cities, and howled from the pangs of hunger, and some got into the city at night and ate people who were sleeping on their porches or in wagons—men, women, and children. And sometimes they even dug through the walls of houses and killed infants in the cradle.

Nobody could believe unless they had seen as I have seen the horrible deeds done during that time, not only by men but by beasts of various kinds. . . .

[198] *The letter of the Emperor of the Tartars to the Pope.*

I wish to record nothing from that book except the aforementioned letter, because I do not have the time. The letter reads as follows:
The letter of the lord of the Tatars[54] *to Pope Innocent IV.*

By the power of God, the Emperor of all men sends a true and veracious letter to the great Pope. In order to preserve peace between us, you, the Pope, and all Christian people have sent your messenger to us, as we have learned from the messenger himself and from your letter. . . . One part of your letter suggested that we ought to be baptized and become Christians.

---

54. Salimbene used Tatar and Mongol interchangeably, and Baird retains his inconsistencies in his translation.

To this we answer you briefly that we do not understand why we should do this. To the statement in your letter that you marvel at the great slaughter of men, and especially of Christians, among the Poles, the Moravians, and the Hungarians, we answer again that we do not understand this. Yet lest our silence should cause you completely to misunderstand, we will answer you in this manner: Because these people obeyed neither the word of God nor the command of Genghis Khan or the other khan, God commanded us to kill them and He delivered them into our hand. And, indeed, if it were not God who did this, what could man have done? Yet you men of the West believe yourselves to be the only Christians, and despise all other men. But how could you possibly know to whom God deigns to grant his grace? We, however, worship God, and by the power of God have conquered the whole world from the East to the West. And if this had not been by the power of God, what could men have done? If, however, you wish to have peace, and will turn over all your power to us, you, the Pope, and all Christian potentates must not in any wise hesitate to come to me and work out the peace. Then we will know that you wish to have peace with us. If, however, you will not believe our letter, and God's, and will not listen to the advice to come to us, then we will know for certain that you wish to have war with us. After this, what the future will bring, we do not know; God alone knows. Ghengis Khan, First Emperor Ochoday Khan, Second Emperor

Cuiuich Khan, Third Emperor

This is the whole of the letter sent by the lord of the Tatars to the Pope.

[343–46] *The ten misfortunes of Frederick II, sometime Emperor.*

Although great, and rich, and powerful, Frederick II, sometime Emperor, had many misfortunes, some of which I shall speak of here. His first misfortune was that his first-born son Henry, who was to reign after him, allied himself with the Lombards against the Emperor's will. Thus Frederick captured him and placed him in chains in prison, and afterward he died a miserable death. Thus the Emperor could say with Job 19[:19]: "he whom I loved most is turned against me."

His second misfortune was that he wished to subjugate the Church, and make the Pope, and Cardinals, and other prelates barefoot paupers. . . .

His third misfortune was that he wished to conquer the Lombards and could not, for when he won them on the one side he lost them on the other. . . .

His fourth misfortune was that Pope Innocent IV deposed him from the empire in full council at Lyons, and made known his evil deeds and maliciousness to the world. . . .

His fifth misfortune was that while he was still living, his empire was given to another, that is to say, to the Landgrave of Thuringia. . . .

His sixth misfortune was Parma's rebellion from the empire and alliance with the Church, which was the cause of his total destruction.

His seventh misfortune was that when the Parmese captured the city of Victoria which he had built near Parma, they threw down, burned, and totally destroyed the city, and even filled up the moats so that not a vestige remained, according to the words of Apocalypse 17[:8, 11] the city "which was, and is not."

His eighth misfortune was the rebellion of his own princes and barons, such as Tebaldo Francesco, who fled to Capaccio, but who subsequently died a miserable death at the hands of the Emperor's torturers. Also, Piero delle Vigne, and so many others that it would take too long to name them all. About these men the Emperor could repeat the words of Job 19[:19]: "They that were sometime my counsellors, have abhorred me: and he whom I loved most is turned against me."

. . . His ninth misfortune was when his son, King Enzio, was captured by the Bolognese. And Enzio's imprisonment was proper and just, because he had captured on the high seas those prelates who were on their way to a council called by Pope Gregory IX.

. . . His tenth misfortune was when he heard that Marquis Uberto Pellavicino wielded more power over the Lombards than he himself could ever do, even though Pellavicino was of his party.

[350–51] *The Emperor Frederick's flaws. God did well in wiping his sons from the face of the earth.*

God did extremely well in wiping the sons of Frederick from the face of the earth, because that was "a perverse and exasperating generation, A generation that set not their heart aright: and whose spirit was not faithful to God" [Psalm 77:8]. . . .

Note that Frederick almost always enjoyed having discord with the Church and fighting her on all sides, although she had nourished him, defended him, and raised him up. He held the true faith to be worthless. He was a cunning, crafty man, avaricious, lecherous, and malicious, easily given to wrath.

Frederick's good qualities and abilities.

At times, however, Frederick was a worthy man, and when he wished to show his good, courtly side, he could be witty, charming, urbane, and industrious. He was adept at writing and singing, and was well-versed in the art of writing lyrics and songs. He was a handsome, well-formed man of medium height. I myself saw him and, at one time, loved him. For he once wrote Brother Elias, Minister General of the Friars Minor, on my behalf asking him to return me to my father.[55] He also could speak many and various languages. In short, if he had been a good Catholic and had loved God, the Church, and his own soul, he would scarcely have had an equal as an emperor in the world. . . .

The Roman Empire was ended in Frederick.

"In that man, also, the Empire will come to an end, because even if he has successors they will be deprived of the supreme honor of the imperial name of Roman." These are the worlds of one of the Sibyls—or so it is said, although I have not found them among the sayings of the Erythraean or the Tiburtine Sibyl.[56] But then I have not seen the writings of the other Sibyls, and there were ten of them. How true that prophecy is, however, is made clear both by the Imperial and the Church party.

The successors of Frederick, both in the Imperial party and the Church.

For in the Imperial party Conrad, Frederick's legitimate son by his wife, the daughter of King John, succeeded to the empire. Conrad never ruled, and was scarcely able to prosper at all. His successor was Manfred, his half-brother, born of the niece of the Marquis of Lancia, whom Frederick married on his death-bed. He also never gained control of the empire, but was always called simply prince by those who had loved his father, and after the death of his father and brother he ruled for many years in Calabria, Sicily, and Apulia. Conradin, the son of Conrad, sought to succeed Manfred, but they were both killed by Charles, brother of the king of France. Moreover, the would-be successors to the empire from the Church party by the will of the Pope, cardinals, prelates and electors—that is to say, the Landgrave of Thuringia, William of Holland; and Rudolph of Germany—never prospered and were never able to gain full control of the empire. Thus the aforementioned prophecy appears to be true.

---

55. This remark is somewhat puzzling in light of Salimbene's own strong desire to remain with the Friars Minor. Perhaps it was not so much the position Frederick took as the fact that he bothered to intervene at all that made a favorable impression on Salimbene.

56. Ancient prophetic writings dating from before the founding of the Roman Republic, in 509 B.C.E.; though many vanished over the years, Roman priests throughout the imperial era would periodically consult those remaining.

[404–5] Many enemies rise up against the Friars Minor and the Preachers, accusing them of four things for which they ought rather to have thanked them.

The clerks gathered together at this council then rose up against the Friars Minor and the Preachers.[57] And they made the following accusations against them: that the Brothers fail to teach the doctrine of tithes; that they act as confessors, which office belongs only to the regular clergy; that they give burial to the dead; and that they exercise the office of preaching, which also belongs only to the regular clergy. In these four ways, the regular clergy are hindered in their means of livelihood.

Both Lord Obizzo, bishop of Parma, and Lord Philip, archbishop of Ravenna, rise up in defense of the Minorites and Preachers.

Then Obizzo of San Vitale, bishop of Parma and nephew of the late Pope Innocent IV of good memory, rose up in defense of the Minorites and Preachers. And he said that none of those things the two Orders were accused of was a hindrance whatsoever to the regular clergy, but rather a help and assistance to them. With sound arguments he defended the Brothers in fine fashion, and confounded the clergy, so that, as it seemed to them, he became their worst enemy. The archbishop also, seeing the Brothers condemned harshly for those four abovementioned deeds, came to their defense immediately, saying, "You stupid fools, I did not call you together so that you could rise up and attack these two Orders, who were sent by God to help your Church and to save the Christian people and all men who will be saved. I called this council together instead so that we might come to some decision with respect to the Tartars, as the Pope commanded me and the other archbishops." But when the clergy continued to murmur, the archbishop became angry and spoke again, saying, "You stupid fools, to whom shall I give the task of confessing the seculars, if not to the Friars Minor and the Preachers? I cannot give it to you with a clear conscience, for when the seculars come to you for confession seeking medicine for their souls, you give them poison instead. For you take the women behind the altar on the pretext of confessing them, and there you know them carnally. . . ." "Shall I," the archbishop continued, "allow the priest Gerard (who is here present) to hear the

---

57. As the arguments on both sides make clear, great competition arose between secular clergy who were fixed in a particular church and the mendicant, traveling orders of the Minorites (Franciscans) and Preachers (Dominicans). At stake were the loyalties and donations of pious Christians throughout Europe.

confessions of women when I know well that his house is filled with sons and daughters? To this man is fitting the prophecy [Psalm 127:3]: 'Thy children as olive plants, round about thy table.' And should such a man, this priest Gerard, be alone in such matters without any witnesses?" After the archbishop had spoken about such matters so openly, all those who knew themselves to be guilty of the same sin blushed for shame. . . .

[412-13] *A terrible, yet true story which Pope Alexander IV recounted to Brother Bonaventure,*[58] *Minister General of the Order of the Friars Minor.*

"Note that the Friars Minor received the privilege of hearing confession from Pope Gregory IX. And, once, Brother Bonaventure, the Minister General, asked Pope Alexander IV whether or not it pleased him that the Friars Minor heard confession, and the Pope answered, 'It pleaseth me very much. And I will give you a horrible example on this subject. There was a certain woman who confessed to the priest of her church. But this priest, wishing to know her carnally, began to solicit her sexually. And so in the very church itself behind the altar near the place where the Lord's body is kept, he sought to rape her. But the lady said to him, "This is neither the time nor the place for the work of Venus. Let us seek a more convenient time when we can do this thing together." She said this, however, merely in order to get away from him. Yet anticipating such future pleasure, the priest desisted from his actions and simply talked with her in a friendly fashion. As she was leaving, however, he said to her, "Remember our bargain, keep in mind our tryst." And she answered, "Oh, I will remember well." When she arrived home, however, she made a pie which appeared beautiful on the outside but which was filled with human excrement, and sent it to the priest as a gift, along with a vase full of fine, white wine. And this was the woman's only fault: she should have sent her own urine to the priest in the vase, just as she sent her own excrement in the pie. When the priest saw this fine pastry, he thought it would make a fine gift for his bishop, and so he sent it to him. Thus when the bishop was dining with his household, he ordered his servant to cut the pie and place it on the table before his guests. When the servant cut the pie in the other room, however, he discovered the excrement

58. Saint Bonaventure (1221–74), often called the second founder of the Franciscan Order, healed many rifts that had arisen among the friars, particularly over the issue of absolute poverty. He was not entirely successful, since a small radical segment persisted in maintaining complete apostolic poverty for decades after his death. Combining great personal piety with profound learning, Bonaventure was proclaimed a saint by Sixtus IV in 1482. *New Catholic Encyclopedia*, 2:479–93.

and was horrified. Then he set the pie aside to show the bishop later, and to the bishop's insistence that the pie be brought to the table, he said, "You have enough for now. Another time, the Lord willing, you will have better." What more can one say? When the bishop saw such a pie, he was "exceedingly angry" [Esther 5:9] against the priest. He had the offender brought before him and said, "Tell me, priest, where did you learn to send such fine pies to your bishop? In what have I offended you? How have I earned such an insult from you? Why have you sent me a pie filled with human excrement?" When the priest heard this, he was stupefied and he said to the bishop, "Father, truly I did not make that pie myself. Such and such a lady sent it to me, and, thinking that such a fine gift was worthy only of you, I sent it to you in order to honor you, believing the whole time that it was a splendid pie." When the bishop "had heard" this "he was satisfied" [Leviticus 10:20]. But after the priest left, the bishop sent for the lady in order to find out the truth of the matter. And she "confessed, and did not deny" [John 1.20], that she was the one who had made the pie, but that she did it to get back at the priest who had attempted to seduce her during confession right in the church behind the altar. Then the bishop praised the lady highly for her deed, and punished the priest grievously.' And it was that very bishop who had received the gift who told the story to Pope Alexander IV, and Pope Alexander told it to Brother Bonaventure, the Minister General of the Friars Minor. Then the Pope added, 'Therefore, with a clear conscience and full permission, I believe absolutely that the Friars Minor ought to hear confession from the people in secular life.'"

[415] *The best response of the Friars Minor and the Preachers to the regular clergy who complain of them.*

"But 'those whose coarse hearts have been hardened by ambition do not believe these things.' For they always believe that whatever is said is said for others, not for themselves. Ecclesiastes speaks of such men, 8[:14]: 'There are wicked men, who are as secure, as though they had the deeds of the just: but this also I judge most vain.' Such are the priests and clerks of our time, who do not want the Friars Minor and the Preachers to live. And this is the height of cruelty, especially since the Brothers are more useful to the Church of God than they themselves, who possess Church goods but do not perform the duties for which they received them. Rather, they go against what the Lord said, Leviticus 25[:36]: 'Fear thy God, that thy brother may live with thee.' For they do not wish to allow us to live on alms, which we beg with great labor and embarrassment, and yet there are many men in these two Orders who, if they were not in the Order, would likely hold the prebends which these men now have."

[474] In that year [1259] I was living in Borgo San Donnino, and I wrote a *Book of Pests* in the manner of Patecchio. And in that same year the mortality rate among men and women was very high, so much so that in the office of Vespers we had two dead at the same time in the church. And this malady arose during Passion week, so that in the whole province of Bologna the Friars Minor could not say the office of Palm Sunday because they were all sick from the cold. And this disease lasted for many months. During this time Lord Rubino de Soragna, uncle of Uberto Pellavicino and brother of Marchesopolo, died, and I heard his confession. Also, from that disease more than three hundred died in Borgo San Donnino, and in Milan many thousands, and likewise in Florence many thousands. And the bells were not rung lest the sick become terrified.

The spiritual movement of the flagellants in the year 1260, and this movement was worldwide, but especially in Italy.

In the year of the Lord 1260, Indiction III, the flagellants arose throughout the whole world, and all men, both small and great, noble and common, went in procession, naked, whipping themselves though the cities, led by the bishops and men in religious Orders. And peace was made, and men restored their ill-gotten gains. And so many went to confess their sins that the priests scarcely had time to eat. And from the mouth of the flagellants sounded forth voices "of a god, and not of a man" [Acts 12:22], and their "voice" was "like the voice of a multitude" [Daniel 10:6]. And men walked in salvation. And they wrote songs of divine praise in honor of God and the Blessed Virgin, which they sang as they travelled about whipping themselves. . . .

[604] And take note that these four men we spoke of above were strong hunters before the Lord, that is, oppressors of men. For Pope Martin was obstinate in seeking to conquer Romagna, and he got what he wanted. But as a result many men fell "with the edge of the sword" [IV Kings 10:25] and much gold was spent. King Charles led an army against Prince Manfred and Conradin and conquered them. And King Peter of Aragon fought against Charles in Sicily, occupied his kingdom, and invaded Apulia. But the kings of France avenged Charles, his uncle, by leading a large French army into Spain against Peter. And yet in one and the same year they have all gone the way of all flesh.

5

The Villani Chronicles

Paula Clarke

The most important chronicle produced in fourteenth-century Italy is probably that written by three members of the Villani family of Florence whose lives spanned over a century. The initial *New Chronicle* of Giovanni Villani (ca. 1280–1348) was so esteemed that, after his death, his brother Matteo determined to continue it; after Matteo's death, in 1363, his son Filippo completed the section on which his father had been working. The resulting two chronicles are, together, a monumental work reaching from the mythical origins of Florence to 1364. They constitute the first major historical work produced in medieval Florence and represent the beginning of serious vernacular history in the city; indeed, they are an important contribution to the development of this genre in Italy as a whole. As the title *New Chronicle* suggests, Giovanni Villani was aware of the novelty of his work, which he intended as a quasi-definitive history of Florence, superior to any of the "few and disordered" chronicles produced before his time (I, 1, for which, see Appendix A).[1] As a historical source, the information contained in the Villani chronicles is subject to the limitations imposed by the material they drew on as well as by their own objectives and presuppositions. Nevertheless, the works remain extremely valuable for the light they shed on medieval European history, especially that of Florence and Italy in the late thirteenth and fourteenth centuries, when the Villani could rely for their accounts on personal knowledge or eyewitness reports. Besides this historical value, the

---

1. All citations refer to book and chapter in the critical editions by Giuseppe Porta: Giovanni Villani, *Nuova cronica*, 3 vols. (Parma: Fondazione Pietro Bembo, 1990–91); Matteo Villani, *Cronica con la continuazione di Filippo Villani*, 2 vols. (Parma: Fondazione Pietro Bembo, 1995). The Porta edition of Giovanni's chronicle contains a book not included in previous editions, and therefore the references do not correspond.

chronicles also offer unusual insights into the attitudes, beliefs, and culture of mercantile circles in fourteenth-century Florence. For all these reasons, they continue to be regarded as among the greatest contributions to medieval Italian historiography.

There are, of course, reasons why such a significant work should have been started in Florence at the beginning of the fourteenth century. By then, Florence had emerged as the major power in Tuscany and one of the leading economic centers of Europe. Its wealth and success aroused immense pride among its citizens, some of whom were consequently inspired to record its deeds and pass on the memory of its success more effectively than had previously been done. Moreover, the cultural situation in Florence by the late thirteenth century served to stimulate the undertaking of major literary endeavors. Higher levels of education and expanding intellectual interests allowed Florence, even without a university, to emerge as a major literary center, with poets of the level of Guido Cavalcanti and Dante Alighieri. At the same time, within learned circles, serious attention was being paid to issues of practical philosophy, such as ethics and politics. Influencing these concerns was the diffusion of knowledge of ancient philosophy, especially Aristotle, and an increasing interest in classical culture and in what it could offer contemporaries in everything from literary forms to philosophical ideas. All this resulted in the emergence in Florence, as elsewhere, of what has been termed a prehumanist movement, in that intellectuals demonstrated an increased admiration for the classics and a desire to imitate classical forms, concepts, and ideals in their own work. The most important Florentine prehumanists were undoubtedly Brunetto Latini, whose *Livres dou trésor* revealed to his fellow citizens the principles of Aristotelian ethics as well as Ciceronian concepts of rhetoric and the orator, and Dante Alighieri, who steeped himself in Aristotelian thought as well as in the poetry of Virgil and who was inspired by Latini to impart his knowledge and insights to his contemporaries through such works as the *Banquet* and the *Divine Comedy*.

Giovanni Villani was influenced by both Latini and Dante. Of the early Florentine chancellor Latini he left the following admiring and frequently cited description: "the beginner and master in refining the Florentines and in making them expert in speaking well and in knowing how to guide and rule our republic according to political [science]" (ix, 10). Of Dante, Villani wrote what was effectively the first biography, in which he showed a considerable knowledge and appreciation of the poet's intellectual and literary achievements, if not of his political position (x, 136). As Villani saw it,

Dante's commitment to the White faction and his consequent exile, in 1302, had led him to inveigh unfairly against his native city. In contrast, Giovanni attempted to dissociate himself from the White faction, which his father had supported, and, while horrified by Charles of Valois's perjury and the destruction carried out by the victorious Blacks (ix, 39, for which, see Appendix A), identified the latter as the true Guelfs, to whose cause he remained permanently committed.

Despite this difference in political views, Villani clearly read Dante's works with great interest, especially the *Divine Comedy,* which was coming out while he was writing the *New Chronicle* and which he quotes in the last portion of his work. The influence Dante exerted on Villani remains a subject of debate, but it is, possibly, evident in Villani's stress on Virgil as a historical source, in his vision of Florence as gradually corrupted by its wealth, and in his emphasis on the year 1300, which Villani presents as the year in which he conceived his work and which Dante saw as the turning point of his own life.[2] Connected with the year 1300 is the rather controversial question of the influence Dante may have had on Villani's conception of his historical enterprise. In the so-called second prologue (ix, 36, for which, see Appendix A), Giovanni attributes his inspiration to write a chronicle to the impression made on him while in Rome during the Jubilee of 1300. He was struck by the contrast between the decline of the ancient city and the rise of his own Florence, a Roman foundation and therefore, to Villani's contemporaries, heir to the glorious tradition of antiquity. This, together with his reading of classical and late classical historians, aroused in Villani, or so he claims, the idea of recording the deeds of his own city and perpetuating its fame, just as ancient historians had that of Rome.

Under Dante's influence, Giovanni probably used this "second prologue" as a clearer enunciation of what was for him a long-term commitment to essentially prehumanist ideals. From the start of his chronicle, Giovanni demonstrates the influence of ancient historians, together with an admiration

2. A considerable literature treats the subject of Dante's influence on Giovanni Villani, which revolves in part around the question of when the *New Chronicle* and the *Divine Comedy* became available to the public. Some historians argue that Dante's influence on Villani was such as to justify a pre-Dante and post-Dante division of Villani's work (see Giovanni Aquilecchia, "Dante and the Florentine Chroniclers," *Bulletin of the John Rylands Library* 48 [1965–66]: 30–55), while others have even suggested that Villani may have influenced Dante (e.g., Nicolai Rubinstein, "The Beginnings of Political Thought in Florence: A Study in Medieval History," *Journal of the Warburg and Courtauld Institutes* 5 [1942]: 198–227). The similarity of themes in their work is at least partly due to the influence of widespread, popular Florentine traditions mentioned below.

for the Roman political achievement and the classical tradition, which he clearly wanted to claim for his native city. Indeed, the idea developed by Giovanni that the Romans themselves deliberately founded Florence in the image of their own city was already present in the earlier chronicle tradition. Thus, while it may well have been only on reading the *Divine Comedy* that Giovanni clearly conceived his own work as a direct imitation of the great historians of antiquity, his vision of the glory of the Roman past and his desire to use it in order to comprehend and elevate his contemporary urban world suggest that, quite independently of Dante, he had been deeply influenced by prehumanist culture and that its ideals informed his work from the outset.

That said, Giovanni's claim to have imitated the style and form of classical historians must be taken in a very broad sense, particularly since he was much less capable, even than Dante, of imitating the stylistic and rhetorical techniques of classical literature. A merchant who spent his life working for two of the major merchant-banking companies of Florence,[3] Villani did not have the opportunity to acquire a higher education in Latin, although he certainly learned enough Latin to be able to read the classical authors whom he cites.[4] His decision to write in Italian may well, in fact, have been influenced by a sense of an inadequate command of Latin, as well as by his expressed aim of making his work available to his less-educated, lay contemporaries, an objective he shared with both Latini and Dante, whose major works were also written in the vernacular.

The influence of classical historians on Giovanni Villani must thus be sought less in language and literary style than in conception and organization of his work. Most fundamentally, while Giovanni encountered an interest in the origins of Florence in the local chronicles he read, his intention of beginning with his city's foundation undoubtedly derived in large part from Livy. Livy's influence probably also lies behind Giovanni's decision to divide his chronicle into books, separated largely according to subject matter, while following a chronological organization within these sections. His reading of the classics may also have inspired Giovanni's conviction that history should explain the causes behind events, rather than simply record them, and his sense that it should provide examples and lessons to its readers. Finally, classical influence most probably lies behind Giovanni's practice of

---

3. The Peruzzi and the Buonaccorsi. See Michele Luzzati, *Giovanni Villani e la compagnia dei Buonaccorsi* (Rome: Istituto dell'enciclopedia italiana, 1971).

4. There is some debate regarding how good Giovanni's Latin was and whether he may, for example, have read Livy in a translation.

pausing, when he records the death of a famous person, to provide a physical and moral description of him and an assessment of his life.

While Giovanni Villani was thus influenced in certain important ways by
classical historians, his work nonetheless developed within medieval historical traditions. Of these, the most important for the *New Chronicle* were
undoubtedly universal history and the collections of annals in which major
events were organized chronologically year by year. Many of the sources
Giovanni Villani consulted would have included one or even both of these
structures, and the influence of these medieval traditions is evident in many
aspects of the Villani's work. For example, the medieval annalist tradition,
as well as the model of Livy, probably led to the strict chronological order
imposed in the Villani chronicles and emphasized by Giovanni's decision,
once he could establish a connected chronological narrative, to insert the
relevant year on each page (v, 18). Moreover, despite Giovanni's declared
intention of recounting the history of his own city, his chronicle rapidly became a quasi-universal history, going back to biblical times and the legends
of Troy and including events worthy of note that occurred throughout the
known world.

One of the major problems facing the Villani was the need to obtain accurate information. This undoubtedly contributed to the rather exceptional
attention Giovanni paid to sources and his recognition of the need to search
out all available relevant material. Certainly, Giovanni did consult a large
number of written works, from the Bible and classical authors to saints'
lives and a wide range of chronicles, including foreign ones, such as that of
Salisbury Abbey (1, 24), which he must have consulted during his business
trips.[5] Rather unusually, Giovanni even looked to archaeological evidence
in order to confirm local traditions, such as the antiquity of Fiesole or the
Roman foundation of Florence. For periods closer to their own, the Villani
could take advantage of written reports by travelers and of merchant letters, as well as a lively oral tradition that preserved memories going back for
generations. All this material, particularly oral memory, presented problems of accuracy and assessment, which the Villani attempted to resolve by
providing alternative views, opting for what seemed most reasonable or by

5. There is still some debate regarding the chronicles Giovanni used. Particularly problematic is the relationship of the *New Chronicle* to a chronicle supposedly compiled in the
late thirteenth century by Ricordano and Giacotto Malispini, for sections of the one repeat
those of the other practically verbatim. In general, historians have dismissed the Malispini
chronicle as a later composition drawing on the *New Chronicle,* but the issue has never been
definitively resolved.

asserting that what they reported had been affirmed by respectable individuals "worthy of belief." While this approach allowed the elimination of some legendary interpolations into Florentine history, it by no means guaranteed the exclusion of fabulous stories or prejudiced accounts, particularly if these coincided with the writers' own political or religious biases.[6] Moreover, Giovanni in particular seems to have shared the popular fascination with the marvelous and the monstrous, with miracles and demons, and clearly enjoyed a good story, a tendency encouraged, perhaps, by reading or hearing recounted the popular romances of the day.[7]

Contrasting with this apparent credulity is the interest displayed by Giovanni, like certain other medieval chroniclers, in the historical accuracy to be gained from documents, some of which he even incorporated directly in his text.[8] Moreover, his mercantile experience encouraged in Giovanni a notable interest not only in economic issues such as coinage but also in statistics as a source of precision and accuracy. His opportunities for gaining statistical information regarding his native city were aided by his appointment, from 1316 to the 1330s, to various municipal magistracies, including the highest executive body, the Signoria. What he learned from public sources formed the basis for his famous statistical description of Florence in the late 1330s (XII, 94) and for his detailed account of prices and poor relief during the famine of 1346 (XIII, 73, for which, see Appendix A).[9]

The inaccuracies in the Villani chronicles could have arisen not only from inadequate or faulty sources but also from the writer's particular objectives and presuppositions. This is especially evident in the first books of the *New Chronicle*, which deal with Florence's origins and earliest history and where Giovanni drew on local legends, which he accepted in large part and possibly elaborated for patriotic and propagandist purposes. A brief consideration

---

6. Consider the highly distorted information on the founder of Islam and the spectacular vices used to blacken the reputation of the Hohenstaufen.

7. On this aspect of Giovanni as raconteur, see Giuseppe Porta, "Giovanni Villani storico e scrittore," in *I racconti di Clio: Tecniche narrative della storiografia* (Pisa: Nistri-Lischi, 1989), 147–56, and idem, "La costruzione della storia in Giovanni Villani," in *Il senso della storia nella cultura medievale italiana (1100–1350)* (Pistoia: Centro italiano di studi di storia e d'arte, 1995), 125–38.

8. On use of documents, especially letters, by medieval chroniclers, see Gherardo Ortalli, "Cronache e documentazione," in *Civiltà comunale: Libro, scrittura, documento*, Atti della Società ligure di storia patria, n.s., 29 (103), fasc. 2 (Genoa: Società ligure di storia patria, 1989), 507–39.

9. Primarily a merchant, Matteo participated less in public office, and hence, perhaps, his less frequent use of statistics. For a summary of the brothers' political careers, see Luzzati, *Giovanni Villani.*

of this section of the chronicle will help illuminate Giovanni's sense of the purposes of history and the way in which contemporary concerns influenced the creation of a collective memory of the past, which could then be turned by someone like Giovanni Villani into a quasi-official history.

For information on this early period, Giovanni drew on local Florentine popular traditions that also can be found in the work of Dante Alighieri, specifically, in those tales of Troy, Fiesole, and Rome that Dante says women recounted as they worked (*Paradiso,* xv). This legendary view of Florentine history probably developed in the twelfth century, and reflects the preoccupations of the early Florentine city-state during the first stages of its territorial expansion.[10] At that time, one of the closest towns blocking Florence's conquest of the territory around it was Fiesole, and a struggle developed between these towns, which ended only with Florence's destruction of Fiesole around 1125. This conflict, coming as it did at a critical moment of Florence's history, when the city was beginning to emerge as an independent state and to form its own consciousness as such, had a decisive influence on its historiography. The struggle against Fiesole was projected back onto the city's earliest history such that, as Villani points out, the origins of Florence came to be wrapped up with the destruction of Fiesole and Florence's growth until 1125 was interpreted in terms of a seesaw relationship with its feared and finally defeated rival.

The material for this interpretation of history seems to have come in part from Fiesole itself and to have reflected the memory of this town's Etruscan past. The legends on which Villani drew depicted Fiesole as the first city built in all of Europe, supposedly founded in the most healthful location in the whole continent. According to these legends, Fiesole would have been the origin of much of ancient civilization, including the foundation of Troy and therefore, indirectly, of Rome itself. However, once these legends were adopted by the Florentines, who were so proud of their Roman origins, the earlier foundation of Fiesole became a motive for casting the rival city as an enemy of Rome and of the civilization Rome represented. For example, in the Florentine chronicles, Fiesole is depicted as a supporter of Catiline's conspiracy against the Roman government. Therefore, it would have been destroyed in 72 c.e. by a Roman army led by Julius Caesar, which then went on to found Florence as a second Rome, modeled physically on the ancient

---

10. Of the vast literature on Villani's treatment of Florence's origins, see in particular Alberto Del Monte, "La storiografia fiorentina dei secoli xii e xiii," *Bullettino dell'Istituto storico italiano per il Medio Evo* 62 (1950): 175–282; Charles T. Davis, "Topographical and Historical Propaganda in Early Florentine Chronicles and in Villani," *Medioevo e Rinascimento* 2 (1988): 35–51; Rubinstein, "Beginnings of Political Thought."

capital and peopled by some of the best of Roman families. Subsequently, according to these Florentine legends (which anachronistically date the Gothic Wars to the period of Attila the Hun), the Gothic king Totila would have destroyed Florence in 450 C.E. and reconstructed Fiesole to ensure that Florence was never rebuilt. To these legends Giovanni Villani may have added an element of his own, drawn from French chronicles, according to which Florence would have been refounded only in 801, by Charlemagne, then in Rome for his coronation as emperor[11] (IV, 1, for which, see Appendix A). Thus, Florence's second foundation would have linked it to the reviver of the Roman imperial tradition, as its first had to the creator of the original Roman Empire, Julius Caesar. Such a connection between France and Florence would have strengthened Florentines' sense of continuity with the most admired political tradition of the Middle Ages. At the same time, it would have reflected the increasingly Guelf sentiments of the Florentines of Villani's age, by which time Florence had emerged as one of the major supporters of the papacy and had been linked to France not only through business connections but also by a common Guelf sympathy for papal, as against imperial, jurisdictional claims.

Ultimately, then, these legends served to justify Florence's destruction of a town that, in the Florentine version of events, had been transformed into a rough and barbaric enemy of Roman civilization. As a result, Giovanni Villani, like Dante and presumably leading Florentines in general, could attribute their tendency toward factionalism and internal conflict in part to the presence in the city of two different and conflicting ethnic traditions—the by now rough and barbaric Trojan one of Fiesole and the virtuous Roman one of the original Florentines. Moreover, Villani adopted the legend that the Romans of Florence had worshipped Mars and built a temple to him (identified with the baptistery, despite the fact that this was a later, Christian structure).[12] This original dedication to the god of war provided for Villani and his contemporaries a further means of understanding their city's notorious tendency toward factional strife. By accepting and developing earlier legends, Giovanni, probably unconsciously, used his history to help construct and preserve an identity for his fellow citizens that satisfied their patriotic pride while also providing interpretive keys through which to comprehend themselves and their city's role in history.

11. See the articles by Davis and Rubinstein cited in the preceding note.
12. This idea, which appears first in Villani's time, may well have been a borrowing from Livy's history of Rome, where (bk. I, chap. 1) he refers to the Romans' claim that Mars was the father of their founder and, therefore, the origin of their martial success.

The Villani also offered other interpretive keys to their readers, the most significant of which are connected with their concepts of historical causation. First, although the Villani were aware of the larger forces acting in history, such as social and economic conflict, they did not possess the modern sense of history as a product of long-term, structural developments. Rather, they interpreted events in terms of the immediate actions and motivations of the individuals involved. Thus, for example, although he was aware of the internal tensions contributing to the formation of factions, Giovanni presented the origin of the Guelf-Ghibelline conflict in Florence merely as a result of the spectacular murder of Buondelmonte Buondelmonti in what was essentially a private quarrel.

Second, the Villani were devout and orthodox Christians who absorbed and reflected the typical religious beliefs of their day. Among these was the idea that the universe, created by God, reflected a divine plan evident in human history and that God could and did frequently intervene in events to ensure that His design was carried out. Such a view was not incompatible with a belief in human agency, for religious thought emphasized that human beings contributed to their own destiny by exercising their free will. However, it does mean that the Villani, like the majority of their contemporaries, tended to see human action in terms of Christian virtue and sin. Illustrating the lessons of history therefore meant demonstrating how the providential plan of God was realized or at least, in the case of the Villani, how virtue was rewarded and sin punished. The latter, in particular, figures in these chronicles, in part, undoubtedly, because the Villani accepted the orthodox idea that, with the Fall, human beings had acquired a natural tendency to sin and to succumb easily to the wiles of the devil. Thus, major events, such as natural disasters or human errors not otherwise easily explicable, are frequently interpreted as divine justice intervening to punish sin or to warn human beings to abandon their sinful ways. As the Villani saw it, God could effect His justice through nature by, for example, sending fires, flood, or plague, or He could act through human beings, whether by taking away their common sense or deliberately guiding their destinies in order to use them as instruments. Here, Giovanni in particular, clearly influenced by the Old Testament, emphasized how God raised up tyrants in order that their oppression might cleanse their subjects' sins.

Third, the Villani possessed a strong sense of the fragility of human happiness and success, which led them repeatedly to moralize about the vanity of trusting to worldly things. Indeed, as Louis Green has pointed out, although the Villani Christianize the concept, they accept a point of view, going back to antiquity, that sees in human success the seeds of its own destruction.[13] In their view, wealth and ease, which perhaps represented the seduction of worldly pleasure, almost automatically engender sins such as envy and pride, and these in turn bring about punishment, whether through destructive factional conflict or through intervention by God. This vision ultimately requires that prosperity be followed by decline, a position that contrasts with Giovanni's initial enthusiasm regarding his city's success but that is in keeping with the more somber attitudes of his later years and with Matteo's more generally pessimistic vision of human life.

In this moral and providential conception of history, there is also a political element, in that Giovanni, at least, naturally tends to see God as supporting His Church, represented ultimately by the papacy. God shows his support, according to Giovanni, in the destruction even of valorous and successful figures like Castruccio Castracane, whose early death, prophesied by the Augustinian friend of Villani (and of Petrarch) Dionigi da Borgo San Sepolcro, becomes in large part a divine judgment for his Ghibelline opposition to the papacy. As a corollary of this view, Florence, as one of the major Guelf powers in Italy, should be specially favored by God, a position that Giovanni, influenced by his fervent patriotism, does tend to adopt. Certainly, he is very aware of the sins of his fellow citizens and repeatedly interprets Florence's setbacks, from fires to bad government, as divine retribution for these. However, it is significant that he tends to view these disasters as warnings sent by God to his favored children in order to urge them to repentance.

In addition to the providential interpretation of history, Giovanni offers another, more ambiguous key to historical causation. He was typical of his day in believing in astrology, according to which both natural phenomena and human actions were influenced by the movements of the heavenly bodies. Such beliefs were sustained by the philosophy of the day, which interpreted the universe as a hierarchy of being to which God imparted life and movement in an action passed down through the concentric spheres of stars and planets to the immobile earth at the center of the cosmos. Thus, the higher spheres exerted vital influences on the earth, and astrology, which concerns these effects, was a source of essential scientific knowledge. Giovanni Villani was clearly fascinated by this subject, which he must have studied with enthusiasm, since he is able to recount with appropriate terminology

---

13. Louis Green, *Chronicle into History: An Essay on the Interpretation of History in Florentine Fourteenth-Century Chronicles* (Cambridge: Cambridge University Press, 1972).

the effects attributed to various planetary conjunctions that were the harbingers of major disasters. However, he was also aware of the dangers of astrological determinism, by which the action of the heavenly bodies might leave no room for human free will or for God to intervene directly in the world contrary to the natural functioning of the cosmos. He was sufficiently concerned about this problem to devote the first three chapters in book XII to a discussion of the debate that occurred in Florence between astrologers and ecclesiastics regarding the origins of the disastrous flooding of the Arno in 1333. After providing a detailed and knowledgeable presentation of the astrologers' position, he nonetheless opts as usual for the side of orthodoxy, asserting that the flood had been sent by God principally as a punishment for sin, that the action of the celestial bodies was really indirectly that of God, and that, while God might choose to act through the stars, He might also intervene to effect His will contrary to the normal course of nature. This commitment to orthodoxy is undermined, however, in a later cryptic chapter (XIII, 41, for which, see Appendix A), in which Giovanni suggests an almost purely astrological interpretation of history, whereby the recurrence of a major conjunction would have been responsible for most of the significant historical shifts in Italy, going all the way back to the decline of the Roman Empire. While he continues in this chapter to make such a naturalistic vision of history subject to the consent of God, his view is in fact dangerously close to the astrological determinism he condemned.

A final point should be made about Giovanni Villani before turning to a short discussion of the views of his brother Matteo. Giovanni's comments reveal something of his social and political attitudes, which were in keeping with both his time and his social status. Though himself a commoner of mercantile training and experience, he seems to have absorbed some of those chivalric values typical of contemporary culture, not least from the romances he must have read and heard. These values are expressed in his admiration for courage and military skill, in his tendency to see these virtues as residing above all in the nobility, and in his sympathy for the aristocracy, even the often unruly nobles or magnates of his own city. Regarding the "people," or commoners, Giovanni's attitude is decidedly ambivalent. On the one hand, he sees them at times as innocent victims of noble oppression, though capable of fighting for justice and liberty and of realizing the contemporary ideal of working together for the common good. On the other hand, he repeatedly presents the people as ungrateful and presumptuous, merely worsening the political situation by seeking influence and power beyond their station. Such a view was undoubtedly reinforced by Giovanni's own experience when, after a term in public office, he was accused of corruption—an event that may have harmed his political career, even though he was acquitted.

Giovanni's rather conservative and hierarchical social attitudes go hand in hand with his political views. He shows little knowledge of or interest in political theory; his sole citation of Aristotle's *Politics* (XIII, 43), which he may have known best through the work of Saint Thomas Aquinas, suggests that he may have been more concerned with the quality of government than with its form. In fact, he does praise good government of any type, whether that of good kings or lords (as opposed to "tyrants") or that of a united republican government serving the common good, as opposed to an incompetent or self-interested ruling group. Only in his later years, as the phenomenon of the lord or tyrant spread into Tuscany and the Florentines found themselves not only fighting against these tyrants but also experiencing the oppression of the duke of Athens, did Giovanni's attitudes seem gradually to shift toward a greater appreciation of republican liberty and a fiercer condemnation of "tyranny." In this tendency, as in his growing hostility to papal policy in Italy, Giovanni undoubtedly reflects the changing attitudes of his day, anticipating the political views more clearly expressed by his younger brother Matteo.

Turning then to Matteo, it is clear that he shared many of his elder brother's views but differed from Giovanni not least because his experience extended into the rather different intellectual and political world developing in the mid–fourteenth century. In addition, Matteo was intellectually more sophisticated than his elder brother and had greater literary pretensions. These are evident in his prologues, which provide a theoretical framework for each book, and in his efforts to craft a more elevated prose style modeled to a degree on complex Latin sentences. Here, he was undoubtedly influenced by the literary world of Florence in his day, where figures like the novelist and protohumanist Giovanni Boccaccio were devoting their attention to the development of Italian prose. Matteo's stylistic interests were undoubtedly inspired at least in part by Boccaccio, some of whose works he cites and whose description of the Black Death in the *Decameron* may have served as a model for Matteo's own (1, 1–4 and 6, for which, see Appendix B).

Matteo's approach to history was necessarily conditioned by the fact that he was continuing his brother's work, which presented him with established forms and principles, some of which, however, he modified. In general, Matteo shared his elder brother's conviction that the historian's goal was to instruct, particularly in a moral and Christian sense, by demonstrating the negative effects of sin and the positive ones of virtue in an illustration of a divine, providential plan. However, as Louis Green has pointed out,[14] Matteo was deeply affected by his experience of the Black Death, which he regarded as the greatest disaster ever to be visited on the human race and therefore proof that human sins had reached a climax in his own time (1, 1, for which, see Appendix B). The fact that human beings, despite this dire warning from God, failed to repent their sins but rather became even more dissolute and wicked led Matteo to a profoundly negative judgment of the human race. His consequent sense of human degeneration led his chronicle to become a pitiless exposé of human weakness, revealing the self-interest, greed, violence, duplicity, and corruption of those involved in events.

Matteo's despair that God's punishments or warnings would ever bring about any improvement in the human race undoubtedly lies behind a relative decline in emphasis, by comparison with Giovanni, on the action of divine justice in the world. Indeed, as Green has indicated, the events surrounding the Black Death seem to have reduced Matteo's confidence that God was really imposing any kind of providential design on human history. He therefore tended to emphasize the inscrutability as well as the absolute nature of the divine will and man's inability to cooperate with it, a tendency that some historians have seen as typical of the postplague era.[15] Further, Matteo lacked his brother's conviction in the explicative and predictive power of astrology.[16] In the case of the Black Death (1, 2, for which, see Appendix B) he rejected the astrological explanation completely, on the rational grounds that similar conjunctions had never before produced anything resembling it.

These tendencies to discount celestial influences and to reduce the action of God in the world provide Matteo's vision of history with a larger sphere for human action and decision in determining events. Moreover, in the absence of a universal order clearly imposed by divine providence or by nature, chance or fortune finds a larger role in his interpretation of history. Indeed, at times, Matteo presents events principally in terms of the human being pitting his own strength or virtue against the changing whims of fortune. A notable example is the admiring description of Nicola Acciaiuoli, whom Matteo presents as rising from almost nothing to become one of the

---

14. Ibid.

15. The clearest statement of these views is by Millard Meiss, *Painting in Florence and Siena After the Black Death* (New York: Harper, 1964). Porta, in his commentary on Matteo's chronicle, makes this same point.

16. For example, in book 11, chapter 44, he lists all the possible effects a comet might have had, only to leave the interpretation of these to astrologers, while he returns to "our coarser matters."

dominant and wealthiest figures in the kingdom of Naples, chiefly through his own high-mindedness and virtue (III, 9). Similarly, in order to demonstrate what human will can achieve, not least against a tyrant, Matteo devotes disproportionate attention to the determined and successful defense put up by the Florentine garrison in Scarperia against the vastly superior forces of the ruler of Milan (II, 23, 29–33).

If Matteo's vision of human history thus differed somewhat from his brother's, his social views were very much the same, since he shared Giovanni's scorn for the lower classes and for the new men recently arrived in the city. The demands of artisans and workers for a higher standard of living and their rise to an economic position that could challenge that of the older families constituted one of the developments that most convinced Matteo the plague had brought about a revolution in the world. Even more than Giovanni, he felt that the entry of such people into government had a deleterious effect, particularly by making the ruling group more corrupt and self-interested. However, his principal concern regarding municipal politics was the threat from the aristocrats of the Guelf party, who used their powerful position to remove their enemies from government, so that Matteo, who suffered such removal himself, could characterize this conduct only as unjust and tyrannical.[17]

On a more general political plane, Matteo's orientation represents a development of those later directions in Giovanni's attitudes mentioned above. Although Giovanni's criticism of the Church and papacy does not reflect loss of respect for these as institutions, Matteo's may. He does not spare churchmen in his devastating critique of human failings. The papacy in particular he treats with the harshest criticism, his attitude toward it undoubtedly affected by two major trends of his time. First was a growing divergence between Florentine and papal political policy, brought about in part by the popes' efforts, criticized by Giovanni, to seek a pacification in Italy through accords with Florence's enemies, especially the generally Ghibelline lords. Aggravating this rift was the goal, best embodied by Cardinal Albornoz, of reinforcing papal control over Church territories in Emilia-Romagna and in Perugia, which conflicted with Florentine interests in these areas. Second, the Avignon papacy's concentration on the secular ideals of greater administrative and financial control of the Church aroused considerable criticism for what was seen as growing worldliness and corruption. Matteo

17. On Matteo's being declared a Ghibelline and thereby rendered ineligible for public office, see Gene Brucker, "The Ghibelline Trial of Matteo Villani," *Medievalia et Humanistica* 13 (1960): 48–55.

was strident in his depiction of a corrupt papacy, whose policies were determined more by bribery and influence than by any sense of the needs of Italy or of Christendom. The old Guelf commitment that represented the principal axis of Giovanni's political thought therefore almost disappears from Matteo. For him, Guelf and Ghibelline have come to mean less pope and empire than republican government and tyranny, and for him the issue dominating Florentine politics is the defense of liberty against tyranny. Here, once again, Matteo represents the new directions in Florentine thought, for this vision of his city as the bulwark of freedom against tyranny was to become the central motif of the civic humanism emerging in the city by the start of the fifteenth century.

The shift in generations from Matteo Villani to his son Filippo marked a period of profound change in Florentine culture that brought to an end the chronicle tradition of the family. Filippo, representative of the early humanist circles in Florence, chose to invest his energies in the study of Dante and in writing a learned Latin study of the origins of his city, together with biographies of its famous men. The humanist trend to exalt the Latin language, as well as the higher standards of humanist scholarship, meant that Filippo regarded the vernacular and popular work of his father and uncle as inferior to his own intellectual aspirations. In his introduction to his portion of the chronicle, he built on his father's initial prologue to present Matteo's work as a mere preparation of material that "higher and more delicate minds" could turn into a "happier and more elevated style" (XI, between 60 and 61). With such an attitude, it is understandable that Filippo did not continue the chronicle beyond the end of book XI but instead turned to his own, rather different intellectual interests. Thus, while the new humanist culture would go on to produce its own historiography, the Villani chronicles remained as enduring monuments to the culture of a preceding age.

APPENDIX A: GIOVANNI VILLANI, *THE NEW CHRONICLE*

Book I, Chapter 1 (1:3–4):[18]

This book is called the *New Chronicle*, which deals with various past events, especially the origin of the city of Florence, then all the changes the city has

---

18. Giovanni Villani writes in long sentences and with liberal use of the conjunction "and," both within sentences and to connect one sentence to another. While an effort has been made to reflect this style, on occasion sentences have been divided and some of the

experienced and will experience over time, begun in the year of the Incarnation of Jesus Christ 1300.

Here begins the prologue and the first book.

Although few and disordered records of the past events of our city of Florence were left by our earlier Florentines, whether because of their negligence or because, when Totila, the Scourge of God, destroyed the city, the records were lost, I, Giovanni, Florentine citizen, considering the nobility and greatness of our city at our present time, thought it appropriate to recount and leave a memory of the origin and beginning of such a famous city, of its happy and unhappy mutations and of its past deeds, not because I feel up to such a task, but in order to give an inspiration to our successors not to be negligent in recording the notable events that will occur in the times after us, and to give an example of past changes and events, and the reasons and why, to those who will be [in the future], so that they act following virtue and avoiding vice, sustaining adversities with a strong mind for the good and well-being of our republic. Therefore I will faithfully narrate in this book in a clear vernacular, so that laymen as well as the educated can draw benefit and enjoyment from it. And if it should be defective in any part, I leave the corrections to those who are wiser. And first we will say whence was the beginning of our city, continuing over time while God concedes us his grace. And not without great effort will I toil to find and draw on the oldest and most diverse books, chronicles, and authors in order to compile the deeds and actions of the Florentines here, starting with the origin of the ancient city of Fiesole, whose destruction was the reason and beginning of our city of Florence. . . .

Book IV, Chapter 1 (1:143–45):

Here begins the fourth book: how the city of Florence was rebuilt through the power of Charlemagne and the Romans, going back a little.

It happened, as it pleased God, that during the time of the good Charlemagne, emperor of Rome and king of France, of whom we earlier gave a long account, after he had overcome the tyrannical pride of the Lombards

---

"and"s eliminated. Translations are based on the critical editions by Giuseppe Porta; see note 1 above. The location of each chapter in the modern editions is indicated parenthetically by volume and pages.

and the Saracens and the infidel of the Holy Church and restored Rome and the empire to liberty and a prosperous state, as was mentioned earlier, certain nobles and gentlemen of the Florentine countryside, of whom it is said the leaders were the Figiovanni and Figuineldi and Firidolfi, descendants of the ancient noble citizens of the first Florence, met together with the inhabitants of the place where Florence had been and with other followers of theirs in the Florentine countryside, and agreed to send ambassadors drawn from the best among them to Rome, to Emperor Charles [i.e., Charlemagne] and to Pope Leo and to the Romans—and this was done—begging them to remember their daughter, the city of Florence, who had been ruined and destroyed by the Goths and Vandals to spite the Romans, so that it be rebuilt, and to supply a force of men-at-arms against the Fiesolans and their followers, enemies of Rome, who would not allow the city of Florence to be reconstructed. These ambassadors were honorably received by Emperor Charles and by the pope and by the Romans, and their petition was kindly and willingly accepted; and immediately Emperor Charlemagne sent his troops of knights and foot soldiers in large numbers. . . . The Romans made a decree and ordered that, as their ancestors had before created and populated the city of Florence, so [the city] should be rebuilt and populated with the best houses, both noble and popular, of Rome, and so it was done. . . . The Fiesolans and their followers, seeing the army of the emperor and the Romans so large and powerful, dared not fight them but, remaining in the fortress of their city of Fiesole and in their castles round about, disturbed the rebuilding as much as they could. . . . And it is said that the ancients believed it was not possible to rebuild [the city], unless first the marble image consecrated by the first, pagan builders, by necromancy, to Mars, which had been in the river Arno since the destruction of Florence, was found and drawn from the Arno; and, found again, it was placed on a pillar on the bank of that river, where today is the beginning of the Ponte Vecchio. We do not affirm this, nor do we believe it, since it seems to us an opinion of pagans and of augurs, and not rational but of great simplicity, that such a stone could work such a thing; but commonly, among the older people, it was said that if it was moved, great change would come to the city. . . .

Book VII, Chapter 39 (1:326–29):

How in Florence the first popular government was created to end the violence and injuries inflicted by the Ghibellines.

Once the army returned to Florence [from a defeat at Figline], there was a great grumbling among the citizens, for the Ghibellines who ruled the town oppressed the people with insupportable taxes and imposts, from which they saw few benefits, since the Guelfs were spread throughout the countryside and held many castles and made war on the city; and, besides that, the Uberti and all the other noble Ghibellines tyrannized the people with heavy extortions and violence and injuries. On account of this the good men of Florence gathered together for action at the church of San Firenze, but then, because of the force of the Uberti, they were afraid to stay there; they went instead to the church of the Minorite friars at Santa Croce, and stayed there, armed, afraid to return to their homes for fear that, once they abandoned their arms, the Uberti and the other nobles would defeat them and they would be punished by the government. So they went armed to the houses of the Anchioni at San Lorenzo, which were very strong, and there [trusting to their] armed force they created thirty-six heads of the people, and they dismissed the Signoria and podestà and all the officials then in Florence. That done, without opposition they created a *popolo* [i.e., a government made up of artisans and modest merchants], with certain new regulations and statutes, and elected as captain of the people Messer Uberto da Lucca; and he was the first captain of Florence, and they created twelve elders of the people, two from each sixth[19] [of the city], who guided the people and advised the captain. These met in the houses of the Badia over the gate, which leads to Santa Margherita, and they returned to their houses to eat and sleep. And this was done on 20 October in the year of Christ 1250, and, on the same day, the captain gave twenty banners to certain heads of the people, who were divided into armed companies according to neighborhoods, with several parishes together, so that, when it was necessary, each would gather armed around the banner of his company, and then they would go with the banners to the captain of the people. And they had a bell made that the captain kept in the Tower of the Lion, and the principal banner of the people, which the captain kept, was divided into two halves, white and vermilion. . . . And, as the people had organized the symbols and banners in the city, so they did in the countryside, giving one to each baptismal church, which were ninety-six, and they organized them into leagues so that one should help the other and they should come to the city armed when it was necessary. . . . And to strengthen the popular government, they

19. Florence was divided into six districts, or *sestieri* (sixths).

decided and began to build the palace behind the Badia, on the square of Sant'Apolinare, the one with the dressed stone and the tower,[20] since before there had been no Palace of the Commune in Florence; rather, the Signoria met now in one part of the city and now in another. . . .

Book IX, Chapter 36 (2:57–59):

How pope Boniface VIII gave an indulgence to all Christians who went to Rome in the Jubilee Year of 1300.

Whereas previously, according to many, every hundred years after the birth of Christ the pope of the time proclaimed a broad indulgence, in the year of Christ's nativity 1300 Pope Boniface VIII, who was then [on] the apostolic [throne], in reverence of the birth of Christ issued a high and solemn indulgence in the following form: any Roman who visited the churches of the blessed apostles Saint Peter and Saint Paul continuously for thirty days, and any non-Roman for fifteen days, would receive full and complete pardon of all his sins, of both guilt and penance, if he confessed. . . . And finding myself in that blessed pilgrimage in the holy city of Rome, seeing its great and ancient remains, and reading the histories and the great deeds of the Romans written by Virgil and by Sallust and Lucan and Paulus Orosius and Valerius [Maximus] and Titus Livy and other masters of history, who wrote of the lesser and of the greater deeds and affairs of the Romans and even of others of the whole world, I took my style and form from them to give a memory and example to those to come, although as a petty disciple I was not worthy to undertake such a work. But considering that our city of Florence, daughter and creature of Rome, was on the rise and would pursue great things, while Rome was in decline, it seemed to me appropriate to bring together in this volume and new chronicle all the deeds and the beginnings of the city of Florence, as far as it has been possible for me to collect and find them, and to continue in the future with the affairs of the Florentines at length and the other notable events of the universe in brief, as long as it pleases God, in hope of whose grace I began this enterprise, more than [trusting in] my limited knowledge. And thus, in the year 1300, after returning from Rome, I began to compile this book, to the reverence of God and of the blessed John [the Baptist] and in commendation of our city of Florence.

20. The present-day Bargello.

Book IX, Chapter 39 (2:62–66):

How the city of Florence was divided and ruined by the White and Black parties.

In this time [1300], when our city of Florence was in the greatest and happiest state it had ever enjoyed since its reconstruction, or even before, whether regarding size and power or number of people, since there were over thirty thousand citizens in the town and over seventy thousand people in the territory able to bear arms, or regarding the nobility of its good cavalry and bold people, or its great wealth, since it dominated almost all of Tuscany, the sin of ingratitude, with the aid of the Enemy of the human race, from this richness brought forth a proud corruption. . . . It happened that, through envy, divisions began among the citizens, and the principal and greatest began in the administrative district of scandal, in the Porta San Piero, between the family of the Cerchi and that of the Donati, the one moved by envy and the other by savage ingratitude. The head of the Cerchi was Messer Vieri de' Cerchi, and he and those of his house were men of great affairs and powerful with influential relatives, very wealthy merchants, for their [commercial] company was among the major ones of the world; the men were soft and innocent, uncouth and ungrateful, like people who had risen quickly to high status and power. Of the Donati house the head was Messer Corso Donati, and he and those of his house were gentlemen and warriors, not of overwhelming wealth, but their nickname was Disrepute.[21] They [the Cerchi and the Donati] were neighbors in Florence and in the country, and because envy encountered that bizarre savagery, there arose a proud scorn between them, and this grew, especially because of the wicked seed of the White and Black parties, which came from Pistoia. . . . The Cerchi were in Florence the heads of the White faction and, with them, held [there follows a long list of the principal, mainly noble clans who constituted the White faction]. And with them sided many houses and lineages of commoners and lesser guildsmen, and all the Ghibellines, whether magnates or commoners; and because of the large following the Cerchi had, the government of the city was almost entirely in their power. On the Black side were [a shorter list of the clans forming the Black faction] and part of all the Guelf houses named above, since those who were not with the Whites joined the opposite side. Thus, all of Florence and the countryside was divided and contaminated by these two factions. . . . For this reason, the Guelf party,

21. "Malefami." This could also be interpreted as "desiring evil."

fearing that this division might favor the Ghibellines, sent to the Curia of Pope Boniface for some remedy to be found. On account of this the pope sent for Messer Vieri de' Cerchi and, when he was before him, urged him to make peace with Messer Corso Donati and with his faction, entrusting their differences to himself and promising to place him and his supporters in great and good state and to grant him whatever spiritual graces he might ask. Messer Vieri, although he was in other respects a wise knight, in this was not wise but too harsh and capricious, for he would not listen to the pope's request, saying that he had war with no one; at this he returned to Florence, and the pope remained very angry with him and with his faction. A little after this, it happened that both sides were going through the city armed and attentive, and with some of the young Cerchi there were Baldinaccio degli Adimari and Baschiera dei Tosinghi and Naldo de' Gherardini and Giovanni Giacotti Malispini with over thirty of their followers on horseback; and with the young Donati were the Pazzi and the Spini and others of their band. The evening of May Day, 1300, watching a dance by women in the square of Santa Trinita, one side began to get angry with the other and push against them with their horses, whence arose a great brawl and melee in which there were several injuries, and through bad luck the nose of Ricoverino di messer Ricovero de' Cerchi was cut from his face; and because of this scuffle that evening all the city was under arms through fear. This was the beginning of the scandal and division of our city of Florence and of the Guelf party, whence followed many evils and dangers, as we will mention over time. . . . And note that the year before these events the houses of the commune that begin at the foot of the Ponte Vecchio on the Arno toward the castle of Altrafonte were built, and, to do this, the column at the foot of the bridge was made, and therefore the statue of Mars had to be moved; and whereas before it had faced east, it was now turned toward the north, whence, because of the augury of the ancients, it was said: "Please God that our city does not suffer some great change."

Book XIII, Chapter 41 (3:392–96):

On the conjunction of Saturn and Jove and Mars in the sign of Aquarius.

In the year 1345, on 28 March, a little after the ninth hour, according to the calculations of Mastro Pagolo di Ser Piero, a great master of this science, there was a conjunction of Saturn and Jove at twenty degrees in the sign of Aquarius with the disposition of the other planets as described below. However, according to the almanac of Profazio the Jew and the Tables of Toledo, this conjunction was supposed to be on the twentieth of this month of March. . . . But following his own calculation, Maestro Pagolo, who is one of the modern masters, said that, with his instruments, he clearly saw the conjunction on 28 March. . . . This conjunction, with this disposition of the other planets and signs, according to the words and writings of the books of the ancient great masters of astronomy, signifies, with God's consent, great happenings in the world, and battles, murders, and great changes in kingdoms and peoples, and deaths of kings and changes in rule and in factions, and the appearance of a new prophet of heresy, and a coming of new lords and new peoples, and famine and consequent illness in those kingdoms, lands, and cities under the influence of these signs and planets. . . .

Now, whoever reads this chapter may well ask what use is this astronomy for the present treatise? We reply that whoever is attentive and knowledgeable and wants to investigate the changes that have occurred in the past in this country and elsewhere, by reading this chronicle, can comprehend a great deal and, by comparison with the past, can prognosticate the future, with God's consent. . . . And in the past 960 or 953 years there have been forty-eight conjunctions, and if one goes back to the first of these, which was the most massive of them all, one will find it followed by the decline in the power of the Roman Empire, the arrival of the Goths and the Vandals in Italy, and many tribulations for the Holy Church. This is enough of these matters, and we will talk of other things.

Book XIII, Chapter 73 (3:466–72):

Of a great famine that occurred in Florence and the area around and in various parts.

In the year 1346, but originating back in October and November 1345 at sowing time, there was excessive rain so that the seed rotted, and then, in April, May, and June of 1346 it never stopped raining, sometimes with storms, so that the seed of that grain was similarly lost and what had been planted was ruined. That occurred in many areas of Tuscany and Italy, in Provence and Burgundy, and in France (so that in these countries there was great dearth and high prices), and in Genoa and at Avignon in Provence, where the pope was with the Roman Curia. This happened, according to the astrologers and masters of natural ⌜philosophy⌝, because of the earlier conjunction of Saturn, Jove, and Mars in the sign of Aquarius, which we mentioned above. From this it happened that, for over a hundred years, there had not been in this country such a bad harvest of wheat and grain, wine, oil, and everything as there was this year. . . . The people would have died of hunger if the commune had not made a generous and good provision, as we shall describe below. . . .

The commune provided for this by buying and making commitments through cash deposits with certain Genoese, Florentine, and other merchants for 40,000 *mòggia* of wheat from overseas, from Sicily, Sardinia, Tunisia, Barbary, and Calabria, and for 4,000 *mòggia* of barley, but only 22,000 *mòggia* of grain and 1,700 *mòggia* of barley could be brought from Pisa, which cost in Florence 11 gold florins per *moggio* of wheat and 7 florins per *moggio* of barley. The reason we did not receive all the grain our commune had bought was that the Pisans also had great need of it, as did the Genoese, so that by force they seized the grain we had bought once it arrived in Porto Pisano, supplying themselves before us. This created a serious shortage for us, and often great straits and fear, but there was nothing we could do about it. . . . It was discovered that some of the treasurers of the officials[22] [responsible for the grain] defrauded the commune by falsifying the measure and weight of the bread and by mixing the wheat with darnel and other grains, so that they netted a large profit, but they were arrested and forced to restore 10,000 gold florins to the commune. Note that all this is a great infamy for these wicked citizens and for those who called them to the offices, if they were guilty, as it was said, and they confessed under torture.

At the beginning the communal officials put on the market every day from 60 to 80 *mòggia* of wheat at 40 shillings per *staio,* though later the price rose to 50 shillings for wheat and 40 shillings for barley per *staio,* but this was not enough for all the country people who had come to the city, not counting the other needy citizens. The communal officials had ten ovens, [surrounded] by scaffolding and closed by doors,[23] built for the commune in the houses of the Tedaldini in Porta San Piero, which is a large complex, and there men and women, day and night, baked bread of flour made from the commune's wheat, without sifting it or taking out the husks, so that it was very gross and cruel to see and eat. Each [loaf] weighed six ounces, so that nine dozen could be baked from each *staio,* and they used daily from 85 to 100 *mòggia.* Then it was distributed in the morning at the sound of

22. The rest of this paragraph may well be a later insertion and probably refers to the officials mentioned in the next paragraph.

23. Villani is implying that these structures were intended to guard the ovens from potential assault.

the large bell of the priors at various churches and warehouses throughout
the city, and outside the main gates for the country people near the city in the
parish of San Giovanni and of other parishes who came to the gates for
it, and they were given two loaves per head at four pence each. The numbers were so great—and they wanted more than two loaves per head—that,
because of the crush, the officials could not supervise [the distribution prop-
erly]. Therefore they ordered that the bread should be given to families on
the basis of written tickets, two loaves per head. In the middle of April 1347,
there were at least ninety-four thousand mouths to which [bread] was distributed daily, and we know this to be true from the chief official of the
piazza, who received the tickets. . . . Despite the shortage and the great need
of the commune and its citizens, no poor person was expelled, even if he
was a foreigner or from the country, but [all] were fed with adequate alms,
considering the extreme dearth and hunger. The richer, good and merciful
citizens gave good and generous alms, wherefore we should hope in God
that He will not consider the inordinate sins of the citizens—for, as we said
earlier, of these our city is well supplied—but that He will compensate for
these with the alms of the good and dear citizens, if He pleases to exercise
His mercy as He did with those of Nineveh, "since alms wipe out sin," *dixit
Domino. . . .*

APPENDIX B: MATTEO VILLANI, *THE CHRONICLE*

Book I (1:3–5):

Here begins the chronicle of Matteo Villani, and first the prologue and the
first book.

Examining in my mind your exhortation, dearest friends, to devote myself
to writing the history and the novelties that will occur in our times, I felt
that my limited ability was too inadequate to pursue such a great task. However, your request makes me ready to obey through a sense of obligation,
and your support adds vigor to my lone mind. Also, [I have] considered
that, because of the stain of sin, the whole human race is subject to temporal
calamities and to much misery and to innumerable ills, which come about
in the world in various ways and through diverse and strange changes over
the ages. [Examples are] the disturbances of war, the confusion of battles,
the uprisings of peoples, the change of kingdoms, the seizure [of power]
by tyrants, plagues, death and famine, floods, fires, shipwreck, and other

disasters. At these, the men of the period in which they occur, if caught in ignorance, marvel the more and understand less the divine justice [behind these events], and they have little sense of how to respond to or remedy the adversity if the memory of similar events in the past does not instruct them. Nor do they know how to act with due moderation when the happy face of prosperity smiles on them, since the uncertain outcome and the doubtful end of mortal affairs is hidden under the dark veil of ignorance. Wherefore, thinking that this work could be fruitful and bring pleasure because of the natural desires of men [to know], I was moved to begin, as best I could with my limited knowledge, in order to encourage the wise to devote some of their time to leaving to others memory of what will seem worthy [of recording] in their day; to give the less learned hope to be able, through labor and study, to achieve virtuous deeds; and to inspire those with greater genius to reduce this, our history, to brevity, with increased pleasure for the hearers. But because everything is imperfect and vain without the aid of divine grace, we call to our assistance divine charity, blessed Christ, who, in unity with the Father and with the Holy Spirit, lives and rules throughout the centuries and gives beginning, middle, and end to every good undertaking.

Book 1, Chapter 1:

On the incredible epidemic.

In the Holy Scripture it is written that when sin had corrupted every aspect of human flesh, God sent the flood over the earth and, saving, through his mercy, eight souls of the human race—Noah, his three sons, and their wives in the ark—submerged the rest of mankind in the Flood. Afterward, over time, as people multiplied, there were some particular floods, epidemics, corruptions and pestilences, famines, and many other evils, which God permitted to afflict men for their sins. Among these epidemics we find the most serious [included] one in the time of the emperors Marcus Aurelius Antoninus and Lucius Aurelius Commodus in the year of Christ 171, which began in Babilonia in Egypt and affected many provinces of the world. And when Lucius Commodus returned with the Roman legions from Asia, it seemed to be attacking by infection the men of the provinces through which they passed, and in Rome it brought widespread death among the inhabitants. And another occurred at the time of Gallus Ostilius Augustus and his son Velosius, who seized the empire and were serious persecutors of the Christians; it began in the year of Christ 254 and lasted, recurring from time to

time, for around fifteen years, and it consisted of diverse and incredible ill-
nesses and affected many provinces of the world. However, from what can
be found in written records, since the general Flood there has been no universal judgment of death that so involved the whole world as that which
occurred in our time. In this epidemic, considering the multitude then alive,
by comparison with those living at the time of the general Flood, many
more died in this than in that, according to the judgment of many knowledgeable people. Since, during this epidemic, the author of the chronicle
called the Chronicle of Giovanni Villani, citizen of Florence, rendered up his
soul to God, and I was closely conjoined to him by blood and by affection,
after many misfortunes, with a better knowledge from experience of the
calamities of the world than its prosperity, I proposed in my mind to begin
our changeable and calamitous history with this event, as though with a
renewal of time and of the world, and to include in each year the events that
appear worthy of memory, according to the ability of my poor intelligence,
and as best we can gain a true report of them.

Book I, Chapter 2 (1:8–12):

How long the plague lasted in each country.

Having to begin with an account of the extermination of the human race
and to describe the time and manner, the quality and quantity, of [the
plague], the mind remains stupefied as it prepares to write about the sentence divine justice delivered upon human beings, and with great mercy,
for they were worthy, with their sinful corruption, of the final judgment.
Nevertheless, thinking of the value this account could have for nations coming after us, with greater confidence of mind we begin as follows. In the year
of the saving Incarnation of Christ 1346, there was seen a conjunction of
the three superior planets in the sign of Aquarius, of which conjunction the
astrologers said that Saturn was the lord. From it, they prognosticated important and weighty changes in the world, but since the same conjunction
had occurred many other times in the past [without producing the same
results], its influence does not seem to have been the origin of this [epi-
demic], but rather divine judgment, according to the disposition of the
absolute will of God. There began, in the Orient, in the said year, toward
Cathay and upper India, and in the other surrounding provinces on those
shores of the ocean, a pestilence among men of every condition, age, and

sex, who began to spit blood and died, some immediately, some in two or three days, while others took longer to succumb. And it happened that whoever served these sick people sickened of the same disease and died similarly, [as if] the malady had fastened onto them [too]. In most the groin swelled, and in many the undersides of the fingers of their left and right hands, and in others other parts of their bodies, as almost always some unusual swelling appeared in the infected body. This pestilence gradually spread from people to people and, within a year, had affected that one-third of the world called Asia. At the end of this period, it reached the nations of the Black Sea[24] and the coasts of the Tyrrhenian Sea,[25] Syria and Turkey and toward Egypt and the banks of the Red Sea and, in the north, Russia, and Greece, Armenia, and the other adjoining provinces. At that time, Italian galleys left the Black Sea, Syria, and Romania[26] to flee the plague and to take their merchandise to Italy, but they could not prevent a large number of people from dying of this illness at sea. And, having arrived in Sicily, they had dealings with the inhabitants and left some of their sick there, so that immediately the pestilence began among the Sicilians. And when the galleys came to Pisa and then Genoa, because of their contact with the men there, the mortality began in these places, but it was not widespread. . . . And in the year of Christ 1348, it had infected all Italy except the city of Milan and areas around the Alps, which divide Italy from Germany, where it did little harm. And in the same year, it began to cross the mountains. . . . And this plague lasted in the country it infected five months continuously, or rather five lunar months, and this we know from the definite experience of many countries. It happened that, because this pestilential infection seemed to attach itself through sight or touch, once a man or woman or child was known to be sick with that swelling, many abandoned them and a vast number died who would have lived if they had been helped with what they needed. Among the pagans there began this inhuman cruelty, that mothers and fathers abandoned their children, and children their parents, one brother another, and other relatives [the same]—a cruel and amazing phenomenon, alien to human nature and detested by faithful Christians, who [nevertheless], imitating barbarous nations, adopted this cruel [behavior]. Once [the plague] had begun in our city of Florence, the wise [*discreti*]

24. Literally the "Greater Sea," as it was then called.
25. This must be an error.
26. The Greek-speaking areas that had been part of the Roman Empire.

criticized the reaction of many who took precautions by shutting themselves off in solitary places with wholesome air, supplied with every good
thing to eat, [and] where there was no danger of infected people. In various areas divine justice (against which you cannot lock the door) smote them
like the others who had not taken such precautions. Many others, who resigned themselves to death in order to serve their sick relatives and friends,
survived the illness and many did not [even] get it, although they continued this service. Therefore, everyone reconsidered and began without fear
to aid and serve one another, from which many recovered and felt more
secure caring for the others.

Book I, Chapter 3 (1:13–14):

On the same subject.

In no part of the world could any doctor, whether through natural philosophy or medicine or through the astrological art, find any explanation or real
cure for this pestilential illness. Some, for profit, visited [the sick], giving
their cures, but the death [of the sick] proved that their art was feigned
and not true, and many, through scruple, declared that the money they had
unfairly taken should be restored. In our city, [the plague] began to be
widespread at the beginning of April the year of the Lord 1348, and it lasted
until the beginning of September of the said year. And there died in the city
and territory of Florence, of both sexes and of every age, three or more out
of five, putting together the lower, middling, and upper classes, for [the
lower classes] suffered somewhat more, since [the plague] began [among
them] earlier and they had less help and more difficulties and privation.
And in general, throughout the earth, the human race diminished in a similar proportion and manner, according to the news we received from many
foreign countries and many provinces of the world. There were certainly
provinces in the Levant where many more [than this] died.

Book I, Chapter 4 (1:14–15):

On the same subject.

We heard from Genoese merchants, men worthy of faith, who had received
news from those countries, that some time before this pestilence, in the area
of upper Asia, there came forth from the earth or fell from the sky a huge

fire that extended toward the West, burning and consuming a vast territory, without any resistance. Some said that the smell of this fire generated the corrupting element of the general plague, but we cannot confirm this. Then we learned from a venerable Minorite friar of Florence, bishop of [blank] in the kingdom [of Naples], a man worthy of belief, that during the epidemic, in the area around the city of Mecca, for three days and three nights it rained bloody serpents who created a stench and corrupted the whole district, and in that storm part of the temple of Mohammed was struck down, as was some of his tomb.

Book I, Chapter 6 (1:15–17):

How people were worse than before.

The few wise men who remained alive foretold many developments that, because of the corruption of sin, did not come about as they expected, but rather, amazingly, the opposite [occurred]. It was thought that those whom the grace of God had kept alive, having seen the extermination of their neighbors and heard that the same had happened to all the nations of the world, would become better: humble, virtuous, Catholic; that they would have avoided sin and iniquity and been full of love and charity to one another. Instead, immediately, once the epidemic ended, the opposite happened, as men, finding themselves few and having abundantly inherited worldly goods, forgot past events as if they had not happened and gave themselves up to a more immoral, dishonest life than they had before. For, living in ease, they fell dissolutely into the sin of greed, [frequenting] banquets, taverns, and pleasures with delicate food and games, abandoning themselves to lust without restraint, creating for their clothes strange and unusual fashions and immoral styles, introducing new forms into all types of dress. And the lower classes, both men and women, because of the overwhelming abundance of goods, refused to work at their usual crafts and wanted the dearest and most delicate food and married as they pleased, while servants and base women wore all the expensive and beautiful dresses of the honorable women who had died. . . . And, from the news we could get, nowhere did those who had escaped the divine fury live in continence, [since they] thought the hand of God was tired. But, according to the prophet Isaiah, the fury of God is not cut short, nor is His hand weary, but He is very eager to use mercy and therefore works gradually in order to draw sinners to conversion and penitence, and He punishes temperately.

Book VIII, Chapter 1 (2:135–37):

Here begins the eighth book, and first the prologue.

It is an ancient question among the wise, on which we have nevertheless tried hard to gain greater clarity by searching out examples in authors of all ages, regarding what is more effective in the world: the force of arms in the hands of powerful commanders and lords without the virtue of eloquence, or noble eloquence expressed through the mouth of princes with much less power. We seem to find, although mine is a superficial and not fixed opinion, that eloquence has exceeded the power [of arms] and done greater things in the world. The eloquence of Nemrod, taught by his master Gioniton, gathered together all the human beings of the Orient in one camp to build the Tower of Babel; the confusion of tongues destroyed their force and their undertaking. Xerxes, intending to conquer Greece, covered the sea with ships and the plain and mountains with an uncountable host; the small force of Leonidas, with five hundred companions emboldened by that man's eloquent leadership, made such an incredible resistance to that huge army that it gave hope to the Greeks of defeating it and [reduced] the king to be happy to return home with [only] a few of his [men remaining]. Alexander of Macedon, with a small number of horsemen enflamed by the inspiration of his pleasing tongue, overcame the infinite forces and treasures of Darius. The noble Roman rulers, more through wise teaching of the military art than by arms or the force of their cavalry, tamed the universe. For example, Tulius Hostilius, king of the Romans, having taken the field to fight against the Etruscans, seeing himself in a desperate situation, abandoned and betrayed by his companions and prey to his enemies, [used] his knowledgeable and effective oratory with great force, encouraging his men with powerful arguments, and turned them into victors. What did the noble Scipio Africanus do? Did he not, with the force of his tongue, defeat the wicked advice of the senators who, through fear, wanted to burn and abandon the city of Rome, and thereby overcome and subject Africa to the Roman Empire? Magnificent Caesar, with a small company by comparison with his enemies, could often expect to become the prey of his adversaries in France, Burgundy, in Saxony and in England, but through the guidance and encouragement of his voice, many times he defeated strong and powerful enemies, whom he subjected to his domination. What can one say of him, when, with a handful of horsemen stirred by his encouragement, he tamed and subdued all the nations of the world on the field at Thessaly? But, turning to lesser things, the old philosopher Zeno, placed on a cross miserably in great torment, by using the force of his magnificent eloquence, brought down the great and unlimited power of the tyrant of Syracuse. Who, then, can move peoples, who instruct great armies, if not eloquence, resounding in the ears of its hearers? And therefore, without doubt, it seems that eloquence, directed to the good, achieves more than arms and, when drawn to evil, does more harm than anything else.

6

Chronicles and Civic Life
in Giovanni Sercambi's Lucca

Duane J. Osheim

At first glance the most remarkable thing about Giovanni Sercambi's chronicles may be the brilliant watercolor illuminations added to the first volume.[1] In the final copy of the chronicles Sercambi had his scribe leave space to add illuminations and chapter titles to each of his entries. He likely had a local artist or artists illuminate what to him seemed the most critical events in Lucca's recent history. The images range from simple line drawings of the castles with which Lucca maintained control of Versilia to elaborate evocations of the death of Pope Urban VI. Some are gruesome—the highly symbolic plague arrows and pots of corruption pouring out of the heavens over prostrate citizens or the mass executions, with rows of rebels being beheaded. Other images are stylized invocations of the Volto Santo, San Paolino, and the Virgin, those saints who protected the city of Lucca. The book was meant to be a centerpiece in Sercambi's significant personal library. In addition to his own writings, he had copies of Donatus's grammar, Cicero's rhetoric, Seneca's tragedies, and numerous books of popular piety and poetry. The chronicles were part of what must have been an unusual library in a provincial Tuscan city.[2]

1. Giovanni Sercambi, *Le croniche di Giovanni Sercambi, lucchese*, ed. Salvatore Bongi, Istituto storico italiano: Fonti per la storia d'Italia, 19–21 (Lucca: Tipografia Giusti, 1892); the illuminations are discussed and reproduced in Ottavio Banti and Maria Laura Testi Cristiani, eds., *Le illustrazioni delle Croniche nel codice lucchese*, Accademia lucchese di scienze, lettere, arti: Studi e testi, 10 (Genoa: Silvio Basile editore, 1978).

2. On Sercambi's library, see Marco Paoli, "I codici," in *Giovanni Sercambi e il suo tempo* (Lucca: Biblioteca statale and Archivio arcivescovile, 1991), 196; the inventory was printed in Salvatore Bongi, *Inventario del R. Archivio di Stato in Lucca* (Lucca: Tipografia Giusti,

In ways that are not so immediately apparent, the chronicles themselves are quite remarkable. Sercambi wrote in a vacuum, in a milieu quite unlike the Florence in which Giovanni Villani and later Leonardo Bruni wrote their works. He began his history with no clear conception of his topic, and his observations often reflect the heat of the moment. Book 1 can be divided into three or perhaps even four sections indicating the stops, changes, and reformulations of Sercambi's view of Lucca's past. Initially Sercambi planned to stop in 1400, but he quickly began a second book, which continued without interruption until his death in 1424. Taken together they show how his view of Lucca and its history changed over the nearly sixty years that he wrote.

Sercambi's chronicles begin in the 1160s and follow events chronologically to shortly before his death in 1424. He says his story tells how Lucca had its liberty, lost it, and then regained it. But analysis shows that he began writing the chronicles almost in reverse order.[3] He first described the dramatic events of the late 1360s and early 1370s, when Lucca regained its liberty. Then it seems he decided to return to the 1330s and the decades when Lucca suffered "under the Pisan yoke." And finally, he went back to narrate what he understood to be Lucca's first period of liberty, from 1164 to 1313. Having completed this background, he then resumed his contemporary narrative following the events of the 1370s and 1380s. His highly detailed narrative of the decade of the 1390s completes book 1. Sercambi initially ended his account in 1400—"on 6 April, as we are celebrating our Festival of the Liberty of Lucca." But Sercambi returned to his topic and began his second book later in that same year. The new book is a continuous narrative combining observations on the court of the Guinigi, the family that had come to dominate the city, with accounts of Italian and European events.

Much of what we know about Sercambi comes from the chronicles. As he tells us, he was born while plague was raging throughout the city in 1348. His was a modest family that had arrived in Lucca at the beginning of the fourteenth century. His father was a poor apothecary, a trade he himself would follow.[4] Sercambi's own wealth and his status came from his

1892), 4:344. Some writers have assumed that since Sercambi finished his life as a courtier for Paolo Guinigi, the illuminated chronicles must have been composed for presentation to him. This seems unlikely because the two volumes are clearly meant to be part of a single work and many of the entries in the second volume are highly critical of the Guinigi.

3. On the organization of the chronicles, see Franca Ragone, "Le 'croniche' di Giovanni Sercambi: Composizione e struttura dei prologhi," *Annali dell'Istituto italiano per gli studi storici* 9 (1985–86): 5–34.

4. On Sercambi's life, see most conveniently Christine Meek, "Il tempo di Giovanni Sercambi," in *Giovanni Sercambi e il suo tempo*, 1–30; Sergio Nelli and Maria Trapani, "Giovanni

fascination with and eventually his participation in Lucca's political life. He was just in his twenties in the tumultuous years of 1368–69, when Lucca appealed to Emperor Charles IV, who eventually freed Lucca from Pisan domination. He tells us that at a critical point in the negotiations he, along with the poet Davino Castellani, presented a petition in verse form to the emperor himself. It seems that it was in the aftermath of these heady days that he decided to compose his chronicles. And from then to his death, in 1424, Sercambi remained an observer of and a player in the political life of Lucca.

Like Giovanni Villani, Sercambi notes that he began to write because he realized how unusual his situation was. Villani, of course, wanted to celebrate his Florence, which he found every bit as glorious as ancient Rome. Sercambi's Lucca was quite a different sort of city. At the end of the fourteenth century it was a small town of perhaps ten thousand, whose best years were behind it. The town was struggling to reestablish its silk industry, which had once produced Europe's most prized cloth. Lucca was still home to numerous commercial and banking families, but Lucchese generally saw the town as small and weak. In the twelfth century, territories under Lucca's influence had stretched from the Apuan Alps north and west of Lucca to far south of the Arno. It was perhaps the leading city in Tuscany. By Sercambi's time these lands largely had been lost to Lucca's neighbors. Sercambi included in his chronicles a long list of castles, villages, and territories taken from the Lucchese by Pisa, Florence, the Estensi in Modena, the Malaspina and other lords in the Lunigiana (1:555).[5]

Sercambi approached his project apologetically, with a clear idea of his own limits. He explains his method in the preface to the second section of book 1:

> [I]t is a good thing to do some good work in order not to waste the time God has given us. And after all, not all men are adept at being spiritual or religious. If they were, then naturally enough the world would wither away.... Clerics should instruct heretics in the true meaning of the Catholic faith, showing them what they should hold to and observe.

Sercambi: Documenti e fatti della vita familiare e sociale," in ibid., 33–100; and Giorgio Tori, "Profilo di una carriera politica," in ibid., 101–34.

   5. *Le croniche* were written in two books, but have been edited in three volumes. Book 1 makes up volumes 1 and 2 of the Bongi edition, and book 2 is in volume 3. All citations refer to volume and page of this edition.

Other masters, experts in poetry and sciences, should put together books on civil law, morals, philosophy, medicine, and on all of the seven sciences. . . .

Those who have not acquired learning but are skilled and wise through practice should compose ballads of battles, songs, music, and other things that give pleasure to simple men. And sometimes they can describe, to the extent they understand them, some of the things that happened in their locality.

And concerning these books, it will not be surprising if they are not entirely correct or if they do not seem entirely grammatical. Yet as they say, "Nothing ventured, nothing gained." . . . And so I have resolved to compose this little book even though I am not educated in theology, philosophy, astrology, medicine, or any of the seven liberal arts. But as a simple man with little knowledge, I have written this book, based in part on the testimony of living and truthful persons, in part on the testimony of truthful but dead persons, and in part on some things I have seen with my own corrupt eyes. I give less credence to what I have seen than to the other truthful witnesses, living or dead.

In this book are recounted some of the many things that were said and done in various parts of Italy and in some other countries. They are primarily things that touch on the city and community of Lucca and its citizens and the residents of its surrounding countryside. These things are explained as best I can, given my little knowledge. . . . And in general I say that no one should take badly anything that they find here. I only find fault with vice. I have not favored one person more than another; but concerning each, if their acts were just, I have justified each as much as I could, given my modest understanding. And so of necessity I have recounted things as they happened. (1:118)

Sercambi concedes that he is not educated. And he admits, as any reader of the chronicles will immediately notice, that his style is rough, basic, and not always clear in meaning or structure. A learned treatise was meant to proceed clearly and logically, in a balanced way. His book proceeds very unevenly. The early parts are very brief and schematic, while the last part of the first book, covering the decade of the 1390s, is told in excruciating detail. This was the period during which Milan and Florence fought for predominance in northern and western Tuscany. Lucca was often a pawn in the dizzying cycle of skirmishes and diplomatic intrigue. It becomes clear that Sercambi is recording his immediate responses to the issues at hand without much consideration of what these events really signify. He includes a description of one of the countless border clashes between Pisans and Lucchese, telling how Lucchese youths "mooned" the Pisans. He says they ran up to the gates and banged on them with their bare asses before stealing what they could and returning to Lucca. Its meaning to the chronicler? "This is how things happen: today to me, tomorrow to you" (1:441).

Although Sercambi promises to use the most trustworthy sources and only then "my own corrupt eyes," it is clear that things were not so simple. The problem for Sercambi was that few sources were available for the early history of Lucca. He did not know the annals of Ptolemy of Lucca, the best source on the town before 1300.[6] He did use several anonymous chronicles in Italian but seems to have found little else. Nor was he familiar with any of the Florentine or Pisan historians. The lack of written sources is especially clear in the second section, dealing with the events between 1335 and 1368. Skipping over large periods of time, Sercambi discusses just a few events and even then with scant detail. He reports little other than popular recollections and, at the very end of the period, his own eyewitness account.[7]

When Sercambi does use other sources, they tend to be moral and political tracts and poems.[8] He seems to believe that they have a probative value that his own narrative lacks. He repeatedly apologizes for his lack of education—*mio pogho intellecto*. And wherever possible he uses other sources, poems, stories, even documents, to explain things that might otherwise be difficult or ambiguous.

The second section of his chronicle begins with the controversial period when Lucca fell under the control of Castruccio Castracane, a Lucchese who attempted to conquer much of Tuscany. Castruccio's reign in Lucca was the last time that Lucchese could dream seriously of dominating Tuscany. But

6. The early annals of Lucca are edited by Bernhard Schmeidler in *Die Annalen des Tholomeus von Lucca in doppelter Fassung, nebst teilen der Gesta Florentinorum und Gesta Lucanorum,* in *MGH: Scriptores rerum germanicarum,* n.s., 8 (Berlin: Weidmannsche Buchhandlung, 1955), 243–323.

7. See Schmeidler's introduction to *Die Annalen.* There is also one fragment probably written by a Pisan resident in Lucca. All of this leads to the conclusion that Sercambi did not search very diligently for sources.

8. See Furio Possenti, *La poesia nelle croniche di Giovanni Sercambi,* Accademia lucchese di scienze, lettere e arti: Studi e testi, 8 (Lucca, 1974), and Piotr Salwa, "Retorica e politica—croniche e novelle di Giovanni Sercambi, lucchese," in *Renaissance Studies in Honor of Craig Hugh Smyth,* ed. Andrew Morrogh (Florence: Giunti Barbèra, 1985), 1:465–79.

Sercambi avoids telling the story of Castruccio:[9] "And as well [as dominating Lucca] Castruccio was lord of Pisa, Pistoia, Luni, San Miniato [al Tedesco], and [everything] up to within five miles of Florence. And he was also senator of Rome, and one could write much else about the many things he did, but to avoid a long speech about him, I will not take note of them" (1:123). Rather than tell the dramatic tale of Castruccio's rise and fall, he begins with transcriptions of the three papal letters by which Pope Benedict XII freed Lucca from an interdict brought on by Castruccio and established the process by which Church and commune should be reconciled.

The three papal letters, transcribed almost completely, are unique in the entire work. Other constitutional documents are mentioned; Sercambi even notes where they can be found, but they are not transcribed. Not even Charles's privilege reestablishing Lucca's liberty receives the same treatment. Of Charles's privilege, Sercambi merely says, "I will not get involved in describing them. Those who wish to see them should look in the sacristy of the Anziani palace, where they will find them" (1:173).

The three papal letters tell the tale of Lucca's reintegration into the Christian community and make a number of points about Lucca that Sercambi seems to find important. They affirm the Lucchese argument that the interdict was the result of tyranny brought on by Castruccio, Emperor Louis of Bavaria, and the heretical antipope Pietro da Corbara. Lucchese ambassadors said, and Sercambi faithfully records, "It was never the intention of the commune, people, men, and the foresaid [ambassadors] to hold the holy Mother Church in contempt . . . [they carried out] the previous excesses involuntarily because of the tyranny and power of Louis and Castruccio" (1:120). The letters make clear that the commune and its citizens did restore all that had been seized from ecclesiastical institutions. And finally, as a sign of good faith, Benedict required, and the commune agreed to build, a chapel dedicated to Saint Benedict and annual celebration of the feast of Saint Benedict as a civic festival. Sercambi says he is beginning with this example to remind the Lucchese of "what must be done in order not to offend the Holy Church, or God" (1:66).

His interpolation of the pope's letters underlines the use he makes of outside sources. It seems that as he read sources, he rapidly integrated them into his story. Fazio degli Uberti's *Dittamondo* may be the most significant example. An exile from Florence living at the north Italian courts, Uberti

9. On Castruccio, see Louis Green, *Castruccio Castracani: A Study on the Origins and Character of a Fourteenth-Century Italian Despotism* (Oxford and New York: Clarendon Press and Oxford University Press, 1985).

composed a long moral tract in which the author, accompanied by Virtue, traveled throughout Italy and the world and recounted the great stories and legends of the past as well as short descriptions of the places he actually visited. Sercambi uses much of Uberti's description of Italy in book 1 of his chronicles; Uberti also provides the itinerary for the imagined journey that is the frame for Sercambi's *Novelliere,* a collection of tales patterned after Boccaccio's *Decameron.*[10]

Sprinkled throughout his chronicles are over seventy moral and political poems. Sercambi apparently wrote none of the poems himself. They are taken from other, mostly Tuscan writers. There are snatches from Davino Castellani of Lucca, from Dante, Nicola Soldanieri, and Frate Stoppa of Florence, as well as from numerous other minor or anonymous writers. It is likely that he met several of these poets when they were residing in Lucca. He also added moral tales, mostly as "notes" directed at people discussed in his chronicle. Sixteen of these notes were taken from his own collection, *Il novelliere.*

Sercambi's use of poems, aphorisms, moral tales, historical commonplaces, and selections of *laude* (popular hymns), which he believed his fellow citizens needed to recall, is not unusual at the end of the Middle Ages. Even hardheaded and realistic Florentine debaters often repeated commonplaces about Roman virtues or added to their discussions homey observations such as "the barking dog does not bite."[11] In Sercambi's hands, however, these observations tend to sum up and conclude sections. After discussing a series of battles in the 1390s in which Lucca found itself threatened by mercenary armies as well as by the Florentines, Sercambi includes a long poem by his friend Davino Castellani on the vices of the Tuscans, which has a simple couplet as its refrain:

> Oh glorious Tuscans, more triumphant than others,
> Do not fight like dogs, for God made you brothers.

(1:438)

---

10. Giovanni Sercambi, *Il novelliere,* ed. Luciano Rossi, 3 vols. (Rome: Salerno editrice, 1974); there are also two editions by Giovanni Sinicropi: *Novelle* (Bari: Laterza, 1972), and *Novelle* (Florence: Le lettere, 1995). On the tangled history of these editions, see Peter Nicholson, "The Two Versions of Sercambi's Novelle," *Italica* 53 (1976): 201–13, and Christopher Nissen, review of Giovanni Sercambi's *Novelle,* edited by Giovanni Sinicropi (1995), *Italica* 74 (1997): 423–25. On the poetry in *Le croniche,* see Possenti, *La poesia.*

11. On the language of political analysis at precisely the time Sercambi was writing, see Gene Brucker, *The Civic World of Early Renaissance Florence* (Princeton: Princeton University Press, 1977), 302–18; and for a later period, see Felix Gilbert, *Machiavelli and Guicciardini: Politics and History in Sixteenth-Century Florence* (Princeton: Princeton University Press, 1965), 7–48.

At another point, in discussing Lucca's endless skirmishes with Pisa even as Florence presented a greater danger, he uses a popular saying to make clear that dangers were often unexpected:

> The frog and the mouse prepared to fight,
> 'til they were eaten by a passing kite!
>
> (1:85)[12]

Relations with the Church and moral reform do seem important to Sercambi. He includes a long discussion of Urban VI's time in Lucca and the townspeople's hopes for an end to the schism that divided the Church. He also provides a long discussion of Lucca's later encounter, in 1399, with the Bianchi—the processions of penitents who moved through many of the larger cities of Italy.[13] Christianity and moral reform came to Sercambi's mind when he thought about his city and the preservation of its liberty. After explaining that the Lucchese should not put their trust in Florentine or any other lordship, he concludes, "our only hope is in the all-powerful God, who we hope will lift us out of our present servitude and make us free" (1:121).

In book 2 Sercambi includes poems and short tales meant to celebrate Paolo Guinigi's domination of Lucca and to remind Paolo of his own obligation to remain loyal to those who aided him in difficult times. One note concludes:

> In good times many are your friends;
> When your fortune turns, their friendship ends.[14]

Moral commonplaces are never far from Sercambi's mind when he reflects on Lucca's public life.

Sercambi's primary theme is, of course, liberty. And the Lucchese did maintain their liberty (after a fashion) until the French came in 1797. Their liberty was remarkable enough that Thomas Hobbes noted that the word "Libertas" was etched on their Baroque walls. Lucca, for the Englishman, epitomized the still living but anachronistic ancient ideas about civic freedom.

---

12. The same couplet figures in Exemplo 135 of Sercambi, *Novelliere*.

13. Daniel Bornstein, *The Bianchi of 1399: Popular Devotion in Late Medieval Italy* (Ithaca: Cornell University Press, 1993), 117–61, on "songs and signs" of the Bianchi, and esp. 123–24, on Sercambi.

14. Tempore felici multi numerantur amici, / Dun fortuna perit nullus amicus erit (Sercambi, *Le croniche*, 3:20).

Liberty has a long history in medieval Italian political discourse. As early as the twelfth century Lombard communes challenged imperial claims in the name of preserving their liberty. The Florentines, of course, used cries of liberty as an excuse for taking control of most of Tuscany. In a Florentine mouth, however, the concept of Tuscan liberty had a number of meanings. It could refer to living freely in a Guelf republic. The numerous Florentines who used the term "liberty" might also mean "freedom from outside domination," or they might be referring to the protection Florence exercised over towns like Pistoia and Volterra and was striving to exercise over Lucca. Finally, Florentine and Tuscan liberty was at the heart of the political and cultural agenda of Florence's first generation of civic humanists, almost exact contemporaries of Lucca's simple apothecary.[15]

The Lucchese story of liberty is quite unlike the Florentine version. Comparing the two reflects the profound differences between the city Villani found in no way inferior to Rome and its neighbor to the west, which by the late fourteenth century saw itself as a small town surrounded by giants. This recognition of Lucca's perilous position is key to Sercambi's discussion of liberty lost and regained. He has a sharp eye for what does and does not pertain to his subject. He tells us, in fact, in the prologue to his work,[16] that he will concentrate on those things that touch on the commune of Lucca, its citizens, and the inhabitants of its district.

We can get a good idea of how he understood his topic if we look briefly at the earliest section of his work, which commences with Lucca's liberty in 1164 and ends with Castruccio's coup in 1313. It seems likely that after he had begun writing in the 1370s, friends showed him fragments of the annals floating around Lucca. Sercambi begins by taking note of the destruction of Milan by the emperor Frederick Barbarossa and the building of Alessandria. But the most important early event was in 1168, when, he says, the war between Pisa and Lucca began. In fact, this first section of the chronicle is concerned almost exclusively with Lucchese attempts to secure Versilia, that is, the Tyrrhenian coast north of Pisa, and with Lucca's ongoing battles with local rural lords.

---

15. On the complex role of liberty, see Quentin Skinner, *The Foundations of Modern Political Thought*, vol 1, *The Renaissance* (Cambridge and New York: Cambridge University Press, 1978), 3–65, and Mikael Hörnqvist, "The Two Myths of Civic Humanism," in *Renaissance Civic Humanism*, ed. James Hankins (Cambridge: Cambridge University Press, 2000), 105–42.

16. Sercambi, *Le croniche*, 1:63–66. Sercambi includes three prologues in book 1, each one tracking his ideas as he expands his topic. This is the prologue to the second section of the book, the place where Sercambi initially expected to begin his book. See Ragone, "Le 'croniche' di Giovanni Sercambi," 12, esp. n. 18.

Lucca's high medieval diocese was vast, extending north into the mountains of Garfagnana, along the coast in Versilia, and far to the south of the Arno. Attempts to bring all of this area under communal control constituted the most important theme in the anonymous annals provided to Sercambi and remained important to him as well. Sercambi follows the annals, carefully recording Lucca's expansion, its arrangements with its bishop over strongholds south of the Arno, and its strategic moves designed to control the roads between Lucca and Pisa.

In one sense this should surprise no one. The theme of the conquest of the *contado* (the countryside surrounding the city) has been a staple of medieval Tuscan history at least since Gioacchino Volpe's first works, published at the beginning of the last century.[17] What is interesting in this context is the way in which the early annals' description of the capture in the twelfth century of what is now Viareggio fits almost seamlessly with Sercambi's later description of communal interests in the fourteenth century. In the decades after Lucca regained its liberty, Sercambi continued carefully to record lands and castles taken or lost—especially to the north and west, but also in the Arno valley. In Sercambi's telling, though, the story takes on a different meaning. After 1368, the commune of Lucca was very aware of its precarious situation and its rapacious neighbors. Its fortresses, roads, and lands did not open out to further conquests but rather served as strategic defensive points to keep Lucca's enemies at bay. Shortly after Lucca regained its liberty, it was once again fighting to hold or regain fortresses in Garfagnana and along the Arno. When Sercambi reports a loss, it is "to Lucca's great damage" (1:219–20).

Sercambi views Lucca's defense of its hinterland as part of an interurban competition. Where the annals often record clashes with various rural lords, Sercambi sees these conflicts as bound up in Lucca's struggles with Pisa and eventually Florence. He ignores the first indications of a commune and its claims to a hinterland, both of which are found as early as the eleventh century. His tale of liberty begins with what he sees as Pisan interference with Lucchese possessions in 1168. The annals,[18] for example, report that Lucca captured the fortress of Corvaia from the rural lords of Versilia, but

17. See Gioacchino Volpe, *Studi sulle istituzioni comunali a Pisa: Città e contado, consoli e podestà, secoli XII–XIII* [1902] (new ed., Florence: G. C. Sansoni, 1970), and especially the introduction written by Cinzio Violante; more recently on the early communes and the countryside, see Edward Coleman, "The Italian Communes: Recent Work and Current Trends," *Journal of Medieval History* 25 (1991): 375–81.

18. Schmeidler, *Die Annalen*, 291.

Sercambi adds that this really was a fight against rural lords allied with the Pisans (1:5).

Modern work on the Italian countryside emphasizes the complex social, economic, and political issues involved in immigration, legal administration, and agricultural trade that continually caused tensions between town and countryside. And Sercambi himself, in his *Novelliere*, recounts common tales of powerful lords, gullible landlords, and crafty peasants.[19] This complexity is lost in the chronicles. Here Sercambi does not believe that the troubles Lucca faces are caused by rebellious locals. Rather, they mask the interests of other powers. These suspicions become a regular feature of his chronicle. Unrest in one village, he says, is caused by a faction in league with the Florentines. When Lucca is ravaged by military companies, Sercambi observes, "they say this is at the request of the Florentines" (1:220). When one castle falls into the hands of some Lucchese exiles, Sercambi assumes it does so because of Florence's or some other power's interference.

In this respect, Sercambi accurately reflects common opinion in Lucca. Christine Meek's discussion of Lucchese diplomacy in this period underlines the timorous and fearful policies regularly advocated in city council debates.[20] Speakers in the city council tended to assume that even when they were formal allies, the Florentines could not entirely be trusted. Further, even in peace, the Pisans and the Florentines were only too willing to feast on their weaker neighbor. A peace treaty, a truce really, between Florence and Pisa involved the transfer of lands in the Valdinievole and along the Arno from Lucca to Florence. "And so in this way," Sercambi concludes, "Lucca sustained greater damage in peace than it had in war" (1:128).

Sercambi also reflects common Lucchese attitudes insofar as he avoids partisanship. During the debates over the form of government in Lucca, it was decreed that Lucchese should avoid inflammatory terms like "Guelf" and "Ghibelline," names that seemed to invite factionalism and division.[21] Sercambi does not entirely avoid the terms, and, of course, he cannot entirely

---

19. Michel Plaissance, "Les rapports ville-campagne dans les nouvelles de Sacchetti, Sercambi et Sermini," in *Culture et société en Italie du Moyen-Âge à la Renaissance: Hommage à André Rochon*, Centre interuniversitaire de recherche sur la Renaissance italienne, 13 (Paris: Université de la Sorbonne nouvelle, 1985), 61–67, and Giovanni Cherubini, *Signori, contadini, borghesi: Ricerche sulla società italiana del basso Medioevo* (Florence: La nuova Italia, 1974), 3–49.

20. Christine Meek, *Lucca, 1369–1400: Politics and Society in an Early Renaissance City-State* (Oxford and New York: Oxford University Press, 1978), pt. II, 115–74, concentrates on foreign relations.

21. Meek, *Lucca*, 229–36.

avoid factionalism. This too must be part of his narrative of liberty. He follows the annals in reporting riots between districts of the city in 1195. He also briefly records the struggles between the *popolo* (guildsmen) and Lucchese aristocrats early in the thirteenth century. And he reports factional struggles in 1300 and the later popular revolution of 1308—misdated in his telling to 1310. But in most cases he reports such matters as briefly as possible. He acknowledges that there were twenty-two families in Lucca who helped Uggucione della Fagiuola of Pisa take control of the city in 1313, and later he adds laconically that Castruccio Castracane returned to Lucca with the Pisans and soon took control of the city himself. His deliberate suppression of the story of Castruccio seems to be a response to the issues of factionalism in Lucca in the years after liberation. He was very aware of how his chronicle was likely to be read by his fellow citizens.

In his introduction he warns his readers that he means to praise virtue and condemn vice. His purpose, he says, is not to anger or shame individuals or families but to provide good examples. He is clearly worried that his readers might react badly to finding relatives treated critically in his narrative. He does sometimes condemn by name individuals whose behavior he finds traitorous, but he is more likely to be circumspect. In describing the tangled events of 1363, when some Lucchese plotted to free the commune and others continued to support Pisan rule, he concludes, "in order not to shame and divide [*dizonestare*] the Lucchese, I will not recount who took part in the plot, who revealed it, or who went to Pisa [to argue for the execution of the plotters]" (1:118–19).

Sercambi's circumspection changes only in the 1380s with the emergence of the Guinigi party. Sercambi makes clear his views when he describes the death of Francesco Guinigi, in 1384 (misdated in Sercambi to 1383), whom he calls Lucca's *maggior Cato*. He credits Francesco with bringing together clergy, great merchants, and artisans. "He was lamented," Sercambi adds, "by all who cherished virtue and maintained Lucca's liberty" (1:238).

In many respects, the death of Francesco did represent a watershed in Lucca's public life. From the mid-1380s the power of the Guinigi faction became more and more evident. In the chronicles the change becomes definitive in 1390, a time when Lucca was reforming its *tasche*, the bags from which officials were chosen. In a long passage that can be read as yet another prologue,[22] Sercambi reminds his readers yet again that he wants to provide

---

22. This may in fact be an indication that Sercambi's interest in his chronicle had waned until these events. See Ragone, "Le 'croniche' di Giovanni Sercambi," 26–28.

good examples for those who wished to maintain Lucca's liberty. But now the problem, he claims, is factionalism and discord brought on by Bartolomeo Forteguerra and his party. He says there were "many arguments, and many people used divisive language [*dizoneste parole*]" (1:260). In fact, it seems that the difficulties of the early 1390s really reflect a more complete assumption of power by the Guinigi faction. Sercambi himself was an important hardliner on the side of the Guinigi, and his criticism of Forteguerra reflects his now evident partisanship. For the rest of this book, Sercambi is less careful to avoid angering one group or another in the community. He describes Lucca's internal problems bluntly. Liberty is endangered not simply by foreign enemies but also by internal factionalism that must be controlled. He says he will impartially write of those who help or hinder Lucca and its liberty.

This shift reflects the second important theme in Sercambi's chronicles, the role of the Guinigi party as guarantors of Lucchese political stability and liberty. Toward the end of the first book, in describing the assassination of Lazzaro Guinigi in February 1400, Sercambi provides a clear idea of how he now thinks factionalism must be handled. The assassination resulted from a complex political crisis, which Sercambi does not entirely explain. Lazzaro's assassins were his brother and brother-in-law. The brother-in-law, Niccolò Sbarra, had once been part of the opposing faction. Lazzaro had apparently at one time intervened to prevent Niccolò's execution, then had enriched him and married him to Lazzaro's own sister. Guinigi strategy generally was to defuse confrontations, and what better ploy than a strategic marriage? Sercambi claims that, emboldened by the Evil One, Niccolò continued secretly to hate Lazzaro and desired his death. The assassins went to Lazzaro's room in the Guinigi palace, murdered him, and then attempted to seize the government. Though the assassination succeeded, the coup failed badly, and the two assassins were publicly executed.

In recounting the tale of the assassination, Sercambi lets his anger explode. In a long and improbable section he compares the betrayal of Lazzaro to the tragic fates of Medea, Dido, Achilles, and others—at least Medea, Sercambi concludes, lived and could take her revenge on the thoughtless Jason! Sercambi follows this tale with advice based on Lazzaro's tragic fate. The lesson of Lazzaro Guinigi, he seems to say, is that the old communal strategy of quietly ignoring the potential hazards of factionalism will no longer work. He warns other leaders—and here he really means the Guinigi leaders—that they cannot afford to tolerate dissidents or quietly act as past communal leaders had. Leaders must not show their true feelings; nor can they afford to allow any potential enemies to get close to them. Most of all, one must respond to injuries "with sword in hand." "You are powerful and have many friends," he assures them, "who will follow your lead." And he concludes, "Wake up! Sleep no any longer! Put aside your sorrows and cares and attend to those things that will secure your person. And recognize that your life is the *libertà* of Lucca . . . !" (2:415).

Sercambi's chronicles imply that it was this tragic assassination that changed his view of politics and liberty. It is probably more correct to say that it was the assassination that prompted him to include these ideas in his chronicle of Lucchese liberty. Sometime after 1392, perhaps eight years before the assassination of Lazzaro, Sercambi had already written a "Note to the Guinigi,"[23] in which he explained to Lazzaro and his brothers what was needed to preserve Lucca's liberty. Much of the advice is not unusual. Sercambi identifies critical defensive points in the countryside, advocates new tax measures, and suggests initiatives that might be taken to revive the economy. In addition to these measures, Sercambi warns the Guinigi that they should make sure that offices "always go to your friends . . . because they can carry out measures more properly so that you shall always have your way." And he goes on to add that "your friends should be understood as those who are united to you in life and death." Finally, aware of his own modest status, Sercambi excuses himself, saying that if any of this "is not in your interest, pardon me, understanding that everything I have done was as your most faithful servant."

Sercambi's continuing service to the Guinigi is a major theme of the second book of the chronicles. He continues to follow the fortunes of the papacy during the schism, and he includes reports from around Europe, forwarded by his uncle Giglio and other Lucchese merchants resident in northern Europe. But the primary topic is the Guinigi court and Sercambi's relation to it. Sercambi tells us that he played a key role when Paolo Guinigi assumed control of Lucca, but it seems that from that point on his influence in the government waned. Sercambi's remarks in book 2 become increasingly bitter. The problem for him seems to have been that he was a tough partisan politician in a period when Paolo was distancing himself from his most partisan supporters and attempting to reach out to the defeated faction. More personally, Sercambi felt embittered when abandoned by Paolo during litigation over the estate of Sercambi's uncle who had died in Paris.

23. The complete title is "Dino, Michaele, Lazzarino et Lazario de Guinigiis: Nota a voi Guinigi." It is included as an appendix to Sercambi, *Le croniche*, 3:399–407; for a newer edition, see Giovanni Sinicropi, "Giovanni Sercambi, *Nota ai Guinigi*, testo critico, introduzione e note," *Momus* 3–4 (1995): 7–45.

The source of Sercambi's anger comes out in a long rambling entry that begins with his discussion of plague in 1422. Sercambi is clear in his view that plague mortalities were always the result of sin. He rejects out of hand talk of astral conjunctions or corruptions. In this case, he asserts, the cause was avarice: "no prince, lord, or community was willing to reject the sin of avarice," and so God sent the mortality (3:317). This passage leads to an extended consideration of avarice, based on selections from Dante. Having warmed to the subject, Sercambi moves on to consider avarice in Lucca, particularly among judges and notaries, whom he even names: twelve judges and lawyers and another twelve notaries, who, he says, "became notaries only because of avarice and lack of knowledge." "Ask yourselves," he cries, "you of the Berindelli family and Simo Turelli, how litigation over less than thirty-two florins consumed over two thousand through the actions of Ser Domenico [Lupardi] and other lawyers?" (3:328). Moreover, the long list of avaricious lawyers seems to have reminded Sercambi of his own legal problems, which he promises to explain later. Thus the section on avarice is followed shortly by a chapter, "Concerning the injuries done to Giovanni Sercambi of Lucca because of his friendship with the house of Guinigi and with the lord Paolo Guinigi." Sercambi tells us he was the object of a murder plot, that enemies of Paolo planned to murder him during a trip to Venice. Most of all, this section describes in numbing detail litigation over his late uncle's properties, litigation in which he expected, but did not receive, support from Lord Paolo. He includes this, he says, because he fully expects that Paolo or his heirs will someday reward him for the dangers he has faced and the losses he has suffered by supporting the family.

It seems that Sercambi cannot quite decide whether he has stepped over the boundaries of the permissible or if he has a just cause. Thus he follows these complaints with an explanation: "I, Giovanni Sercambi, author of this book, am melancholy because of the things I have recounted and said above. I have seen myself abandoned in my need by people, especially by him whom I had most hoped would help me. My hope is in God, who will always aid me. I am zealous and have a full heart and love for the position of the magnificent lord Paolo and his sons" (3:348).

So in the fifteenth century Sercambi remained an ardent champion of Lucchese liberty. But his version of liberty did not closely resemble the proud civic liberty of the Florentines. In addition, civic liberty in Sercambi's Lucca was not quite what it had been. To be sure, Sercambi still fretted over foreign designs on traditionally Lucchese lands. Toward the end of the book he even included a lachrymose enumeration of all the lands stolen by Lucca's rapacious neighbors.

But what had changed was Sercambi's ideal of the role his fellow citizens should play in the preservation of *libertà*. When he began his chronicles, he assumed that when freed from foreign influence, citizens would naturally cooperate to preserve their liberty. By 1400, he had concluded that Lucchese liberty depended on internal tranquillity—a tranquillity that only the Guinigi could guarantee. Even more fundamentally, the governance of the Guinigi should be built on a reciprocal loyalty between the ruler and his party. Sercambi's chronicles, then, are a history of Lucca and Italy at the end of the fourteenth century, but a history that makes clear the profound transformation of ideas about commune, factionalism, and politics at the end of the Middle Ages.

APPENDIX: GIOVANNI SERCAMBI, THE CHRONICLES[24]

173 . . . In this book I will write of all that follows about the liberty of Lucca and of matters pertaining to Lucca, and some touching other places, assuming most of the subjects treated matter to Lucca and its liberty. Begun in the year 1368 and finished afterward, as you will see from this book. [1:141]

The Divine Power moved the hearts of the most Holy in Christ Father messer Urban V, by divine providence pope, and the most illustrious prince and lord messer Charles, by divine clemency emperor of the Romans and king of Bohemia. He compelled them to free the city of Lucca and its *contado*[25] from the servile yoke of tyrannical Pisans under which it had been placed for so long a time. Lucca was removed from tyrannical servitude and put in a state of liberty. . . .

201. How the emperor freed Lucca. . . . [1:172–74]

In the month of June 1369, at the request of the Holy Father and of many lords and many citizens of Lucca, messer lord emperor appeared in imperial court in the church of San Michele in Mercato [in Foro], on the steps before the Porta Maggiore, with the cardinal, many barons, counts, princes, and lords of many localities. The Anziani[26] of Lucca and many venerable

---

24. Translated from Sercambi, *Le croniche*. The numbers following the chapter titles indicate the volume and page from the Bongi edition.

25. The *contado* was that area surrounding an Italian city which was under the city's jurisdiction.

26. The Anziani, or Elders, were the administrative council that headed the government of Lucca.

citizens appeared in his presence, asking his majesty to concede a privilege and grace such to preserve Lucca in liberty, remaining always subject to the imperial majesty. At the request, the emperor again freed the city of Lucca and conceded to it a privilege with many dignities. In order not to get too detailed, I will not get involved in describing them. Those who wish to see them should look in the sacristy of the Anziani palace, where they will find them. . . .

Ever after the emperor was in Lucca, the Pisans were entirely excluded from the Signoria of Lucca. That resulted in more and more riots, in which many citizens and others were robbed, wounded, and killed. But because they were not persons of much account, I will not tell of them here. But I will say that many citizens returned to Lucca, and [among them were] Bartolo-meo Faitinelli, Nicolao del Caro, Ponsando Sornachi, citizens and merchants of Lucca who were elected to the Anzianate. Before they could take office, they died, and many said there were poisoned by the Pisans. And it was entirely credible because many times that art was practiced by the Pisans. Because of that the other citizens were careful, hoping that Lucca would remain free. And since it pleased God, things went from good to better.

. . . Then the holy emperor left the city of Lucca. But before he left, he wanted a great quantity of florins from the citizens of Lucca. And beyond that, he wanted a promissory note worth 100,000 gold florins, which obligation and payment are found in the privilege held by the Anziani. And he wanted the same for the freedom of [the town of] Massa, which at that time was given to Lucca. So that the facts are known, these are the sums borrowed by the commune of Lucca, in addition to those which the citizens and countrymen of Lucca have paid, in order to satisfy the sum they owed to the emperor. . . . And in truth, the liberty of Lucca cost the citizens of Lucca more than 300,000 florins in cash, not counting the dangers.

214. *How they began to tear down parts of the fortress and castle of Lucca.* [1:187–88]

On 26 March 1370, the cardinal and his troops left Lucca and went toward Rome, leaving by the San Gervasio gate. And when they had left, the mob of the *gonfalone* of Cecino[27] immediately began to tear down some of the fortifications of that gate, although guards were still there. The citizens were of one mind, that they should grind to earth the castle of Agosta,[28] because they thought it was the reason Lucca and the Lucchesi had been

27. A *gonfalone* was an administrative district of the city.
28. The Agosta was the citadel within the city walls that was used as a military stronghold.

subjects and subordinates for more than forty-eight years. And since some, because they desired to dominate [Lucca], did not think it was a good idea that this castle should be destroyed, they ordered that a ban be published that on pain of death no one should presume to destroy or even remove bricks from the wall of the castle.

215. *How the friars of San Romano destroyed the gate of the castle that was opposite the church of San Romano.* [1:188–90]

Then those who had lived under the yoke of servitude because of the fortress returned to San Romano. There they showed themselves useful to the church that was dismantling the San Romano gate of the castle. They paid no attention to the ban because it was clear that the whole commune of Lucca, or the major part of it, was happy about the dismantling of that castle. They came to that gate and threw down the gates, and they pulled down the walls such that before Vespers [i.e., by late afternoon] no man or woman, great or small, remained who had not climbed upon the wall. Some with smith's hammers, some with small hammers, some with other iron bars, and some with their bare hands tore down the merlons of that wall. There was not a priest or friar who did not tear down something. In that spirit of merriment, many cried for joy and many seemed mad or beside themselves. Truly there was such joy that the tongue of man cannot describe it. And so all that day everyone took pleasure in going up to the wall and tearing down whatever they could. And those who had nothing else used their hands to dislodge bricks, rocks, and mortar from the wall, cursing that it was because of that [castle] that they had been made subjects. And because I cannot truly describe what went on there, I will not speak of everything they did. Some danced; some just sat; some sang; some pretended to fight; some called out as if the guards were still there; others issued orders just as a lord would; some recalled when the lords were still there; some wept because of the damage that had been done. Many grieved at the deaths of fathers and relatives, some for possessions taken from them, some at the violence, some for the dishonored women, some because of the fortunes they had preserved. Some took pleasure in having lived so long that they could trample down and destroy [the castle]. Some said it seemed like they were in the second level of paradise: "Now that I have seen Liberty, I do not fear death. And when death comes, those who consider themselves richer than the emperor will not give it regard." And it seems that all citizens in that movement were lords. In order not to dull the mind, many other things that men generally acquire when they receive liberty are being left out. And so I will not describe them here.

238. *How in Lucca discord over government by "a popolo" or by "a commune" was born. And for that reason several were beheaded.* [1:204–5]

In February 1371, discord arose between citizens who took no notice of the recent past. Because it was not a good thing to name everyone [who was involved], it is best to keep quiet. But it can be said at least that many wanted Lucca governed in the manner of the *popolo*,[29] and so they painted the arms of the *popolo* wherever they could. Many [others] said that they should live [governed] by a commune, without any role for the *popolo*. For a long time this difference had been great, and people had strong opinions about it. Now, when they saw that things were going badly, the council met. Many notable citizens took part, and they concluded that they should be governed by the *popolo*. There was a riot after. People took up flags and banners [for their own factions]. The podestà of Lucca was Messer Ugolino Galuzzi of Bologna. During the riot he captured the tailor Nicolao Lippi and Nuccino Sornachi, both citizens of Lucca and friends of the Guelf party. He also took the weaver Pierotto. The podestà caused Nuccino and Nicolao to be beheaded in the piazza [San Michele] of Lucca. Pierotto lost his right hand. . . . All this happened because they wanted to change the government by the people to a government by commune. And so the anger between citizens began to grow in such a way that it has not ended.

677. *How Lazzaro di Francesco Guinigi was killed.* [2:405–8]

The Enemy of Human Nature, who because of his pride was driven from heaven and sent into the deepest Hell by the Divine Power, had the power to stimulate an evil nature. And in his envy of human nature, he seduced Adam and Eve, our first parents, to sin and thus like him to be deprived of the eternal good and the glory of Paradise. He thought therefore that all human nature would be deprived of that eternal good and glory of Paradise. . . . He has no other purpose. The greater the evil, the greater his pleasure, because the penalties [of sin] continue to grow. . . . I will say no more of the past and return to that which recently happened in this our city of Lucca on 15 February 1400. It was a Sunday, as I will recount below:

The house of Guinigi, and especially Lazzaro di Francesco Guinigi, had supported the person of Nicolao di Benedetto Sbarra, and furthermore [Lazzaro] enriched him with thousands of florins. And more than that he made Nicolao his brother-in-law, giving him his sister as a wife. He showed him

29. "Governing in the manner of the people" meant a government dominated by wealthy merchant families and excluding proscribed noble families. The most modest artisans and laborers had no role in government. Meek, *Lucca*, 179–93, esp. 182.

such love that had Nicolao been Lazzaro's son, he could not have treated him better. While he was living in that condition, Nicolao had ill will toward the house of Guinigi and their friends. . . . And that is how things were when it happened that Antonio Guinigi, by his own fault and for no reason, took a dislike to his brother Lazzaro. When he made his dislike known to Nicolao, Nicolao tempted Antonio with false replies that inflamed him and maintained in him the hate for Lazzaro. Nicolao showed such love toward Antonio so that his own evil intentions might be carried out. Antonio's ill will was so inflamed that he resolved with Nicolao that Lazzaro should be killed. And so that he could carry this out, Nicolao now showed in his conversation a false friendship for Lazzaro. As a result Lazzaro confided a great deal in Nicolao in the belief that he was what he was not. Lazzaro made his thoughts known to Nicolao. He let him know about his life, his daily routine of living and sleeping, where his room was located, and how he was guarded. When the time seemed right to Nicolao to put his evil plans into effect, he put his trust in the Devil rather than in God, and he told Antonio that it was a good time to carry out their plans. On Sunday, 15 February, excited by the Devil, Nicolao said to Antonio, "Tonight will be the time to accomplish our intentions. I want to be the one to do it." Having agreed on the betrayal, Nicolao, that afternoon before supper, about three, when Lazzaro had entered the house and was writing at his desk on the third floor, came to the door of the house with Antonio. He knocked, and Lazzaro asked who was knocking. Nicolao responded, "It is I. I want to speak with Lazzaro." And as to a true friend, Lazzaro had the door opened, and [Nicolao] along with Antonio entered. When he had climbed the stairs, Nicolao entered the room and stood before Lazzaro. "Good evening," he said. And Lazzaro responded, "What's new?" To which Nicolao responded, "Traitor! You will die!" And he drew out a sword from his cloak and struck Lazzaro on the head. At that point Antonio reached him and wounded him with more blows. Not content with this, Nicolao cut his throat with a stone chisel.[30] This is how the most excellent and wise Lazzaro ended his life. And before we go on to recount some of the things that should be said about such a death, I will tell you what happened to these malefactors.

678. *How Antonio Guinigi and Nicolao Sbarra attempted to raise a revolt in Lucca.* [2:408–10]

After Lazzaro had been killed, Antonio, wearing a cuirass bearing the Guinigi arms, and Nicolao, wearing a breastplate under a red jacket [short

---

30. A *bazolare*.

coat], and both well armed, went into the Piazza San Michele at the second hour of the night [i.e., about two hours after dark]. They went to the loggia where the flags and the officer of the guard stood. When they reached them, Antonio spoke in desperation, "Our enemies have entered Lucca, and I think they want a revolution. I say to you that I think it would be a good thing for us to punish those who would bring us down." And when he had said these words, Antonio shouted and caused the constables to shout, "Long live the Ghibelline party!" since they all believed what Antonio had said was true. Hearing these voices and also hearing of the death of Lazzaro, the friends of the house of Guinigi then armed themselves. . . . When the Guinigi heard of Lazzaro's death and of who caused it, they armed themselves and joined their friends and soldiers. When they had armed themselves and were protected, they could think about what the surviving Guinigi should do: the house of Guinigi needed revenge, first, because Lazzaro was dead; second, because the murder was committed by Antonio, brother of Lazzaro, Bartolomeo, and Paolo Guinigi; and finally, because this is what the Guinigi wanted done. And therefore discussions were held in that house. Those of that house, principally Bartolomeo and Paolo Guinigi, Lazzaro and Antonio's brothers, armed themselves and went with the other Guinigi to the palace of the Anziani. Then they resolved that the malefactors should be captured by command of the Anziani of Lucca. . . . After much debate it was decided that they should carry the banner of the *Popolo* into the piazza. All the mounted and foot soldiers and many citizens carrying torches were to go with Bartolomeo and Paolo Guinigi to capture the malefactors. This was about the fifth hour of the night. And they did it just as they had decided. The banner of the People was put in the hands of Bonacorso Bocci, who was the standard-bearer. And Bartolomeo and Paolo Guinigi, with the mounted and foot soldiers and the Lucchese carrying lit lanterns and torches, left the palace and marched toward the piazza, shouting: "Long live the *Popolo*." And this is how they entered the piazza. . . . [Lacuna in the manuscript.] Antonio Guinigi and Nicolao [were captured] . . . by Bartolomeo and Paolo and taken before the lords Anziani in the palace. Then the lords Anziani as well as the Standard-bearer of Justice Giovanni Testa turned Antonio and Nicolao over to the podestà, who examined them and in the course of the examination made them confess how they committed that murder.

681. *An oration of the memory of Lazzaro.* [2:411]

Now I will speak of the memory of Lazzaro as an example to his relations and friends. How much your friendship and family connections cost you!

You made friends with your enemy, hoping in that way to sweeten what was a most bitter poison. Truly your hopes were dashed. And it will be the same for anyone who expects to use a good heart to reconcile with an enemy. Because hatred is hidden, the more one draws [the former enemy] near with pleasing acts or family relationships, the more toxic the poison of such hatred will become. And so every lord, count, duke, prince, commune, and person with authority or influence would do well not to show or give to his enemy any power over him. Nor should he undertake to offer to an enemy such friendship, personal relationship, or family connection that would grant normal relations or associations. In this way no enemy can put his evil designs into effect in the midst of normal relations or while the lord is eating or sleeping. But following the example you set toward your enemies, Oh Lazzaro! most people, like you, would find themselves deceived.

685. Counsels of friends. [2:414]

Dearest friends![31] Why do you have such sorrow? And if there is good reason for such grief, it is still not proper for wise men to show publicly the secrets of their hearts. If they show clearly the pain they feel when things go wrong, it gives sorrow to their friends and makes their enemies swell with happiness. Pretend! Appear pleased when your sorrows abound! Do not let yourself be tormented by these things that must torment you when you think about them. It is not honorable to respond by shedding tears. Rather, a man must defend himself from all these injustices with a sword, by revenge, not by whimpering! And in this way, you can show the valor of a wise man in adversity and in contrary times. When you think of wrongs [done to you], your soul should rise up so that you will not again receive the same injury. If you do so, it will calm your souls and ours. And such a vendetta should not be demanded with tears, but with great virtue and a strong heart. But as you know, you are strong, and you have many friends who would follow your lead. And you should be willing to call on nearby and distant friendships so that no more can ill-intentioned persons in their malevolence affect any of you. We will also move against those who want to offend you. And if in the future you do not let down your guard, it will be difficult to drive you from Lucca; rather, all the malevolent will suffer harsh penalties, and their evil deeds will be undone through your wisdom and power. And whoever would want to do evils such as these that have been done or similar deeds should suffer a hard death, like an evil thief. So arise! Do not sleep! But put

---

31. Sercambi writes, "charissimi magiori," by which he seems to be referring to the Guinigi family and their party.

aside your grief and anguish! Look to those things that will be the salvation of your person. Thus you know that in your lives you hold the liberty of Lucca, the good of all citizens who wish to live well, the comfort of your friends, and the confusion of your enemies.

2:374. On the injuries that I, Giovanni Sercambi, have received for being a friend of the house of Guinigi and of Messer Paolo Guinigi. [3:333–36]

I will speak no more about the things in Italy, but I will now recount the damage endured by me, Giovanni Sercambi, and by him who lives in other lands where there are divisions of opinion and sects. And since one could speak from the experiences of many people of the great cost to those who found themselves in one of the factions, and assuming that many found themselves defending one of the parties for good reasons, nonetheless it is not true that those of the other party do not hold ill will toward their opponents. And when they have the means and time to avenge themselves, they have no regard for the pardons and graces they have already received from the victors.

Although that which I will describe does not seem honorable, yet I will describe how things came to pass up to this year 1423. I will say how much was done by me for the salvation of the house [of Guinigi], for the community of Lucca, and also for the magnificent lord Paolo Guinigi. . . .

From 1370 to 1383 [actually 1384] Lucca remained free from Pisan servitude through the wisdom of Francesco di Lazzaro Guinigi, father of the magnificent lord Paolo. . . .

And in order to continue this good life, the city council ordered that an office of the *balìa*[32] be established that was maintained so long as Francesco Guinigi lived. When Francesco died, the Devil began to insert into the hearts of many citizens the desire to bring down completely the position of the house of Guinigi. And this inclination was found in a great number of citizens who, if you wished to note them all, would take a long time to list. . . . When the city council met, the [pro-Guinigi] *balìa* was quashed and canceled. So there was little or nothing the council could do in Lucca. And that is how things stood until the death of Matteo Guinigi, as I explained in the first book. Since the Guinigi remained surrounded by friends, no expulsion from Lucca took place. That is how things stood until 1390, when a new faction, including those named earlier along with many others, desired to have the entire house of Guinigi and their friends driven out of Lucca.

---

32. A *balìa* was an ad hoc committee with wide ranging extraconstitutional powers to deal with emergencies.

I myself, Giovanni, concluded that the government of the Guinigi was useful, good, and the salvation of Lucca, since I had observed that those who made themselves enemies of that house were themselves divided: some Guelfs, some Ghibellines, some Dugali,[33] and some blackguards wanted to make themselves lords, to become rich by theft and evil deeds. I placed myself in God's hands, and I resolved in all things to be a friend to the Guinigi and their friends. I and my relatives and supporters would be loyal in council as well as with arms. This was not with an expectation of gain but for the well-being of that house and for the salvation of Lucca.

. . . And as I explained, that is how things remained until the death of Lazzaro di Francesco Guinigi. Because of his death, that house became much weaker. Their external and internal enemies were happy because of it, and they thought they could return to Lucca greatly strengthened.

And after this the mortality began in Lucca and in the *contado,* as was described at the beginning of this volume.[34] I, Giovanni Sercambi, saw that the mortality had carried away Lazzaro di Nicolao Guinigi, his son Giovanni, and Bartolomeo Guinigi, brother of Lord Paolo Guinigi. Paolo was ill with plague swellings and fever; Dino [Guinigi] was old; and Michele Guinigi was ill with an incurable infirmity. Learning of the rebels' plans to destroy Lucca and moved by a zealous love for the salvation of the city and of the house, I went to Michele Guinigi and told him of the danger to them and to the city. I said that to save the city and his house a *balìa* must be established. And so it happened, as I have recounted.

And using the influence of my office, I, as standard-bearer [of justice], made the magnificent lord Paolo captain and lord of Lucca. God preserve him in that lordship as long as it is his desire and that of his sons! May it please God, amen!

. . . Having recounted all of this, I must tell clearly how much this friendship has cost me. I do not say this in disrespect for the magnificent lord Paolo, but to confirm what has been said by authorities, beginning with my first injury:

375. *First injury.* [3:338–39]

When I went to Venice for my own business, there were many exiled Lucchesi and many others from Lucca who opposed the house of Guinigi. These [people] decided to murder me. I was in Venice less than a day—it

---

33. The Dugali were the faction of the descendants of Castruccio Castracane, the adventurer who dominated Lucca and much of Tuscany until his death, in 1327.

34. An infestation of plague in 1400.

was the [feast] day of Santa Lucia—before I was assaulted and wounded on the head by a number of them who said, "Traitor! Supporter of the Guinigi! . . ."

376. *Second injury.* [3:339]

The second injury happened as follows. I had an apothecary shop. One night when no one was there, several enemies of the Guinigi set it on fire. Because of that, everything burned. I lost goods valued at more than 1,800 florins. And there was no thought to make things right, and I had to absorb the loss.

377. *The third injury sustained.* [3:339–40]

The third injury I received is that I was deceived and misled by the executors that Master Gilio Sercambi, my uncle, while in Paris, realizing he was dying, had named, after which making me, Giovanni Sercambi, and my brother Bartolomeo his heirs. . . .

The will was made in 1404. Since the magnificent lord Paolo was already lord of Lucca, I took the letter informing me that my brother and I had to go to Paris to the magnificent lord. And when the magnificent lord considered the situation, it did not seem to him that I should go. But he did advise that my brother Bartolomeo should go. And Lord Paolo sent along with him a letter to the executors. . . . The executors refused to obey the recommendations of the magnificent lord Paolo. Rather, there were such labors, expenses, and regrets that Bartolomeo died in Paris after spending 700 florins.

388. *Note to the magnificent lord Paolo of Lucca.* [3:348]

I, Giovanni Sercambi, author of this book, am melancholy because of the things I have recounted and said above. I have seen myself abandoned in my need by people, especially by him whom I had most hoped would help me. My hope is in God, who will always aid me. I am zealous and have a full heart and love for the position of the magnificent lord Paolo and his sons. . . .

7

Fourteenth-Century Lombard Chronicles

Sharon Dale

Lombard chroniclers were describing an eventful and often chaotic time in the fourteenth century.[1] Trapped geographically within the competing and often devastating papal-imperial and later Franco-German territorial rivalries, Lombardy was also caught politically between Guelf and Ghibelline ideologies regarding temporal power. Milan dominated the region, yet other cities, such as Pavia, had long, often glorious histories and resisted such subjugation. Mostly Ghibelline, Lombard cities favored the emperor in principle, but lingering anti-German sentiment dating from the destruction wreaked by Frederick Barbarossa's invasions in the twelfth century made them wary of the imperial presence.

Lombardy's continuous struggle to define and maintain independence came to be entwined with the family history of the Visconti. They were imperial vicars yet wary of emperors, proud patrons of churches but at war against popes, and seeking marriages with French royalty while endeavoring to keep the French from annexing northern Italy as they had Naples. Lombard chroniclers necessarily reflected these tensions as they struggled to define their Visconti lords. The chronicles describe the Visconti as brilliant, powerful, and rich, but also violent, ruthless, and amoral. A tortured relationship with the Church, from which numerous members of the family were excommunicated, some for years, others for decades, yet others for eternity, forms a counterpoint to the story of Visconti hegemony in northern Italy, a narrative of nearly ceaseless warfare.

---

1. The best account of this period, in English, remains Peter Partner, *The Lands of St. Peter* (Berkeley and Los Angeles: University of California Press, 1972), 311–65. While the book's focus is the Papal State, it includes much pertinent information on the larger historical picture.

Yet on the eve of Giangaleazzo Visconti's sudden death in 1402, this duke of Milan was the most powerful lord in Italy. His glittering court, anchored by a massive castle in Pavia, was a hub of learning and art patronage. He had assembled two colleges of eminent legal scholars, who were attempting to codify and systematize the jumble of laws throughout his territory, laying the legal groundwork for a unified Visconti dynastic state.[2] Politically, he was well on his way to controlling most of northern and central Italy, including parts of the Papal State and Tuscany, not by conquest but by voluntary submission to his seignorial authority, which many preferred to annexation by republican Florence.[3]

Because the Visconti archives were destroyed during the 1447–50 Ambrosian Republic, chroniclers have largely shaped the Visconti historical persona. Contemporary anti-Visconti writers, most notably the Florentine Villani chroniclers, have informed us about some of the family's less appealing traits, such as their alarming predilection for poisoning one another.[4] Ironically, the Villani texts are the most oft cited sources regarding Visconti action in Italy, so that Milan's bitterest enemy, Florence, has provided the historical lens through which to view the Lombard past.

Two Lombard chronicles form the foundation of our knowledge of the Visconti: Galvano Fiamma's *Opusculum de rebus gestis ab Azone, Luchino et Iohanne vicecomitibus,* written by 1344, and Pietro Azario's *Liber Gestorum in Lombardia,* finished in 1364.[5] Both writers were employed by the

2. Giangaleazzo's father, Galeazzo II Visconti, founded the University of Pavia in 1361. Giangaleazzo expanded the university's law faculty by attracting to Pavia many notable jurists, including Baldus de Ubaldis. On the latter, see Joseph Canning, *The Political Thought of Baldus de Ubaldis* (Cambridge: Cambridge University Press, 1987), 221–27. Giangaleazzo also organized a law college in Milan that was mainly deliberative, offering him legal counsel. The main evidence for this is an opinion offered to Giangaleazzo by twenty-nine named jurists regarding a boundary dispute in Piedmont. The unpublished document is in Turin, Archivio di Stato, *Monferrato,* Ducato, Mazzo 10, 2.

3. On Giangaleazzo, see Daniel M. Bueno de Mesquita, *Giangaleazzo Visconti* (Cambridge: Cambridge University Press, 1941).

4. Giovanni Villani, *Nuova cronica,* ed. Giuseppe Porta, 3 vols. (Parma: Fondazione Pietro Bembo, 1990–91); Matteo Villani, *Cronica con la continuazione di Filippo Villani,* ed. Giuseppe Porta, 2 vols. (Parma: Fondazione Pietro Bembo, 1995).

5. For the Fiamma chronicle, see *Opusculum de rebus gestis ab Azone, Luchino et Iohanne, vicecomitibus ab a. 1328 ad a. 1342, RIS,* n.s., 12, pt. 4, ed. Carlo Castiglioni (Bologna: Nicola Zanichelli, 1938). For the Azario, *Liber Gestorum in Lombardia, RIS,* n.s., 16, pt. 4, ed. Francesco Cognasso (Bologna: Nicola Zanichelli, 1925–39). Other Lombard chroniclers of the Visconti include Buonincontro Morigia (*Chronicon Modoetiense, RIS,* 12 [Milan: Società Palatina, 1728], cols. 1061–184), Giovanni Cermenate (*Historia Iohannis de Cermenate, Notarii Mediolanensis,* ed. Luigi Alberto Ferrai [Rome: Forzani, 1889]), Johanne de Mussis (*Chronicon Placentinum, RIS,* 16 [Milan: Società Palatina, 1730]), and Andrea

Visconti: Fiamma was an intimate of Azzo, confessor to Luchino and chaplain and scribe to Giovanni; Azario was a notary, chancellor and judge under several Visconti lords and their appointed podestà.[6] While both writers were Visconti insiders, they had markedly different approaches to their stories. Fiamma was hardly a dispassionate observer and offered little criticism of the Visconti lords. A Dominican friar at the church of Sant'Eustorgio, site of much Visconti patronage,[7] Fiamma agonized over the strained relationship between the Visconti and the papacy. The notary Azario, by contrast, ignored religious conflict and was far from uncritical in his account. His worldview was conditioned by observing, often firsthand, the war-ravaged landscape of northern Italy. In his estimation, wise leadership by legitimate Italian rulers, namely the Visconti, was the only solution to the chaos, but Azario arrived at this conclusion reluctantly, and even tentatively. His career success, although tethered to the Visconti, seems only slightly to have tempered his ambivalence.

Galvano Fiamma's chronicle spans the entire lordship of Azzo and lightly touches upon those of his successors, Luchino and Giovanni.[8] His narrative tells of heroes and villains who remain consistent through history. So, for example, one of the Manichaean dualities for Fiamma is the enmity between Milan and Pavia, exacerbated by the sacking of Milan by Frederick Barbarossa in 1162. Fiamma observes that every city in Lombardy except Pavia helped rebuild Milan. He does not dwell on the issue; after all, Pavia and Milan will always be enemies. This stylistic technique is consistent. What is included or excluded, which events are discussed, and above all the narrative sequence reveal Fiamma's intentions and opinions.

The chronicle opens with the coronation of Louis of Bavaria as king of the Romans in Milan in 1327:

Biglia ("In exequiis Iohannes Galeatii Vicecomitis ducis Mediolani laudatio funerea," *RIS*, 19 [Milan: Società Palatina, 1731], cols. 9–158). Also useful is the anonymous *Annales Mediolanensis, RIS*, 16 (Milan: Società Palatina, 1730), cols. 641–840. See also Luigi Alberto Ferrai, "Gli annali mediolanensis e i cronisti Lombardi," *Archivio storico lombardo* 7 (1890): 277–313, and Paolo Chiesa, ed., *Le cronache medievali di Milano* (Milan: Vita e pensiero, 2001).

6. On these authors, see the entries in *Dizionario biografico degli italiani*, 4:740–42 and 47:331–38. On Fiamma, see too Luigi Alberto Ferrai, "Le cronache de Galvano Fiamma e le fonti della *Galvagnana*," *Bullettino dell'Istituto storico italiano* 10 (1891): 93–128, and Chiesa, *Le cronache medievali di Milano*.

7. See Anita Fiderer Moskowitz, *Italian Gothic Sculpture, c. 1250–c. 1400* (Cambridge: Cambridge University Press, 2001), 201–7.

8. Giovanni's promotion to archbishop of Milan in 1342 occasioned Fiamma's completion of a history of Milanese archbishops, now at the Biblioteca Braidense in Milan, MS A.H. XI. 38.

The first year of the coronation of Louis of Bavaria in Milan. And the same Louis installed as his vicar-general William of Montfort, a German, and then he named as podestà of Milan Gozius the German, and thus the city of Milan had three Germans, that is Louis, William, and Gozius. At this time the treasury of the church was stolen. At this time the legate of the Roman Church Cardinal Bertrand [du Poujet] resided in Piacenza, fighting frequently, spewing the harshest sentences, and preparing a severe process against the enemies of the Church.[9] (1:3)

This account is followed immediately by the information that the papally dispatched money "for the business of the Church" was stolen in Pavian territory by soldiers from Milan (1:3). Thus from the start Fiamma establishes a cast of villains, namely Louis, his German appointees, Pavia, and the papal legate. Each villain will eventually get his just desserts, usually delivered by Azzo Visconti. Louis will be paid off and forced to retreat to Germany, his Teutonic minions will be bought off, and Pavia will be triply humiliated as it first shelters the hapless and fleeing Louis, is defeated in battle, and then finally subjugated by Azzo. Bertrand du Poujet, the papal legate, will be run out of Bologna by an angry mob. Most important, Milan will be freed from German domination and have its status as the enemy of the Roman Church overturned by Azzo's actions, which then serve as a prelude to Fiamma's account of the glorious years of Azzo's rule of Milan.

Fiamma's chronicle proceeds chronologically but steps backward frequently to fill in historical information relevant to the discussion. Following the details of Louis's coronation, he traces Azzo's rise to lordship of Milan, including an account of his battlefield bravery (if not success) against Florence and Bologna before Louis's arrival in Milan—"These glorious victories having been completed, he returned to his father in Milan with glory"[10] (1:5)—and in the process providing a telling comparison with Louis's less distinguished behavior: "In the meantime Louis of Bavaria, who called himself king of the Romans, girded himself with soldiers in the church of Sant'Ambrogio in Milan on the feast of Pentecost" (1:5).

9. Text citations from Fiamma and Azario cite chapter number followed by page in the *RIS*, n.s., editions.

10. Johanne de Mussis, *Chronicon Placentinum*, col. 494, with a decidedly anti-Visconti orientation, describes Azzo's loss of Bologna as a "true miracle." At this time Piacenza was the subject of the Church in both temporal and spiritual realms, and the chronicler provides a strongly Guelf account of these events.

Fiamma records that Louis later imprisoned Azzo and his father, Gale-azzo Visconti, in Monza, deprived them of the lordship of Milan, and exiled them. Only after these humiliations did he restore their dominion. The chronicler comments, "for Louis, counsel was not served by wisdom; never trust your enemy." And then he concludes, "What height of insanity this was will be proved by his own deeds" (1:5).

Fiamma notes that, in excommunicating Louis, Pope John XXII deprived him of the kingship of Rome and freed all from loyalty or allegiance to him. He then takes a distinctive tack, declaring that Louis warred against both the church and the city of Milan, thus elevating the status of the Visconti and their city. Then Fiamma poses a question: Was this a just war against Milan? In other words, was Louis the legitimate emperor? Reviewing the controversial election of 1314 that produced two contenders for emperor, Louis and Frederick, the duke of Austria, Fiamma agrees with the pope that Louis was not legitimately elected. Further, due to his "excesses," foremost among them his crowning an antipope, he was excommunicated and de-posed. Therefore, no one should obey him. Thus Fiamma establishes the rationale for Azzo's betrayal of Louis—he owed him no loyalty, since he was not a legitimate emperor (1:6).

Fiamma is also able to foist the responsibility for Milan's interdict onto others as well:

> At that time many heresies sprang up in that city; false and evil religious of Milan were wagging their tongues in public against the pope and preaching that he was not the pope, indeed that he was a heretic under excommunication, deposed, and the worst mur-derer. And they extolled Nicholas the antipope with great praise. Moreover, at that time, the Apostate was called the Apostle, and all Catholics were called heretics. Thus truth was overthrown in the street, and the city that had formerly been full of the just had now become a wet nurse of pollution and a nest of heretics. (11:6)

Azzo Visconti will rescue Milan from this poisoned state. "With Milan riven from the Church of God and its men rent with hostility, Azzo began to rise by means of good counsel against Louis, once duke of Bavaria and now usurper of empire" (III:6).

Learning of Azzo's change of loyalty, Louis left Pisa and came to Lom-bardy "drunk with fury" and "desiring to extirpate the Visconti *genus* (clan)" (III:7). Despite some assistance from the della Scala lords of Verona, Louis was "deprived by God of help and counsel." Seeing himself at a military disadvantage, he abstained from war and signed a peace pact with Azzo instead. Fiamma then avers that Azzo, a prudent man like his father, offered Louis foods and wines and a certain quantity of money. Louis's dire need for cash was almost legendary, and his months in Italy had been financially disastrous.[11] Tempting Louis with what he most craved, Azzo succeeded in freeing Italian Ghibellines of his embarrassing presence. Fiamma tersely notes that Louis went to Monza and then Pavia, where he spent 21 June, the feast of Saints Gervasius and Protasius, and then retreated to Germany, where he now contentedly resided.

The very next sentence informs us, "At this time, Marco Visconti, who had lived in Rosate, came to Milan on 15 August, and suddenly, on 5 September, he died and was buried in the cathedral, in the chapel of St. Agnese" (III:7). We know from Buonincontro Morigia that Marco Visconti had informed Louis of Azzo's peace overtures to Avignon.[12] Once again, Fiamma's inclusion of certain facts and, as important, their sequence communicate a great deal. Marco's sudden death must be related to his act of betrayal.

The next chapter is entitled "Of peace between the Church and Milan" and reviews the sins of Louis, who committed the "gravest schism and raved in madness against the Church" (IV:7). Visconti recognition of Louis's disputed claim as king of the Romans had elicited the strongest possible opposition from Pope John XXII, as had Louis's crowning of an antipope. Yet, recognizing that Azzo had served him by expelling Louis from Italy, the pope tempered his hostility toward the Visconti. Azzo then sent a delegation of ambassadors to Avignon asking that Milan be absolved from the interdict. After receiving assurances that Azzo would keep Louis out of Italy, John XXII showed clemency and forgave Milan and, in time suspended the interdict. Thus Fiamma has managed the unthinkable; the Visconti are transformed into defenders of the church.

Fiamma is surpassingly charitable toward John XXII, whose mission had been to destroy Visconti control of Lombardy.[13] Ironically, Fiamma reserves far more venom for his successor, Benedict XII, whose policy toward the

---

11. "Impecunious kings were not rare in fourteenth-century Europe. But [Louis's] lack of money was chronic and desperate to a degree which sets him apart from most of his contemporaries." Hilary S. Offler, "Empire and Papacy: The Last Struggle," *Transactions of the Royal Historical Society*, 5th ser., 6 (1956): at 31.

12. Morigia, *Chronicon Modoetiense*, chap. XXXV.

13. On the Visconti and the papacy, see Sharon Dale, "Contra damnationis filios: The Visconti in Fourteenth-Century Papal Diplomacy," *Journal of Medieval History* 33 (2007): 1–32.

Visconti was conciliatory in both military and political arenas, confirming their vicariates and *signorie,* but demanding in the religious sphere; while lifting the interdict on Milan and other Visconti-held territories, he refused to absolve Azzo from excommunication. To the friar Fiamma, no less than to the Visconti themselves, the damnation of Azzo's soul was serious business (see Appendix A, xiv).

Like other chroniclers, Fiamma ascribes political significance to natural and unnatural phenomena. In a chapter concerning the "reintegration" of Cremona into Visconti dominion, Fiamma describes the appearance of a "stupendous monster" in the snow, whose form disappeared into the Ticino river, which then, "it was believed," altered direction, appearing to flow toward the mountains of Germany (xiii:14–15). The passage leaves unsaid the message that the Visconti were now committed to keeping Italy free of German control.

As Louis Green has illustrated, Fiamma explicates a theory of magnificence for Azzo whereby art and architectural projects commissioned by the Visconti lord were testaments to "princely greatness" and his role as a "benefactor of his community, whose generosity towards it served the Aristotelian notion of the common good."[14] The theme of magnificence will continue to define the Visconti *signorie* and serve as a trope for later Visconti chroniclers.

Pietro Azario was a notary, not a friar, and far less preoccupied than Fiamma with personal salvation. His *Liber Gestorum in Lombardia* presents a dynastic history of the Visconti often imitative of the style of Roman epic poetry. As much a literary conceit as a thematic one, this conscious classicizing creates a framework for Lombard history beginning with Aeneas, who founded a Roman kingdom in Lombardy *in magnificentia fuit erecta* (built in magnificence) (1:8). But, the *civitas* of Rome, that is, the Christianized Roman Empire, brought infamy to the kingdom of Aeneas, for it was rent with discord, having had from the beginning two competing swords, a spiritual one held by the pope and a temporal one held by the emperor. Azario portrays Lombardy as "stabbed" by these sharp swords, personified as two demons, one called Gualef and the other Gibel, whose followers were respectively the Guelfs and the Ghibellines. Azario has little good to say about either faction, although he observes that the Guelfs were worse to each other than they were to the Ghibellines (1:8). Azario advocates a return, not to the Roman republic, as Florentine writers desired, but to the pure kingdom

14. Louis Green, "Galvano Fiamma, Azzo Visconti, and the Revival of the Classical Theory of Magnificence," *Journal of the Warburg and Courtauld Institutes* 53 (1990): 98–113.

of Aeneas. For Azario, peace was the overarching goal. Writing during the 1362 plague, Azario reveals at the end of his account that he has lost his wife and two children to the disease. Yet, in his view, the greater threat to his remaining children and to Lombardy was the Anglicorum Societatem, the English company of mercenaries that was ravaging Italy in the third quarter of the trecento.[15] Revulsion toward foreign mercenaries in Italy, as well as toward those who hired them, permeates Azario's account. Although cognizant of the Visconti's flaws, Azario reluctantly looks to them as Lombardy's best hope for peace; and if not peace, then at least a defense against plundering mercenaries. Azario's ambivalence is revealed by his title "The book of the story of Lombardy and especially for and against the lords of Milan."

While dependent on Fiamma for the details pertaining to early members of the Visconti family, Azario is selective about what to include and what conveniently to omit. He begins his Milanese history with an account of how the della Torre, the Guelf magnates of Milan in the thirteenth century, were proud, raped pretty women, and, because they were dissatisfied with mere secular domination, usurped the power of the Church in Milan (III:15). The archbishop of Milan at this time was Ottone Visconti, who exceeded his successors in virtue, morals, eloquence, temperament, and perseverance (I:10). Matteo Visconti, who "saved" Milan from the della Torre, is described by Azario in almost Vergilian terms: He was an industrious youth, and of the greatest morality and virtue, big hearted, with a happy face, affable, benign, generous, and gregarious—we fully expect to see a jubilant Roman god spring from the pages (I:11).

Azario rarely dwells on the actions of the papacy, a rather astonishing omission, given the aggressiveness with which the papal legate Gil Albornoz pursued the Visconti lords, a campaign that Azario witnessed firsthand.[16] Unimpressed by most popes, he typically sums them up in a single sardonic sentence. For example, Pope John XXII was "the Servant of the Servant of God most wise and powerful . . . who sought to deprive the Visconti of all their power through sentences of excommunication" (IV:20). Azario views this as a temporal challenge to the Visconti and concludes that they were obligated to fight the papacy to defend their rule. Azario is no less critical of

15. For a modern account of the impact of these mercenaries on Italy, see William Caferro, *Mercenary Companies and the Decline of Siena* (Baltimore and London: Johns Hopkins University Press, 1998).

16. Azario was employed as notary by Giovanni d'Oleggio Visconti in Bologna. Some time after Giovanni betrayed his Visconti relatives, Azario changed employers, going to work for Galeazzo II Visconti.

intemperate leadership at the imperial level. He complains that Charles IV of Bohemia encouraged warfare between the lords of northern Italy and the Visconti. In Azario's view, both popes and emperors had failed Italy. They were shepherds who neglected their flocks and refused to "tune their lyres to one sound" (see Appendix B, conclusion).

Azario, like Fiamma, is careful to ascribe serious character or behavioral flaws only to rogue members of the Visconti family. He has a multitude of different uses for Marco Visconti, who, he says, exceeded his brothers in probity. Further, he was not fearful of war but rejoiced in going to war, for, sounding like Julius Caesar, that which was carried willingly was carried lightly. For Azario, fame was acquired not by fighting against *rusticos* (countryfolk) but rather against kings and princes while defending one's *patria et penates* (fatherland and household gods, whom the ancient Romans believed protected one's family) (IV:21). Azario uses this heretical epithet to explain that Marco and his brothers were defending their land and family against the tyranny of the pope. Thus Azario introduces a distinctly antique and pagan trope upon which he can construct his new Visconti mythology with little risk, for Marco is doomed to die.

Though suspicious of religion as a source of discord rather than salvation, Azario is quite moralizing. A husband and father of seven children, he is highly critical of men who move from bed to bed, frequently interrupting his historical account for a seeming digression about salacious activity by a dissolute Visconti. When Azario mentions someone's sex life, death is usually imminent. Eros and Thanatos are indivisible in these embedded morality plays, as the discussion of Marco Visconti's virtues and vices illustrates.

Azario says that Marco Visconti, the great soldier, was fierce, impatient, and ambitious, but his real flaw was that he was without a marriage bed, while he defiled many. And one night he died in his bed (VI:33). We know from other chroniclers that Marco was actually murdered by his family, tired of his repeated betrayals, but Azario is silent about these charges, saying he knows nothing about his death.[17] Moreover, in a lengthy aside he introduces Lodrisio, an illegitimate cousin, to whom he attributes traitorous deeds that Marco himself committed (VI:33–34). Marco was a flawed hero who had to die, but his death must be due to lust rather than betrayal.

Azario portrays Azzo's successor, Luchino Visconti, in heroic terms suggesting that, had he not exiled his nephews, Matteo, Bernabò, and Galeazzo,

---

17. Morigia, *Chronicon Modoetiense*, chap. XLII, for example, discusses Marco's betrayal of Galeazzo and his demise.

Luchino would have been honored as a saint ("posset sanctus Luchinus per omnes Mediolanenses titulari") by the Milanese (vii:46). Azario reprises Fiamma's notion of magnificence, using the verb *magnificare* to describe Luchino's architectural patronage, which subsidized the building of the church of San Giovanni in Conca, as well as a palatial house with many towers and a bridge of ten *braccia* connecting two buildings. Azario praises the public good that derived from castles built in towns like Vigevano. Luchino also had constructed a large wooden bridge across the Ticino river at Pavia, which, Azario marvels, was the longest and strongest wooden bridge ever built. The Pavese burnt it, an example of bad civic behavior in need of Visconti correction (vii:46).

If Azario glorifies the reign of Luchino, he tempers his praise of the archbishop Giovanni Visconti. Giovanni is portrayed as a skilled leader, trying to keep Italy from chaos caused by renewed papal interest in Italy and the disastrous arrival of the mercenary companies. Yet, Azario finds him too concerned with material things. Noting that Giovanni built a beautiful home, Azario observes that he spent enormous sums on the finest food and wine (viii:64). Azario may also have been especially critical of Giovanni for making his natural son Leonardo the podestà of Novara, Azario's hometown. The chronicler reports that Leonardo was both inept and weak and had been rejected as unfit to serve by the Novarese. Nonetheless, Leonardo served four terms as podestà during his father's lifetime (viii:65).

Upon Giovanni Visconti's death, in 1354, Charles IV named the Visconti nephews as vicars-general of Milan, but he transferred the vicariates of Novara and Pavia to the marquis of Monferrato. Azario's laconic commentary is unflinching: "And thus the invincible Charles, king of the Romans and always august in Germany, made massive errors of judgment in Lombardy so that Lombardy would be cruelly lacerated and devastated by wounds" (ix:74).

Most of Azario's chronicle is devoted to warfare, the dominant condition of northern Italy in his lifetime. He recounts at some length the protracted warfare over Bologna, which he finally dismisses as not worth the struggle (viii:53). But concerning war close to home, in Novara, Azario cannot be objective. He is prolix in his discussion of its history because, as he says proudly, "I am a notary from Novara" [ego notarius sum novariensis] (ix:92). While Novara suffered at the hands of both the marquis of Monferrato and Galeazzo II Visconti, Azario's account of their struggle for the city reveals why he was a Visconti partisan, if a reluctant one. He harshly condemns the Visconti-appointed podestà and vicar for imprisoning large numbers of Novarese and transferring much of the professional class and intelligentsia to Milan and Pavia (IX:108). And the financial toll of Visconti lordship on the city was devastating and personally known to Azario. He says, "I know that in the time of the said podestà Giovanni [Pirovano],[18] over one hundred thousand florins were extracted from the city and district of Novara for the lord of Milan; the tax on bottled wine that year counted at nineteen thousand imperial pounds" (IX:109).[19] Despite these Visconti exactions, Azario condemns the marquis of Monferrato for hiring two thousand mercenaries who raped women and robbed with impunity. These mercenaries were partly paid by Pope Innocent VI, a fact alluded to by Azario, who notes that the English company was led from Avignon to Lombardy by the marquis of Monferrato (IX:110).[20] Papally dispatched or not, these mercenaries, in Azario's view, were a plague of locusts destroying Italy. But the story does not end here. In order to eliminate the "perfidy" of the English company from Novara, Galeazzo Visconti burnt down numerous towns in the district so that the company would have no place to hide and no villages to plunder. It was a Pyrrhic victory: The Novarese defeated the company, but "Novara was buried by devastation and imprisoned by injustice."[21]

Lest we think that Novara was an isolated situation or that only the mercenary companies were to blame for Italy's misfortune, Azario turns first to a short comment on Pope Innocent VI, who "devastated the Curia" (IX:112), and then to an account of the Visconti struggle for Pavia. His discussion of this city is emblematic of his pessimistic view that the highly imperfect Visconti might bring peace to Italy by military dominance that would lead, he hopes, to law and order in this treacherous landscape. Most important to Azario, the Visconti could repel mercenary armies.

18. The podestà was a chief magistrate, appointed for a fixed short term, usually six months. He was usually a nobleman from another city and thus relatively detached from local affairs, a condition meant to encourage impartiality. Appointing the podestà was one of the most important means of asserting Visconti control over a city. See Jane W. Black, "The Limits of Ducal Authority: A Fifteenth-Century Treatise on the Visconti and Their Subject Cities," in *Florence and Italy: Renaissance Studies in Honour of Nicolai Rubinstein*, ed. Peter Denley and Caroline Elam (London: Westfield College, 1988), 154. Giovanni Pirovano was the second Visconti podestà in Novara, succeeding Ottino de Marillano, whom Azario harshly criticized earlier.

19. Azario tells us that he was serving as chancellor to the podestà and a judge of the *dazio* (direct tax). Thus he was perfectly situated to calculate the financial toll on the city that Visconti control entailed.

20. A document substantiates Azario's suspicions: On 23 October 1358, a payment of one thousand florins was made by the papacy to the Great Company. Archivio Secreto Vaticano, *Inst. Misc.* 2139.

21. Azario, *Liber Gestorum in Lombardia*, IX:112: "Et sic Novaria ducta est a lacubus infra in eclipsin, et a lacubus supra de justicia nulla respondetur civitati."

Azario begins his discussion of Pavian history by declaring *Papia parum pia dicta fuit,* an epithet that he repeats several times (IX:112). (This ambiguous phrase can mean that Pavia either was said to have little piety or denoted little piety.) The word "Pavia" etymologically derives from a historical condition, lack of piety, that Azario both accepts and condemns in his own time, establishing a model of Pavese decadence that the Visconti would be obliged to reverse through conquest.[22] Azario finds much to criticize in Pavia. Their Beccaria lords were corrupt, beset by some unspoken scandal. They betrayed both the Visconti and their own Ghibelline faction, and they were inconsistent, as they lurched between the Visconti and the marquis of Monferrato and then back again (IX:116–17). Most despicably, they fled Pavia without fighting when challenged (IX:121).

In stark contrast to the dynasty of rational lordship that he has shaped for the Visconti, Azario points to the corruption and cowardice of the Beccaria family in Pavia as the reason for their failure and the concomitant rise to power of Jacopo Bussolari, a fiery Augustinian Hermit who was the de facto ruler of the city between 1356 and 1359.[23]

The chronicles of the Florentine Matteo Villani and the Lombard Pietro Azario provide a telling contrast in recounting the story of Jacopo Bussolari. Tailoring their accounts to fit disparate political models, these chroniclers respectively heroize and vilify their subject. In a well-known prologue to his *Cronica,* Villani presents Bussolari as an exemplar of the power of eloquence. He opines that the armies of the most powerful lord who lacks the

22. The evilness of the Pavese seems to be something of a trope. Even early biographies of Archbishop Lanfranc of Pavia, who died in 1194, cite the corruption of the city. Gualtiero Tacchini, *San Lanfranco Beccari: Vescovo di Pavia, 1180–1198* (Pavia: Giovane Artigiano, 1998), 22. Carlo Magenta frames instances of Pavese defiance of the papacy as assertions of independence. Magenta, *I Visconti e gli Sforza nel Castello di Pavia* (Milan: Hoepli, 1883), vol. 1, pt. 2, 11 n. 5.

23. Bussolari was an Augustinian friar. The formal name of the order was the Hermits of Saint Augustine. Thus its members were called Hermits. Bussolari is known almost entirely from secondary sources; none of his writings or sermons survive. A handful of contemporary documents, mostly in the registers of his order and of the papacy, trace his career. He is first documented in 1341. See Giacinto Romano, "Eremitani e canonici regolari in Pavia nel secolo XI e loro attinenze con la storia cittadina," *Archivio storico lombardo* 4 (1895): 39. Four contemporary chroniclers, including Azario and Matteo Villani, have defined the image of Bussolari. Each portrait is shaped by its author's particular political bias. Modern historians are similarly afflicted, so that Bussolari is hailed (or reviled) as a democrat, republican, demagogue, or, most inventively, proto-anti-Fascist. Carlo Magenta, for example, compares him to Savonarola. Magenta, *I Visconti e gli Sforza nel Castello di Pavia,* 1:63. Giancarlo Ceriotti, "Interpretazione storica di Fra Jacopo Bussolaro," *Bollettino della Società pavese di storia patria* 24 (1972): 3–34, is the most complete modern account.

virtue of eloquence might be more than matched by a less powerful prince blessed with "noble eloquence." Citing the examples of Alexander the Great and Scipio, Villani suggests that despite being outnumbered, they were militarily successful due to their extraordinary oratory.[24] With these grand antecedents, Villani introduces Bussolari, the son of a barrel maker and now a simple friar, who inspires the Pavese to defeat a large Visconti navy and establishes a republic in Pavia.

In contrast, Pietro Azario, his opinions shaped by Lombard patterns of seignorial government, portrays Bussolari as a pious and articulate Hermit who went mad with power, forgot his true calling, and led Pavia to misery and privation in his misguided quest for temporal power. Exhorting his fellow Pavese with examples of heroism from Roman history, Bussolari convinced them that it was preferable to die for one's *patria* than to be reduced to weakness by an alien force (ix:120). Azario tacitly draws a telling comparison with the cowardly Beccaria, who would soon flee in shame. The model also recalls his own account of the brave Visconti of the 1320s, who could, in his construct, legitimately look back to Roman examples because they were part of the family heritage. Bussolari was, by contrast, a demagogue, a mere commoner and a friar no less, who was misappropriating a Roman model.

Azario portrays the Pavese as twice betrayed: first by Bussolari, who convinced them to sell their worldly goods to pay mercenaries to resist the Milanese, and then by the marquis of Monferrato, who seized the money for himself (ix:123). The Visconti masterfully exploited the situation: after signing a peace treaty with the marquis of Monferrato in 1358, they successfully invaded the city the next year. But Azario does not depict the Visconti as violators of the peace treaty. Instead, Bussolari bears the burden for the invasion. The Pavese women resembled "beguines" in their somber black dresses and privation. Moreover, Bussolari forbade married couples to have sex, and pregnant women had to hide from his view (ix:123–24). Previously in Azario's chronicle, extramarital sex signaled an individual's demise. Apparently, interfering with marital sex was equally risky. Azario introduces Bussolari as a most excellent preacher (*excelentissimus predicator*). Then he calls him an evildoer (*maleficus*). In the end Bussolari is the diabolical friar (*diabolicus Frater*), "for what else can be said of one who not only caused thousands of men to die but also caused vast numbers of children not to be born" (ix:126). After the Pavese surrendered to Galeazzo II Visconti, Bussolari was dispatched to prison in Vercelli.

24. Villani, *Cronica*, bk. 8, chap. 1 (2:135).

Azario is most critical as well of the marquis of Monferrato, who had hired the mercenary army of the count of Landau to "depopulate the city of Milan" (IX:78) and was arranging to bring these same mercenaries to Pavia. Azario condemns them as *Alamanni,* that is, Germans, who "came out of love not for the Lombards or Lombardy but for the Lombard florin, and these they acquired and stole, stealing from rich as from poor" (IX:80). Azario thus tempers Visconti aggression by condemning the treachery and duplicity of their enemies. He particularly notes the marquis of Monferrato's opportunism, shifting allegiances repeatedly as a means of exerting his own power over Pavia. Inconsistency and betrayal, in Azario's view, should be defeated, as should anyone unleashing foreign mercenaries on Italy.

Azario writes with a mixture of awe and disgust about Galeazzo's immediate construction of a new *castello* (castle) in Pavia, whose height, size, and thick walls could only be described as *mirabilia* (marvels) (XII:166–67). Thus, Azario reintroduces Fiamma's concept of magnificence as a princely virtue. But rather than emphasize the public good that might obtain from extravagant private splendor, such magnificence had apotropaic powers, meant to repel evil. The impervious castle would be an emblem of Visconti authority, power, and stability. Yet, Pavia would see more hardship when plague appeared in the city and devastated the population. Were this not enough, the marquis of Monferrato led the English company to the territory between Tortona and Pavia. They pillaged, as was customary, to which the Visconti responded with more soldiers, as was also customary (IX:128). And the endless warfare ground on.

While Fiamma's chronicle optimistically praises the emerging Visconti domination of Lombardy, Azario has a more temperate and nuanced view of his Visconti lords: They are far from perfect, but their opponents are much worse. Fiamma ends his chronicle with a celebration of the "natural dignity" of Visconti lordship over Lombardy (XXVIII:45). Azario, in contrast, closes his chronicle with heartrending anguish. Writing from Tortona, he is overcome by grief and desperation. Fleeing plague with his sons, Azario leaves his wife and daughters behind. He soon learns that his wife and a daughter have perished. Fearing both plague and the mercenary armies surrounding the city, Azario is immobilized by his own fear and by the blockade of his city. He cannot rescue his abandoned children. He says he is tormented and knows that the dangers of hell will find him (see Appendix B). Yet Azario's chronicle suggests that hell could not be much worse than Lombardy in the middle of the fourteenth century. While the idyllic kingdom of Aeneas was a worthy model to which Italy might strive, the troubled Lombard chronicler harbored few illusions. Italy in Azario's day could look for salvation only to tyrants strong enough to dominate other, worse tyrants, dangerous popes, and their more dangerous mercenaries.

APPENDIX A: GALVANO FIAMMA, *THE HISTORY OF AZZO, LUCHINO, AND GIOVANNI VISCONTI*[25]

VIIII. On the magnificence of Giovanni Visconti, bishop of Novara [11]

In the year of Christ 1333. His eminence John XXII was on the apostolic throne. Brother Aicardo was installed as the archbishop of Milan, where Lanfranco Mussi of Novara had been podestà . . . for half a year. Subsequently the podestà was Zanto Fieschi of Genoa. At this time, after Giovanni Visconti had been made bishop of Novara, he entered the city of Novara and personally seized Cazino di Torniello, the lord of the city, and put him in prison and thus obtained the lordship of the city, both temporal and spiritual, where he erected an exceedingly strong fortress and restored the city and the *contado,* long abused by the Church.

When Pope John heard that Cazino di Torniello, a declared enemy of the Church, had been captured and that the city had begun to return to the rule of the Church, he was very pleased and appointed the aforementioned Giovanni, bishop of Novara, as conservator of the archbishopric of Milan, so that when he took control of the temporalities of the archdiocese, he would provide an annual pension of fifteen hundred florins to Brother Aicardo, the archbishop of Milan.[26] Moreover, he himself, having followed in the footsteps of his [great-] uncle, Archbishop Ottone Visconti, restored the city of Milan to the Church, with all of his vigor: he recovered revenues that had been lost, rebuilt archiepiscopal palaces, homes, and halls, built two new palaces that faced each other on a square cloister of the archiepiscopal courtyard. In the countryside he built halls, homes, and palaces throughout the lands of the archbishopric. This Giovanni, the bishop of Novara, was magnificent, more than is possible to be believed, in households, chapels, horsemen, servants, falcons, hawks, and sparrow hawks in the greatest quantity, and in other diverse furnishings of food and clothing. There was not a

25. Fiamma, *Opusculum.* The number in brackets following each chapter title indicates the page number from the Castiglioni edition.

26. Aicardo, while serving as an inquisitor, had been responsible for excommunicating several Visconti in the 1320s. Despite the financial inducement, Aicardo did not leave the see. Giovanni succeeded to it only in 1342, three years after Aicardo's death, in 1339.

prelate so glorious in Italy or even in the College of Cardinals. He conducted himself well in divine matters, honored religious persons, loved justice and fairness. He won over many heretics to the service of faith. He stood out as one who gives alms to the poor.

XII. The legate of the Church was expelled from Italy [13]

Beltrand of Ostia, the episcopal legate of Italy, who was then in Bologna, lamented when he heard about the massacre of his own people, and blamed the whole matter on the Milanese, and sent letters that agitated the mind of the pope against Azzo Visconti. A little later, on the day of 17 September, the citizens of Bologna rebelled against their own lord, the legate himself, with the help of Rainaldo, the marquis of Este. Then it was proclaimed, "Let us kill the legate who exposed the people of Bologna to so many dangers." And they besieged the legate in his fortress, attacking with missiles and fire for ten days; at last, driven by hunger, the legate abandoned his fortress. Then they eviscerated a certain Bolognese, who was a member of the legate's household. They threw his limbs to the dogs. They robbed chaplains and prelates and inflicted various torments on them. They ejected the legate with insults, on account of which they incurred the charge of lèse-majesté from the apostolic see. For this reason, the pope placed the city of Bologna under ecclesiastical interdict, and he excommunicated the guilty persons by name, closed the university, suspended all privileges, either papal or imperial. He suspended all judges, notaries, and other officials from any legal activity, notwithstanding whatever privileges and indulgences had been conceded to Cistercians, Preachers, or Friars Minor. Liable to all these sentences as well was Rainaldo, the marquis of Este, with all of his supporters. This year, on the twenty-third day of November, Giovanni Grassi left Cantù, attacked the city of Como at noon, where he carried out several armed attacks from ambush in fields of cabbage. Nevertheless, the city could not be overcome.

XIV. Benedict XII becomes pope [15]

The same year of 1335, Pope John, who spent on the church twenty-three million florins, not to mention other treasures, died in Avignon on the day of 12 December. Nor did the world have a richer Christian. He retracted his opinion of the beatific vision as was stated above.[27] Then the cardinals in

27. John XXII asserted that before the resurrection of the flesh, the souls of the just would not see God or the "beatific vision." For the papacy this was a major controversy that the pope tried to defuse by indicating he had only been speaking as a private theologian. The best work on the subject remains Marc Dykmans, ed., *Les sermons de Jean XXII sur la vision béatifique*, Miscellanea Historiae Pontificiae, 34 (Rome: Gregorian University Press,

conclave on 16 December elected Benedict XII of the Cistercian order as pope. If anyone wishes to know this Pope Benedict and his qualities, let him look in contrast to the nature of his predecessor, John, because that pope, John, was small and lean in body; this pope was large, obese in neck and all his limbs, so that his appearance was horrible. That one ate and drank sparingly; this one was a great eater and egregious drinker. That one was gracious in granting favors, was benevolent beyond measure; this one was very cruel. He withheld, moreover, 380 episcopal benefices [keeping the revenue for the Curia], and so he was not the pastor of churches but their destroyer.

John was altogether a very rapid expeditor of business; Benedict never expedited business, [but was] a man of whom it could be said he did nothing more right than to die but ruled [as pope] for six years, four months, and four days. He died in the year of our Lord 1342, on the feast day of Saint Mark, and the papal throne was vacant for thirteen days. Then Azzo Visconti, wishing to show himself as a son of the Church, sent a noble embassy to the Curia, among whom was Friar Lanfranco of the order of Hermits [of Saint Augustine], of the Settala [family] and a master, licensed at the University of Paris. The pope received them with honor. Then Guidolo di Calice, the syndic and procurator of the city of Milan, swore in the presence of the pope, on the part of Azzo Visconti, lord of the city of Milan, and on the part of the community, to preserve a treaty made between the pope and the city of Milan, which has been mentioned above. And in this vein, he sought absolution in this way: "If the pact shall have been preserved until the feast of All Saints, Pope Benedict absolves the Visconti, the clergy, the commune, and the population of the city and district from all lawsuits, penalties, sentences of law or of man and from interdiction. Otherwise, if [the pact is] not preserved, everything is void, invalid, and null and will be considered completely unfinished. In the same year, around the feast of All Saints, the syndic of the city went to the Curia and solemnly ratified everything mentioned above, that is, the treaty, the deeds done, what had been promised, and the oaths, and he gave his approval, and then the interdict was removed.[28]

1973). The pope only partially recanted this belief on his deathbed. See G[uillaume] Mollat, *The Popes at Avignon, 1305–1378*, trans. Janet Love from the 9th French ed. (London: Thomas Nelson & Sons, 1963), 22–23.

28. In fact, not until 1341 was the interdict permanently lifted from Ghibelline cities that had supported Louis the Bavarian. Fiamma's hostile evaluation of Benedict XII is partially based upon the pope's refusal to reverse Azzo Visconti's excommunication, even after his death, in 1339.

XXXVIII. Concerning the two signs of the love of the people of Milan for Azzo Visconti [27]

From all of these difficult and terrible wars a very great fear arose in the city, and a very shameful flight took place. All the inhabitants of the outlying places and villages surrounding the city transferred themselves with all of their worldly goods within the walls of the city, and because there were no workers to run the mills, within three days prices in the city became high. I am not speaking of the price of grain but of flour, so a bushel of a mixture of flour and wheat sold for ten lire; there was no bread to be found for sale or for consumption.

Even in the city itself a terrible fear gripped the people. Nevertheless all prepared themselves for defense. Along with the regular soldiers, there were found in the city . . . noble young men who, without being compelled, of their own accord were ready and at their own expense produced as many great warhorses covered with noble caparisons.
They themselves also gleamed with sparkling armor from the soles of the feet up to their heads. For the honor and government of their lord they were prepared to risk the danger of death. On account of which this Azzo himself became greatly indebted to the people of Milan. For from this he proved that he was their lord not only in body but in mind, not only temporally but spiritually, an infallible sign of love.

Likewise the Milanese people demonstrated another sign of their love to their lord because when Lodrisio Visconti occupied our countryside with all his might and with great bravery for twelve days, no citizen of Milan, neither brother nor cousin, neither Ghibelline or Guelf, neither lowly or great, went over to his side, nor did they lend him aid or favor or counsel, but all to a man took up arms against him and fought bravely to maintain the rule of their lord. Nothing like this has been heard of for generations, because, if any enemy would have occupied our *contado* for even three days, many of our citizens would have gone over to him. And by this sign of love similarly was Azzo Visconti able to prove himself to be the lord of their souls.

APPENDIX B: PIETRO AZARIO, *HISTORY OF LOMBARDY* [29]

VII. Luchino and Giovanni Visconti [36–39]

Moreover, Luchino Visconti together with his brother Lord Giovanni, then bishop of Novara and lord general of the city itself, sons of the aforementioned

---

29. Azario, *Liber Gestorum in Lombardia*. The number in brackets following each chapter title indicates the page number(s) from the Cognasso edition.

late lord Matteo, held the lordship of Milan in common.[30] This Luchino governed with moderation the aforementioned cities, apart from Novara and those recently acquired.

He feared an uprising against his lordship, since until then the aforementioned Lord Luchino had led a prodigal life, associating with evil people rather than with good people and sleeping for the most part during the day and staying awake at night. And he had taken as a wife one of the Spinola, whom he was said to love greatly because she was young and because he contrasted her with his wife from his first marriage.

She having died, he married her ladyship Elizabeth Fieschi, who was a maiden stately and beautiful, sister of Giovanni Fieschi, who had earlier died. And from this wife he had a son, also named Luchino, and a daughter, Orsina. But he had several bastards, gotten from various women, who were named Bruzio, Foresto, and Borso, some of whom were notable for their ability, as will be narrated in its place.

In fact, he allowed the Milanese people to complain about the things mentioned before and others not mentioned regarding the authority that had been given to him. Thus he became eager to practice virtue and to favor good people, to the extent that he surpassed his other brothers in ruling. He favored, but silently, the Ghibellines. He reintegrated the state of Milan, to the extent that Milan came to be seen not as a city but as a province. He delighted in peace and loved impartial justice and showed that he cared for the lowly people and the many. First he reformed his household and ordered them to desist from their accustomed ways. He continued to maintain a great number of mercenaries, and it was said he always prospered from making war. He kept the territory that he had in such a peaceful state that one could travel anywhere at night as during the day and even in isolated places. Finally, he had such cunning that he absolved robbers and those accustomed to plundering of their deeds, and rewarded them with money so that they took care of those places they customarily harmed. In fact no fortress or man making war for himself could endure against him. He was a man of forceful appearance and deeds, liberal, sparing in his promises and generous in patience, and he never lost property once he had it. He loved only his children and cared little for his other relatives. He was intensely suspicious and never pardoned those whom he thought were harming him, nor did he trust them. That this is true is proved by a true example:

30. Giovanni and Luchino Visconti jointly ruled their territories from 1339 until 1349, the year of Luchino's death. Giovanni himself then ruled until he died, in 1354, to be succeeded by his nephews, Matteo II, Galeazzo II, and Bernabò.

The brothers Matteo, Bernabò, and Galeazzo, sons of the deceased lord Stefano and a noblewoman of the Doria clan of Genoa, their mother, were growing up. And while they were still young, they were handsome, and they considered they ought to rule Milan; and already one, namely Lord Matteo, had married Lady Ziliola, daughter of Filippino Gonzaga, lord of Mantua. [Luchino] hated them secretly, and finally it became necessary for him to act. He expelled his nephews from Milan and from his territory, and I believe that by the request of those lords of Mantua, the aforementioned Lord Matteo was not expelled from Lombardy but was sent to the territory of the marquis of Monferrato, that is to say, mainly in the vicinity of Morani.

On the other hand, the others, although younger, he expelled from Lombardy, and with such hatred did he persecute them that they found it necessary to flee to distant parts, settling in different areas apart from one another for two reasons: first, on account of their poverty and, second, because of the cleverness of their uncle, so that he would remain ignorant of where they had gone. Indeed, up to the day he died, he did not wish to hear anything good about them, and he hated their supporters as well.

Moreover, he bore grievous animus against the feudal nobility who had been in league with the aforementioned Azzo, and it was said that he did this on account of either of two reasons, either because they had consulted and agreed on the death of the aforementioned Marco, his brother, or, as narrated above, because during the rule of the lord Azzo he himself had few profitable positions and titles of authority. For the aforementioned lord Azzo trusted greatly his advisers, and with him they were made extremely wealthy. And for this reason Luchino treated these advisers badly, even though they were among the most powerful people of Milan.

And among these men was the lord Franceschetto Pusterla, who was richer and more fortunate than any other Lombard, as if worldly things can make a man truly happy. And that it was true you shall hear.

For he had taken as his wife the most beautiful and noble woman of Milan, very noble because she was a Visconti, and very beautiful because she was called Margarita, or pearl, and that was certainly a wonder. In lust there was no other person equal to him, to the degree that he used to arise from lunch and have intercourse with this Margarita. (He used to do the same when riding, if he had to dismount and have sex with prostitutes.) With this wife he had three male children more beautiful in appearance than anyone in the city of Milan, and if it had been otherwise, nature might have fallen short, because each of them, as much the man as the woman, was extraordinarily handsome and very beautiful. Moreover he had a very beautiful house in Milan and possessions and so much furniture that their amount cannot be established. Certainly he could be called another Job.

And because it is too long to narrate fully, let me finish briefly. The aforementioned lord Franceschetto was accused of plotting against Luchino, and certainly it could have been true, for it was said that his wife had been sought out by that lord Luchino, who wished to besmirch her noble birth by vile intercourse. For the aforementioned lord Luchino was very lustful, and what was more serious, on account of Franceschetto's hostility, which Luchino saw, he doubted the other's loyalty. And certainly if the aforementioned lord Franceschetto had completed the things that he planned, he would have succeeded easily; but because so many powerful citizens consented to this plot, it was inevitable that it be made public, and with bad results. For Luchino took many of them as prisoners, and they were immediately decapitated or died from starvation and other torture. Because it would take too long to tell, I will be silent about the whole story for now. However, the aforementioned Franceschetto fled and betook himself with many of his children to Avignon, but he was not permitted to live out his days in Avignon or in exile, and it was necessary for him to flee for his life elsewhere. For spies followed him, and what is true is that he was captured with two of his sons on the coast, north of the port of Pisa, and they were taken to Milan. Luchino accused many others, whose property he had seized and whom he executed, and finally he had Franceschetto decapitated along with his sons, so beautiful, and his kin in Broreto and anyone related, man or woman, and finally Margarita herself he murdered. For this Margarita was another Hecuba, as is read in the poem of the Trojans.[31] Finally, Luchino purged them with such obstinacy that I think the Milanese never dared to conspire against the Visconti again, especially because they are timid by nature.

X. Bernabò Visconti [133–35]

I now turn to Bernabò Visconti, the second brother of the three Visconti, the great and lofty lord of Milan and of other cities. I have already discussed his succession after the death of his brother Lord Matteo and also the division of the cities formerly under his rule. He had from the aforementioned wife Regina [della Scala] many children and mostly sons, the firstborn named Mark, who, it was said, in his early years never laughed. . . . "The deep voice of the lion roars through the desert": this quotation mystically associates the name and the words of the Evangelist Mark.

---

31. Hecuba was the wife of King Priam, to whom she bore nineteen children, including Paris and Hector.

The lord Bernabò is a genuine lord, a lover of justice, constant, impatient, and extremely virtuous, but nevertheless sometimes strong willed. For he applies himself above all to run the government of his cities by his own efforts, and in difficult situations he possesses sound counsel. For he has always governed, and he governs his own cities and the other places by never losing them in some way. Even if by chance he loses a castle or a village or a town, he resolves immediately to recover what was lost, postponing everything else.

For he had in his part of Milan the house that was constructed by Luchino Visconti next to San Giovanni in Conca, as has been described above, which house and church he embellished very greatly. In fact, he enlarged the house itself beyond the limits of the first walls, in a great space with strong crenellated walls about twenty-five *braccia* high, and constructed within the walls a courtyard where his mercenaries could exercise their mounts.

He constructed a stable for his horses, for he had a large number of horses within the new walls. That house was not a residence but seemed like a towering fortress, very strongly built with multiple gates and many courtyards. He decorated that church with walls, chapels, paintings, and altars, and especially the high altar, and above that high altar, I declare, on the altar itself, he placed a likeness of himself in armor, as for war, sculpted in marble stone, and very appropriately he was depicted with the scepter of dominion in his hand, and supporting the side were sculpted two maidens, namely Justice and Fortitude, and this was because he adheres to the aforementioned virtues in exercising power [and] against which virtues it can be said that he does not act unless they hinder his power. For he took pains to recover the lands that had been lost by his magnificent brother lord Matteo, with the greatest effort, paying no attention to the expense.

He also took pains to make peace if he were able with the aforementioned Giovanni d'Oleggio, who had taken over the government of the city of Bologna, as I have said above, that was earlier acquired by Lord Giovanni the archbishop. Since peace had been promised, he endeavored to be at peace with Giovanni d'Oleggio;[32] to keep the peace he restored to that lord

---

32. Giovanni d'Oleggio had been the Visconti captain in Bologna. Taking advantage of the archbishop Giovanni's death, in 1354, he rebelled against Visconti control. For Giovanni d'Oleggio, see Azario, *Liber Gestorum in Lombardia*, 56, and Villani, *Cronica*, bk. 5, chap. 5 (1:612–13), and bk. 5, chap. 12 (1:619–23). The former suggests ("plures credebant suum esse filium") and the latter asserts that he was a son of Giovanni. He was, in fact, the son of Filippo Visconti, as is made clear in a long missive by Urban V regarding the Visconti in which Giovanni d'Oleggio is referred to as "Johannes quondam Philippi de Vicecomitibus de Oleggio nati militis Novariensis"; Archivio Secreto Vaticano Reg. Vat. 261, fols. 71v–75r. On this period, see as well Partner, *Lands of St. Peter*, 346–47.

Giovanni d'Oleggio the fortress of Bazzano, which he had occupied against the will of Lord Giovanni himself, and then both of them began at this time to be on friendly terms. And in order that the aforementioned lord Bernabò might be assured of his loyalty, he appointed as podestà of Bologna Lord Guglielmo degli Arimondi, a doctor of laws from Parma who, for a long time, had been the vicar-general of the lord archbishop Giovanni. When Lord Guglielmo ruled Bologna as podestà, he began treating well and according to their rank the servants of the household of the aforementioned Bernabò when they came to Bologna.

Now, the lord Bernabò legally held the territory of Lugo in the middle of Romagna. For this reason he had often sent to Bologna his servants, acting as officials and sometimes collectors and heads of the household, who for recreation would remain many days in Bologna. And while all this was happening, the lord Giovanni d'Oleggio, who was still the lord general in Bologna, like a clever and vigilant snake, thought that his own officials might be tempted to defect to Milan and feared that he would be betrayed as he had betrayed others. So one day he was not able to resist the bad plans he had conceived, and he thought to do that which would make him more feared and seem more astute. And thus captivated by his own cleverness, he armed his mercenary soldiers, and he arrested lord Guglielmo, the podestà of Bologna, and Duke Enrico, the son of the former lord Castruccio [Castracane] of Lucca, and Benno di Valgrana, a servant of that lord Bernabò and some others, and he immediately imprisoned them and subjected them to torture so that they would write in their confession what he wished. Thereafter, in the piazza of Bologna, he had them decapitated in public as traitors on the eighth day of February 1356, no other judge being present. He had tortured and decapitated certain others, and especially one [who was] his own ex-chancellor, from whom he obtained all of the aforementioned confessions. It was horrible to lose in such a way such a nobleman as Lord Enrico, who was unable to defend himself. Now, since the aforementioned lord Castruccio had dominated many cities, he was known as and was the head of the Ghibelline party in Tuscany, so that the aforementioned lord Giovanni d'Oleggio had to proceed carefully with these executions. The executions and indeed others worse did not help his cause. On the contrary, how much thence was he able to gain boasting more of unjust deeds than being silent, so that he terrified the Bolognese and his allies even more? Moreover, the aforementioned lord Bernabò was pained by these executions, and until his death he mourned the loss of so noble a man, Lord Enrico, his bodyguard and his ally. He mourned also for the podestà, such an old sage and long in loyal service to house of the Visconti, and for his most loyal servant. Then taking a breath and putting aside everything else, he set his mind to recovering Bologna, which formerly belonged to him, and, more, to avenging the death of his officials.

Conclusion [177]

The pains of death surrounded me and the dangers of hell found me. I, Pietro Azario, the aforementioned notary, was anchored in my agony and saw the ship of Peter lacking oarsman and sailor and tossing in the deep, and moreover it was battered in the midst of its perils, especially in parts of Italy and chiefly Lombardy. This was happening all the more through the failure of the two shepherds who tended their flocks badly and did not seek to tune their lyres to one sound. And as if without hope, I had to express my grief in order that I might derive from it the blessing of health, by writing for the sake of relief, [that] the sting of pain might be removed, but it has been of no use to me because a chronic disease has not a cure.

Alas, by what grief and anxieties was my soul crucified! What physical pain did I bear because of the unspeakable things I have heard and seen! And also these dead from the plague and the persistence of bad decisions coming together at the same time! No remedy has been given for these things by the aforementioned bad shepherds or by a doctor in order that Lombardy might undertake sane or healthy remedies in the midst of these bad deeds, fires, destruction, and murder. Which wickedness prevailed like a disease to the extent that the human race in the regions of Lombardy, as it were, weakened and perished.

Remaining moreover in the office of notary in Tortona, as described herein, I was surrounded by the pains of death. When I was leaving Borgomanero, where I had to prolong my stay with my family, since stones had been placed before the gate of the city, I saw my son Ambrogio, seven years old, die. Then, with the three other sons, to wit Filippo, Jacopo, and Giovanni, the older ones, I escaped from the city and fled the plague. I left behind in my house my wife, Franceschina, the daughter of the late Ardicino da Fossato, with a very young daughter named Antonia, four months old, and Caterina, three years old, and Giovannina, nine years old, whom I was not able to take with me, since I did not know where I was going, first because of the plague now spreading from that place and second because of the aforementioned English [company], who were then residing in the territory of Cavali.

Having seen these things, I fled with those whom I could and left my wife and daughters under the protection of Jesus Christ. Soon I was informed in Tortona that my wife and my daughter Caterina had perished and the other girls, the baby and the older, were without any assistance or a nurse. I neither could nor dared help them, because of the plague and because of the strife of the present war that even now encircles Tortona. Because of that, the dangers of hell found me, and because of accursed letters sent and received, I was crucified with fear, since, according to rumor, four times that week the city was agitated by the depraved English company's doing such things that any inhabitant of Tortona had to fear for his safety, and many times I could not believe what I heard.

Moreover, in the city itself it was impossible to restore order for many reasons. There were shortages of everything, not only food but clothing. Because of this, this stay in Tortona was hell on earth. Thinking about what I have recounted and other, similar things that have happened elsewhere, I have thought it best to take the advice of the Psalmist, "I will grieve with those who are grieving and rejoice with those who are rejoicing." If, more-over, what is written above should prove to be defective, let the hand of the corrector amend it. Written in the Fifteenth Indiction,[33] in the month of November 1362. Therefore, I, Pietro Azario, son of the deceased lord Gia-como Azario, notary of Novara by public authority, while I was in the city Tortona a judge of the *dacita*,[34] in the said city also chancellor of the noble lord Giovanni Pirovano, honored as podestà of the city of Tortona for the magnificent and exalted lord Galeazzo Visconti of Milan, the imperial vicar-general, have compiled and written about these events that took place at var-ious times, and in witness of what I have written, I have affixed my usual seal.

33. An indiction is a fiscal period of fifteen years. Public documents in Italy were often dated both from the year of the birth of Christ and by the year of the indiction.
34. That is, a judge in settling inheritances.

8

Venetian History and Patrician Chroniclers

John Melville-Jones

Just as Venice, glittering serenely on myriad islands, is a city like no other, its chronicle tradition too is distinctive and unusually rich. Venetians believed that their city, established on a lagoon in the Adriatic, was independent of the medieval Christian empire, that it was founded by noble exiles from Troy, and that its future greatness was foretold to Saint Mark. Moreover, as a result of a Venetian-dominated conquest of Constantinople in the Fourth Crusade, Venice acquired a maritime empire, fundamentally altering the Mediterranean world.[1] Its earliest historians sought to explain Venice's unique position in Christian Europe and justify its maritime hegemony.

The oldest of these chronicles, which celebrates the emergence of the unique Venetian culture in the lagoons of the northern Adriatic, is attributed to John the Deacon (Giovanni Diacono). Along with other early accounts, the chronicle of Grado (*Chronicon Gradense*) and the chronicle of Altino (*Chronicon Altinense*), which focus on the neighboring coastal cities of Grado and Altino, John the Deacon's chronicle marks the emergence of the Venetian commune by crafting a distinctive early history. These foundation myths reach back to the Lombard conquests in the seventh century, to the devastations wrought by the Huns in successive invasions in the fifth century, or even to the mythical arrival of exiles from the East after the conquest of Troy by the Greeks.[2]

Later chronicles differ in both form and content. Writers of the numerous

---

1. Thomas Madden, *Enrico Dandolo and the Rise of Venice* (Baltimore and London: Johns Hopkins University Press, 2002), 195–200.
2. An excellent synopsis of this aspect of the chronicles is to be found in an article by Gina Fasoli, "I fondamenti della storiografia veneziana," in *La storiografia veneziana fino al secolo XVI: Aspetti e problemi*, ed. Agostino Pertusi (Florence: L. S. Olschki, 1970), 11–44.

minor chronicles honored the ancient history of the Venetian Republic but did so in a way that emphasized the political role of the patrician families. As James Grubb has noted, Venetian chroniclers "established the history of Venice as the cumulative deeds of the city's nobles."[3] Their histories were usually not written in Latin, but in *volgare* (the vernacular). Often copied into elegant volumes and decorated with family crests, they were meant to be material demonstrations of a family's preeminence. The chronicle of Antonio Morosini, whose codex is the focus of this chapter, synthesized both these traditions. Taking full advantage of the rich Venetian chronicle tradition, Morosini liberally copied from earlier accounts, but he also crafted a version of history that emphasized the accomplishments of the patrician class, of which he was a part.

The general circumstances that led to the writing of chronicles in Venice and the Veneto were much the same as elsewhere, but the Venetian chronicles share certain distinctive elements. In the first place, Venetians could take pride in the city's rise to prominence, but compared to many other towns, Venice was a fairly young city. Padua, Treviso, Grado, or Aquileia, or, further afield, Ravenna, Florence, and Milan—all could claim a longer history and a more prestigious Roman heritage. Many Italian cities claimed to have been settled by refugees who fled Troy after its destruction by the Greeks. Rome is the obvious model. The poet Virgil's great epic, the *Aeneid*, recounts the story of Aeneas, who settled along the coast near Rome and whose descendants eventually founded the city. A Trojan pedigree was quite common in the late Middles Ages. London and Paris both have Trojan foundation myths. Indeed, some German families still claimed Trojan ancestors in the sixteenth century. Several Venetian chronicles begin with the legendary arrival of Trojans in the Veneto. If Venetians could not claim foundation by a specific Trojan, as did the Paduans, who claimed Antenor as their founder, at least they could associate themselves generally with the Trojan myth.

The Genoese created a respectable antiquity for their city in a similar manner. A Genoese chronicler of the later thirteenth century, Jacobus de Voragine, used the medieval Latin form of his city's name, Ianua, as the basis of a claim that Genoa had been founded by the Roman deity Janus (who, as he then delightfully declared, was actually the biblical patriarch Noah). Genoa, unlike Venice, had been a port of some importance in Roman times,

---

3. James Grubb, "Memory and Identity: Why Venetians Didn't Keep Ricordanze," *Renaissance Studies* 8 (1994): 377.

so the invention of an early history was not imperative, but it demonstrates the importance of an ancient lineage to the historians of both cities.

Alternatively, Venetian chroniclers might link the city with Saint Mark, its patron saint. This approach was followed by one of the greatest Venetian chroniclers, Andrea Dandolo (doge, 1343–54). His work begins with Saint Mark's establishment of a bishopric at Aquileia. Chapters are then organized around the reigns of succeeding bishops, until the year 697, when Dandolo begins to divide his work according to the reigns of doges (leaders elected for life), beginning with that of Paulicius, which he presents as a decisive moment in the history of Venice.[4] This approach provided, as well, a needed Christian past for Venice. Rome was of course the city of Saints Peter and Paul. Milan was the city of a Church Father, Saint Ambrose. Dandolo recounts Saint Mark's founding of Aquileia and his revelation in dream of the founding of Venice and the construction of the church of San Marco. Thus Venice could claim a religious status similar to that of other great Italian cities.

The foundation of Venice on 25 March 421 c.e. is commonly recorded in the Venetian chronicles. On this date, refugees from the mainland escaping the invading forces of Attila the Hun supposedly established themselves on the islands at a site called Rivo Alto (the present Rialto district of Venice). In fact, Attila was not the first northern invader to chase mainlanders into refuges offshore; and whatever settlement took place there in the late fourth and fifth centuries was of a very insubstantial and impermanent nature.

No exact foundation date can be established for Venice. By 639, however, the islands must have had a larger population than originally, because the church of Santa Maria at Torcello was established by a certain Isaac, the reigning exarch, or imperial vicar. The emperor in Constantinople at that time was Heraclius, and a tradition is repeated by later Venetian chroniclers that the emperor gave the city of Grado a most marvelous gift, the throne of Saint Mark. Later writers appreciated this story, since after the eighth century Grado replaced Aquileia as the most important center of the cult of Saint Mark. How much of this story is sheer invention is not known, and no such throne exists today at Grado. Foundation tales of this kind are not uncommon in Venetian chronicles, and their existence makes clear the desire for religious status that particularly characterized eleventh- and twelfth-century cities.

---

4. Paulicius was not truly a dux but rather an exarch, an imperial officer ruling on behalf of the Roman emperor in Constantinople. It was convenient for the Venetians to blur the distinction, in order to portray themselves as an independent community as early as possible.

Venetian chronicles of the thirteenth century begin to reflect a wider and more complex world.[5] For example, the *Historia Ducum Venetorum* anachronistically celebrates the eminence of the Venetian doges precisely at the time when the doge's power was being limited by communal institutions. Its author clearly intended to credit the doges with the transformation of Venice. The Venetian world had been expanded by the conquest of Constantinople in 1204 and the subsequent allocation of Crete and other parts of the Byzantine Empire to Venice. Venice was no longer merely an Italian power; its influence now extended throughout the Mediterranean.

It was against this background that one of the major Venetian chronicles, *Les estoires de Venise* (Histories of Venice), by Martino da Canal, was written. The chronicle covers the period up to 1275 and celebrates the beauty and wealth of Venice, emphasizing her prominence in the Christian and Mediterranean worlds. Martino began writing in 1267, an anxious time when Venice's status in Western Christendom was threatened. The writer is especially interested in telling the story of the expansion of Venetian power along the Dalmatian coast and its dramatic expansion into the Mediterranean. The Fourth Crusade and the story of the conquest of Constantinople by Western crusaders are the central events of this history. As a result of the capture of the capital of the Eastern Roman Empire, Venice came to dominate the trade of Constantinople and much of the eastern Mediterranean. Later, when the combined forces of the Byzantine Greeks and the Genoese navy retook the city, Venice found itself diplomatically and economically threatened. Martino's history celebrated Venice and underscored its role as a loyal supporter of the papacy and Western Christendom to justify its assertion of military and economic hegemony.

The Venetian empire is also at the center of the so-called *Chronica per extensum descripta* (Extended chronicle), by Doge Andrea Dandolo. This was a sequel to *Chronica brevis* (Brief chronicle), which he had composed before becoming doge in 1343. Dandolo's chronicle combines some traditional mythic tales (such as Saint Mark's missionary journey to the lagoons) with quotations from official documents, thus producing a narrative designed to create what one commentator has called an "authentic" or perhaps even an official history of Venice.[6] This is not unusual. Many of the major chronicles were known to and likely approved by Venice's rulers. Martino

5. Giorgio Cracco, "Il pensiero storico di fronte ai problemi del comune veneziano," in *La storiografia veneziana*, 45–74.

6. Girolamo Arnaldi, "Andrea Dandolo doge-cronista," in *La storiografia veneziana*, 133.

da Canal had also used records that could not have been seen without official approval.

Alongside Dandolo's semiofficial history and the other major chronicles that preceded and succeeded it, a lively and informal tradition of semiprivate chronicles evolved.[7] Many hundreds of minor chronicles, often copied from one another with modest variations, were written by members of noble families, sometimes embellished with a family crest. They can be organized to some extent by subject and style, but it is now virtually impossible to establish their sequence. It was obviously normal, perhaps even expected, that a Venetian noble family would create a chronicle by copying one or more existing chronicles with slight variations. The variations might be purely stylistic, giving the writer the feeling that he was creating an original text; or they might be designed to emphasize the history of the writer's own family or show events in as favorable a light as possible. To a great extent, the tradition was as much about celebrating a family as it was about celebrating the city. In general, the family chronicles concentrate on victories rather than defeats or natural disasters; if these are mentioned at all, they are passed over quickly.

The vibrant Venetian chronicle tradition is characterized by several important features. All authors whom we can identify (though most of the surviving manuscripts are anonymous) came from patrician families rather than from the general populace or the priesthood. In a process begun in 1297, social and political distinctions were sharply drawn in what is often called the *serrata* (the closing of the Grand Council).[8] Those who managed shops and served in government offices were defined as citizens and given limited political influence. Patricians were generally those who controlled the largest mercantile ventures and, most important, the only ones eligible to sit in the Grand Council or hold the highest administrative offices. Defining and maintaining status as a patrician family was a critical task in the fourteenth century. And possession of a family chronicle was one mark of patrician status.

Thus, in Venice, not only was chronicle writing suitable for the nobility, it became almost obligatory. Besides the chronicle of Andrea Dandolo, we

---

7. Antonio Carile, "Aspetti della cronachistica veneziana nei secoli XIII e XIV," in *La storiografia veneziana*, 75–126.

8. On the complex debate over the *serrata*, see Gerhard Rösch, "The Serrata of the Grand Council and Venetian Society, 1286–1323," in *Venice Reconsidered: The History and Civilization of an Italian City-State, 1297–1797*, ed. Dennis Romano and John Martin (Baltimore and London: Johns Hopkins University Press, 2000), 67–88.

also have one by Nicolò Trevisan, a governor of Crete and a procurator of the basilica of San Marco (the latter being an office reserved for those of the highest status). Another patrician chronicler was Gian Giacopo Caroldo, a member of the senate who became the secretary of the Council of Ten, the highest council of the republic. Antonio Morosini came from a family that produced more than one doge. These typify the sort of men who wrote chronicles at Venice.[9]

The Venetian chronicles were therefore primarily the products of a political upper class, intended to be read by members of that same class. There is nothing literary or humanistic about them; indeed, one of the reasons that they continued to be produced in the fifteenth and sixteenth centuries was probably that Renaissance humanism was slow to take root at Venice. For this reason, the emphasis of the chronicles is on action, military, political, and commercial, and on recording and justifying the activities of men from the patrician families of the city. Except for the earliest histories, the reigns of the doges provide the framework for their accounts of historical events. These are histories for politically involved men; the activities of women scarcely rate a mention.

The earliest chronicles were written in Latin. The first chronicle to depart from this practice was the chronicle of Martino da Canal (listing events up to 1275), which was written in French. The writer makes it clear that while he had considered writing in Latin or the Venetian *volgare,* he chose French because it was the most commonly understood language in Europe at that time. Andrea Dandolo, however, whose chronicle extends to 1280, used Latin. Nicolò Trevisan, who composed a chronicle extending to 1366, did write in the Venetian language. Nonetheless, for a considerable time, the vernacular did not displace Latin, the established language of formal communication. For example, the major chronicle written in the 1420s by Lorenzo de Monacis, a chancellor of Crete, still employed the Latin language.

The patrician texts frequently copy earlier chronicles, with minor omissions, additions, or changes of emphasis. Selective copying is normal in chronicle composition at Venice and elsewhere. The authors of these texts initially acted as copyists, but then made the work their own by selecting, by introducing additional material into the text, and by extending one or more existing chronicles chronologically.

This is the rich tradition within which Antonio Morosini created his codex,

---

9. A possible exception to this general rule is Martino da Canal, whose first name was not generally used by patrician families.

a combined chronicle and diary.[10] Morosini was a patrician whose brother Michele was doge in 1382. But apart from his will, he is known today only for the extensive chronicle that he wrote. Morosini was not a well-known public figure in Venice, and did not, so far as we know, figure in any major events, hold any public office, or engage in any major commercial ventures. He was born about 1365 and enrolled in the senate before he was twenty years old. As a member of one of Venice's leading families, Morosini was well placed to acquire information. The length of his work (561 folios written on both sides) and the fact that he was not a public figure and is known to us otherwise only from his will have suggested to some that he may have suffered a physical or mental infirmity that prevented him from taking part in public life and activities outside Venice. But this cannot be proved.

Morosini's work exemplifies the transition in Venetian historical consciousness from a focus on the Venetian commune to a celebration of the status of patrician families that dominated fourteenth- and fifteenth-century Venetian government. It is a combination of the traditional chronicle with a diary of the events of his own time. Although later historians of Venice knew the work and occasionally used it in the sixteenth century, the codex is not well known. It was eventually acquired by the eighteenth-century scholar-doge Marco Foscarini, but only after he had written his authoritative and influential book on Venetian literature, *Della letteratura veneziana* (1752). It is now held in the Austrian National Library, Vienna, together with a great deal of other material that was transferred there when Venice was ceded to Austria in 1797. It has been only partly published.[11]

---

10. A long-term project to publish the whole of this work in a dual English-Venetian text is now in progress; the first two volumes have appeared. Michele Pietro Ghezzo, John R. Melville-Jones, and Andrea Rizzi, eds., *The Morosini Codex*, vols. 1–2 (Padua: UniPress, 1999–2001). In addition, Andrea Nanetti is producing a critical edition in Venetian that should appear shortly.

11. Two French scholars, Germain Lefèvre-Pontalis and Lèon Dorez, printed a large number of extracts from Morosini's text, accompanied by translations into French, in a work entitled *Chronique d'Antonio Morosini: Extraits relatifs à l'histoire de France*, 4 vols. (Paris: Librairie Renouard, 1898–1902). The first three volumes contain the extracts they selected and the translations; the fourth volume contains a number of essays on the text and its history. As the title shows, the selection of extracts to be included was confined to material of interest to French readers, particularly those passages which reported the exploits of Joan of Arc. The proportion of the Morosini codex that was published in this way was about 15 to 20 percent. A few short extracts were included by Nicolae Jorga in his work *Notes et extraits pour servir à l'histoire des croisades au xve siècle* (Paris: E. Leroux, 1899–1902), and many other historians have either quoted the text or at least shown that they knew of its existence. The codex's 561 sheets of paper are of approximately American letter size, and the writing on both sides is in a fifteenth-century hand (probably Morosini's). In addition

Lacking the first forty-eight folios of the manuscript, we cannot know how it began. Perhaps there was a prologue or a narrative of one of the traditional foundation myths. The surviving manuscript begins with a fragment from the late eleventh century and quickly moves on to the thirteenth. The first portion of Morosini's extant text is a conventional chronicle of Venetian history, largely dependent upon earlier chronicles, particularly those of Nicolò Trevisan, Andrea Dandolo, and Rafaino (or Rafaelo) Caresini. Morosini's discussion of the conquest of Constantinople is a radically simplified account of this complex tale. Historians still debate how a combination of Venetian sailors and Frankish crusaders was diverted from a Crusade to the Holy Land to the conquest of Constantinople and its Christian empire.[12] A complete explanation of the conquest would have to take into account the interests of the papacy as well as the diplomatic and political goals of the Venetians, the crusaders, and the Byzantines themselves. In contrast, Morosini's narrative is laconic. For him, the primary actor is the doge, Enrico Dandolo. It is to Dandolo himself that the young claimant to the Byzantine throne offers two hundred thousand silver marks for Venetian aid. During the attack on Constantinople, it is Dandolo's shrewd plan that secures victory. And it is Dandolo who eventually calls a council of the allies to select a new emperor and to divide the spoils of victory. Morosini does not ignore his own family's contribution: Domenico Morosini was involved in the early battles, and Tommaso Morosini became patriarch of Constantinople. The Morosini family thus figures prominently in his version of Venice's great achievement.

The second part of the codex (1361–88) is copied from the chronicle of Rafaino Caresini. This section includes the battle of Chioggia, a turning point in the struggle between Genoa and Venice for control of the eastern Mediterranean. Long enemies, Venice and Genoa had engaged in intermittent struggle for predominance in the Mediterranean. Morosini understood the struggle in the following terms:

> And here I wish to speak of the insane revenge of the Genoese, which was this: that purely through envy they had to chase the

---

to the original, in the Austrian Nationalbibliothek, Vienna (mss 6586–87, bound in two volumes), a manuscript copy made in the nineteenth century is held by the Biblioteca Marciana, Venice (ms it., cl. vii, 2048/49, also bound in two volumes). This copy is usually reliable, and most modern scholars have preferred to work from it rather than from the original, which is much more difficult to read.

12. Many still question whether the conquest of Christian Constantinople was Dandolo's goal from the beginning. See most recently Madden, *Enrico Dandolo*, 155–72, who believes Dandolo was more pragmatic than disingenuous.

Venetians and all other nations from the Black Sea, occupying the empire and every kingdom, so that there should be no place where they could go on commerce except Babylonia, which was subject to the sultan.

And for this reason then, it is clear that the Venetian struggle was manifestly just and famous. And this justice and equity which [the Venetians] love brings forth peace. And for this reason people of all nations, catholic and barbarian, should support them [i.e., the Venetians].[13]

This conflict came to a head in 1379, when Chioggia, a strategic island on the southern edge of the Venetian lagoon, was occupied by a combined Paduan-Genoese force. Genoese galleys blocked the sea access to Venice. Hungarian troops pressed from the north, and Padua blocked the western approaches to the city. This was the gravest threat that medieval Venice had yet faced. Food and provisions were in short supply as the blockade strangled the city. The ensuing war lasted nearly a year. In contrast to his brief account of the takeover of Constantinople, Morosini accorded the War of Chioggia an expansive narrative. He believed that Venice's ultimate triumph was God's will, and he recognized the centrality of this event in shaping the Venetian identity.

Morosini's history changes as he notes the major events of the years following 1404, that is, events from his own lifetime. He begins to write in his own words. This portion of the codex contains a diary of noteworthy events as they occurred or were reported in Venice. Some are recorded regularly— for example, the annual auctions of the right to operate merchant galleys on the five main voyages that took place each year. Galleys, as opposed to ships, were built and owned by the Venetian government, were manned by large crews that could fight as well as row, and were used for carrying cargoes of small bulk and high value. The success of their voyages was of great importance for the Venetian economy. Morosini, like other chroniclers, also recorded epidemics (*pedimie*) of plague, unusual weather conditions, and floods in Venice.

A notable feature of his work is the inclusion of copies of letters sent by Venetian commanders or governors residing overseas. Some of these letters have survived elsewhere (for example, some are also quoted by Marin Sanudo in his *Lives of the Doges of Venice*), but others have not and are known only

13. *Morosini Codex,* 2:67.

from Morosini's quotation of them. The text presents us with an enormous amount of other material: wars and battles, debates of the Venetian cabinet and council, embassies and expeditions, trade relations, processions and religious festivals, state visits, and reports from external sources on events in Europe, Africa, and Asia. A constant stream of messages flowed home from Venetian outposts around the Mediterranean, brought by individual merchants or by the convoys of armed galleys carrying precious cargoes that sailed each year in many directions. Likewise, many reports reached Venice by land from northern Europe, sent by individual Venetians who were engaged in trade there and knew that their fellow merchants needed to be kept informed of current events in areas where Venetians traded. Morosini reports the news as it arrived in Venice. He includes, for example, reports of a merchant convoy to Flanders in 1416–17:

> And then it was decided by the members of the council to put up for public auction four galleys of the large size used for the voyage to Flanders, two of them for London and two for Sluys and Bruges. The first went to the noble messer Girolamo da Canal, the second to Messer Polo Pasqualigo, the third to Messer Tomaso Duodo, the fourth to Messer Marco Zen. The first was auctioned for 39 *lire* 18 *soldi di grossi,* the second for 34 *lire* 13 *soldi di grossi,* the third for 45 *lire* 2 *soldi di grossi,* the fourth for 43 *lire* 1 *soldo di grossi.* The captain was the noble Andrea da Molin. They left Venice on the fourteenth of the month of April [1416] with a cargo worth 120,000 gold ducats. May Christ bring them home again safely![14]

And he followed this entry with letters about the movements of these merchants between Flanders and England.

When Morosini wrote, Venice was creating an extensive state in northern Italy, the *terra ferma.* The composition of the second half of the codex also coincided with the reign of one of Venice's best-known doges, Francesco Foscari, who pursued an expansionist policy in the eastern Mediterranean, not always successfully. Venice was a major European center, so people knew about and discussed events in England and France (for example, the Hundred Years' War and the rise and fall of Joan of Arc), as well as events in the East, such as the collapse of the Byzantine Empire. All these topics are

---

14. Venice, Biblioteca Marciana, MS it., cl. VII, 2048/49, II:311B.

discussed in the later part of the codex, which the author sometimes refers to as a diary or journal.

Morosini does not explain his changed method. He has not simply run out of sources to copy. The section covering 1388 to 1404 also was to an increasing extent based upon his own observations. Perhaps, like the later Marin Sanudo, he intended to use his diary as a source for a later history. Unlike the synthesis that marked the earlier sections, this part of the diary includes, without much reflection, whatever information came Morosini's way. A survey of the materials he collected for 1406 will clarify his method. His first entry of the year was 17 January, when he noted the death in a Venetian prison of Francesco Novello Carrrara, former tyrant of Padua. He repeats the official version of the events: "At Vespers the ducal council reported that just yesterday Ser Francesco da Carrara passed from this miserable, mortal life in prison. He was found to have died of a painful illness or catarrh. He had wasted away and was horrible to see. The ducal council saw that he was carried honorably to his burial in the monastery of Santo Stefano of the Hermit Friars."[15] In truth Francesco had been savagely beaten and strangled by Venetian authorities. It seems likely that rumors of what had actually happened were circulating at the time, but Morosini chooses to ignore them.[16]

Morosini then reports on actions to protect the Gulf of Venice, the disposition of merchant convoys, and fortifications of Venice's newly acquired mainland possessions. He goes on to record diplomatic initiatives in Sicily and others involving relations with Genoa. And finally he records the election of the Venetian Angelo Correr as the Roman pope Gregory XII. Morosini writes that he hopes that Gregory will be able to end the Great Schism, which had left claimants to the papal throne in both Rome and Avignon. He ends the year with a translation of a letter Pope Gregory sent to the other papal claimant, Benedict XIII, together with Benedict's reply. None of these materials are organized into a broad context, a task he must have assumed would be done later.

It is in relation to this diary, or journal, that a most unusual event took place in 1418, when Morosini was ordered to destroy some pages of his work. The problem seems to have been his access to official documents. These

---

15. Ibid., 1:192B.

16. See Benjamin G. Kohl, *Padua Under the Carrara, 1318–1405* (Baltimore and London: Johns Hopkins University Press, 1998), 335–36, for a graphic description of the execution. Although there is no firm evidence, Kohl believes that rumors of what really happened circulated at the time.

official sources make the Morosini codex more closely resemble the semi-official chronicles of Martino da Canal and Enrico Dandolo than the many minor patrician chronicles. Morosini does not simply repeat the information that is available in official Venetian documents. He also narrates minor happenings recorded nowhere else, reports rumors both true and false, and preserves the text of now-vanished private letters. The senate must have been aware that this combination of privileged official information, public documents, and rumor might compromise government interests. On 7 July 1418, the Venetian senate passed a motion commanding Morosini to hand over his writings for examination, for in them "many things are contained that are burdensome to our government." A few days later they made another decision: "Some of the pages of the books of Messer Antonio Morosini in which there are noted certain matters causing scandal are to be burned."[17] Scholars still are unable to say just what was destroyed or how this destruction affected Morosini. We may hazard a guess that he had recorded something that reflected badly on the current doge, Tommaso Mocenigo, or that the government considered too politically sensitive. Oddly, the surviving manuscript shows no sign that any folios are missing from this portion of the text.[18] It has been suggested that the fragmentary and incomplete coverage between 1388 and 1404 may be related to this problem. In this period Morosini ignores several important challenges to Venice's status—for example, the rise of the Carrara dynasty in Padua and the French acquisition of Venice's traditional rival, Genoa. Despite this official displeasure, Morosini not only continued writing but also retained access to official documents. The government permitted Morosini to continue his compilation, within limits.[19]

The senate's order and Morosini's access to official and private correspondence are probably a good indication of the codex's value. What began as a fairly standard Venetian family chronicle developed into a much more significant historical resource. Morosini does not provide the careful analysis typical of the best of the fifteenth-century historians, but his diary allows readers to follow the transformation of a Mediterranean sea power into one of the great states of Renaissance Italy.

17. *Morosini Codex*, 1:xix.

18. As indicated above, the first forty-eight folios, which probably contained a recital of the early stages of Venetian history based on the chronicles of others, are lost. As well, three pages dealing with events much later than 1418 are missing.

19. On the controversy, see Lefèvre-Pontalis and Dorez, *Chronique d'Antonio Morosin*, 4:120–21, 168.

APPENDIX: ANTONIO MOROSINI, *THE MOROSINI CODEX*

1. The Fourth Crusade[20]

This lad,[21] who was a nephew of the emperor, that is the son of a daughter of his, the wife of the emperor Isaac, who was chased from his empire by the Grifoni,[22] was carried safely by a tutor of his to Germany and grew up in the court of the emperor. So the young man made a request of the doge or his barons, saying that on the recommendation of this monarch he wished to travel with the fleet and return to his empire, which was his by right. The words were very pleasing to misier[23] the doge, and they were accepted, with an agreement on the following terms, that when he regained his empire he would give misier the doge 200 thousand silver marks, and in addition to this repay every expenditure that the fleet made in this service and trouble, and so all the barons departed with a great fleet from Venice in 1202 in the month of October, and first in Istria in the city of Trieste and in Muggia under the control of the doge they forced and constrained them to render a certain tribute to be maintained by all future doges, then they passed into Sclavonia and attacked Zara[24] in such a manner and fashion that they captured it and razed it to the foundations and punished many of the rebels with the affliction of death, and the Hungarians escaped to their own country, and were unable to defend it, and then winter came upon them and so they all stayed there. The following year misier Francesco Mastropiero left Venice with 18 galleys and went to build a castle where Zara was, and stayed there as castellan, after driving the Zaratini from Zara, together with the count who was there, the noble misier Domenico Morosini.

Then, when the new sailing season came, the fleet left Sclavonia and sailed in the direction of Romania and arrived there safe and sound. When the Grifoni, that is the Greeks, of the mountains, who had chased away the emperor called Isaac, or had put out his eyes, heard of the arrival of misier the doge and the barons, they reinforced themselves without delay as strongly

20. *Morosini Codex*, 1:7–11.
21. Alexius IV. Morosini states incorrectly that the young claimant was a nephew of the Byzantine emperor Isaac II.
22. "Grifoni" is a word of obscure origin that was used by some writers in Italy at that time to refer to the Greeks; it may be a perversion of "Graeci" or "Graecanici," or it may be connected with "grifone" (vulture) in the sense of "hook-nosed."
23. Venetians often wrote "misier" instead of "messer," with the meaning of "sir" or even "signor" or "lord."
24. "Sclavonia" is the term Italians use for the Balkans. Zara is a coastal town along the Adriatic.

as possible, but to little avail, since the Franks were able to land about 800 cavalry (although there were more than 1,000 when they left Venice, some died on the ships, but they had foot soldiers in abundance). But in truth, in the whole army of the Venetians and Franks there were no more than 20,000 persons, but the number of armed men in Constantinople could well have been 40,000, among whom there were at least 20,000 cavalry. Now as it pleased God, when battle was joined by sea and on land according to the command of misier the doge, the Franks made an attack on land, and the Greeks were expecting a different result, thinking that they would defeat them because they were few; then misier the doge with his ships and galleys approached the walls and attacked the city in such a way that they entered over the walls. Then the Greeks, seeing that they were in a dangerous situation, turned back in most places to regain the city, but the Franks were at their backs and defeated them completely, and the Venetians, when they had burned the greater part of the city and killed a great number of them, returned to their ships joyfully. And after a few days had passed, seeing that they could not depart, they came to an agreement with misier the doge and the barons to take the said boy in as their lord and emperor, and so it happened, then the empire was handed over at once to the boy emperor, and he had a relative of his who was called Mourtzouphlos brought out of prison and made him his High Chamberlain and Marshal. Then the Venetians decided, with the Franks, to go on their voyage, and they passed into the parts of Egypt to the Holy Sepulcher, but first they received part of the treasure owing to them, and the emperor said to them, "On your return, may it please you to visit these regions, and I will be ready to complete the payment of what I should give you," and so it was done.

So on the return of misier the doge with all those Frankish barons, after doing many marvelous and wonderful deeds against the infidels, which it will take too long to relate in full, I return to our subject. It seemed that the aforesaid Mourtzouphlos, chamberlain of the new emperor, had left him dead with the agreement and assistance of the Greeks, which greatly displeased misier the doge and his barons, and they wanted to enter the city although it was well guarded and well ordered, but they were refused entry by Mourtzouphlos and the Greeks. Then misier the doge decided to recover the city completely and take the whole empire from the hands of Mourtzouphlos and the Greeks. He prepared his ships and when those in the city saw this they were afraid, and one day this Mourtzouphlos, who had elevated himself to the position of leader and emperor, sent to misier the doge, saying that he would like him to come with his galley to a certain place in the city to speak with him. Misier the doge agreed to this, and armed himself, and advanced to the middle of that place, and asked Mourtzouphlos what had happened to the emperor his master and kinsman who had done him so much good, and he dissimulated, saying that he was sick and could not speak with him, but that he was ready to give him willingly the remainder of what was due to him, and in addition whatever else he wanted, but misier the doge, who knew of the whole betrayal and understood his words, replied, "If this is true, then allow me, Sier Mourtzouphlos, to enter and visit him. We wish to give whatever aid can be given, and afterwards we will take what is due to us and go on our voyage." But this Mourtzouphlos, with his usual duplicity, answered that the physicians had given orders that because he was so sick no one could speak to him, and that the empire was not in his hands, and that was the whole of his reply. Misier the doge then took counsel with his barons about what should be done, and when the discussion ended, on the advice of misier the doge the city was attacked vigorously, but in the first battle, because the Franks did not hold to the advice given on the orders of Misier the doge, their barons suffered a great defeat on land, and when the Greeks saw that it was the Venetian fleet at sea that was doing them damage and they had little to worry about elsewhere, they decided to make every effort to destroy it, so on the orders of the said Mourtzouphlos about 18 ships full of brushwood and reeds were sent at once against the Venetian fleet one day, when the wind was favorable at the right time for doing this. There was only one man on board each of these ships to steer it, and a *saettia*,[25] which they could sail back against the wind and reach safety. The Venetians at once with their yard-arms and boat hooks protected themselves so effectively that nothing could harm them, and now an attack was made by misier the doge from the seaward side, and when the Venetians entered by one of the gates and the Franks also entered, the Grifoni made an exit through another part of the city, a great number of them being killed. Among them Mourtzouphlos, while escaping over a palace and being pursued, was stoned on top of a column, and in the end was catapulted down to the ground and there he died. With grievous difficulties, thus the whole city remained without any resistance in the hands of misier the doge and the barons.

After misier the doge and the barons and all the others in the army had stayed at Constantinople for some days, the property that they found, I mean

---

25. A *saettia* (from the Latin "sagitta" [arrow]) was a fast light craft suitable for making a getaway in these circumstances.

the money, was at once divided among them with great joy and cheerfulness. And misier the doge took the jewels and other things of the greatest value which had all been acquired by the emperors of olden times from many countries, and when he arrived in Venice they were given with much reverence to the Chapel of misier Saint Mark, and up to the present day they are placed on the great altar at the great festivals and will be so placed in the future. And when Misier the doge was preparing to return to Venice after winning such a great victory and allegiance, he held a council to choose an emperor, since at that time no one of the imperial blood could be found, and count Baldwin of Flanders was worthily elevated by misier the doge and the barons, and one of the relatives of misier the doge, a priest, was made patriarch by him there and then joyously confirmed by the pope, and at that time the city and the empire were divided, and the agreement which was made was that misier the doge should have half, and the city and the empire were divided in this way, that the part of Constantinople on the sea which was under the control of the patriarch would remain unclaimed by misier the doge, and in the same way all the parts of Greece that fell to the doge and the Venetians. And it is true that in order that misier the Count Baldwin could better protect the empire, out of his liberality he gave him a quarter of the empire as his share; and for this reason the Marquis of Monferrato was granted the lordship of Thessalonica and made ruler of it under the authority of the emperor. So misier Enrico Dandolo, Doge of Venice, added to his title "Doge of Venice and of a quarter and a half of the whole of the Empire of Romania," and so all the doges after him up to the present time added it to their letters and edicts, and had it written afterwards in this manner.[26]

2. The Conspiracy of Marino Falier 1354[27]

Marino Falier, a man of great nobility of the ancient Falier Dononi family, a knight and count of Valmareno, possessing an enormous abundance of wealth, was elected doge following the usual form of election by the 41, and when he had been elected he was confirmed by all the people. He was at that time at the court of the Pope, sent as an ambassador in the name of the Commune of Venice. He received 36 ballots for the dogeship and was acclaimed

26. The addition to the title of the doges of Venice of "a quarter and a half [of a quarter]" implies that they now ruled over three-eighths of the Greek part of the Byzantine Empire.

27. *Morosini Codex*, 2:3–5.

almost universally because of the splendid reputation which he had at the time. And after coming to Venice he was received with marvelous honor during 1354 on the 5th of October.

And when that doge had held office peacefully for 8 months and 6 days, he found himself almost without supporters, and also an injury had been done to him by some young men, sons of Venetian nobles, who had been punished unjustly. Either for this reason, or because he was urged on by the spirit of the Devil, he collected some men of the people, sailors and other persons of the lower class, and plotted to have the city of Venice subjected to his domination like a tyranny, but God and the Evangelist St Mark, who by their divine grace have never allowed this to happen, nor will they ever allow it, inspired some men who were in that conspiracy to reveal it; so at once the dogal Signoria, as quickly as they could, secured every entrance to the square, and the Doge was brought to justice on the staircase of the palace, and was at once decapitated. A similar fate befell those followers who were disposed to follow him in his wicked intention: they were hanged in the same fashion from the red columns of the Palazzo Vecchio, being 11 in number, and the city of Venice remained in a tranquil state. Everything belonging to the conspirators was confiscated, except that a concession was made as an act of grace to misier Marino the Doge, allowing him to retain from his property 2,000 ducats in gold, and everything that remained went to the Community. And after this he was dishonorably buried in the monastery of Sts Giovanni and Paolo of the Fra' Predicatori [i.e., the Dominicans] in his tomb before its school, and this was during the course of this year, the 17th of April, and he reigned as doge in the palace, as I have said above, for just eight months and six days.

3. The Battle of Chioggia 1380–81[28]

It was a great marvel that after the Genoese seized Chioggia, their galleys had never been so united that some of them were not at sea, also two galleys or one alone were accustomed to stand guard over the harbor, but on this day all of them were enclosed at Chioggia; and it was even more remarkable that our fleet stayed for several days within the canal of St. Mark, and remained there, and all this was not hidden from the enemy. And misier the doge of Venice had sailed out with the intention of fighting at sea against the enemy. And the eyes and understanding of the enemy could not believe that they had set out with such a fleet of galleys, because they were awaiting

28. Ibid., 2:101, 103, 105.

the noble captain misier Carlo Zeno who was expected to return from overseas. Now we will say that anyone who does not exercise caution, thinking he is safe, not surprisingly often breaks the net.[29]

The enemy, hearing the sound of trumpets and then the shouting of men's voices, aroused themselves at once, astonished at so many galleys and regretting their own negligence, and realizing that at the very moment that they were keeping us besieged conditions had now changed and they were enclosed even more closely, and in such a manner that the sea and rivers which had previously been closed to us were now open, and now they were completely at a disadvantage.

Hearts of stone would have been moved to compassion seeing two such notable and powerful communities which for the sake of destroying each other had placed all their forces on land and on sea, and on one side and the other were well supplied with noble Lombard men, cannon, mangonels and crossbows with which many were killed, among them the brave captain misier Pietro Doria of the Genoese who, wishing to go outside from there with his galleys, was killed by cannon fire.

The hotheadedness or the fiery nature of the enemy, made them all like a bird which is enclosed in a cage, as they sought for the opening to escape from Chioggia; so they dragged out fourteen light galleys, digging a trench for a day and a night in the sandy soil by way of Santa Caterina del Deserto, up to a place near the canal of Brondolo, all of them believing they could escape secretly by this route and not be detected, and some of our galleys opposed them and did not let them pass.

4. A Sea Battle off Sapienza, October 1403[30]

The following is an example of the official letters to which Morosini gained access. It is the report of Carlo Zeno, procurator of Saint Mark and captain general of the sea, who sailed east to Venice's maritime possessions with fifteen galleys. The skirmish he describes is part of the ongoing hostilities between Genoa and Venice. It is clearly only one part of the story of a complex battle.

"Most Serene Prince: I inform your dogal Signoria that while I was here with eleven galleys and your two from Romania, on the sixth of this month, toward midday, signals indicating five galleys were made by the guard stationed at

29. Morosini misunderstood his source, who had written "is deservedly caught in the net."
30. Venice, Biblioteca Marciana, ms it., cl. vii, 2048/49, i, 147B–149A.

Sapienza,[31] because of which I swiftly set sail from where I was, going toward them, and I found there three vessels, one coming from Chanea and the other two from the direction of Coron, and I asked them whether they had seen any armed vessels, and they answered that they had not, so I took myself to Porto Longo, because the day was already well advanced; but a little afterward, toward sunset, the *Loredana* came, which I had sent to Modon, and they reported to me that they had seen nine galleys, which had passed Cape Gallo and were coming toward Ziaglo; there were in fact eleven their galleys. I swiftly left the harbor because it did not seem to me to be a safe thing to allow oneself to be found in the harbor, and I came to the rock of Saint Nicholas near the Cabrera islands, and I summoned the captain of Romania there, and all the *padroni*,[32] asking them what they thought we should do. And the galleys were now near Grizo and heading for the land, and there were eleven, with their lanterns hoisted aloft. And they arrived at Sapienza and anchored there, and stayed the whole night. And my captains and *padroni* and I decided that we would stay there that night and organize ourselves well, and we arranged that we should be supplied with stones and in the morning come to Modon to take the two great galleys from there and then go to meet the galleys of the Genoese, and so we did. The galleys of the Genoese stayed all that night at Sapienza with their lanterns hoisted aloft, and there was such arrogance in them that they did not think it necessary to give me any notification of their presence there, neither to me nor to the castellans, and I knew of it from a boat that Misier Almorò Lombardo sent to me where I was. So in the morning we left the rock and headed toward Modon in order to find the two great galleys, according to the orders that had been given. And as we went on our way, we came across those galleys, which had departed a little earlier without having given me notice of their arrival, and this seemed to everyone to be a sign of the ill will and animosity that they had against our Signoria because of the damage and the pillage they had done at Beirut, after invading our establishment there. And if they had been well disposed, they would have wished to speak with me or with the castellan because of this pillaging. So when I saw that they had departed, I took with me the two great galleys, following the decision that had been taken, and followed them under oars, and when they had traveled for eight

31. An island off the Peloponnesian coast of Greece. The other places named in the letter are difficult to identify but must be nearby.

32. A *padrone* can be any one of a number of different people. Morosini at times means the captains of the vessels in the fleet and at other times the owners of a boat or those who have a financial interest in it.

miles toward the bay of Zonchio, the galleys, seeing that they were being followed, suddenly lowered their sails and started coming toward me. I certainly imagined, when they lowered their sails, that Misier Boucicaut[33] wished to send me a galley, as he had done at another time, when I received it amicably and sent another back to him; and then we would have approached each other, so that in tranquillity and peace some good arrangement could be made regarding the pillaging. And so I hoisted my flag, according to our instructions. But his arrogance or that of his advisers was so great that they came against me most vigorously, well organized and in good order. So, since we saw that nothing else could be done, we went against them bravely, and so we attacked each other, them and us, and us and them, with great courage. At this a fierce and great battle began, between one side and the other, which lasted for around four hours, and it is certain that never has so hard a battle been seen. In the end, through the grace of Misier Domeneddio[34] and of the Evangelist Saint Mark, we defeated three of their galleys, and eight fled, greatly damaged, and many were wounded and killed, and if all our men had done their duty, not one galley would have escaped. And so, with regard to our men, if God sends me to Venice safe and sound, I will ask the Signoria to agree to make an investigation through their Avogadori del Comun,[35] so that those who were the cause of my being prevented from having an outright victory should be punished. I could not pursue the galleys that fled, because of the very great number of wounded men on the galleys that did the fighting and also because, when the next day came, they were exhausted.

"As to what I myself did, I have no hesitation in writing about it, because what I did was done in full view of everyone, and everyone saw clearly that I attacked the galley of Misier Boucicaut, which had on board at least 280 to 300 fighting men, and I grappled with it and would have totally overcome it if another two galleys had not arrived, one ahead of the other, to attack me, the first at the prow and the other in the region of the poop on the starboard side, so that while the battle lasted, for more than an hour, they boarded my galley with three galleys and drove me back as far as the ship's cuddy, and their trumpeter came on board with two flags. And as it

33. Genoa was at this time under the control of the French king. Boucicaut was a royal commander who had been sent to Genoa.

34. Italians turned the phrase "Lord God" (i.e., Domine Dio) into a single name, Domineddio.

35. The Avvogadri, or the "Advocates of the Commune," were a committee of three charged with the maintenance of the laws and with conducting public prosecutions.

pleased God, thanks to the courage of my men, among whom was my *armi-raio*,[36] who fought like a lion, and the others who rallied by the cuddy, their trumpeter was cut to pieces with another five men who had boarded us, and others were thrown into the water, and I remained free. In that great confusion all my men at the bows of the galley died, and the press of bodies that I had there was so great that they broke the gunwale on the port side and many fell in the water. Then the battle began again, and no one ever came to my aid, except Misier Leonardo Mocenigo, who was at my side and had attacked one galley and damaged it; and then he left it and came stern foremost to challenge one of the galleys that was upon me. Because of this Misier Boucicaut began to retire, and if even a brigantine, not a galley, had come to attack him when he began to withdraw, he would have been taken, because, as everyone saw, when he disengaged himself from mine, he had no more than twenty oarsmen rowing on one side, and he made his crossbowmen take oars in their hands to get away from there, that is, while he disengaged himself from my galley, because that was the best that he could do. Having another galley, as I have written, on my starboard side, I decided to call on someone whom I will not mention, someone who would go to attack Misier Boucicaut, and by the true God, I stayed on the galley fighting for more than two hours, and this is proved by the fact that I did not have thirty on the galley who were not all wounded, and fourteen to fifteen were killed. I give thanks to God, who has granted me as much grace as this, that we extricated ourselves from so fierce an attack as I had from these three galleys, and if they had been only Genoese, we would have defeated and routed them at the first engagement.

"Next, Most Serene Prince, I say that I have told your Signoria the facts completely in relation to my own actions, point by point as they happened. And I am not writing about the rest, because I can say little about them, since I had so much to do with my own affairs that I concerned myself little with those of the others. And may God pardon anyone who had the guilt of not having done his duty in these actions; and I have said to them, in their presence, that surely, as far as it is within my power, your Signoria will make seen and known anyone who was to blame in this matter. The reasons that moved me to pursue these galleys were these: first, to obey the order of your Signoria, which I do not repeat now, because it is well known to you and to everyone; second, to preserve your honor and fame, because when

---

36. The *amiraio*, or "admiral," was not a naval commander in the English sense, but rather a lower-level official with limited powers of command.

those galleys had done so much damage and so pillaged your people, and when they had come with such haughty pride into your possessions, if we had let them go in this way without pursuing them, there would have been little honor for your Signoria. The damage that we have received from them is manifest to all the world, and if we had not responded to that outrage, it would have given a great reputation for cowardice to all your galleys, since we were numerically superior and had the advantage. This affair [as it turned out] will be a great reason for the Genoese not to have such arrogance and steal in every place and with contempt, as they were doing every day. And now that they have tested our bravery and our ardor, they will be careful not to undertake any war so lightly against us, but will always be content to remain peaceful, as is reasonable.

"The prisoners whom I should mention to your Signoria are, first, three *padroni*, that is, Misier Pietro, Misier Cosma de Grimaldo, and Misier Leonardo Sauli, and Misier Cassano Doria, who was going as an adviser to the Levant, and several others of no particular importance. And as for the oarsmen and foot soldiers, there are at least four hundred, and many French were taken, and of the notable ones there is Misier Jean Château-Morand, Misier Louis de Normandy, and many others of their knights."

After those who were on board the eight galleys of the Genoese had departed, defeated and badly treated, and after Misier Carlo Zeno had the victory, he came on the next day to Modon and gave all the crew who were wounded medical attention and had the three captured galleys unloaded, in which many valuable goods occupying a small space were found, silver objects and money, and around fifty pounds of every type of spice: eleven of pepper, twenty-eight of ginger, five of cloves, six of cinnamon, and everything was kept safe under lock and key by the castellan and his counselors, under the seal of the commune, according to the usual procedure. Meanwhile it happened that the Genoese prisoners protested to the government of Modon, saying that the merchandise that had been taken came from their own purchases at Famagusta and not from the sacking of Beirut, but they received the answer that all these things would be saved for them if it was established that this was really the truth.

Afterward, so great was the fear that they had, and that continually, of still being pursued that three of those eight galleys separated themselves and went to Romania, and the remaining five, of Misier Boucicaut, as I have said earlier, went to Genoa without ever lighting their lanterns through fear that Misier Carlo might be at their backs. And in truth, not a single man of them would have escaped from being taken prisoner. But may Christ pardon those *sopracomiti* who did not fight! If they had, all the Genoese galleys would have been captured, and as a result the losses that happened afterward would not have occurred.

On the seventh of October 1403, the above-mentioned five galleys of the Genoese, very badly equipped, left to return to Genoa, but as chance would have it, they found one of our large cargo galleys, loaded with oars and a supply of biscuit, and they took it through a great trick by showing the ensign of Saint Mark, so that as it approached them, as we have said, they deceived it and took the supplies and the bread, because of the great disaster that they suffered, since indeed they had a great need of those things.

5. News of Joan of Arc Reaches Venice[37]

This letter, of which the first part is presented below, was written on 9 July 1429 and received on 2 August 1429. It is one of a number of similar letters written from northern Europe to Venice during this period and quoted by Morosini. It was most likely sent by Pancrazio Giustiniani, a Venetian resident in Bruges, to his father Marco, as were a number of similar letters also quoted by Morosini and attributed to Pancrazio. The letter is partly based on correspondence sent from Brittany to Bruges, written on 4 June. This speed of travel was normal for all but the most urgent news.

News of the maiden Joan [*Zaneta poncela*] who came to the kingdom of France in the year 1429, about whom we had a number of letters from Brittany, of 4 June, from certain respected persons who have seen and heard her and speak with confidence, and not only from this source, but from many others who have seen her—and to sum it up, I will say to you about these things, that they are quite miraculous, if they are true, and it seems to me that they are, and because her way of life is as it is said to be, I believe that the power of God is great indeed.

This maiden is of the age of eighteen or thereabouts. She is from the country of Lorraine, on the borders of France, and she was a beguine[38] [*begina*], a shepherdess, born from a man in the village. At the beginning

---

37. Venice, Biblioteca Marciana, ms it., cl. vii, 2048/49, ii, 504A.

38. "Beguine," or "begina," had a number of possible meanings in the fifteenth century. For one, it signified a member of a religious order of women, most commonly in the Low Countries and Northern Germany, who had taken vows of chastity and lived in religious communities of women. The term could also indicate a woman who had taken some sort of semireligious vow and perhaps continued to live outside of a religious community. These last sorts of beguines were often assumed to be heretics. Morosini's source is not quite clear on what the term means in this letter.

of the month of March she left her flock and prayed to God and her parents and two gentlemen that they would agree not to oppose her, saying that she was acting as she did to them through divine inspiration.

When she came before the presence of the noble prince Charles the Dauphin, son of the king of France who has recently died, she informed him on behalf of Jesus our Savior that he should accept her for three things (and these, as she said, would follow if he had complete confidence in her), if, after relinquishing his present manner of life, he amended his ways and governed himself according to her, through the grace of God, by whose commandment she was moved.

She had come, first, to raise the siege that the English were conducting at Orleans; second, to crown him freely as king of France and all its associated territories; third, to make peace between him and the English; and also [to see to it] that the duke of Orleans should leave prison in England for the sake of friendship. But this last item contains something that, if God's mercy is not applied to it, will be very difficult to achieve without much shedding of blood on both sides. And if, in the end, the English do not consent to hand over the duke of Orleans except by force, she will cross over into England and remove him against their will, and she will subjugate the English, to their great shame and loss.

When the Dauphin heard all these things proceeding from the mouth of a young woman, he mocked her, believing her to be mad and possessed by demons, because she was so ardent in her manner. And when she saw that no one would believe her, it is said that she told him that no one other than God and herself knew of these things. On account of this, he had many wise men brought together and began to have discussions with her and test her in many ways, subjecting her both to physical discomfort and to conversations with the gentlemen, and finally with grand masters in theology, for the space of as month, and in the end they concluded, seeing her manner of life, and in particular how she spoke and replied to the questions and statements that they put to her, that this creature was nothing less than holy, and all of them held her to be a servant of God, and they counseled the Dauphin that he should believe her with all his heart. And many other things are written, and it is also reported of her that before they believed her, they made many tests. One of these, performed when she took Communion, was that the priest had one consecrated wafer and one wafer that was not, and he decided to give her the one that was not consecrated, and she took it in her hand and said that this was not the body of Christ her Redeemer but that it was the one she knew instinctively he had hidden about his person.

She lives on no more than two ounces of bread a day. She drinks water, and if she drinks wine, she puts three quarters of water in it. Each Sunday she makes her confession: she is very devoted, very pious, and completely filled with the Holy Spirit. Her instructions to anyone in a position of high rank are that that person, with all his captains and lords of his court, should go to confession and should confess to fornication, with all the ladies. And among those men and women, those who go against God with their bodies, the most cruel and wicked in every vice that ever existed—she has brought them with all the others to do her will, so that they are not in danger; and I will not extend myself in telling this, but they are coming to the mercy of God and to their salvation.

As soon as she was made captain and governor of all the army of the Dauphin, she commanded that no one should dare to take by force from his subjects anything for which he had not paid—otherwise, he would risk being put to death—[and issued] many other orders, all honorable, which I will not take time to relate.

She then wanted the Dauphin, when he took communion, with all his subjects, to promise freely and willingly to pardon every man who had acted against them, and all their enemies and rebels, and to treat peacefully all the lands into which they had entered, without taking revenge on anyone, or their persons or their property, making it clear to them that if they said this with their mouths and then acted in a different manner, they would be the ones who would suffer all the harm, and that certainly in a very short time the Dauphin would then be driven out of France with all his men, with no hope of staying there; but if they did this, in a little while God would show grace to them through His mercy, and would make him ruler of his country.

The maiden has had armor made to fit her. She rides and goes fully equipped like a soldier, and even better. And it appears that she has found an ancient sword, which was in a church, on which it is said that there are viiii †,[39] and this is the only weapon that she bears.

She also bears a white standard on which Our Lord is placed in the manner of the Trinity, and in one hand He holds the world, and with the other He bestows blessing, and on each side there is an angel, who offers two lily flowers, like those borne by the kings of France.

39. That is, nine signs of the Cross.

9

Chronicles into Legends and Lives: Two Humanist Accounts of the Carrara Dynasty in Padua

Benjamin G. Kohl

The title of this essay is intended to convey a certain irony and caution about earlier scholarly interpretations of the changes in the historiography of Italian cities in the fourteenth and early fifteenth centuries as well as to highlight the obvious propaganda purposes of most early accounts of ruling dynasties of Renaissance Italy. In his classic essay of 1946, "Leonardo Bruni and Humanistic Historiography," B. L. Ullman pronounced Bruni "the first modern historian" on the basis of his critical use of sources and attempts to determine the underlying causes of events.[1] Even Louis Green's more nuanced account of the transformations of fourteenth-century Florence's historiography depicts a transition from the traditions of the medieval universal chronicle to the realistic political narratives of Giovanni and Matteo Villani.[2] In short, students of the historiography of the republics of Renaissance Italy have stressed growing critical methods of these early historians and have assumed an attitude of Whiggish approval of their incipient modernity and concern for objectivity. Yet, a consideration of two humanist historians of the Carrara regime reveals the propagandistic value of these accounts in bolstering the legitimacy and grandeur of the family's rule over Padua, an

1. Berthold L. Ullman, "Leonardo Bruni and Humanistic Historiography" (1946), in *Studies in the Italian Renaissance*, 2nd ed. (Rome: Edizioni di storia e letteratura, 1973), 343.

2. Louis Green, *Chronicle into History: An Essay on the Interpretation of History in Florentine Fourteenth-Century Chronicles* (Cambridge: Cambridge University Press, 1972).

objective that became the norm for historians of princely regimes of the Renaissance.[3]

This title is something of a misnomer. First, in composing his own new version of the origins of the Carrara dynasty, Giovanni Conversini da Ravenna (1343–1408) relied more on oral traditions than on chronicle accounts. His short work, the *Familie Carrariensis natio* (The birth of the Carrara family), is an imaginative retelling of older family traditions, that is, legends, about the origins of the Carrara dynasty that were circulated at the Carrara court in the 1370s, and relies little on the earlier chronicle accounts of the Paduan commune. The somewhat later work of Pier Paolo Vergerio (1370–1444), *De principibus Carrariensibus et gestis eorum liber* (The Carrara princes and their history), is a series of lives of the first seven Carrara lords, modeled after Petrarch's *De viris illustribus* and ultimately Suetonius's and perhaps Plutarch's *Lives*. Vergerio uses some local city chronicles but relies more on recent biographies of members of the family, the *Gesta magnifica domus Carrariensis* (History of the distinguished Carrara house), in his own polished accounts of the lives, deeds, and personalities of the Carrara lords. Written in elegant (if often complex) Latin, the Conversini and Vergerio works attempt to bolster the legitimacy of Carrara rule over Padua by appealing to the ancient imperial origins of the family and depicting the achievements of the first seven Carrara rulers.[4] Both were the products of scholars residing and working in the Carrara court during the reign of Francesco Novello, who ruled from 1390 to 1405; both were written specifically to praise and legitimate Francesco Novello's rule in Padua.[5] And most interesting, each humanist knew the other's work. There is some evidence of intertextuality, with cross-references in the prefaces to each work on the nature and reliability of their sources.

Giovanni da Ravenna, who came to be known by the patronymic surname

3. See Gian Maria Varanini, "Propaganda dei regimi signorili: Le esperienze venete del Trecento," in *Le forme della propaganda politica nel Due e nel Trecento*, ed. Paolo Cammarosano (Rome: École française de Rome, 1994), 313–43, for an assessment of some early histories of the Veneto lords, and Gary Ianziti, *Humanistic Historiography Under the Sforzas: Politics and Propaganda in Fifteenth-Century Milan* (Oxford: Oxford University Press, 1988), for a classic account of the service of humanist history in promoting the greatness of the Sforza.

4. The standard account of Padua in this era is now Benjamin G. Kohl, *Padua Under the Carrara, 1318–1405* (Baltimore and London: Johns Hopkins University Press, 1998).

5. Oddly, the works of Vergerio and Conversini are not treated in the standard survey of historians of Carrara rule in Padua, Lidia Capo, in Girolamo Arnaldi and Lidia Capo, "I cronisti di Venezia e della Marca Trevigiana nel secolo xiv," in *Storia della cultura veneta*, vol. 2, *Il Trecento* (Vicenza: Neri Pozza, 1976), 311–27.

Conversino (or Conversini), was the most enigmatic, obscure, and troubled of the humanists of the generation that came after Petrarch.[6] Born in 1343 in Buda, where his father Conversino da Frignano was the court physician to King Louis of Hungary, Giovanni was, after the early death of his mother, sent to Ravenna under the guardianship of his uncle, the Franciscan prelate Tommaso da Frignano. There he studied under several cruel masters, finding his first real mentor in Donato Albanzani, who ran a school in Ravenna before he settled in Venice and later Ferarra. To provide a home life for his nephew, Tommaso betrothed Giovanni at ten to an older child in Ravenna, one Margherita Furlan. But the early deaths of his wife's parents soon deprived the young couple of any adult supervision. By age fifteen Giovanni became the father of an infant boy, named Conversino after his grandfather, and he soon abandoned his wife and son for the life of a goliard (wandering student). After a visit to Ferrara, Giovanni studied rhetoric at Bologna, and then followed a two-year course in the notarial arts from 1360 to 1362. By the summer of 1364, Giovanni was in Padua, where his first maestro, Donato Albanzani, introduced him to the aged Petrarch and where he attended Pietro da Moglio's lectures on Valerius Maximus, before returning to Bologna.

At Bologna, Giovanni Conversini created his own commentary on Valerius Maximus from a set of lectures probably given in 1365, under the direct inspiration of his revered master Pietro da Moglio.[7] In the numerous exempla of Valerius Maximus organized around pithy sayings, ancient religious and political practices, and Roman virtues and vices, the Greek past came alive. In his own histories, dialogues, autobiography, and moral treatises, Conversini mined the *Facta et Dicta Memorabilia* (Memorable deeds and sayings) relentlessly for telling anecdotes and memorable events from Greek antiquity. From his letter of consolation on the death of Petrarch, sent to Donato Albanzani in 1374, down to his dialogue on the preferable way of

6. The most complete survey of Giovanni Conversini's life and works remains Remigio Sabbadini, *Giovanni da Ravenna, figura insigne d'umanista (1343–1408)* (Como: Tipografia editrice Ostinelli, 1924), 3–118; the second half of the volume has excerpts from his works. More recent brief accounts of his career include Luciano Gargan, "Il preumanesimo a Vicenza, Treviso, e Venezia," in *Storia della cultura veneta*, 2:161–67, and the entry by Benjamin G. Kohl, "Giovanni Conversini da Ravenna," in *Dizionario biografico degli italiani*, 28:574–78 (Rome: Istituto dell'enciclopedia italiana, 1983), on which this summary draws freely.

7. On his commentary, see Benjamin G. Kohl, "Valerius Maximus in the Fourteenth Century: The Commentary of Giovanni Conversini da Ravenna," in *Acta Conventus Neo-latini Hafniensis,* ed. Rhoda Schnur et al. (Binghamton, N.Y.: Medieval and Renaissance Texts and Studies, 1994), 537–46.

life, written thirty years later, Conversini illustrated his message with exempla taken from Valerius Maximus. In his "mirror for princes," the *De dilectione regnantium* (On the respect due rulers), addressed a quarter century later to Francesco Novello da Carrara, Conversini discussed the effects of youthful corruption that were overcome in later life.

Following his lectures at Bologna, Giovanni Conversini traveled to Ferrara, where he was employed as a preceptor in the household of the lord of the city, Niccolò II d'Este, and in 1366 accepted the post of schoolmaster of Latin grammar in Treviso. A year later he returned to Ravenna, whose lord, Guido III da Ravenna, had him appointed as one of the foreign notaries to serve in the court of the podestà of Florence. While he served in this post, in 1368–69, he also gave lectures on Virgil's *Georgics* and the rhetorical text *Ad Herennium* at the Florentine studium. In the summer of 1369, he left his posts at Florence and returned to Treviso to teach Latin grammar in the communal school. Here he was joined by his wife and young son from Ravenna, who were suffering from the deprivations his wandering life had caused, and had fallen ill. His wife soon died, and the son, Conversino, was only gradually nursed back to health. After a stint teaching Latin in the Veneto hill town of Conegliano, Giovanni visited his uncle Tommaso in Venice, where he had recently taken up residence as patriarch of Grado. The nephew and uncle quarreled violently, and Giovanni left in the fall of 1373 for visits to Padua and Arquà, where he stayed briefly with his hero, Francesco Petrarch, before taking up residence in Belluno, where he held the post of master of the communal school for five years. Here he married a wealthy widow and formed a new family with the birth of a second son, Israele. When the commune did not renew his teaching contract in 1379, Giovanni left with the intention of visiting his uncle Tommaso in Rome. But his way was barred by the uncertainties of the War of Chioggia raging between Venice and Genoa and its allies, the lord of Padua and the king of Hungary.

More by accident than by design Giovanni Conversini found himself in Padua, where he briefly taught Latin grammar and soon became a member of the Carrara household government. From 1379 to 1382, he was a constant and intimate companion of the ruling lord, Francesco il Vecchio. In an arresting account of a typical day at the Carrara court, Giovanni describes how at meals he would discuss important matters with the lord, listen to his stories, tell some of his own, fan him, massage his feet and legs during his afternoon siesta, and attend the lord as he gambled and caroused into the night.[8] During these years of intimacy he heard a primitive version of the noble origins of the family from the elopement of the daughter of the emperor, who is understood to be Charlemagne, with a French knight.[9] Their wanderings take the couple to northern Italy, where they settle in a wooded area of the Padovano and live by building carts (*carri*). The tale ends with the discovery of the couple by imperial officials and their eventual reconciliation with the father-emperor, who conveys rule over Padua and its district to this first Carrara lord. A draft of these legendary origins of the Carrara dynasty was apparently Giovanni's sole literary composition during his first sojourn in Padua.

Shortly after the end of the War of Chioggia, Giovanni Conversini left Padua for Venice. He eventually served as chief notary of Ragusa and later as schoolmaster in Udine from 1389 to 1392, only to return to Padua for further service in the chancery of Francesco Novello from 1393 to 1404. Discharged as a result of economies forced on the Carrara regime during its final war with Venice, Conversini used his enforced leisure to compose a polished draft of his earlier version of the family's origins.

Giovanni Conversini discussed the delayed completion of his work in two letters addressed to two of Francesco il Vecchio's illegitimate sons, both of whom made their careers as mercenary captains. The first letter was written in the early 1390s as a reply to a request from the condottiere Conte da Carrara (ca. 1350–1421) for a copy of Conversini's account of the origins of the Carrara family. From internal evidence it is clear that Giovanni was still master of the communal school in Udine, while Conte was probably in the service of Pope Boniface IX in Lazio.[10] Apparently Conte wanted a copy of the treatise to bolster his own prestige, since, as we have seen, the work

8. See Giovanni Conversini da Ravenna, *De primo eius introitu ad aulam,* in *Two Court Treatises,* ed. and trans. Benjamin G. Kohl and James Day (Munich: Wilhelm Fink Verlag, 1987), 34–37.

9. I use the text of Conversini's *Familie Carrariensis natio* that was edited, with Italian translation, by Libia and Dino Cortese, *Giovanni Conversini di Ravenna, 1343–1408: L'origine della famiglia di Carrara e il racconto del suo primo impiego a corte* (Padua: Centro studi Antoniano, 1980), 40–73. This "edition" is actually only a literal transcription of one of the oldest surviving manuscripts of the work, Venice, Biblioteca Querini-Stampalia, IX, no. 11 (= 1006), fols. 6r–10v, and presents many problems of interpretation. A full critical edition of this text, with Italian translation by Letizia Leoncini, is forthcoming in Giovanni Conversini da Ravenna, *Le prose narrative,* ed. Gabriella Albanese and Letizia Leoncini.

10. The letter to Conte da Carrara is available in Cortese and Cortese, *L'origine,* 26–29, with the editors' discussion on dating in ibid., 20–21. On Conte's career, see Kohl, *Padua Under the Carrara,* 297–99.

averred that the Carrara family arose from the elopement of a daughter of
Charlemagne, or another medieval emperor, with a French knight. Hence
it was claimed in Giovanni's account that the Carrara were descended in the
matriline from the Carolingians, one of greatest dynasties of Western Christendom. Conte had offered to have his agent in Padua, one Baldo Bonafari,
procure the history from Giovanni in Udine.[11] But Giovanni argued that the
work was still unpolished and that he was engaged "in very tiresome occu-
pations and similar nuisances of life [that is, school teaching], which grow
worse daily, so that he never has sufficient time to carry out the necessary
work [of revision]."[12] Recalling his affection for Conte's "delightful father,"
Giovanni stated that he hoped he would be able to revise the work for publication soon.

In any event, the final revision of the *Familie Carrariensis natio* had to
wait for more than a decade. Only after Conversini had left service at the
Carrara court in the spring of 1404, when he was tired of the hazards of
court life and saw his position of chancellor compromised, did he have time
to complete the *Natio*.[13] He continued to curry favor with members of the
Carrara family and, in the second letter mentioned above, dedicated the revised work to another of Francesco il Vecchio's illegitimate sons, the knight
and captain Rodolfo da Carrara (ca. 1360–after 1425).[14] Here he announces
that he had returned to the composition he had put aside when burdened
with the duties of chancellor and is now publishing his account of the illustrious origins of the Carrara family. He repeats his claims of being Francesco
il Vecchio's intellectual companion and avers that the then ruling lord told
him the story on which the account is based. Conversini asserts that he has
written up a polished version, not for material reward, but to glorify the
family, which he claims with all too typical exaggeration he has served for
"almost forty years [*octo prope lustris*]."[15] Clearly service to the Carrara
dynasty loomed as the central event in Giovanni Conversini's life (otherwise

11. On Baldo Bonafari as an agent for Conte in the 1390s, see Silvana Collodo, *Una società in trasformazione: Padova tra XI e XV secolo* (Padua: Editore Antenore, 1990), 288–91.

12. Cortese and Cortese, *L'origine*, 29: "Ego enim occupationibus permolestis ac vite
similiter tediis ita deteror deteriorque quotidie, ut ad id opportuno labore peragendum
nequaquam ipse sufficiam."

13. Giovanni Conversini provides his own version of the reasons he left the Carrara
court in 1404 in a passage of his *Dragmalogia de Eligibili Vite Genere*, ed. and trans. Helen
Lanneau Eaker, with introduction and notes by Benjamin G. Kohl (Lewisburg, Pa: Bucknell University Press, 1980), 66–81.

14. On Rodolfo's career, see Kohl, *Padua Under the Carrara*, 259, 299–300.

15. The letter to Rodolfo da Carrara is available in Cortese and Cortese, *L'origine*, 32–
37, with the quotation on 35.

spent mainly in the degrading posts of Latin teacher or tutor for unruly boys). The publication of this work provided the opportunity for Giovanni to honor and flatter a dynasty he esteemed, perhaps to regain his post at court, and to showcase his skills in historical research and in the imaginative reconstruction of distant events, using his favorite literary genre, the dialogue, to carry forward the action.[16]

But the composition of the *Familie Carrariensis natio* as a work of accurate history presented special problems. First, as Conversini states in his preface, the true origins of the family are difficult to know because they lie buried in the distant past (see Appendix A). According to the best traditions (as maintained by Francesco il Vecchio), the Carrara family originated from the elopement of Landolfo of the Roussilon nobility near Narbonne with the Holy Roman Emperor's daughter Elizabeth. The couple was of surpassing beauty and wildly in love. But because of Landolfo's status as a mere knight, Elizabeth was unable to secure her father's permission to marry, and the couple eloped. After a time of wandering, the two settled in a dense forest some six miles from Padua. Here Landolfo made his living building carts (*carri*), and the village soon took the name of Carrara from its sheltered position, the Casa Rara. Here Elizabeth conceived and bore twin sons, named Rodolfo and Milone. The family lived happily in harsh, rustic seclusion. Some years later the emperor (whose actions resemble Charlemagne's but who is never named as such) annexed Italy to his empire. Upon hearing this, Landolfo, fearful of the emperor's wrath on account of the forbidden elopement, sought to hide himself and his family ever deeper in the woods. Here Conversini recounts the prophecy of Elijah, with the appearance of his wheel in the sky, which is the origin of the Carrara coat of arms.

When the emperor reached northeastern Italy, his majordomo, Conrad, went hunting in the wooded area south of Padua, and the chase took him by chance to the home of Elizabeth. At her invitation he took a meal with her and the twin sons in their rustic home. At the end of the day, Conrad returned to dine with the emperor in his castle and described meeting the twins and Elizabeth. Here Conversini inserts a digression on man as subject to divine providence and describes how he earlier chanced to meet Duke

---

16. Seven of Conversini's fifteen major works are dialogues or use internal dialogues in their narration; see Benjamin G. Kohl, "The Works of Giovanni di Conversino da Ravenna: A Catalogue of Manuscripts and Editions," *Traditio* 31 (1975): 355–57. On Conversini's use of the dialogue form for his novellas, see Gabriella Albanese, "Per la storia della fondazione del genere novella tra volgare e latino, edizioni di testi e problemi critici," *Medioevo e Rinascimento*, n.s., 9 (1998): 279–80.

Leopold of Austria at Belluno. To prove that the emperor would recognize his own daughter, Conversini adduces a contemporary anecdote from Belluno. He tells the story of a young woman employed as a wet nurse in a household in Belluno, who had an affair with a man of the town and became pregnant. After the birth of her illegitimate son, the mother left town with her lover, but her employer took pity on the abandoned child and provided for his support. Some years later the mother returned and observed her son on the playground at school. The young boy immediately recognized his birth mother and rushed to embrace her at their reunion. In like fashion, the emperor foresaw that the young mother and twins might be his lost daughter and his unknown grandsons, and Conrad confirmed this fact. With this revelation, Conrad advised a meeting with the couple and their sons and urged the emperor to forgive their flight.

Further developing the theme of divine providence and good coming from apparent evil, Conversini inserts a digression on wandering heroes as the founders of great cities, such as Antenor of Padua, Aeneas of Rome, and Cecrops of Athens. Still, the reunion rekindled the emperor's anger at his daughter's flight, but the arguments of Conrad, Landolfo, and Elizabeth, and the unrestrained affection of the twins for their grandfather, eventually brought about a reconciliation (see Appendix A, "The Reunion of the Emperor with His Daughter"). Conversini lets the arguments for forgiveness "speak for themselves" in a series of imagined dialogues. Especially touching are Elizabeth's final requests of her father. She realized that with her headstrong insistence that she marry the young knight she loved she had offended her father's high sense of his own majesty. But she was not troubled by the lack of kingdom or a king's marriage bed, because the man she wed, though a commoner, possessed every royal attribute, which she defined as the Roman and knightly virtues of loyalty, generosity, justice, upright character, and moderation. Since her husband, the first Carrara lord, was in effect a king without a kingdom, and a man of the highest virtue and nobility, it was easy for the emperor to accept him into the imperial family and sanction his daughter's marriage. With her father's final pardon, the daughter was completely happy.[17] With his forgiveness, the emperor bestowed Padua and its district on the house of Carrara, making Landolfo and his male descendants the dukes of Carrara, and his grandsons the counts of Pernumia and Anguillara, rewarded with their own castles. A final digression

---

17. A paraphrase of the text of *Familie Carrariensis natio*, based on that in Cortese and Cortese, *L'origine*, 65, 67, is given in the text below.

foretells greatness for the Carrara family and prophesies that Giacomo il Grande will become the first lord of Padua. In this concluding prediction of the Carrara family's future just rule over Padua, Giovanni's account functions as a most transparent piece of propaganda. The ultimate irony was that the family that he asserted was the most worthy to rule Padua was soon to suffer extermination in a Venetian prison.

Pier Paolo Vergerio's account of the lives of the ruling lords of Padua is as critical and scholarly as Conversini's is novelistic and fanciful. Written between 1403 and 1405, when Vergerio was a tutor in the Carrara household and sometime official in the Carrara chancery, the *De principibus Carrariensibus* is a reworking of the available sources, mainly earlier chronicles, to bring prestige to the Carrara lords and document their rule over Padua.[18] But Vergerio's account is scarcely a roseate vision of virtuous and heroic lords. Rather, it presents vivid examples of their flaws, cruelty, and ambition, as well as their lust for power, genius, and cunning. Vergerio begins his preface with a review of the sources available for his lives and finds each wanting. The earlier historian of communal Padua, Albertino Mussato, was too much an enemy of the Carrara family to provide an accurate account of their careers. His successor Guglielmo Cortusi was also more concerned with the course of events than with individual motivation. Concerning the origins of the family, neither author provides any information. In this context, Vergerio cites Conversini's *Natio* as the standard work but is agnostic about what is really to be believed concerning the family's foreign origins. One version has the Carrara coming from Germany, while Conversini's account ascribes their origins to the emperor's court in Transalpine Gaul. In the end, Vergerio admits that Conversini's account is probably to be preferred, if only because this is the version of the family's origins that the forebears of the Carrara told so often.

The body of the work lies in the detailed sketches of the lives of seven lords, beginning with Giacomo il Grande, who was the first ruling lord of Padua, elected in 1318, and ending with Jacopino, who was coruler with his elder brother Giacomo II and his nephew Francesco until he was deposed and imprisoned for treason in 1355.[19] Despite Vergerio's criticism of his

18. I use the critical edition of Pier Paolo Vergerio, *De principibus Carrariensibus et gestis eorum liber*, ed. Attilo Gnesotto, *Atti e memorie della R. Accademia di scienze, lettere ed arti in Padova* 41 (1924–25): 327–475, which has been reprinted, with Italian translation and commentary, as *Liber de principibus Carrariensibus et gestis eorum incipit feliciter* (Fasano, Brindisi: Schena, 1997). Page numbers cited are from the later edition.

19. The standard monograph on Vergerio is now John M. McManamon, S.J., *Pierpaolo Vergerio the Elder: The Humanist as Orator*, Medieval and Renaissance Texts and Studies,

predecessors in the preface, his own work is often derivative. For the early lords, Vergerio used the communal history of Rolandino of Padua in addition to Mussato's history. For the Carrara lords after Giacomo il Grande, he adapted the work of Cortusi and especially the anonymous *Gesta magnifica domus Carrariensis,* which survives in four different redactions in both Latin and the vernacular.[20] The first version of this work was compiled at the Carrara court by a local functionary, Bernardo de Caselle, around 1375, probably at the behest of Francesco il Vecchio.[21] The most complete Latin version was redacted in 1390 to celebrate Francesco Novello's reconquest of Padua, and greatly used by Vergerio in his lives of Marsilio, Ubertino, Giacomo II, and Jacopino da Carrara. In fact, Vergerio's dependence on the *Gesta* and other chronicles is so massive that several scholars have largely discounted the value or originality of his lives of the Carrara lords.[22]

Though dependent largely on a few older histories, Vergerio's lives are novel in their insight into character and motivation, their critical use of other material to provide a clear narrative of events, and their inclusion of a few new anecdotes from an oral tradition of family history that was alive at the Carrara court. In the presentation of each life, Vergerio follows Suetonius's model that Petrarch had adopted in his *De viris illustribus:* an account of parentage and birth, followed by career, domestic situation, and mode of death, and concluding with a description of appearance and character.[23]

The most interesting of the lives is that of Ubertino da Carrara (lord, 1339–45), which Vergerio treats as a moral transformation from a corrupt and headstrong youth to an energetic, cunning, and impressive ruling lord. As a youth Ubertino had been deprived of adult supervision by the early death of his father and uncles, corrupted by the inheritance of great wealth,

163 (Tempe, Ariz.: Medieval and Renaissance Texts and Studies, 1996), which contains an extended discussion of the lives on 109–16. David Robey, "P. P. Vergerio the Elder: Republicanism and Civic Values in the Work of an Early Humanist," *Past and Present* 58 (1973): 3–37, is a closely argued essay on the chronology and values of Vergerio's early works.

    20. The standard edition is *Gesta magnifica domus Carrariensis,* ed. Roberto Cessi, *RIS,* n.s., 17, pt. 1, vol. 2 (Bologna: Zanichelli, 1942–48).

    21. Bernardo de Caselle was a Paduan notary who was responsible for putting together several versions (or redactions) of the *Gesta,* but the actual author of the work is not known. On Bernardo's role, see Cessi's preface to the *Gesta magnifica domus Carrariensis,* xviii–xxii.

    22. Carmela Marchente, *Ricerche intorno al "De principibus Carrariensibus et gestis eorum liber" attribuito al Pier Paolo Vergerio* (Padua: CEDAM, 1946), 11–37, demonstrates Vergerio's massive dependence on earlier sources, while Roberto Cessi in the preface to his edition of *Gesta,* xxv–xxxiii, condemns Vergerio for his lack of originality.

    23. On this model, see Benjamin G. Kohl, "Petrarch's Preface to *De Viris Illustribus,*" *History and Theory* 13 (1974): 132–44.

and enthralled with other violent young men who were his boon companions. As a result, Ubertino grew up a violent, libertine spendthrift, ever ready to visit his violence and lust on members of the Paduan populace, and especially on his hated political enemies, such as the Dente clan. Stories abound of his desire for attractive young matrons, his thefts from priests, his threats to nuns, and violent murder of hated political rivals, such as Guglielmo Dente. For this crime, the current podestà, a Bolognese jurist, exiled Ubertino and his roughneck companion Tartaro da Lendinara to Chioggia. But after the Dente faction was defeated in a pitched battle in Padua by other Carraresi and their allies in the summer of 1325, Ubertino and his friends returned to Padua to wreak vengeance on the podestà and his staff. Ubertino and his gang chased the podestà to the roof of his own palace, whence he leaped to his death rather than face capture, torment, and death at the hands of his archenemy.[24]

Even when Ubertino assumed the lordship of Padua upon Marsilio's death early in 1339, he continued his violent and cunning ways. One of the stories that is original in Vergerio tells of Ubertino's treatment of a Venetian senator who had attacked him and his policies. Irritated by the senator's criticism, Ubertino had the man drugged and brought secretly to Padua, where he was placed in Ubertino's own bed in the Carrara palace and awakened in a chamber decorated with the *carro*, the feared coat of arms of the family he had just criticized. Terrified when Ubertino entered the room, the senator fell on his knees and begged for mercy. Feigning surprise, Ubertino asked how the senator had come to Padua and why he had criticized him so harshly. Tormented with fear, the senator asked for Ubertino's forgiveness, which was granted, with the understanding that the senator would never again poor-mouth the house of Carrara.[25] Vergerio documents Ubertino's change of heart from lustful youth to just lord with the story of his execution of his own sister, a nun, for her indulgence in lovemaking with a priest. But Vergerio's conclusion also shows that Ubertino never lost his capacity for riotous living or his clever wit:

> Endowed with an extraordinary sex drive, Ubertino, from excessive use of his genital member, came to be afflicted with a disease, which troubled him for a long time and eventually killed him. Sensing the

24. See Vergerio, *De principibus Carrariensibus*, 208.

25. Ibid., 218, and retold with relish by Horatio Brown in "The Carraresi," in his *Studies in the History of Venice* (New York: E. P. Dutton & Co., 1907), 1: 122.

weakening of his powers, he decided to provide for his successor in ruling the city. Since he had no legitimate male heirs, he selected as his heir Marsilietto Papafava dei Carraresi and took pains while he was still alive to ensure that the lordship of Padua would be bestowed on him. Near death, when he was about to receive the last rites of the Church from the hand of a priest, he was asked whether he was truly penitent for all those sins he had committed in this life, as the teachings of the Church hold. He replied, "Certainly I will tell you the truth and not deceive you, since it would be pointless to try to do so. You should know that I have never done anything for the success of my family that I would not do all over again for the same reason. I am certain that God himself will pardon me for this act. Therefore, I have nothing to fear when I shall come before him."[26]

Written under the patronage of Francesco Novello da Carrara, Vergerio's lives obviously display partiality toward the ruling family of Padua. The lords who challenged the successful rule of Novello's direct forebears are given short shrift. Marsilietto Papafava dei Carraresi, who was murdered by Novello's grandfather to secure his own rule over the city, is depicted as weak and greedy. And Jacopino da Carrara is said to have plotted to assassinate his popular nephew out of jealousy and his wife's prodding. Novello's great-grandfather Niccolò, founder of the dynasty's stem family but never a lord of Padua, is accorded a long and favorable biography. The whole series of lives constitutes an invaluable history of Padua and its ruling family that probably would have gained wider recognition if the Carraresi had not been executed in a Venetian prison shortly after Vergerio completed his work. Even Conversini's fanciful version of the family's origins plumbs the depths of human emotions, with its accounts of star-crossed lovers, family formation under difficult circumstances, generational conflict, and the reconciliation of a headstrong daughter and her imperious father. Setting the events in a distant past, Conversini appeals both to divine providence and to the pagan Fates to explain the justice of Carrara rule over Padua. Together, the works mark the beginnings of the dynastic history that will become a standard approach to celebrating and explaining political change in early modern Europe.

26. Vergerio, *De principibus Carrariensibus*, 220–21.

APPENDIX A: GIOVANNI CONVERSINI DA RAVENNA, ON THE ORIGINS OF THE CARRARA FAMILY [27]

PREFACE

It is well known that the Carrara family is famous for the glory of its deeds, its valor, its wealth, and all the other attributes of good fortune. But this fact can be understood more from the evidence of their present splendid deeds and actions than from written works of history. Indeed, in earlier times no rewards, grants, or stipends were offered to scholars so they might be encouraged to create fairly accurate histories. For this reason and because of a lack of gifted writers who might strive to note down the family's deeds, their achievements usually went unrecorded. Therefore, many honorable deeds of this family have been forgotten, obliterated by time, and also because of the lack of those scholars who would have been able to set them down in writing. The earlier ages lacked a faithful custodian of literature, which is almost a divine estate, and since there were no rewards for praise by writers, almost all memory of great deeds was lost in obscurity. Therefore many outstanding deeds of this family, and its very splendor, have been buried in oblivion for the lack of those who would be able to make them known to our own age. And though it would seem rash to venture into such a distant and glorious past, of which, as they say, the memory is very meager, still, because of the debt I owe and the great benefits conferred most generously by this family, especially by Lord Francesco [il Vecchio],[28] it is right for me to use all my talents on its behalf. Driven by my great love for the family to undertake daily this difficult task, and overcoming any idleness and fear of hostile critics, I have decided it would be the highest honor for me to describe the origins of this great family. I hope that with this undertaking I will bestow on the seventh prince of this dynasty, who wields the scepter of rule over Padua, a gift that is more splendid and more enduring than any he could ever hope to have received.

---

27. Cortese and Cortese, *L'origine*, 41, 59, 61, 63, 65, 67, translated by Benjamin G. Kohl.

28. This reference to Francesco il Vecchio da Carrara (1325–93), who ruled Padua as the seventh lord of the city from 1350 to 1388, shows that Conversini is presenting the version he composed in the 1380s. In reality this text was retouched in the early fifteenth century for presentation to the condottiere Rodolfo da Carrara about 1405.

THE REUNION OF THE EMPEROR WITH HIS DAUGHTER, AND
THE FUTURE GREATNESS OF THE CARRARA FAMILY

At once Conrad [the emperor's majordomo] dismissed all normal use of words and said to the emperor:

"Look here, sir, these are your grandsons."

"But what are you saying? What have you found out? How can it be that my grandsons are raised in this region?"

"By your daughter," Conrad added, and he explained the whole chain of events. The old man, struck by the unexpected joy fell into a kind of stupor, and for a moment he fainted. He eventually recovered his senses and began to be assailed with doubts about his early decision [to execute his daughter for deserting him]. Should he end his own lineage by destroying those who had abandoned a parent in flight, or, finally at peace, should he admit them back to the family? Love and the senseless end of his race argued for the latter; injury, shame, and offense for the former. The conflict vexed his countenance and his soul. In the end, he lashed out and said: "My friend, Conrad, you have brought me great harm. I had promised. [My daughter's] punishment is fixed. But what should we do now? Please give advice in such a difficult matter."

[Conrad replied:] "Let you, the father, pardon his daughter; you must recognize your grandsons. The Fates decree that you must accept your son-in-law. Any complaint by you now would be too late. To commit an act of vengeance now would be an impiety. Your daughter ran away, but that is past history that cannot be changed. She is now joined in marriage with the man she loved. She follows an honorable life. Here she gave birth; here are her children. If there were no other reason, the children's innocence and the hope for their future happiness should merit your forgiveness. You cannot be just to the guilty except by being most cruel to the innocent. Control yourself, O Caesar, and let your holy estate excuse the guilt of youthful lovers. Choose clemency that will make you beloved rather than unwavering justice that will only make you feared. Can you really believe that without God's protection your offspring would have been able to overcome such dangers of travel, of different places, of men, and of toil and settle in these very fields? God abided, guided, and ruled. Let us obey, therefore. We mortals should not attempt to struggle against the degrees of the Fates, even when we believe we are right. Necessity is unconquerable.

"Who will deny that an illustrious race of your descendants will issue forth here in a grand and imposing future and will be made immortal by their great works? Here they will continue to cultivate the soil that the Fates have showed to be theirs; here they will rule those lands which fortune has so favorably granted them. In this very region, the wandering Antenor found peace and founded a city with his laws and peoples. Another wandering hero [that is, Aeneas] was guided by fate to the Tiber, where he laid the foundations of the empire, which earlier was granted to Evander coming from Arcadia. An exile founded Boeotia.

"The same fate founded Salamis and Carthage. An unexpected matrimony led to the founding of Massilia [Marseilles]. And Cecrops, fleeing the vengeful furies, founded the city that they later would call Athens. The same reason gave to Argos its free founder.[29] Let us, therefore, yield to the Fates, and as nature gives to every seed the soil where it can best flourish. In the same way, the power of the stars or of some hidden force or a wise and perfect numen distributes the various regions to mortals as is most convenient and appropriate for each one. Rather, I should think that very few could develop their powers in the fullest when they remain in the households of their fathers. In like fashion, plants and olive trees do not grow strong and bear unusually high yields except when they are transplanted. Submit, therefore, with equanimity to what was pleasing to the lovers, and what the gods decided to favor. Do not get carried away by the desire to avenge injury. The power of love is unconquerable.

"Your daughter was certainly not the first to be abducted from her home, nor will she be the last. Let her keep in peace and safely her sweet husband. Act manfully after her elopement. Act for the increase of your own majesty. Let your wealth grow. Add your assistance to the favors they have gotten from other people. That these of your family will be alone there, that they

29. This catalog of wandering heroes and mythological characters who founded great cities derived from Giovanni Conversini's reading of such ancient Roman poets as Ovid, Horace, and Virgil, and historians such as Valerius Maximus, Hyginus, and Justinus. The Trojan warrior Antenor was the legendary founder of Padua, Aeneas the founder of Rome. Evander was a demigod who left Arcadia for Italy and landed at the Tiber, where he settled on the Palatine Hill. Cadmus, the son of the king of Tyre, was sent to find his sister, Europa, and in the process was led to the site of Thebes, in Boeotia, where he built its ancient citadel. Teucer, the son of the king Telamon of Salamis, was banished after the fall of Troy and came finally to Cyprus, where he founded another city named Salamis. Dido, the legendary daughter of the king of Tyre, came to Carthage following the murder of her first husband and there perished on a pyre when her love was rejected by Aeneas. Cecrops, a mythical figure that was half serpent, half man, was, according to legend, the first king of Athens. The king and queen of the Ionian town of Phocaea (Foggia) fled to escape Persian domination and founded the city of Massilia (Marseilles). The marriage of Inachus led to his founding Argos and becoming its first king.

will remain distant from you, and will be deprived of the solemnity of your glory—these penalties are already more than enough.

"Therefore, Caesar, let yourself be moved by a friend's persuasive advice, and ask that your daughter and son-in-law come before you, and then embrace the two boys most tenderly, kiss them as your true grandsons, and love them as your own members, with that very sweet joy that is lodged in your breast, so you will not be able to gaze upon them or caress them enough."

The mediator, Conrad, saw to it that the parents should come in, and they obeyed, and entered the first room of the inner chambers and thus were secluded from the crowd. In this way, it was planned by Conrad that if the father were by chance to say something harsh at the first meeting, when he would scarcely be able to restrain himself, on looking back at past injuries, reproaching and blaming fate, and thus criticize his daughter and son-in-law, all this would not reach the ears of the large retinue.

Landolfo, confident of his good fortune, stood before Caesar, with his outstanding wife, and presented their children. They knelt down before him, adored him, and begged his forgiveness. The monarch scarcely knew how to contain the force of anger he felt. Immediately when he saw them, the memory of past wrongs and crimes began to blaze forth again in his breast. First he criticized the husband's injuries, first as abductor and seducer, then as forgetful of past benefits, finally as ingrate. Then he turned on his daughter, calling her impious, one who had deserted her father, her homeland, and her honor, a sordid example of womanhood and the shame of her noble rank. They said nothing to contradict, confessed their faults, and implored his forgiveness. At that moment the children, who had formerly behaved familiarly with the emperor, began to speak. They were accustomed to his caresses and embraces, and they now asked the grumbling old man to play with them. The children's appearance and their boyish high spirits as well as Conrad's intercession and speech served to banish every cloud of acrimony from the mouth and mind of the indignant old man. He said, "I am defeated, and you are forgiven."

And as his attitude changed to one of affection, he added at once: "Daughter, I had hoped that from you kings would be born, just as you were born from a queen. Thus I wished that you would have a king for a husband and a kingdom. But my hopes were in vain, and we must follow our fate. At the same time, a well-disposed spirit has conveyed to you this region by fate, and may it always remain yours. You have your husband, my daughter, and that is both happy and fortunate. So love him, follow him, honor him, and be faithful to him alone. And you, Landolfo, I love, honor, and have you as my son-in-law, and this woman I commend and give over to you. Love and protect her, I beg you. And I order you to acknowledge that I am your father-in-law, for the entire world knows it."

To all this, Elizabeth responded thus: "Until now, dear father, what has happened today with your clemency and divine kindness has quite overwhelmed us and deprived of our speech. You have treated us, father, most humanely, and by forgiving our faults and sins, you have prevented us from taking up one topic. I must speak, however, of this one thing, father, that especially troubles me and has always troubled me and now troubles me more than ever. Because of the high sense of your own majesty, you are offended, father, that I acted contrary to your own desires. But I am not disturbed by the fact that I lack a royal kingdom or a king's marriage bed, because I have gained that king whom I want the most, and more than the kingdom that you have wished for me. For me it is more sacred to have wed a man with a royal soul who lacks a kingdom than a commoner who holds several kingdoms. I consider and believe that my husband is a king because, except for a kingdom, he possesses every royal attribute; he has solid virtue, constancy, magnanimity, justice, upright character, moderation. The one thing that he lacks, father, is your peace and pardon. And if you will deign to grant him these, by the gods here present, you should know that you have given your daughter the greatest gift.

"When I was at court, I lacked any hope of possessing him, and when I was in that high position, I considered what I wanted most rather than what was best for me, and so quite out of my mind and desperate, I chose love, not as an adulteress or some lewd mistress, but as a wife accompanying her husband. And I now have him with your sacred pardon and assent, father; all my desires are fulfilled, and I will live happy. Having obtained this last pardon, father, I can think of nothing else to ask of you."

This said, Landolfo added only a little. "Now I can die happy, dear father-in-law, since I have obtained your clemency and your forgiveness. Nor am I able to repay your indulgence and kindness with sufficient humility and respect, or ever praise your love and honor enough. Be sure that I will always carry out gratefully all that you have commanded. It will seem to me that we have suffered enough already by lacking you who has been so good and generous in granting us mercy. O Caesar, I have never considered your daughter an adulteress or a runaway bride, but I have always seen her as a lady and a queen of the highest nobility, and as such I have venerated her. Henceforth, I will strive ever more fervently and tenaciously after virtue, so that you, my father-in-law, will never be ashamed that you have accepted me as your son-in-law."

With this, the emperor's countenance began to soften, and, with his good-will restored, he started to behave like a father. Thus moved by the compassion of old age as well as by feelings of mercy, and burning with parental affection, he embraced his daughter, weeping with joy, and asked her for a kiss. He was not able to restrain himself from caressing now his daughter, now his grandsons. He ordered that they all be clothed in imperial dress and accompany him to the royal palace.

Meanwhile the news that the prince of the world had found his daughter filled the ears of the nobles and the townspeople. Thereafter, everyone was overjoyed, praising the gods, and rejoiced in the honor of competing to fill the temples with offerings, and especially of congratulating the emperor. Four whole days were set aside so everyone could participate in the celebrations. The event became very famous among the people both for enthusiasm of partying and the wealth expended. Particularly amazed by these celebrations were the neighboring peoples, those from the Euganean Hills, from Padua, and from Venice. The first were very impressed by the enthusiasm for celebrating and well-wishing, the others were now able to understand and observe that an important and unexpected event had occurred. As a result, the event became famous among a great many people from all walks of life.

On one of these days of great celebration the emperor went forth in the morning to make a divine sacrifice. Accompanied by the applause of all for the occasion, first came the daughter, decked out in clothes bearing the imperial coat of arms, followed by a long line of noble matrons in their most festive attire. Immediately after came her father, resplendent in his sacred diadem and holding the grandsons by the hand—the great hope and symbol of his dynasty. Next came the son-in-law with the first minister of the empire, his rank next in the procession showing the esteem the father-in-law held for him. The line of march continued with the other notables and nobles.

When he had completed the rite of thanksgiving, the emperor took his place on the throne, surrounded and honored by the foremost princes of the world. Ordering the crowd to become silent, he declared that Landolfo was his son-in-law and that his marriage with his daughter was valid forever. Then he appointed his grandsons, Milone and Rodolfo, as imperial counts and conferred on them [the towns of] Pernumia and Anguillara, which at that time were famous strongholds. He also ordered that the forests where by fate their parents had settled, namely the area called Carrara, was to be free from all other jurisdictions and thereafter, together with the nearby regions, under their perpetual rule.[30] Then, he bestowed on his daughter and son-in-law a thousand pounds in gold and silver, together with many precious ornaments. Finally, he conferred on the grandsons, and all who would descend from them, the highest imperial privileges, dignities, and honors. When he had finished his speech, the emperor proceeded to the banquet table, and everyone spent the next days in feasting and the greatest merriment.

APPENDIX B: PIER PAOLO VERGERIO THE ELDER, CONCERNING THE CARRARA PRINCES AND THEIR DEEDS[31]

PREFACE

From the most ancient writings, it is not possible to known for certain whether the distinguished Carrara family, from whom have arisen the current lords of Padua, descended from among the most powerful of lineages in this region, or whether they grew up from the modest beginnings of an unknown progenitor of their clan and only gradually reached their present greatness.

Certainly, after the empire was violently overthrown in Italy and Rome destroyed by the barbarians, for a long time there was (if I am able to recall correctly what I have read) no one who described the events of his age in any distinguished sort of composition. This happened, not because there were no great or important events worthy of being remembered in this period, but rather because there was no enthusiasm among the men of the age to set down in writing the events that occurred. Nor was there scarcely any appreciation for the craft of literature. As a result, for the most part, this early history of events and of men remains quite unknown or of doubtful validity.

Concerning the older history of the city of Padua, there is almost nothing known except the few facts that are mentioned in the books of the ancients,

30. Carrara, Pernumia, and Anguillara had long been historic centers of the Carrara family's landed wealth, just as Landolfo, Milone, and Rodolfo were names of early nobles of that house. And Rodolfo was, of course, the name of the contemporary Carrara captain to whom Giovanni had dedicated this history.

31. Translated from Vergerio, *De principibus Carrariensibus*, which has been reprinted, with Italian translation and commentary, as *Liber de principibus Carrariensibus et gestis eorum incipit feliciter*. Translations are from 47–50 and 219–21 of the latter edition.

or, indeed if I may dare to speak frankly, quite little of the events that occurred before the tyranny of Ezzelino da Romano. But the period of Ezzelino's reign was noted for such unbelievable cruelty and so many miseries that it could not very well be forgotten. For that reason, these events have been well documented.[32] At that time, the Carrara family was much less wealthy and powerful than several other clans in the Padovano, but it was among the first families in the antiquity of its origins and the nobility of its stock. After this period, Albertino Mussato, a Paduan who was distinguished both for the glory of his learning and his services to the commune, compiled a fairly accurate chronicle of his age that contains much concerning the Carrara men and their undertakings. But angered by the injuries he had received at the hands of the Carrara, this author took many liberties with the facts.[33] Later, Guglielmo Cortusio, who was Mussato's contemporary and fellow citizen, undertook to compose and collect in a single narrative what he had witnessed both of local events and foreign affairs, both in Mussato's lifetime and, since he outlived him, much that came after Mussato.[34] But while he recorded the events in detail, he was clearly not able to equal the elegance of Mussato's style. Further, though both these authors recorded much concerning the men of the Carrara family, neither treated the origins of the clan.

On the question of origins, Giovanni Basilio followed the common opinion of many and affirmed that the Carrara family came from Germany. But

32. The tyranny of the Ghibelline vicar Ezzelino III da Romano over Padua from 1237 to 1256 was the cruelest chapter in the civil strife of the communal period. The standard chronicle account favoring Ezzolino's rule is by the Vicentine judge Gerardo Maurisio, *Chronica dominorum Ecelini et Alberici,* ed. Giovanni Soranzo, *RIS,* 8, pt. 4 (Città di Castello: S. Lapi, 1914), while opposing narratives are Rolandino Patavino's *Cronica in factis et circa facta Marchie Trivixane,* ed. Antonio Bonardi, *RIS,* 8, pt. 1 (Città di Castello: S. Lapi, 1906), and *Chronicon Marchiae Tarvisinae et Lombardiae,* ed. L. A. Botteghi, *RIS,* 8, pt. 3 (Città di Castello: S. Lapi, 1916).

33. The Paduan judge and historian Albertino Mussato (d. 1329) was a champion in the struggle of the commune against the growing power of the Carrara faction, which he chronicled in his partisan account *De Gestis Italicorum post mortem Henrici VII Caesaris,* written between 1314 and 1328. On Mussato as historian and defender of communal values, see John Kenneth Hyde, *Padua in the Age of Dante* (Manchester: Manchester University Press, 1966), 295–303, and Ronald G. Witt, *"In the Footsteps of the Ancients": The Origins of Humanism from Lovato to Bruni* (Leiden: Brill, 2000), chap. 4.

34. The Paduan judge Guglielmo Cortusi recounted the history of Padua from the fall of Ezzelino to shortly before his death, in 1358, in his *Chronica de novitatibus Padue et Lombardie,* ed. Beniamino Pagnin, *RIS,* n.s., 12, pt. 5 (Bologna: Zanichelli, 1941). For assessments of Cortusi as a historian, see John Kenneth Hyde, "Guglielmo Cortusi" in *Dizionario biografico degli italiani,* 29:806–7 (Rome: Istituto dell'enciclopedia italiana, 1983), and Capo, "I cronisti di Venezia e della Marca Trevigiana," 313–19.

he is a very recent author and cannot have much information about earlier times.[35] Moreover, he does not support his views with written documentation, and besides, he is accustomed to embellish the events with many fabulous particulars, so that one does not have faith even in that part of his history which is otherwise believable. Thus, of the three authors, the first two say nothing concerning the origins of the Carrara family, while the third states nothing reliable, so I shall limit my exposition to the two theories that have commonly been handed down concerning the origins of the family.

The most commonly held belief is that the family traces its origins back to Germany. But it is not clear why the family emigrated from its homeland, or who was the leader of the family who first came into this region, and when he came. If I were to give credence to this theory, then I would have to believe that the Carrara descended from Lombard stock. If I were to hold to the old and common notion that the Carrarese are said to come from Germany, then they came here first with that tribe which was under the leadership of Ibor and Aione and which occupied a large part of Italy for many years by force of arms and ruled it with their kings and their own laws. This view is further attested by certain old annotations of charters that state that the early members of the family lived under the laws of the Lombards. Those who think this way and have them coming from Germany recall from these accounts that they first held lands at Sossano in the Vicentine countryside. That they for a long time called themselves counts of this region is also witnessed in certain poems that I know about. Thereafter, the clan was enlarged by a number of in-laws and powerful friends, and supported with all sorts of wealth and riches; certain members of the family penetrated the Paduan countryside. Here first they had the village of Carrara, later many castles, and finally they obtained lordship of Padua itself.

Others scholars, on the contrary, believe that the Carrara family migrated from Transalpine Gaul, from the Rousillon nobility, which in the time of Charlemagne boasted a number of illustrious men, both from the antiquity of their stock and the greatness of their deeds. Even before the Carrara gained the lordship of Padua, this opinion was treated with respect by old men of the family and often repeated as a story that was handed down through the generations from the earliest forebears. Although this version of the

---

35. See Giovanni Fabris, *Cronache e cronisti padovani* (Padua: Rebellato Editore, 1977), 35–36, on Giovanni Basilio as the misattributed author of the works of Giovanni da Nono (d. 1347), and on the value of da Nono's "social chronicles" of Padua, see John Kenneth Hyde, *Literacy and Its Uses: Studies on Late Medieval Italy,* ed. Daniel Waley (Manchester: Manchester University Press, 1993), chap. 2.

family's origins may not be the absolute truth, it should be noted that it is recorded elsewhere. In this regard it is worth mentioning that Giovanni [Conversini] da Ravenna has written up this version with great diligence and in an elegant style.[36] Certainly it can be agreed that nothing in his narrative is inconsistent with the probable events. Thus, the forebears thought that this version of the origins of the family was the more believable, adducing as an argument that both the ancient right of hospitality and the law of friendship were always present in those times. I am also prone to accept this second hypothesis, persuaded by nothing more than that it is more plausible that those who really care about the antiquity of the family would cultivate more than others a memory of their true origins. Though the fact that they profess to have lived under the law of the Lombards probably says nothing about the origins of the clan, still it does indicate the customs under which they agreed to undertake governing the area. For anyone who at that time governed a civil society ruled either by the Lombard or Gallic law.

And even if nothing of this hypothesis is valid, still the nobility of the family is beyond question, since it was famous in all of Italy and rather ancient. The cause of these differing opinions can perhaps be attributed to the fact that at different times, as many remember, the Carraresi were driven from their home by wars and uprisings. Some were forced to flee to southern France, others to Germany. At these places, they collected allies, and with the help of friends who had remained at home and with the support of clients, they returned to Italy and retook possession of their lands from which they had been driven. But what use is it to investigate the early history of a family when everyone can observe so much evidence of its greatness? For indeed it is the first sign of nobility to have the origins of one's nobility lost in its antiquity. And why should we seek this family's splendor in foreign parts when there is such great splendor at home? Indeed, there are many of us who harbor the vain notion that no one should be judged noble in Italy except that their nobility has been conferred on us by some foreigners, who lie in wait to claim our own nobility. For there are many foreign princes who boast that their family arose from Italian stock, and among these both the dukes of Austria and the counts of Vigilio glory in tracing their origins from ancient Roman patrician families. Likewise, several of our own citizens who have studied the matter for a long time venture to derive the Carrara family from the ancient Roman tribune Milo, who murdered another powerful and noble Roman citizen, Clodius. For this criminal act

---

36. A reference to Conversini's *Familie Carrariensis natio,* discussed in my essay above.

of murder Milo was brought to trial, where he was defended by the eloquence of Cicero and the authority and might of Pompey the Great. But this claim, it seems to me, has been based on nothing more than the fact that Milo has been often used as a given name in the Carrara family and that from the distant past there have been many Carrara males who were named Milo.

Among so many uncertain and conflicting interpretations, each person is of course free to put forward his own conjectures. Certainly everyone agrees that for a long time now the Carrara family has been illustrious in the power of its men, the extent of its riches, and the glory of its arms, as is also proved by the coats of arms [insignia] that earlier emperors have bestowed on them and the grants of property they have from time to time conferred. Especially famous is the charter of donation, made over four centuries ago in the time of the emperor Conrad I, of the monastery of San Stefano da Carrara to Litolfo, son of Gumberto.[37] And to this donation was added other property given to Litolfo's two sons and other members of the family. Over this monastery, which was founded by the family and enlarged by later generous grants, the Carrara are now by legal right the perpetual patrons. Indeed, the rather handsome village of Carrara is situated in the Paduan countryside about seven miles from the city, on fertile soil, watered by many streams, whose cultivated fields are surrounded by pleasant meadows and woodlands interspersed with glades. Therefore, this area is especially suited for fishing, hunting, and falconry. It is a place where rustic peasants are employed in providing the necessities of life and energetic nobles can take delight in agreeable pastimes. Moreover, I believe that the name Carrara was given to the village because here carts [carri] were constructed. Before that time, it was called Village of the Woods [Villa Nemoris].

THE LIFE OF UBERTINO (CONCLUSION)

[Ubertino] constructed walls to protect the city [of Padua], and he adorned it with buildings and promoted the study of the liberal arts. Indeed, he largely completed the work on the walls, which his predecessor Marsilio [da Carrara] had begun. He constructed a squared portico of the highest columns in the palace (where Cangrande [della Scala] had begun to built the first residence of the ruling family), and he required that it be two-storied,

---

37. Vergerio probably derived the story of Conrad I's grant of rights over the monastery of San Stefano to Litolfo from redactions B and C of the *Gesta magnifica domus Carrariensis*, 155–56.

so that anyone who wanted could stroll on the ground and the second floor, shielded from the rain.

On the other side of the palace, he added another portico, of equal height and with the same symmetry of the columns. But he ordered that this loggia be open only on two sides, the north and the west, so that it would give the viewer a prospect on those parts of the heavens. And he caused to be placed in the top of the city's tower a large clock, thanks to which the twenty-four hours of the day and night would always be visible.

He also undertook to enlarge the woolen industry, whose guild would thus reap the greatest profit. He endowed the other guilds with privileges and immunities so that these would also grow larger. Indeed, he particularly favored academic studies, and he hired at an enormous salary Rainiero Arsendi of Forlì, who was the most outstanding law professor of his age. He paid special attention to the well-being of the countryside and commissioned the paving of the road that went [from Padua] to the town of Camposampiero. Other roads that had been cut or were crooked he repaired, completed, and straightened. He also constructed dikes on the riverbanks so that high waters would not flood the nearby fields. And he built a navigable canal from Este to Montagnana, but unfortunately the maintenance of this has been neglected by his successors.

The following anecdote illustrates Ubertino's domestic situation. Now, as a child he had inherited a slave named Longhetto, and the two were raised together. At that time it was still the custom in Italy to be able to inherit domestic slaves, a custom that has now largely fallen into disuse. Ubertino had complete faith in this slave and confided in him in all matters. But at one point, Ubertino's concubine, an extraordinarily beautiful woman named Carentana, got into a domestic spat with him and as an insult called him "slave." To her Longhetto replied, "Yes, I am his slave, and you also are his whore." Certainly nothing could have made Carentana angrier than to hear this accusation. Now, trusting in her own good looks (for she in fact had a very beautiful body) and in the declarations of love she had received from Ubertino, she resolved that no one could inflict such an insult on her who was not a member of her own family. Therefore, she sent her little daughter, who was the apple of her father's eye, to Ubertino to complain of the insult the mother had received. But the slave had also appealed to certain of Ubertino's friends, who were always present at the lord's councils, that they should take his side in the matter. Thus, when the little girl began to lodge her complaint, she was immediately interrupted by the counselors. Now the mother, who was looking at the entire scene from an upper loggia, became angry because no one was listening to the complaint, hurriedly came downstairs, and herself lodged the complaint that she had been insulted by Longhetto. Ubertino, who was not at all disturbed by this unusual boldness in a woman, ordered that Longhetto be brought before him so that he could hear the matter for himself. When he had heard the case, Ubertino said, "Inasmuch as this case of insults affects me, I absolve both of you." And he ordered a notary to be called who would record what was said. Then he said to Longhetto, "Do you wish to be free." And he replied, "No, I don't want to be free from you, if you simply let me go. I was born your slave, and I am not ashamed of my condition, because I serve such a lord as you. If indeed you manumit me, and at a great price you buy me back from my own freedom, so I shall never be able to be free from you." Ubertino said, "I give you what you wish, and as will be right for you. From the necessity of the condition by which you were tied to me, you are free." Then he turned to the woman and said, "And you also, since you were ashamed of your ties with me, you are free to leave. You are absolved of all ties to me." Then she began to cry, and greatly upset by the unexpected turn of events, she said, "I beg you, and for your own child, do not reject or send me away. I am indeed not worthy to have you as my lord." And when she continued to wail and speak thus, he ordered that she should return to her quarters and never trouble him with such complaints in the future. Thus, with a single judgment, he rewarded the man who deserved it and admonished the woman that she should not be ashamed of her status, which she should have not just willingly accepted but even ardently desired.

Endowed with an extraordinary sex drive, Ubertino, from excessive use of his genital member, came to be afflicted with a disease, which troubled him for a long time and eventually killed him. Sensing the weakening of his powers, he decided to provide for his successor in ruling the city. Since he had no legitimate male heirs, he selected as his heir Marsilietto Papafava dei Carraresi and took pains while he was still alive to ensure that the lordship of Padua would be bestowed on him. Near death, when he was about to receive the last rites of the Church from the hand of a priest, he was asked whether he was truly penitent for all those sins he had committed in this life, as the teachings of the Church hold. He replied, "Certainly I will tell you the truth and not deceive you, since it would be pointless to try and do so. You should know that I have never done anything for the success of my family that I would not do all over again for the same reason. I am certain that God himself will pardon me for this act. Therefore, I have nothing to fear when I shall come before him."

Ubertino died on the twenty-ninth of March 1345. The next day he was borne with great pomp and buried in the church of Sant'Agostino. As a young man, he dressed as an elegant foreigner and did not follow the norms of his homeland, but as an old man he dressed very conservatively. Moreover, he was of medium height, with a pleasant face, a round and prominent chin, and sharp nose; he was much given to lovemaking, quick to anger, vindictive to insults, but magnanimous, eager for glory, someone who preferred to be feared rather than loved.

10

Challenging Chronicles: Leonardo Bruni's
History of the Florentine People

Gary Ianziti

Leonardo Bruni (1370–1444) is generally regarded as the central figure in the early-fifteenth-century cultural movement known as Renaissance humanism. Not a Florentine by birth, Bruni came to Florence at a relatively early age and was adopted into the circle of the chancellor and man of letters Coluccio Salutati (1331–1406). Under Salutati's tutelage Bruni developed into one of the leading lights of the new generation, a young man who came to regard Salutati and his trecento (fourteenth-century) legacy as somewhat outmoded. Like others of his age, Bruni learned Greek, which set him apart from earlier humanists, who had not. Bruni in fact first earned fame as a translator of Greek classics: Plutarch and Plato among others, and, most important, Aristotle.[1] Along with producing translations of and commentaries on such authors, Bruni also read widely in Greek historiography. He was the first modern Western historian to read Thucydides and Polybius. These authors significantly affected Bruni's own historical writing.

Bruni may best be described as a member of the humanist avant-garde of the early quattrocento (fifteenth century). He was part of a group of radicals whose links to earlier city culture had suddenly become problematic. At a date that still remains controversial, Bruni articulated the dilemmas he and his circle faced. How were they to judge their trecento predecessors: Dante, Petrarch, Boccaccio, and (implicitly at least) Salutati himself? Bruni's dialogues offer a portrait of the younger generation involved in prolonged

---

1. Cesare Vasoli, "Leonardo Bruni," in *Dizionario biografico degli italiani*, 14:621–23 (Rome: Istituto dell'enciclopedia italiana, 1972).

disputes on this topic. The subject of the debates was essentially the relationship between the new humanist movement and the city traditions so central to Florentine identity. However one chooses to interpret Bruni's answer to the question, the very fact of its being posed represented a major transgression. Bruni and his circle were seen as having deviated from the revered Florentine traditions of old, and were thus subjected to a barrage of criticism.[2]

This background is crucial to understanding Bruni's masterpiece, the still widely misconstrued *History of the Florentine People*. A superficial glance at this work might suggest that it represents little more than a recasting into classical Latin form of the material contained in the city's fourteenth-century chronicle tradition. On closer inspection, however, Bruni's *History* turns out to be something quite different: a challenge to the chronicle tradition and an attempt to develop a new paradigm for the telling of Florentine history.

Why was such a new paradigm necessary? To answer this question, we need to consider first the type of city chronicles being written in 1415, the year in which Bruni wrote what became the first book of his *History*. By this time Florentine chronicle writing had undergone the evolution described by Louis Green in his classic study, *Chronicle into History*.[3] Green shows how in the preceding century chroniclers in Florence experienced increasing difficulty in relating local events to the Christian providential scheme characteristic of Western medieval historiography. This difficulty resulted in a gradual decline in the ability of chroniclers to produce meaningful accounts within the traditional framework. Chronicling had entered a crisis. The Villani chronicle was not continued beyond 1364, even though the final author, Matteo's son Filippo, lived on until 1405. This crisis inaugurated a period of experimentation in which accounts of the city's history became fragmentary and contemporary in focus. Memoirs, family records, and biography replaced the chronicle. A synthesis of the city's history *ab origine* no longer seemed possible, at least not along the traditional lines set down and followed by earlier generations.

It is little wonder then that in the early fifteenth century the need for a new synthesis arose within humanist circles. First, the new learning had revealed fresh vistas on the foundation and early history of Florence. Second, humanists grew increasingly impatient with the cultural and linguistic

2. Riccardo Fubini, "All'uscita dalla scolastica medievale: Salutati, Bruni, e i *Dialogi ad Petrum Histrum*," *Archivio storico italiano* 150 (1992): 1088.

3. Louis Green, *Chronicle into History: An Essay on the Interpretation of History in Florentine Fourteenth-Century Chronicles* (Cambridge: Cambridge University Press, 1972).

limitations of their forebears. As early as his *Panegyric* of 1403/4, Bruni had hinted at the possibility that he might write a history of Florence in the humanist mode.[4] He was naturally less inclined to do so after accepting an appointment as secretary in the papal Curia in 1405. He even coyly suggested to those who continued to encourage him that they look elsewhere.[5] Only a decade later, in 1415, when he returned to settle permanently in Florence, did Bruni finally set himself to the task of writing his *History*.

Furthering humanist scholarship, however, was not his sole motivation. Beyond Bruni's personal commitment to the project, other powerful forces were at work. One of these concerns Bruni's links to the ruling Albizzi oligarchy. It used to be fashionable—following the lead of Hans Baron—to regard Bruni as politically neutral. The implication for the field of historiography is that Bruni wrote as an independent scholar, unlike the official historians of the other Italian city-states, whose role was to write what they were told to.[6] Subsequent scholars have discovered, however, that Bruni had close ties to a number of the leading oligarchs and had therefore in writing his *History* already identified himself with the city's rulers. Not surprisingly, the resulting work was tinged with official ideology. Bruni received no official commissions as such for his labors but nonetheless was handsomely rewarded for his troubles. Upon completion of the first book, in 1416, he received a significant tax exemption that was valid for his descendants as well. Subsequent installments led to more explicit forms of recognition. In 1427 he became chancellor; by the end of his life his *History* had been adopted and enshrined as the official, state-sanctioned version of the Florentine past.[7]

Wider social questions also underlay the composition of Bruni's *History* and help explain why an updated interpretation of the city's history was required. The political processes that governed and determined the city's power structure were changing during the late fourteenth and early fifteenth centuries. Gene Brucker has characterized these changes as constituting a passage from communal forms of government—based on the collegial sharing of responsibilities—to the more closed and corporate style of rule typified

4. Leonardo Bruni, *Panegyric to the City of Florence*, trans. Benjamin G. Kohl, in *The Earthly Republic*, ed. Benjamin G. Kohl and Ronald G. Witt (Philadelphia: University of Pennsylvania Press, 1978), 163.

5. Leonardo Bruni, *Epistolae*, bk. II, 4, as cited in Hans Baron, *The Crisis of the Early Florentine Renaissance*, rev. ed. (Princeton: Princeton University Press, 1966), 253.

6. Ibid., 496.

7. Riccardo Fubini, "Osservazioni sugli *Historiarum florentini populi libri XII* di Leonardo Bruni," in *Studi di storia medievale e moderna per Ernesto Sestan* (Florence: Leo S. Olschki, 1980), 1:429–32.

by the Albizzi oligarchy.[8] A premise of the latter system was its contempt for certain features of communal government such as the rotation of offices and selection by lot. By contrast, proponents of the corporate polity sought to bypass such procedures in the interest of favoring political competence, which fostered professional standards. They believed in government by an elite body of experts, flanked by trained cadres, steeped in the arts of peace and war. Within such an environment, a new city history had at least two possible functions: (1) to celebrate and legitimize the values of professional government; (2) to teach *prudentia*, or the supreme art of political management. Bruni promotes both themes as priorities in the course of his *History*.

Bruni's *History* is thus a highly specific product designed for a highly specific audience. It is not an all-purpose history. Much has been made of the fact that—compared to Villani, or even to Machiavelli—Bruni offers little information on the social and economic history of Florence.[9] Yet Bruni's very viewpoint distances him from the social and economic and focuses instead on the political. In so doing, Bruni is not only meeting the requirements of his audience but also conforming to the broad patterns of historical writing as codified by the great classical masters, Thucydides, Polybius, and Livy. The dovetailing of classical standards with the most urgent needs of the moment is one of the striking features of Bruni's particular brand of historiography. Bruni's classicism was not an end in itself but a means to an end or ends. These ends are best identified with the historiographical requirements of the new ruling elites.[10]

A clearer picture of this point emerges if we consider the areas where Bruni's *History* diverges from the chronicle tradition. Because Bruni's *History* is largely reliant on the Villani chronicles, many believe that it might be classified as a mere recoding. According to this view, Bruni's *History* would represent continuity with earlier traditions, rather than change.[11] The main

8. Gene Brucker, *The Civic World of Early Renaissance Florence* (Princeton: Princeton University Press, 1977), 283.

9. John Najemy, "*Arti* and *Ordini* in Machiavelli's *Istorie Fiorentine*," in *Essays Presented to Myron P. Gilmore*, ed. Sergio Bertelli and Gloria Ramakus (Florence: La nuova Italia, 1978), 1:163–68.

10. Bruni does not let classicism interfere with historiographic expediency. While preferring not to use such terms as "Guelf" and "Ghibelline," he does so when he has no viable alternative: e.g., *History of the Florentine People*, ed. and trans. James Hankins (Cambridge, Mass.: Harvard University Press, 2001), 1:264. Moreover, he uses the Christian dating system, *ab incarnatione* (from the incarnation), and refers to events as occurring on Christian feast days such as Easter Sunday (e.g., Bruni, *History of the Florentine People*, 1:172, 218).

11. Eric Cochrane, *Historians and Historiography in the Italian Renaissance* (Chicago: University of Chicago Press, 1981), 14.

burden of the present analysis is to explore the ways in which Bruni's *History* differs from the previous chronicles and to determine how such differences relate to the more general themes discussed so far.

The most convenient starting point is Bruni's famous account of the foundations of Florence. He begins his *History* by brushing aside the myth—duly enshrined in the city chronicles down to the time of Villani and indeed well beyond—of Florence's foundation by Julius Caesar.[12] According to this time-honored tradition, Florence was founded in the aftermath of Caesar's deliberate destruction of the ancient yet rebellious city of Fiesole. Thus Florence began life as a Roman colony on the Arno. The town was originally named after Caesar, and only later came to be called Florence. Bruni pays no homage to this legend. In the preface to his *History* he warns readers that his account of the city's foundation will "involve rejecting some commonly held but mythical beliefs."[13] Book 1 opens immediately with the shocking news that Florence—known in these early years as Florentia—was founded not by Caesar but by veterans of Sulla's campaigns much earlier. The break with established city traditions could hardly be more abrupt.

There has been a long-standing tendency in Bruni studies to present this instance as an example of nascent historical criticism.[14] It seems appropriate, however, to bear in mind some of the contextual features covered thus far. The idea that history should deal critically with myths and commonly held beliefs is something Bruni could find spelled out in the first book of Thucydides. As for the repositioning of the city's origins in the time of Sulla, Bruni was in fact building his case on the achievements of earlier humanist classical scholarship, including that of his former mentor, Salutati.[15] What is truly striking is the boldness of Bruni's break with accumulated tradition in a genre of writing where there had been an expectation that such tradition would be respected. Such a break was possible only within the wider context of social and political dislocation alluded to earlier. Bruni's recasting of Florentine origins should thus not be viewed only as a matter of critical scholarship but rather as mirroring wider processes of change. It also reflects a reevaluation of a range of issues regarding Florentine politics, identity, and the interpretation of subsequent city history.

---

12. Nicolai Rubinstein, "The Beginnings of Political Thought in Florence," *Journal of the Warburg and Courtauld Institutes* 5 (1942): 215–25.

13. Bruni, *History of the Florentine People*, 1:7.

14. Rubinstein, "Beginnings of Political Thought," 225.

15. Ronald G. Witt, *Hercules at the Crossroads: The Life, Works, and Thought of Coluccio Salutati* (Durham, N.C.: Duke University Press, 1983), 246–53.

This last point can be illustrated by analyzing Giovanni Villani's treatment of the tale of Florence's foundation by Julius Caesar. Villani stresses that the original inhabitants of the city were drawn from two distinct racial groups: one Roman, and thus of civilized stock, the other Fiesolan, and therefore of warlike and barbarian origins.[16] In later chapters, Villani frequently returns to this racial mixture to explain the causes of subsequent conflict. Florentine civil unrest is thus presented as an inevitable fate whose roots can be traced back to flawed origins.

Distancing himself from the original myth, Bruni also rejects Villani's racial explanation of Florentine civil strife. Party strife was not to be seen as a congenital curse; in Bruni's view it was susceptible to rational analysis. Essentially, it drew its sustenance from the larger struggles for control of the city between the papacy and the empire. And since it was not a congenital defect, party strife could be eradicated. The primary condition for its eradication was Florentine *libertas,* defined by Bruni as comprising two features: first, independence from external control; second, enforcement by a public authority of respect for law.[17]

The development of these two features constitutes the main thrust of Bruni's *History.* Unlike Villani, whose Guelf sympathies were visible at all times, Bruni opts for a more independent stance. He is critical of party politics that override civic authority and that deliver the city to external masters, be they popes or emperors. Here too it is possible to discern the coincidence of Bruni's views with those of the Albizzi oligarchy, whose rationale for governance was based on just such principles. By claiming to exercise public authority the leaders of the oligarchy both rationalized and legitimized their control of the city and its territory.[18]

Bruni's rejection of the imperial Roman origin of Florence as enshrined in the chronicle tradition is thus not to be seen as a matter of mere rectification, but signals a wider reorientation in respect to Florentine history. This same observation applies to other areas where Bruni's account diverges from Villani's. The two differ, for example, over what might be called the issue of Roman legacy. Villani makes much of the fact that Florence is descended from Rome. Florence is, as he writes, "figliuola e fattura di Roma in tutte

16. Giovanni Villani, *Nuova cronica,* ed. Giuseppe Porta, 3 vols. (Parma: Fondazione Pietro Bembo, 1990–91), 2:1 (citations to the *Nuova cronica* refer to book and chapter).

17. Riccardo Fubini, "La rivendicazione di Firenze della sovranità statale e il contributo delle *Historiae* di Leonardo Bruni," in *Leonardo Bruni cancelliere della Repubblica di Firenze,* ed. Paolo Viti (Florence: Leo S. Olschki, 1990), 40.

18. Riccardo Fubini, *Italia quattrocentesca* (Milan: Franco Angeli, 1994), 46–47.

cose" [daughter and creature of Rome in all things].[19] In Villani's perspective, Florence is to be regarded either as part of the Roman Empire or, alternatively—from the Guelf point of view—as reliant on the papal system of power placed under the protection of the French monarchy.

Bruni does not share these views. In his eyes, Florence was founded by Romans, but the city had no chance to develop its potential as long as Rome prospered. Far from seeing Rome as a positive force with which Florence could and should identify, Bruni stresses how from the very beginning Roman power overshadowed the struggling Florentia and actually prevented the city's expansion. This observation applies to the Roman republic as well as the empire: under each, Florentia saw her prospects dwindle. Only with the decline of Rome was it possible for cities like Florentia to flourish and grow.

> Only the nearness of Rome in her grandeur limited Florentia's rise to power. As mighty trees overshadow young seedlings that grow nearby and keep them stunted, so did Rome overwhelm her neighbors with sheer size, allowing no greater city to arise in Italy. Other cities that had once been great were oppressed by their neighbor Rome, ceased to grow, and even became smaller. How, then, might Florentia's power increase? Being under imperial rule she could not augment her borders by war, nor indeed wage war at all; nor could she boast splendid magistrates, since their jurisdiction was narrowly circumscribed and subject to Roman officials.
>
> As to commerce—in case anyone thinks that this activity is somewhat relevant to the growth of the city—in those days it could most profitably be carried on in Rome. That was the place where men gathered and where there were markets. Rome had ports, islands, tolls, privileges, and official protection. Nowhere else was there so much privilege and power. If a man of solid worth was occasionally born elsewhere within the general region, he would see the difficulties that stood in his way at home and invariably move to Rome. Thus Rome drew to herself everything wonderful that was engendered in Italy and drained all other cities. The proof lies in any comparison of pre-Roman and Roman times. Before the Romans took over, many cities and peoples flourished magnificently in Italy, and under the Roman Empire all of them declined. After the fall of

19. Villani, *Nuova cronica*, 2:4.

Rome, on the other hand, the other cities immediately began to raise their heads and flourish. What her growth had taken away, her decline restored.[20]

In reading this passage, one is struck by two things: first, the radical departure Bruni's views represent with respect to entrenched city traditions; second, the extent to which such concepts match the ideology of state sovereignty as articulated by the early fifteenth-century oligarchy. Of particular interest in this latter respect is Bruni's formulation of the attributes of sovereignty denied to Florence and to other cities by Roman authority: "she could not augment her borders by war, nor indeed wage war at all; nor could she boast splendid magistrates, since their jurisdiction was narrowly circumscribed and subject to Roman officials." These were the very rights and prerogatives that the Florentine oligarchy of the early fifteenth century claimed for itself. Bruni's *History* was meant to bolster such claims through its references to the waning of Roman power as a historical reality. Once the decline of Rome became a recognized fact, it presaged the establishment of the Florentine territorial state.

But what of the Roman empire of Bruni's day? In subsequent books of the *History*, Bruni treads carefully. Yet he makes abundantly clear that the German-based empire of his time is but a shadowy fiction. In his correspondence, by contrast, Bruni could afford to be entirely blunt: he describes the Roman empire of the fifteenth century as "dead and buried."[21]

Florentine sovereignty—or *libertas*, in Bruni's term—cannot be grounded in Rome, either in the German empire or in its alternative Franco-papal form. Both of these imply structures of authority that amount to a denial of Florentine claims to statehood. Bruni's *History* functions as a rationalization of the claims to sovereignty through a sustained reinterpretation of the city's past. His history becomes the vehicle for the embodiment and codification of such claims.[22] He invests heavily in a reconfiguration of the fundamental moments of the Florentine past, and thus his *History* diverges widely in form and content from the chronicle tradition.

Bruni systematically rewrites key episodes in Florentine history. A fine example is Villani's tale of the destruction of Florence at the hands of Totila and the city's second founding by Charlemagne. This story fits neatly within

20. Bruni, *History of the Florentine People*, 1:16–18.

21. Riccardo Fubini, "Cultura umanistica e tradizione cittadina nella storiografia fiorentina del '400," in *La storiografia umanistica* (Messina: Sicania, 1992), vol. 1, pt. 1, 413.

22. Fubini, "Osservazioni," 425.

the themes under discussion. For example, it fits squarely with the old Fiesole-Florence dichotomy. According to Villani, Totila, after completely destroying Florence, restored Fiesole to its pristine splendor. Thus did barbarism once again triumph over civilization. Florence lay empty of inhabitants for some 350 years, before Charlemagne resurrected it, populating it with the usual mixture of Romans and Fiesolani.[23]

Again we find the racial explanation for civic strife reaffirmed. More important perhaps, Villani's story—borrowed from earlier Florentine tradition—places the French monarchy at the origins of the renewed city. In a symmetrical twist, Florence owes its original foundation to Julius Caesar and its renewal to Charlemagne, the restorer of Roman power. The city's identity thus hinges solidly on its allegiance to the Franco-papal system.

Bruni's divergence from this scheme deserves careful scrutiny. It, like his recasting of the founding myth, has often been promoted as a breakthrough in critical scholarship. Yet what is striking is the absence, rather than the presence, of source criticism. Bruni's rectification instead combines pure common sense and simple reasoning. Bruni does not deny that Totila ravaged the city. What he shows, apart from correcting chronology and other details, is that the city could not have been completely destroyed, as is traditionally claimed. Nor, by the same token, could Charlemagne have refounded it: "Rather than refounded, in my opinion, it was essentially restored."

> Florentia was razed (according to some) by Attila the Hun or (according to others) by Totila and later restored by Charlemagne after a long period. To us, however, it seems abundantly clear that Attila the Hun was never in Tuscany at all, and that he never crossed to this side of the river Mincio, which flows from Lake Garda to the river Po. Totila, king of the Goths, did, as we have shown, ravage the Tuscan cities, which had rebelled against the Goths after Belisarius' victory. I am convinced, therefore, that a confusion of names has led some authors erroneously to mistake Totila for Attila. It may plausibly be supposed that, quite apart from Florentia's recent defection, an old rancor burned in Totila's heart and made him want to destroy this city, for it was here that, still earlier, so many thousands of Goths under Radagaisus had been killed. The memory of it would have rubbed raw in his mind, and he would have wished to destroy Florentia, a city that stood like a monument to

23. Villani, *Nuova cronica*, 3:1–3, 21; 4:1.

the defeat of his people in Etruria. If so, Florentia must have lain in ruins for two hundred years, from Totila to Charlemagne. Anyone will be justly struck by the question of where the citizens lived in the meantime if the city lay empty of its people for so long. For it is completely useless to imagine that Charlemagne brought new inhabitants in from Rome, especially as that city had been recently involved in great calamities and had already been so much afflicted by earlier devastation that it needed to gain new inhabitants itself and could not possibly supply them. About that time, in fact, it is recorded that Ostia, a city critical to the Roman state, needed inhabitants, and that colonists were brought there from Sardinia because the city of Rome itself was empty.

I think, therefore, that Totila had indeed done great harm to Florentia, slaughtering many of her citizens and tearing down her walls, but I don't believe that he destroyed the city altogether nor that it was entirely without inhabitants in the intervening period. I see standing yet the rich and extraordinary temple of Mars and other buildings from before the age of Totila, and when I consider these unharmed remains I cannot believe that the whole city was destroyed nor that it stood uninhabited for so long. More likely, I think, the walls were restored by Charlemagne and he recalled the nobility, which, lacking confidence in the city's fortifications, would have defended the numerous castles on their estates. I think, therefore, that the city was put back together as a city after having been variously dismembered. Rather than refounded, in my opinion, it was essentially restored.[24]

The contrast between Bruni and Villani on this point is significant. It has perhaps less to do with critical scholarship—though that element too is present—than with radically different ideological patterns. Because in Villani the city's identity is grounded in the Roman inheritance, its history begins and begins again with Roman intervention, the second time in the form of Charlemagne's supposed refounding. In Bruni's view, however, Rome—for all its credit in the historical origin—does not constitute the touchstone of the city's identity. Rome is actually, as we saw, a hindrance to the realization of Florentine sovereignty. Recognition on Bruni's part of complete destruction by Totila and refoundation by Charlemagne would not only violate historical

24. Bruni, *History of the Florentine People*, 1:94–96.

logic, it would also be counterproductive in terms of Bruni's overall objective: the development of a city identity independent of a Roman legacy.

Yet another reason explains why Bruni is so keen to deny the myth of Florence's destruction or refoundation at the hands of Totila-Charlemagne. Bruni's denial of the myth relates to his extended coverage of pre-Roman Etruria.[25] The Etruscan section constitutes a significant share of Bruni's first book, again independent of Villani's meager account. Why Bruni indulges in such detail becomes clear if we consider the implications of his rejection of the traditional Roman link. If Florentine identity is not to be founded on a strictly Roman basis, then what is the justification for an independent Florentine state? For Bruni and his generation the answer could come only from remote history; thus the extensive passages on the power and authority of the Etruscans. Bruni in fact realigns Florentine identity with an Etruscan past that reaches back before the rise of Rome. The argument that the city was neither destroyed by Totila nor refounded by Charlemagne is meant to establish an unbroken line of continuity between remote Etruscan origins and the present.

The point should be clear: Bruni's *History* may rely on material collected in the previous chronicle tradition, yet it also breaks radically with the basic fabric of that tradition. Bruni wishes in essence to recast the core moments of city history in order to bring the past into line with the new values of the early fifteenth century. Such a process involved the renegotiation of the fundamentals of the Florentine story. But to what extent does this represent the introduction of a new historiographical paradigm? Answering this question requires a closer scrutiny of the procedures and methods used by Bruni. Specifically, what features have changed with respect to the chronicles?

One should begin with Bruni's own program, as spelled out in the preface to the *History*. There he makes clear that he aims not to continue but to leave behind the traditional forms of history writing, by which he means the city chronicles. Bruni's use of Latin and his return to a stricter application of classical standards of composition signal a break with tradition. So too does his title: it promises not a chronicle but history (*historiae*), not a municipal history (as in the chronicles) but one of the Florentine people. *Populus* here is used not in its medieval sense of *popolo* but in the classical Roman legal sense of public authority.[26] Bruni's project is thus to write the history not of the city but of the Florentine state.[27]

25. Ibid., 1:18–48.

26. Fubini, "La rivendicazione," 39.

27. Donald J. Wilcox, *The Development of Florentine Humanist Historiography in the Fifteenth Century* (Cambridge, Mass.: Harvard University Press, 1969), 34.

Such features indicate a radical departure from the chronicle tradition. Yet it would be wrong to exaggerate their significance in the opposite direction and to draw lines of continuity leading from Bruni to Ranke. Early attempts to establish a correlation between Bruni and modern historiography of the late nineteenth and early twentieth centuries remain unconvincing and are also misleading. Bruni's *History* is not a leap into modernity but a product of its time. As such, it contains both important elements of innovation and also the conventions Bruni shared with the classical writers of history who were his models.

One example concerns the use of signs and portents. It used to be claimed that Bruni completely eliminated these in favor of rational causal explanation.[28] A careful reading of the *History* reveals that Bruni often cites comets and other signs as announcements of revolutionary change on the horizon.[29] He is also willing to acknowledge prodigies and miracles of various kinds, even transforming and embellishing them in accordance with classical examples. The mysterious voice heralding the Florentine victory at Campaldino in 1289—at the very hour in which the battle ended—represents a good case in point.

> It is established that the battle of Campaldino took place on 11 June, and that news of the victory arrived in Florence on the same day and hour. It was mid-day, and the priors, exhausted from anxiety and sleepless nights, were taking a nap, when there came a great pounding on the doors and a messenger's voice was heard: "Get up! The enemy is beaten; you have won!" The priors sprang up joyfully at the voice, and opened the doors with gladness and thanksgiving. The news flew through the streets, and there were throngs of rejoicing citizens running to and fro, filling the piazzas. But when the author of the tale was sought for, no one came forward, so the story collapsed as an empty and unproven rumor. Yet on the following night when the true report at last arrived from the army, and the manner and time when the battle took place was told, it was discovered that victory was achieved in the very same hour it was announced to the sleeping priors. This seems marvelous, but we have read of this happening in other places, too. And it is by no

---

28. Eduard Fueter, *Storia della storiografia moderna,* trans. Altiero Spinelli (Milan: Ricciardi, 1970), 21–22.

29. E.g., Bruni, *History of the Florentine People,* 1:192–93.

means inappropriate to believe that the divine power by whose generosity victory was won, with an equal generosity announced his propitious favor instantaneously to the very persons he had favored. During the Macedonian War, when the Persian king was defeated in battle, we read that the news was announced in Rome by means of a similar miracle. And in the time of Domitian, when Rome was full of apprehension, an extremely positive report was spread in the city on the very day that a victory was won over the Germans. There are many other traditions of this kind, if one cares to indulge in this prolix sort of research and collect domestic and foreign examples of the phenomenon.[30]

What Bruni does in the *History* is not so much eliminate the irrational as limit its importance. If this shift of emphasis is less pronounced than many have claimed, it is nevertheless significant. In his preface, Bruni takes up the position—ultimately derived from Cicero—that history writing (*historia*) requires not only narration but also "causal explanation of each particular event, and the public expression of one's judgment about every issue."[31] Such a proposition implies an attempt to provide rational explanations for events. The declaration denotes an extremely important divergence from what was frequently, if not always, the case in chronicles, where, barring a better explanation, events could always be ascribed to divine causation.[32]

A comparison of Villani's and Bruni's explanations for the abandonment of the city by the leading Florentine Guelfs after the defeat at Montaperti in 1260 provides an excellent example of the contrast. Villani criticizes the decision as senseless, given that Florence was well fortified and thus able to withstand the force of any imminent enemy attack. He labels the decision to leave an act of pure folly and suggests that God was punishing the Guelfs by making their leaders panic and lose their wits.[33] Villani, in other words, sees the decision as so unwise as to be incomprehensible. Bruni's response represents a fine piece of historical reasoning. It is a mini-essay on a particular historical situation, which both vindicates and explains the Guelf decision.

30. Ibid., 1:340–43.
31. Ibid., 1:5; see also Cicero, *De oratore*, trans. E. W. Sutton and H. Rackham (Cambridge, Mass.: Harvard University Press, 1988), bk. ii, xv, 63.
32. Bernard Guenée, *Histoire et culture historique dans l'occident médiéval* (Paris: Aubier Montaigne, 1980), 36.
33. Villani, *Nuova cronica*, 7:79.

I am well aware that certain great men have judged this action of theirs imprudent and timid: abandoning without a fight a fortified city, girt with powerful walls, before the enemy had even arrived. They could have defended it for some time (it is alleged); and the passage of time can extricate you from many desperate situations. For my part I should never condemn for cowardice and imprudence illustrious men whose brave deeds were later famous throughout Italy; I prefer to think that the condition of those times is imperfectly understood by those who do condemn them. With partisan passions boiling up anew, certain of the more eminent citizens had gone over to the other side. The common people could not be counted on; they had been pledged to neither party for any great length of time, and always tended to favor the victorious party. They considered the exiles their fellow-citizens no less than those who were staying inside the walls. If there had been a fight with some entirely foreign, external enemy and not with fellow-citizens, the common danger both to the ordinary folk and to the optimates and a resolute devotion to country would have united them in the common defense. The return of exiled citizens to the city, while it presented great danger to their adversaries, presented none to the commons; to them it appeared that the city was returning to the control of the citizens, not coming into the power of enemies. Hence the commoners and the masses were unwilling either to undergo a siege or subject themselves to hunger and other discomforts. So for the men of distinction to hide within the walls awaiting the enemy was simply to offer themselves up to certain death; to withdraw and preserve oneself for a better fate seemed to be a course of action that was at once prudent and bold.[34]

Here Bruni again offers no original research material but, as with the story of Totila, uses simple reason to reinterpret events. His hypothesis is that the Guelf leaders must have acted correctly in deciding to abandon Florence. Bruni's whole passage is structured around a reversal of Villani's statements. Whereas the latter characterizes the move as "imprudent and timid," Bruni shows that it was in fact "prudent and bold." The argument he presents to support this thesis reveals a deep understanding of the political and historical situation he is describing. Bruni applies political analysis to achieve

---

34. Bruni, *History of the Florentine People*, 1:170–72.

what he calls an appreciation for "the condition of those times," that is, Florence in 1260, after the Ghibelline victory at Montaperti. Perhaps this deeper level of understanding is attained through a sort of empathy mixed with a heavy dose of historical imagination. The result in any case is a picture that stands in sharp contrast to Villani's. Not only does it offer a rational explanation for Guelf behavior, it also probes the internal dynamics of the political situation unfolding within the city. It justifies a seemingly irrational decision by appealing to a plausible sequence of cause and effect. The scenario of divine punishment concocted by Villani is replaced by more sophisticated tools of analysis.

"Prudence" is a key term in the passage quoted above. Prudence and its opposite, imprudence (*imprudentia*) are fundamental elements of Bruni's political vocabulary. For *historia* is above all the school of prudence, where examples of previous political conduct can be studied with profit. As Bruni writes in his preface, history confers wisdom: "For there the deeds and decisions of many ages may be scrutinized; from its pages we may learn with ease what behavior we should imitate and avoid, while the glory won by great men, as therein recorded, inspires us to perform acts of virtue."[35] The term "virtue" here should be understood in its classical, rather than in its Christian, sense.[36] It refers to the ability to carry out effective action. It does not refer to a moral standard of conduct, as is clear from the context: the primary concept is "the glory won by great men." What should be imitated and what should be avoided do not relate to good and evil in any abstract sense but relate rather to the human endeavor to succeed in this world. Bruni's point is that history provides a gold mine of examples—both positive and negative—regarding prudent political decision making.

This is true, of course, only of a history that focuses its attention on human motivation and agency. Bruni did not invent this approach; he revived such principles, thanks to his reading of the Greek classical authors, above all Polybius.[37] Polybius achieved the most cogent expression of what is often referred to as "pragmatic" history, that is, history that deliberately sets out to teach political lessons.[38] In contrast, classical Roman historiography tended to be moral and patriotic, with exhortation toward correct moral behavior

---

35. Ibid., 3.
36. Fubini, "Osservazioni," 413.
37. Arnaldo Momigliano, *Essays in Ancient and Modern Historiography* (Oxford: Blackwell, 1977), 79–88.
38. Bruno Gentili and Giovanni Cerri, *History and Biography in Ancient Thought* (Amsterdam: J. C. Gieben, 1988), 28–33.

as a central theme. Moral corruption was frequently blamed for cycles of decay and decline. The existence of such a moral framework explains why the classical Roman historians were so easily assimilated into the medieval Christian ethos. Villani, for example, was a great admirer of Livy.

But Polybius employs a different framework that explicitly rejects patriotic history in favor of an impartial, analytical stance.[39] Bruni, to be sure, is not so strictly Polybian as to forget his role as official Florentine historiographer. His *History* has the Florentine view at its core, yet it also displays strong elements of Polybian "pragmatic" history. One would indeed be hardpressed to say which of these two aspects prevails. They coexist in a delicate and sometimes improbable balance. It is nevertheless to the pragmatic side of the work that we now turn. How does Bruni set about achieving the goals of pragmatic history? What devices does he use, and how do these differ from the practice of chronicle writing? One of Bruni's devices has already been noted: the extended commentary, in which Bruni offers a sample of political analysis. In addition, however, there is a feature whose contribution to the analytical side of the work may be less obvious, the set-piece speech reproduced in full, according to the classical model.

Cicero provides perhaps the best key to where the set speech fits into the classical framework of history. In the *De oratore*, Cicero lists the desiderata of historical writing, including the historian's duty to include an account of *consilia* (the decision-making processes), *actus* (the enactment of policy decisions), and *eventus* (the outcomes, or results).[40] Political activity is therefore to be examined according to a tripartite scheme, where the planning stage (*consilia*) holds importance equal to the other two. The intellectual exercise of making decisions is thus elevated to an area requiring careful analysis in works of history.

Certainly this is how the speeches function in Bruni's narrative. An example occurs in book 2, where deliberations are under way in Florence about how to address the renewed Ghibelline threat centering on Siena in 1260. Bruni at this point presents a lengthy speech delivered by Tegghiaio d'Aldobrando Adimari, who argues against the Florentines' taking any military action. Tegghiaio builds his case on the dangers and uncertainties of such a course of action. The plan to meet the enemy in the field he brands as unnecessary and "more audacious than prudent." Bruni adds that the

---

39. Polybius, *The Histories*, trans. W. R. Paton, 6 vols. (Cambridge, Mass.: Harvard University Press, 1922–27), bk. I, 14.

40. Cicero, *De oratore*, bk. II, xv, 63.

view expressed by Tegghiaio was shared by other "outstanding men . . . schooled in practical activity and astute from long experience." Through both context and presentation, Bruni makes clear that Tegghiaio's advice indicates the right path. To underscore this point, Bruni inserts a brief contrasting speech counseling war. And Bruni also follows Cicero's advice by letting the reader know that the counsel for war came from rash and inexperienced elements, "the sort of person unrestrained liberty can sometimes produce."[41]

Bruni's oligarchical prejudices are clearly on display here. The clash of opposites allows him to explore contrasting policies and to assess their effectiveness. He repackages Villani's material and highlights two distinct points of view emanating from different segments of the leadership of the time. The whole presentation moves away from the incidental nature of Villani's account[42] and becomes instead an apology for the rule of the best men.

Bruni also uses paired speeches to contrast opposing political ideologies. In such cases, he skillfully makes his orators speak in character, as when in book 3 he has Pope Gregory X address the Florentine Guelfs in language that reflects the usage and values of the Curia.[43] Similarly, Bruni has the Florentine Guelfs answer according to their own quite different values: "aliter enim caelum, aliter terra regitur" (it is one thing to rule heaven; another, earth).[44] Along with paired speeches, Bruni also uses single set-piece speeches, strategically placed, as a means of showcasing issues he deems worthy of special note. Perhaps the best-known example is the speech of Giano della Bella that explicates a key thematic statement of the *History,* clarifying concepts such as *populus, libertas,* and citizenship and extolling the principle of state authority against the abuses perpetrated by the nobility.[45]

Bruni's *History* is meant to supply lessons, both positive and negative, regarding political decision making. Though officially sanctioned, Bruni's *History* is not a mere celebration of Florentine successes. The work is, on the contrary, studded with accounts of mistakes and errors of judgment, which Bruni singles out for emphasis. At times he blames the incompetence of the inexperienced. The oligarchical prejudice waxes strong. At other times, however, Bruni adopts a neutral posture, where the lessons to be learned take precedence over all polemical intent. Such is the case in book 6, with Bruni's account of Walter of Brienne's brief and ill-fated lordship over Florence in

41. Bruni, *History of the Florentine People,* 1:153, 159.
42. Villani, *Nuova cronica,* 7:77.
43. Bruni, *History of the Florentine People,* 1:260–66.
44. Ibid., 1:270.
45. Ibid., 1:362–70; compare Villani, *Nuova cronica,* 9:1.

1342. Bruni stresses that the affair holds instruction for both citizens and rulers. Citizens will learn from it not to entrust themselves to the rule of one. Rulers will learn to avoid offending their subjects with willful and immoderate behavior.[46] Machiavelli himself could not have been more detached. Such statements prefigure the author of *The Prince*, who was to be one of Bruni's most avid readers.

The mention of Machiavelli indicates the distance we have traveled from Villani and the trecento chroniclers. Or does it? Recent studies have suggested that Machiavelli's own *Florentine Histories* may be seen as a reestablishment of a link with the earlier chronicle tradition.[47] Yet this view in itself implies that that link had been severed, or at least challenged, by Leonardo Bruni. If so, it was a challenge that was fostered and sustained by a particular moment in the early-fifteenth-century equilibrium of social and political forces in Florence. Bruni expressed an outlook—antitraditional and technical—that was congenial to the Albizzi oligarchy, which supported his enterprise. How well it fit the Medici ethos that came to dominate the city after 1434 is an issue that remains to be clarified. One thing, however, is certain: Bruni's *History* did not achieve its primary ambition of replacing the Villani chronicles within the city tradition.[48] The fortunes of Bruni's *History* lay elsewhere, in the chanceries and among the ruling elites throughout northern Italy and Europe. Bruni's outlook was too radical to meet with widespread popular approval in Florence itself. Its success was confined to a limited audience of those who grasped its potential, both as a model of official state history and as a source of political expertise.

APPENDIX: LEONARDO BRUNI, *HISTORY OF THE FLORENTINE PEOPLE*

THE FOUNDATION OF FLORENCE[49]

The founders of Florence were Romans sent by Lucius Sulla to Faesulae. They were his veterans who had given outstanding service in the civil war

---

46. Bruni, *History of the Florentine People*, 2:269.

47. Fubini, "Osservazioni," 446.

48. Emilio Santini, "La fortuna della storia fiorentina di L. Bruni," *Studi storici* 20 (1911): 177–95.

49. Translations are from Bruni, *History of the Florentine People*, 1:9–13, and are used with permission of Harvard University Press.

as well as in other wars, and he granted them part of the territory of Faesulae in addition to the town itself and its old inhabitants. Such a relocation of citizens and assignment of lands was called a colony by the Romans, because the estates cultivated and inhabited by the citizens were granted to them as homes. Why new colonists were sent to this area, however, must be explained.

Not many years before Sulla's dictatorship, there was a general rebellion among the peoples of Italy against the Romans. They had been allied with the Romans on every campaign . . . , they had not shared in the rewards. Hence their indignation. After much complaining among themselves, they finally sent a delegation to Rome to discuss their common problem, and to demand a share in honors and offices for themselves. . . . Their demands were ultimately rejected, however, and then the peoples involved rebelled openly and declared war on their ungrateful allies. Because the war was made 91 B.C. by former allies of Rome, it is known as the Social War. The Roman people emerged victorious and severely punished the leading provinces involved in the rebellion. They dealt most harshly with Picenum [the modern province of the Marche] and Tuscany. The flourishing city of Asculum in Picenum was razed like an enemy town, and in Tuscany, Clusium was likewise leveled to the ground. The people of Arretium and Faesulae also suffered heavy blows above and beyond the war damage itself, for many people's property was confiscated and many were forced to flee, so that these towns were almost emptied of inhabitants.

Such was the occasion—almost, in fact, the invitation—for Sulla's later action as dictator in granting his veterans these lands in particular. That is how Sulla's veterans came to Faesulae and divided the fields among themselves. Many of them decided, however, that amidst the security of the Roman empire it was unnecessary to inhabit an inaccessible hill town. So they left the mountain and began to form settlements along the banks of the Arno and the Mugnone in the plain below. The new city located between these two waterways was at first called Fluentia and its inhabitants Fluentini. The name lasted for some time, it seems, until the city grew and developed. Then, perhaps just through the ordinary process by which words are corrupted, or perhaps because of the wonderfully successful flowering of the city, Fluentia became Florentia.

. . . Out of nostalgia or love for their old home, the colonizers seem to have consciously imitated Rome in their planning of the city and in the construction of buildings. They built themselves a capitol and a forum, in the same configuration as was found in Rome, and they had baths for public cleanliness and an arena for watching games and spectacles. The temple of Mars was built in the same spirit of emulation, for it was to this god that the Romans, superstitiously, traced their ancestry. They were so eager to affirm their relationship to Rome, in fact, that they liked to copy less important structures as well, even at tremendous expense. They brought water in by aqueduct, which was reasonable in Rome where all the local water was chalky, but superfluous in Florentia where perfectly pure water springs up in abundance. It seems likely, moreover, that their private houses matched their public buildings in magnificence, though the evidence that this was the case is less abundant. The above-mentioned ruins of the public buildings prove how ample those, at least, were.

THE ORATION OF GIANO DELLA BELLA, 1292[50]

Towards the end of the year the foundations were first laid for an infinite number of domestic innovations, and the constitutional form that we have used in the commonwealth now for more than 130 years was first instituted. For after a happy ending was brought to the Aretine war, as we have related, and the victory there achieved had greatly advanced the city's position, and then when the Florentine people were considered to be the undoubted winners of the Pisan war, the People began to grow conscious of its own power, and to turn its attention from foreign wars to domestic liberty. The nobility, which up to that time had been the leading force in the city, had never acted as an equal partner with respect to the people. Superior in wealth and arrogant in manner, its haughtiness was unsuited to a free city, and it could be restrained from committing unjust acts only with the greatest difficulty. Supported by their vast clienteles and assisted by their numerous family connections, they reduced the weak to a state resembling honorable servitude. Many were the men of modest fortune whom they attacked physically; and many were despoiled of their goods or expelled from their estates. Although the city tried from time to time to punish these offenses, the nobility were upheld by the shameless favoritism of their relations, and men shrank from denouncing their unjust acts, fearing the power of their families and dreading wounds and death more than the loss of their patrimonies. Indeed, it seemed that the only obstacle to the complete servitude of the common people was the nobility's own internal divisions, riven as it was by envy and competitive rivalries.

50. Ibid., 1:359–71.

One man tried to stop the corruption and decline of the commonwealth: Giano della Bella, who showed greatness and wisdom during that stormy time. He was descended from distinguished ancestors, but was himself a man of moderation and strongly populist in his sympathies. This leader first complained privately with individual citizens about the power of the nobility and criticized the inertia and passivity of the People, how they kept letting individuals suffer injustice, how they failed to realize that they were all as a group being threatened by shameful servitude. He said it was the height of stupidity to believe that violence would not affect one personally, as once the first people were brought to heel, violence would then strike others too, spreading like fire. Resistance was necessary now; the evil must not be allowed to grow. For though the disease had been allowed to spread, it had not yet so taken root that it could not be healed. But if they neglected the situation further and everyone waited for someone else to act, in the end they would find themselves hoping in vain for help against an endemic plague. By raising these issues over and over he fired up men's spirits and stiffened their resolution to take the commonwealth in hand. The popular classes arose and supported the effort, going forth to take the matter to the magistrates. And finally, when the people had been summoned, and different opinions were being canvassed and expressed concerning the issue in accordance with each man's temper, Giano della Bella arose and addressed the crowd on the issue in the following general terms:

"I have always been of the same mind, fellow citizens, and the more I consider public affairs, the more I am convinced that we must either check the arrogance of the powerful families or lose our liberty altogether. Things have reached the point, I think, where your tolerance and your liberty are no longer compatible. I think too that no one of sound judgment can be in doubt which of the two is to be preferred. It does not escape me that it is dangerous for me to speak of these things. But a good citizen, I think, puts aside his own interests when his country needs his advice, and he does not cut down his public statements to suit his private convenience. Therefore I shall speak my mind freely. It seems to me that the liberty of the people consists in two things: its laws and its courts. Whenever the power of these two things prevails in the city over the power of any individual citizen, then liberty is preserved. But when some people are permitted to scorn the laws and the courts with impunity, then one has to conclude that liberty is gone. For in what sense are you free when there are people who, with no fear of judgment, can lay violent hands on you and your property whenever they please? Therefore consider now what your condition has come to, and review the crimes of the nobility. Then tell me, any one of you, whether you think the city is free or whether it has long existed in a state of oppression. The answer will be easier for those who have a neighbor in the city or the countryside who is one of this mob of powerful men. Is there anything we possess that escapes their greed? And what objects of their greed have they not immediately claimed for themselves? And what have they claimed for themselves that they don't feel justified in taking, whether by fair means or foul? Our very bodies, if we will only admit it, are no longer free: just remember the citizens who have been beaten or chased from their property, and the numerous examples of arson, plunder, bloodshed and killing in these last years. Some perpetrators of these evil deeds do them so openly that they don't bother to deny them, while others have been caught in the act and are unable to deny them. So they remain at large: we see men who deserve prison and punishment strutting like lords around the city with crowds of armed retainers, terrifying us and the magistrates. Is anyone going to tell me that this is liberty? How is this condition different from tyrants who kill, expropriate, take whatever they want without fear of judgment? And if one man of this sort can destroy liberty in one city, what shall we think of our city where it happens simultaneously at the hands of so many? We have certainly been oppressed for some time, believe me, and we keep up the appearance of liberty with empty words, while in reality we suffer the most shameful servitude.

"Someone may object, however, and say: no one doubts that that is the case, but we want solutions, not hand-wringing. To this I say: we can find a way to shake this shameful servitude from our backs with no great difficulty. For if the corruption of the laws and the courts has caused the death of liberty, the rebuilding of those institutions will bring liberty back to life. If you wish to be free, therefore—and we should all desire freedom as much as we do life—restore those two things to their proper authority, and be strenuous and strict in keeping them in force. You have many laws restraining violence, killing, theft, assault, and other crimes. These laws must be renewed to take particular notice of the powerful, I say, and new measures must be added. For who can ignore the need for new, additional precautions given the daily increase in human wickedness?

"The most necessary step, I think, is for criminal punishments to be increased in the case of the powerful. Surely if you want to tie up both a giant and a midget, you don't use the same kind of bonds. You tie the giant with chains and cables, the midget with ropes and thongs. Punishments are the bonds of law, and likewise must be made stronger for great and powerful men. The punishments we have on the books now don't hold them. I would add the further stipulation that family and kin are to be included in punishments. We should consider clan and kinsmen as complicit in the crime, for it is his reliance on them that encourages the nobleman to commit crimes. Two things usually hinder the effectiveness of our courts: the difficulty of proving cases and the failure to execute sentences. Witnesses are afraid of testifying against powerful men, and nearly all judicial procedures are subverted by this single fear; and even if the case is proven, the magistrate shrinks from executing sentence. If you do not change these things, you will have no republic. What good are even the finest laws in a state if legal proceedings are made void? So you must first of all, I think, curtail the problem of witnesses; in the case of powerful men, public notoriety must be admissible as evidence. Thus when some malfeasance has been committed, and there has been a public outcry of the neighbors, when the very fields and woodlands cry out that it was done by some powerful man, in my view let the judge not seek scrupulous proofs, which he knows will not be forthcoming owing to fear of power; but let notoriety alone suffice for him.

"As to the difficulty of executing sentence, please pay careful attention, for I think this is a greater matter than people realize, depending less on the magistrates than on the strength of the people. For if the People really wants, as it should, to keep its predominance in the commonwealth, the sentences of the courts, even against powerful persons, will readily be carried out. But if the people is dazzled by the nobility and defers to it, this will make both the magistrates and the courts lukewarm in their efforts. All this was noted and understood a while back when the Standard Bearer of Justice was created, but I marvel that his power has so rapidly fallen into abeyance. But it is stupid to complain, I think, when the People itself is spiritless and negligent, that the People's agents lack keenness. Yet at that time so many things were passed over that the matter seems to have been left in an uncompleted state. So I believe the authority of the Standard-Bearer of Justice needs very much to be strengthened. In my view he should, first of all, have at his command, not a thousand armed men as heretofore, but four thousand, to be recruited from the whole people by turns. I also think that the Standard-Bearer himself should reside in the public palace together with the priors, so that he will personally hear and understand the complaints of the citizens and provide for the needs of the commonwealth. If he remains at home he will either lack full knowledge of the situation or he will be slow to act because of interventions from private individuals, such as we know to have happened hitherto.

"I should add a third provision which was overlooked at that time: that no powerful man, even if he pretends to be a tradesman, can be raised to become a prior, and thus put into a position to help criminals and to impede justice. Their existing power is sufficiently burdensome to us, without adding the armor of public authority. In this way, if you resuscitate the laws, establish severer punishments against the powerful, and strengthen the courts, you will force them to stop their tyrannous behavior. Certainly, if they continued unchecked, you will have to root them out with iron and fire as you would incurably sick limbs, putting aside that excessive patience of yours which is leading you with open eyes and ears into slavery.

"I have said what I think are the measures that will save the commonwealth and are necessary for our liberty. If they were difficult and expensive and involved great labor, I would tell you that they had to be carried out anyway because of their usefulness. As they are easy, however, and lie within your power, who is so corrupt that he would rather serve in humiliation and injustice than be equal to others in rights and honors? Our ancestors forbore to serve even Roman emperors, although the title to which the emperors pretended and their rank made the servitude less dishonorable. Shall you continue serving the vilest of men? Our ancestors bore death and wounds and the loss of their patrimonies and endless strife for the sake of their dignity and preeminence. Shall you, out of fear and baseness, place over yourselves, of your own free will, tyrants who ought to be subject to you? Should a whole people, that is, a vast multitude of strong men, who have conquered by their warlike valor all their neighbors and have smashed a thousand enemy legions, not be ashamed, returning home, to fear the power of this or that family and basely suffer the nobility's pride and contempt to make us slaves? I shall stop now, so that I do not become carried away by my own vehemence. The respect I feel for the People prevents me from chiding them, yet when I call to mind this degenerate passivity of yours I cannot remain silent and calm. I am asking you only to take thought for your own liberty and welfare.

11

From the Roman Empire to Christian Imperialism: The Work of Flavio Biondo

Nicoletta Pellegrino

On 6 June of this year Flavio Biondo passed away. He was a historian born in Forlì; he was apostolic secretary for a long time and was most dear to Pope Eugenius IV. He wrote a universal history, starting at the time of the emperors Arcadius and Honorius—which is said to be the beginning of the Roman Empire's decline—up to his own times. It is a complex work, undoubtedly useful, but in need of someone to edit and correct it.[1]

In this curious epitaph, Pope Pius II revealed his ambivalence toward Flavio Biondo. While often disparaging Biondo's style and accuracy, the pope considered Biondo's *Decades* important enough to revise it for a wider audience.[2] In fact, Flavio Biondo remained an influential source for historians well into the sixteenth century; only in the eighteenth century did his work

---

1. Enea Silvio Piccolomini (Pope Pius II), *Commentarii rerum memorabilium*, ed. Luigi Totaro (Milan: Adelphi, 1984), 2:2256: "Pridie Nonas iunias huius anni Blondus Flavius obiit, historiarum scriptor, natione foroliviensis, qui diu secretarium apostolicum gessit et Eugenio quarto pontifici maximo acceptissimus fuit. Ab Honorio Archadioque Caesaribus, quo tempore inclinasse Romanum imperium memorant, usque ad aetatem suam universalem scripsit historiam, opus certe laboriosum et utile, verum expolitore emendatoreque dignum."

2. *Epitome supra decade Blondi,* published in 1463. Pope Pius II was a well-known humanist in his own right, and is among the authors read and annotated by Christopher Columbus; see Eugenio Garin, *Ritratti di umanisti* (Florence: Sansoni, 1967), 20. His interest in Biondo—and the interest of other contemporaries—was often expressed via corrections and refutations, but the attention they accorded his work bolstered his importance and increased his reputation.

seem to become obsolete.[3] Yet, Biondo's *Decades* suggested a conceptual framework—and a celebrated title—to one of the most famous historians of Rome, Edward Gibbon, writing in 1776.[4]

Flavio Biondo was born in Forlì, a small town between Venice and Bologna, in 1392.[5] He earned a law degree, probably at the University—or Studium—of Piacenza, near Milan, but unlike his father, he never became a professional notary or lawyer. After working a few years for the Republic of Venice and obtaining Venetian citizenship, in 1427 he returned to Forlì, in the Papal State. Biondo was then hired by the papal governor, Domenico Capranica. At the end of 1432 he was called to Rome as notary of the Camera Apostolica, or papal treasury, and early in 1434 he also was made a pontifical secretary, combining the two positions, and grew close to the cardinal *camerlengo* (treasurer), a papal relative. The papacy of Eugenius IV (the Venetian Gabriele Condulmer, elected 1431) was the most intense and rewarding period of Biondo's curial career.[6]

In 1447 Nicholas V was elected pope. Shortly thereafter, Biondo vacated the office of pontifical secretary, regaining it only in 1453. Biondo argued that his work as a writer, historian, and humanist had compromised his position in the Curia. However, it is more likely that his search for new patrons after Eugenius IV's death jeopardized his status at the papal court.[7] Biondo's

3. Ludovico Muratori's *Annali d'Italia, dal principio dell'era volgare sino all'anno 1500* (Rome: Appresso gli eredi Barbiellini mercanti di libri, 1744–49) would take the place of Biondo's work.

4. Edward Gibbon, *The History of the Decline and Fall of the Roman Empire* (London: Printed for W. Strahan and T. Cadell, 1776–88).

5. Biondo, or Blondus, meaning literally "blond-haired," was his real family name and was duplicated as his first name, so that he was called Biondo Biondi, while Flavius (from "flavus," the Latin translation of "biondo") was just a literary name. However, in papal bulls and in other official documents, he is called Blondus; see Bartolomeo Nogara, ed., *Scritti inediti e rari di Biondo Flavio*, Studi e testi, 48 (Rome: Tipografia poliglotta vaticana, 1927).

6. Biondo's influence on the pope is evidenced by the various requests made for his recommendations. The apostolic legate in England, Pietro del Monte; the chancellor of the king of England, Thomas Bekynton; and even Leonardo Bruni, probably the most famous humanist of his time, asked for his assistance. Furthermore, it is explicitly "ex procuratione . . . Biondi" (through Biondo's patronage) that his brother Matteo got an abbacy. It was due to this same influence on the pope that he lost his possessions in Forlì, which were seized in 1434 by the ruler of the city, Antonio Ordelaffi (s.v. "Biondo Flavio," in *Dizionario biografico degli italiani*, 10:541–42 [Rome: Istituto dell'enciclopedia italiana, 1968]).

7. Biondo's relationship with King Alfonso of Aragon was the inspiration behind his writing of the *Italia illustrata*, while his relationship with Venice produced only a fragment of a *History of Venice*. However, it is probable that Biondo intended to devote more attention to Venice in his future work. He was offered the position of lecturer at the school of San Marco but died shortly afterward. See Felix Gilbert, "Biondo, Sabellico, and the Beginnings of Venetian Official Historiography," in *Florilegium Historiale: Essays Presented to Wallace*

last years were spent in relative poverty, writing commercially viable works to support himself as he tried to complete the *Decades*.[8] He died in Rome on 4 June 1463.

Flavio Biondo was one of the humanists who gravitated to the papal Curia at a propitious time. Disputed papal elections had left Christendom with two and then three claimants to the papal see during the Great Schism. In response, many theologians, churchmen, and secular rulers advocated a Church council to solve the crisis. The Holy Roman Emperor Sigismond took the lead in calling for the general council of the Church that convened in Constance in 1414. In resolving the schism, the council itself claimed the right to reform the Church "in head and members." Conciliarism thus became a threat to papal leadership of the Church. Yet, the heirs of Saint Peter were not about to surrender their preeminence without a struggle. Certainly the election of Martin V (1417–31), a member of the powerful Colonna family, historically one of the most prominent in Rome, augured well for the Curia and the city. Yet a complete restoration of papal power was still to come.

After more than a century of papal exile, schism, and conciliarism, Rome's position as a satellite of the empire threatened to become permanent. Certainly the Roman Curia of this time compares poorly with its predecessors at Avignon and its Renaissance successors, both in terms of wealth and cultural activity. Still, despite its recent eclipse in prestige, Rome was the capital of the *respublica Christiana,* and it is the central subject of Biondo's work; but his Rome is much more than a city. Though Biondo fully understands Rome's geography and politics, they are secondary to his larger vision, which casts the city as an explanatory paradigm for history itself. The Rome of the *Decades* is part allegory and part romance. A *genius loci* (spirit of a place) pervades Biondo's work; it is an alluring ghost, a centuries-old literary device that explains the perennial appeal of places like Rome or Delphi, in contrast with the transient attraction of other famous cities, like Troy or Carthage.[9]

The myth of Rome is the historian's starting point, but the informing spirit of Biondo's work is Rome as a metaphor for culture, human values, and intellectual prominence; an ideal space inhabited by artistic beauty, rational

---

K. Ferguson, ed. John Gordon Rowe and W. H. Stockdale (Toronto: University of Toronto Press, 1971), 275–93.

8. See Ricardo Fubini, "Biondo Flavio," in *Dizionario biografico degli italiani,* 10:536–59.

9. Jerry H. Bentley, *Politics and Culture in Renaissance Naples* (Princeton: Princeton University Press, 1987), 165. For a recent literary evocation of the ghost, see Peter Ackroyd, *London: The Biography* (New York: Nan A. Talese, 2000).

law, and morality. As narrated by Biondo, the dynamic unfolding of events occurs over the static image of a center—Rome—that slowly changes and adapts, without ever losing its true identity. Biondo did not promote a cyclical view of history, in which structures and events continually repeat. In fact, the metamorphosis of the Eternal City through history transforms the splendors of pagan Rome into the greatness of Christian Rome, the world capital of the true religion.[10]

Biondo's work never specifically addresses the problematic relationship between the concepts of restoration and renewal. This may be intentional, for unlike many of the north Italian communes where Biondo spent the first part of his life, Rome did not, in its recent past, possess a history of laudable exploits. Rome's credentials were centuries old, tied to the deeds of Caesar and the emperors, as the recent brief attempts at revolution led by Cola di Rienzo and Stefano Porcari had amply demonstrated.[11]

In addition, Biondo never analyzes the papacy, the political and religious institution that he celebrated and served so well. Nor does he examine its ideological basis. He was part of a ruling group faced with the difficulty of rebuilding a political consensus founded on a papal primacy that had only recently and shakily been reaffirmed. The papacy's political and religious enemies were numerous and powerful enough that they were in fact able to exile Biondo's pope from 1434 to 1447. Humanists and other intellectuals at the Curia used their skills to provide ideological justification for a political project: the creation of a powerful papacy, whose primacy would be undisputed inside and outside the Church, and in Rome itself.[12]

10. Virgil's "Roma Aeterna" had come to be known as Eternal Rome, the foreordained see of the popes, during the Middle Ages. Already in the fourth century, while the pagan Symmachus depicted Rome as feeble and weak, the Christian poet Prudentius reversed the image and portrayed Rome as "rejuvenated" by Christianity. See Averil Cameron, "Remaking the Past," in *Interpreting Late Antiquity,* ed. Glenn W. Bowersock, Peter Brown, and Oleg Grabar (Cambridge, Mass.: Harvard University Press, 2001), 1. What is peculiar to Biondo is his elevation of this transformation to be the main theme—in fact, the true paradigm—of the *Decades.*

11. Their revolts were the only two notable attempts to substitute a commune for the papacy. Cola di Rienzo had moderate success during the absence of the popes in the fourteenth century, whereas Stefano Porcari's enterprise (1453) was doomed from the start. The universal appeal of the myth of Rome consistently hampered any elaboration of a municipal spirit construed as separated by its millenarian motifs, like the majesty of law or the sacrality of the popes. See esp. Andrea Giardina and André Vauchez, *Il mito di Roma: Da Carlo Magno a Mussolini* (Rome: Editori Laterza, 2000).

12. The celebration of papal power is easy to recognize in many of Biondo's works. On his followers, see Eric Cochrane, *Historians and Historiography in the Italian Renaissance* (Chicago: University of Chicago Press, 1981), 47–49, which still offers the most comprehensive survey of this subject. In fact, Biondo's proposition was more than a celebration: it

The real Rome had suffered grievously from the absence of the popes in the fourteenth century and from the ensuing schism; when Biondo arrived in 1432, estimates of the resident population were as low as fifteen thousand. From the time of Pope Martin V, Rome's population increased steadily due to immigration, which significantly affected its demographic composition: the newcomers were mostly Italians, but Frenchmen, Germans, and other foreigners also migrated to the city. The presence of these latter groups made Rome more cosmopolitan but less truly Roman; a simultaneous shift within the Curia corrected this tendency to some extent, as the papacy, and especially the humanists in its employ, adopted the identity and ideological aura of ancient Rome. This trend both inspired and depended upon a political belief that fused Rome's imperial past, the Christian religion, and humanist culture.[13]

Biondo believed that he was living in momentous times. He was eager to fill the void of the past twelve centuries, and above all, he wanted to write history.[14] In fact, he explicitly meant to demonstrate that historiography was a discipline of pragmatic relevance. Its relevance arose not from its use of rhetoric, as Cicero had claimed, which would persuade the audience to live morally through the right choice of words and examples,[15] but from a rigorous analysis of the real past—its problems, triumphs, crises, and even failures—which offered the best model to affect the present. Biondo thus agreed with Cicero's reasons for writing history, but rather than extrapolate principles from a few well-chosen examples from Roman history, as Cicero had done, Biondo treated the past as one continuous great example, one integrated model of dos and don'ts.

Biondo's method was a significant departure from that of the earlier historiographical tradition, as well as its exegetical mode, a change that has long since been recognized in Machiavelli's and Guicciardini's works, where "history was placed in the context of politics rather than in that of literature."

---

was a "militant" project, an exhaustive ceremonial model. See Maria Antonietta Visceglia, *La città rituale* (Rome: Viella, 2002), 193.

13. For the cosmopolitan amalgamation that made up the population of Rome, see Anna Esposito, "La minor parte di questo popolo sono i romani," in *Effetto Roma: Romababilonia* (Rome: Bulzoni, 1993), 41–60, and Egmont Lee, "Foreigners in Quattrocento Rome," *Renaissance and Reformation*, n.s., 7 (1983): 135–46.

14. Biondo's belief that he was living in a significant historical period is stressed in the letter he wrote to King Alfonso of Aragon on 13 June 1443. He explained that he was composing the *Decades* starting from the end—the fifteenth century—lest he die before coming to write about contemporary events. Nogara, *Scritti inediti e rari di Biondo Flavio*, 148.

15. Cicero and Plutarch's "pragmatic" idea of history was prevalent in the fifteenth century: see Massimo Miglio, *Storiografia pontificia del Quattrocento* (Bologna: Patròn, 1975).

However, it is clear that this change started much earlier. Flavio Biondo in Rome, like Leonardo Bruni in Florence and Lorenzo Valla in Naples and Rome, worked with "a pragmatic concept of history" and tried his best to clarify the connections between historical events.[16]

Humanist historians had no doubt that the real past could be recovered in its entirety. They collected and read their sources with painstaking attention, and they treated these sources as transparent mediums; there was no contradiction between giving an empirical description and seeking meaning, because the latter would follow the former quite naturally. Although Biondo was not naive and took time to consider his authors' geographical provenience, political inclinations, and actual circumstances, he believed that he would eventually strip his source texts of all their secondary layers, to find the true events behind them.

A consistent element in Biondo's work is his attention to language, and especially to names (particularly geographical and toponymic names) and their etymology. He does not consider them neutral words or historical accidents but instead some of the best indicators of historical change: language is a creation of the social world of which it is a part and whose reality it reflects. For example, he explains how the Huns, after many defeats, started to hate their name and changed it to Avari, not only to erase their painful memories of defeat but also to transform their own perception of themselves.[17]

It is paradoxical that a scholar so finely in tune with the complexity of words should have been widely criticized, both by his contemporaries and modern readers, for his shabby language and style, which produced an uneven Latin prose and alternated convoluted sentences with ones that were too brief.[18] In his defense, it could be stressed that he used language as a

---

16. Gilbert, "Biondo, Sabellico, and the Beginnings of Venetian Official Historiography," 287 and 286. Unlike Cochrane, Gilbert dates the historiographical shift much later than the fifteenth-century humanists: in fact, not before the early sixteenth century (see also, by the same author, *Machiavelli and Guicciardini: Politics and History in Sixteenth-Century Florence* [Princeton: Princeton University Press, 1965]). Although I fully agree that "the philological emphasis in humanistic studies coincided with a new pragmatic interest in history aroused by the events of the recent past" (287), Biondo and his colleagues were already pragmatically motivated.

17. *Decades*, bk. IV, chap. XXIV.

18. Many humanists of his time described Biondo's style unflatteringly, and some contemporary scholars have supported this opinion. See esp. Denys Hay, "Flavio Biondo and the Middle Ages," *Proceedings of the British Academy* 45 (1959): 118. Not everybody agrees: "Biondo, . . . to a remarkable degree combined the best qualities of Bruni and Valla with Livian narrative and Varronian erudition." Donald R. Kelley, "Humanism and History," in *Renaissance Humanism: Foundations, Forms, and Legacy*, ed. Albert Rabil Jr., vol. 3, *Humanism and the Disciplines* (Philadelphia: University of Pennsylvania Press, 1988), 242.

means to an end, a tool to forge truth rather than elegance: he was more than willing to sacrifice style in order to make the past intelligible. Biondo even argued in the *Decades* for the need to mint new words (*barbara verba*) in order to name modern inventions and contemporary institutions, for the sake of better precision. For example, if the name *imperator* in Roman times denoted a leader of armies, in Biondo's time it indicated the emperor; and while "captain" might be vague, the appellation *dux* might confuse a military man with a duke.[19]

The importance of Rome as the central ideological concern in Biondo's literary activity is evident in his first important work, *De verbis romanae locutionis* (On the words of Roman speech), (1435). Biondo puts some of the *Decades'* fundamental theses to the test in this work. For example, he explicitly challenges the claims of some of his fellow humanists. By making Leonardo Bruni the book's interlocutor, he examines Bruni's contention that Latin was the learned language of philosophy, literature, and political debate, the language of the elite. Italian, he concludes, was the language of everyone else. Biondo maintains that Latin had, in antiquity, been used by all Roman people, regardless of their social status.[20] It was only after the decline of the state and the beginning of the Lombard invasions that the language had begun to decline. This corruption, which Biondo explicitly labels as a change for the worse, had, in fact, already begun in the time of the republic. If at first the invasions affected only the people who lived outside Rome, they soon transformed the entire empire. The Lombards, Biondo argues, aimed to do more than conquer Rome politically; they wished to obliterate Rome's prestige as well, a goal they could attain by changing its language and thereby erasing its memory.

Biondo's thesis, that the vernacular stood as the unfortunate corruption of Latin, resulted from his sound historical analysis of relevant sources, from Cicero's writings to contemporary surviving examples of Latin expressions found in the different Italian vernaculars. In the end Biondo's conclusion, not Bruni's, gained wide acceptance as the more historically persuasive. Biondo's ideas regarding language would reappear in some of his future works, such

19. This was also Valla's position: "Since he was writing 'for men of the present and the future' rather than for men of the past, [he] did not hesitate to use modern rather than ancient place names [. . .] and to avoid the anachronistic overtones of old words (*dux*) by borrowing more appropriate words (*capitaneus*) from the vernacular." Cochrane, *Historians and Historiography*, 149.

20. Bruni's position was that there had always been two languages, Latin and a vernacular (or Italian), spoken by the upper and lower classes respectively: two parallel languages, instead of Biondo's two successive languages, Latin slowly evolving into present-day Italian.

as the *Decades,* the *Italia illustrata,* and the *Roma triumphans,* in which
language, institutions, and customs were understood as the result of a single, homogeneous evolution.

In 1443 the papal court returned to Rome, and in 1446 Biondo published
his *Roma instaurata* (Rome renewed), a complete reconstruction of ancient
Roman topography and architecture drawn from literary and monumental
sources. In this work he takes the topography of the city as the starting point
from which to write about Roman institutions, monuments, customs, daily
life, and archeology, paying careful attention to his sources and divesting the
monuments of their medieval magic.[21] Monuments, even those in ruins, impressed Biondo with their technical achievements, but even more with what
they represented. Ancient aqueducts, bridges, and baths were the material
manifestations of a culture unparalleled in history. They stood before him now
as the ruins of a great civilization, whose destruction was not easily explained.

Confronting this dilemma provides Biondo with an opportunity to expand
on one of his favorite themes, the decline of greatness. Roman leaders, both
patricians and popes, bore the brunt of his condemnation because of their
neglect and dishonesty: they even took bits and pieces of ancient monuments
for the decoration of their own buildings.[22] The ruins of ancient Rome sym-
bolized its civic superiority, but Biondo carefully balances this image with the
uniqueness of Christian Rome, which, built over the remains of the pagan
city, could truly be said to be its heir as *caput mundi* (the world's capital).[23] Biondo pushed the correlation between the two Romes to its limits,

21. Many descriptions of Rome appeared during the Middle Ages, but the genre of the
Mirabilia Urbis Romae consisted generally of a list of monuments and some imaginative
information about their origins. See Maria Accame Lanzillotta, *Contributi sui "Mirabilia
Urbis Romae"* (Genoa: D.AR.FI.CL.ET, Dipartimento di archeologia, filologia classica e loro
tradizioni "Francesco della Corte," 1996); Cristina Nardella, *Il fascino di Roma nel Medioevo: Le "Meraviglie di Roma" di maestro Gregorio* (Rome: Viella, 1997); Nikolaus Muffel,
Descrizione della città di Roma nel 1452, with Italian translation and commentary by Gerhard Wiedmann (Bologna: Pàtron, 1999); and Francesco Albertini, *Opusculum de mirabilibus novae & veteris urbis Romae,* in *Five Early Guides to Rome and Florence,* ed. Peter
Murray (Farnborough: Gregg, 1972).

22. Romans' use of the monuments of their city as towers, houses, and marble caves was
a constant thorn in the side in the city's history. Although ancient monuments were used
extensively during the Middle Ages, when there was very little new building activity going on
in Rome, perceptions of systematic looting reached their peak in early modern times. It was
then that the Barberinis (nephews of the pope) were accused of completing the barbarians'
past deeds, this condemnation probably owing to a mixture of greed and phonetics.

23. See esp. bk. i; Bondo here also notes that in some cases Christian churches were
built from scratch, not on the ground of a previous building. This was especially true for the
basilicas, which became the most tangible elements in the metamorphosis of Rome, and
thus received much attention.

positioning the pope as the consul, the emperor as the *magister militum* (the head of the army), the cardinals as the senators, and the bishops as the provincial governors of the Roman Empire.[24] The parallel between the political body of the Church and ancient Rome became a grandiose program to recapture Rome's glory. Biondo appealed to the Curia at the end of *Roma instaurata* to work exclusively for the Church's benefit. He believed that if it did, Asia and Africa would once again become Rome's subjects.

An ideal continuation to *Roma instaurata* was *Italia illustrata* (Italy described), written after the Neapolitan king Alfonso of Aragon had commissioned Biondo to create a catalog of the celebrated men of their time. Biondo accepted the commission, enlarging the project to include the history and geography of the places considered.[25] Italia was clearly a meaningful cultural and political concept for Biondo. In fact, his understanding of Italia has been called "the ablest Renaissance attempt to view Italy as a unit."[26]

It is interesting to note how this notion started to blur when he reached the southern parts of the peninsula, which were given less attention and eventually omitted entirely, together with Sicily and Sardinia.[27] The attention given to each site was determined by various circumstances: knowledge of the place, firsthand or through literary sources, was of course of great importance in determining its inclusion. However, another factor in the selection of one place over another was patronage; King Alfonso may have been its original patron, but many different people were involved in its progression. An early section on the Romagna was dedicated to Malatesta Novello of

24. This synthesis between the two Romes was a bit too extreme to be convincing, but the figure of the cardinals/senators was used for another century: see esp. Paolo Cortesi, *De cardinalatu* (Castro Cortesiano: Symeon Nicolai Nardi senensis, alias Rufus Calchographus imprimebat, 1510). And it would linger much longer: canon law would define cardinals as the "Senate of the Roman Pontifex" up to Pope John Paul II's reform in 1983 (*Corpus iuris canonici*, 1917, canon 230).

25. The *Italia illustrata* was one of the most successful of Biondo's works; it was published, translated, and imitated, and became the model for all the historical-geographical surveys that appeared in Europe for more than a century after. Together with the *Roma instaurata*, in the words of one German historian, it "furnished the models used by the sixteenth-century German topographers." Quoted by Cochrane, *Historians and Historiography*, xiii and 40. A few pages of the *Italia illustrata* were published recently in English: see *Images of Quattrocento Florence*, ed. Stefano Ugo Baldassarri and Arielle Saiber (New Haven and London: Yale University Press, 2000), 316–21.

26. Catherine J. Castner, "Direct Observation and Biondo Flavio's Additions to *Italia Illustrata:* The Case of Ocriculum," *Medievalia et Humanistica*, n.s., 25 (1998): 101.

27. Biondo justified this omission by claiming that he had to rush the release of the *Italia illustrata* because an unauthorized edition was already circulating. However, it is clear that his knowledge of the southern part of Italy was in no way comparable to his knowledge of the central and northern regions.

Rimini, where Biondo was then living, and the section on Latium was at first dedicated separately to Cardinal Prospero Colonna, who remained one of his supporters in the Curia and figured in the *Italia illustrata*. Biondo was writing it in the years after he had lost his position in the Curia, and he needed support. Financial necessities thus determined not only what to include in *Italia illustrata* but also what to exclude, based largely on whether a location enjoyed the "crucial criterion of association with a patron."[28]

The issue of language, which had been the topic of Biondo's first work, resurfaced here, anticipating an analogous consideration in the *Decades*. His concern was how to choose between ancient and modern toponyms. Biondo championed the use of modern words for modern innovations and inventions—whether arms, techniques, or institutions—because this was the best way to be understood by his public, and he always chose to write with clarity rather than with style. But if he did not want to seem obscure, neither did he want to appear ignorant of the classical world and of its culture. In many instances, he decided to use the different names with which a specific place had been known in different times, discussing the changes from one to another.

In fact, for Biondo to surrender his prose completely to modern denominations would have had a more poignant consequence: usually, a place had changed its name from the original Latin after the German invasions, when the political unity of the empire had been broken. To call places with names other than their Latin ones, then, would jeopardize the common identity, Italia, that Biondo was trying to foster. This was indeed a significant concern for him, although he did not force linguistic homogeneity. In fact, he included in "his" Italy some communities where people spoke different languages, like German in the northeast or French in the northwest or Greek in the south. Unlike the prince of Metternich, who in the nineteenth century still dismissed Italy as only "a geographical expression," Biondo conceived of Italy as a reality built out of the peninsula's geography, culture, traditions, language, and above all its preeminence within Christendom.[29]

Cities, always an essential element in Italian history, attracted Biondo's strongest interest, as they would again in the *Decades*, where they would be invested with the mission of preserving Roman culture.[30] In the *Italia*

28. Castner, "Direct Observation and Biondo Flavio's Additions to *Italia Illustrata*," 101.
29. Italy's prominence within Christianity followed, of course, from its being the seat of the popes, but it was also deeply ingrained in the territory, through the many churches spread within and outside of the cities, and it was won through some remarkable men, like Saint Francis.
30. See esp. bk. III, chap. I.

illustrata, cities have lost much of their medieval character. Notably, Biondo dispenses with the founding hero, which had been much beloved in medieval tradition and had lent Rome its own legendary authority and status. Instead, Biondo endows his cities with a more complex legacy of material structures, cultural values, and individual actions. Men shape their cities' characters by continuously participating in urban cultural and political affairs. Thus, Biondo does not ascribe a static identity to cities, fixed at their founding by a mythical hero, but rather emphasizes the dynamics of contemporary political power and consensus.

The importance of cities in the peninsula appears first in the introduction, where Biondo emphasizes the steady decline in the numbers of Italian cities after the fall of Rome. He notes that Rome's collapse had directly affected even the provincial towns, whose monuments began to decay and whose dire situation improved only in the fourteenth century. To illustrate his point, and the chronology of ruin and rebirth, Biondo turns to Florence. Its recovery began with its new founders, cultural innovators like Dante and Giotto. According to Biondo, the city's prestige reached its zenith in 1438/39, with the Church council summoned there by the author's patron, Pope Eugenius IV.

Italia illustrata is not only a remarkable catalog of Italian cities, though it is that; it also accurately demarcates the geographical limits of different Italian regions—where, once again, Biondo collected information about the famous men who ennobled these cities: soldiers and ecclesiastics, doctors and artists, and, of course, intellectuals and scholars. The book opens with praise for the great politicians from the past who were also great historians: Quintus Fabius Pictor and Caius Julius Caesar, the emperors Hadrian and Severus Alexander. They are followed by the long millennium of barbarity, which buried all the arts until Biondo's time, when the restoration of culture encouraged a renewal of intellectual activity. Biondo's reader could therefore draw a parallel between those illustrious politicians writing history then and this other politician writing history now.

The *Roma triumphans* (Rome triumphant) was "the earliest expression" of a change of attitude by humanists: "from the extirpation of the classical city perpetrated by Christians, now they saw the remarkable pre-figuration of the capital of Christendom portended by the classical city."[31] It was also one of the first projects systematically to analyze the institutions of ancient

---

31. Charles L. Stinger, "Roman Humanist Images of Rome," in *Roma capitale (1447–1527),* ed. Sergio Gensini (San Miniato: Pacini, 1994), 25.

Rome, and, as a consequence, it has more weaknesses than Biondo's other works. Written between 1457 and 1459, *Roma triumphans* compares republican institutions with those of the empire in order to identify the seeds of Rome's future decline.[32] Livy was Biondo's main source, and the goal of the work was to explain the extraordinarily long-lasting success of Rome through the analysis of all of its concrete elements. The economic and monetary structures and civil law were examined individually, but also for their role in creating local customs, including even eating habits. In this work, Roman political and military systems receive the highest places of honor. Here Biondo reflects the typical Renaissance interest in the perceived greatest achievement of the Roman republic: the interaction and equilibrium it had created among different social groups. This stability fascinated quattrocento Italians, to whom social tensions seemed an inescapable reality.[33]

After the analysis of the military, detailed to the point of describing Roman arms, comes an examination of religion. He describes paganism first, its material and aesthetic worth and its temples and funerary trappings. He attributes its decline to a moral crisis, which contributed to the demise of the empire. The extraordinary way in which Christian Rome had truly vindicated pagan Rome's role of *caput mundi* is the main subject of the chapter. Here, as in *Roma instaurata*, Biondo organizes his materials so as to conclude with another hortatory message to the popes: let Christianity reaffirm Rome's primacy in the world.[34] One of the most significant passages occurs in the prologue of the work, which uses the metaphor of the city (*civitas*) to describe the Roman Empire. The image had already appeared in the work of the fifth-century historian Orosius (*Hist.* bk. 1, chap. 2), but Biondo infuses the image with more passion than had his predecessor.[35] As

32. See esp. bks. III and VIII.

33. Eventually, it was Machiavelli who would try to reconcile the social upheavals of his time with the realization of a thriving city-state, like republican Rome, concluding that the social conflicts were one of the main reasons for Rome's civil equilibrium.

34. The connection between morality and Christianity in history was more problematic for other Christian intellectuals in this period. A few decades later, Erasmus from Rotterdam would distinguish evangelical Christianity, classical culture, and moral depravity in the world as distinct moments that had been crossing each other since the time of the Incarnation. See István Bejczy, *Erasmus and the Middle Ages: The Historical Consciousness of a Christian Humanist* (Leiden and Boston: Brill, 2001).

35. Paulus Orosius, *The Seven Books of History Against the Pagans*, trans. Roy J. Deferrari (Washington, D.C.: Catholic University of America Press, 1964). Orosius, a Christian priest, was born between 380 and 390 C.E.; he wrote his *History* in 417–18. He was close to Augustine, and his image of the empire as a *civitas* was not so much a literary metaphor as the expression of God's providential design for mankind. Although Orosius appeared often in Biondo's work, his idea of Providence is conspicuously absent.

he explains, Rome's expansion brought with it the end of linguistic particularism and opened the way to improved communication and commerce. Rome was an unabashed bearer of progress and civilization, which would spread throughout the world.

Roma instaurata and *Roma triumphans* served as a sort of preface for the most ambitious of Biondo's works, the *Historiarum ab inclinatione romani imperii decades,* spanning the years between the sack of Rome by Alaric's Goths in 412 and 1441, Biondo's own time.[36] Biondo at one point intended the *Decades* to conclude with King Alfonso of Aragon's triumphal entry into Naples on 26 February 1443, but this was certainly not always his intent. For Biondo began writing in 1439 and was working in reverse chronological order.[37] The narrative eventually reached the Peace of Cavriana and the wedding of Francesco Sforza and Bianca Maria Visconti (24 October 1441). It was only at the end of 1453—fourteen years after he had started it—that Biondo finished and published all thirty-two books of the *Decades.*

The homage paid to Roman history begins with Biondo's choice of format—the "decades" made famous by Livy. The decades were technically a chronicle, intended to present history partitioned by special dates.[38] Biondo's *Decades* also recall the *historiae,* which similarly organized the flow of a chronological narrative by dividing the past into distinct periods. Moreover, the term "historiae" suggests a thesis—in Biondo's case, the eminence of Rome in history—and illustrates it with concrete lessons.

At the outset, the *Decades* take the reader to a crucial moment in Rome's past: the beginning of its decline. Setting a date for this decline was not easy, however; Biondo had to confront at least two major traditions. Did Rome's glory begin to fade with the loss of republican freedom in the first century, when widespread civil wars led to the tyrannies of Marius, Sulla, and Julius

---

36. The Goths entered Rome in 410, but Biondo's choice of 412 is probably due to a systematic frame of mind. At the beginning of his project, he meant to end the work in 1412, the date of Filippo Maria Visconti's accession to the principate (see *Dizionario biografico degli italiani,* 10:543), so he needed a symmetrical starting point. He did not consider the year 476—when the barbarian Odoacer deposed the last emperor of the Western Roman Empire—as significant, probably because he considered Odoacer's seizure of power to be only a formal ending.

37. First he wrote on contemporary history, the third and fourth decades; then he went back to ancient history, writing all of the first decade and the beginning of the second, and finished with the last nine books of the second decade. Nogara, *Scritti inediti e rari di Biondo Flavio.*

38. The chronology of the *Decades* was not evenly spaced, and Biondo's way of dating his material changed with his narrative: from *ab inclinatione imperii* to *anno Domini,* which constituted another validation of Rome's metamorphosis into the capital of Christianity.

Caesar and finally to the beginning of the empire, under Octavian? Or was the empire the pinnacle of Roman greatness, characterized as it was by the extension of Roman institutions, laws, roads, and language from Scotland to Libya, from Portugal to Germany? In other words, was the essence of Rome's achievement its republicanism or its imperial dominance?

During the Middle Ages, the latter assessment had prevailed. Many people believed in the *translatio imperii,* the transfer of empire by which imperial authority passed to the German emperors as designated heirs of Rome. Many medieval thinkers, including Dante, had reflected in their works the theological necessity of the Roman Empire as the means through which Christianity prevailed.[39] Already in the fourteenth century the intellectual vitality of many Italian communes had encouraged reappraisals of Roman history. The internecine struggles in the first century B.C.E. brought an end to the republic and came to signify for many Italians the end of Rome itself.[40]

In the very first pages of his work Biondo acknowledges his predecessors' views. He understands how simple it is to see the decline of Rome in Caesar's political success, which led to a lack of respect for the law and general political corruption—topics very close to the hearts of humanist intellectuals.[41] It is equally fair, he writes, to consider the intrinsic frailty of world empires like Rome, which were structurally fated to fall because they were true political monstrosities. Biondo has no doubt that Rome's demise occurred on a set date: that "memorable April" in 412 when the Goths arrived in Rome. Although Petrarch and Bruni had suggested a "dark age," Biondo was the first to describe the fall of the Roman Empire (*inclinatione Romani imperii*).[42]

39. "Fu stabilita per lo loco santo / u' siede il successore del maggior Pietro." (*Inferno,* canto II, lines 23–24); and also "E sarai meco senza fine cive / di quella Roma onde Cristo e' romano" (*Paradiso,* canto XXXII, lines 101–2). Dante gave poetic expression to a special sort of "Roman nationalism" that dated at least from Pope Leo I, in the fifth century, who explicitly said: "Rome has become the Head of the World through the Holy See of St. Peter." See Richard Krautheimer, *Rome, Profile of a City (312–1308)* (Princeton: Princeton University Press, 1980), 46.

40. See Hans Baron, *The Crisis of the Early Italian Renaissance: Civic Humanism and Republican Liberty in an Age of Classicism and Tyranny,* rev. ed. (Princeton: Princeton University Press, 1966), 55, who found in Ptolemy of Lucca's work (early fourteenth century) a shift of attitudes: Rome's power had been built during the republic, when there was no emperor. Yet it is true that the commune was a flourishing reality since the twelfth century, and some interest in republican Rome was a consequence of the communes' fights for survival against the empire.

41. Humanists and politicians often lamented the loss of Roman freedom in the first century B.C.E., and some of them argued that the true heir to Roman greatness was republican Florence.

42. Still unknown in the West, this concept had been advanced by the fourteenth-century Greek historian Nicephorus. See Cochrane, *Historians and Historiography,* 37.

Biondo is aware of the relative novelty of his position, and he emphasizes this new starting point by means of a comparison. Just as his ancestors began their stories with the foundation of Rome, Biondo maintains that Renaissance historians begin theirs with its decline, in order to illustrate better the events that happened later, which they deemed magnificent and almost incredible. Fifteenth-century Romans had become what they were because of their unique ancestral heritage.[43] Moreover, for Biondo, the topic of decline allows for a better definition of his own times. That is, the humanists' deference toward antiquity does not mean slavish imitation of it; rather, the demise of ancient Rome was essential to the idea of the Renaissance itself.

Biondo also tries to set a date for the decline of the eastern part of the Roman Empire, but does not find anything so convenient or resounding as the sack of Rome in the West. He notices that many locate the beginning of the end in the imperial tenure of Heraclius, two hundred years after the attack on Rome. According to Biondo, however, the emperor had not started out too badly, having even recovered the fragment of the True Cross that had been captured by the Persians. That same year, Heraclius had reconquered all of northern Africa, with the exception of the Arabian peninsula, from which would come Islam, the greatest threat to the Christian world. In fact, although Biondo overtly attributes the emperor's death to his lust and senility, he implies that Heraclius's primary defect was his religious insincerity. The emperor's lack of true faith was crucial to the success of Islam; in Biondo's analysis, this shortcoming allowed Mohammed to preach and thus convert people, which led to the loss of much of Christianity's rightful inheritance.

Still, if the geographical magnitude of the *Decades* separates it from Biondo's previous works, where territorial unity only loosely derived from the Roman Empire, his overall approach remains consistent. The nations and people of the Roman Empire still constitute one unit even after the fall, held together as they were by the common heritage of Christianity. Within this expansive framework, Biondo's narrative ranges from events in Italian history to squabbles among the Franks and to the complicated circumstances of Byzantine history, where the Roman Empire still existed, at least nominally.[44] The consideration of such a wide geographical area, together with the scrupulous attention Biondo dedicates to his sources, is daunting,

43. *Ab urbe condita* ("since the foundation of the city" in 753 B.C.E.) was the usual prefix used by Roman historians.
44. In fact, the empire of the East was called Roman for many centuries.

to put it mildly. To lighten the burden, Biondo communicates to his readers that because part of France, Spain, Germany, Britain, and central Europe ceased to follow Roman jurisdiction, he has no obligation to consider the "decline of the empire" in those regions.[45] And for Biondo, in the final analysis, "Italy [was] the only province left from the former Roman Empire."[46]

The *Decades* do not ignore the conflicting imperial and papal claims to authority in the Christian West. Biondo does deal with the idea of *translatio imperii*, but its relevance is subordinated to the recounting of the relationship between successive popes and emperors. In fact, Pope Leo III bears responsibility for the crucial decision to bestow the imperial crown on a secular ruler, Charlemagne. Even before that, as Biondo mentions later in the work, Pope Hadrian had decided to transfer the Roman *imperium* (sovereignty) from Constantinople back to the West, with the approval of the clergy, the Roman people, and the more prominent Italians.[47] This claim is more startling than convincing, and is based on spurious evidence; it is, however, perfectly consistent with other claims made by Biondo regarding papal rights to lands and the Holy See's special jurisdiction.

The *Decades* offer the best opportunity to consider Biondo's use of his sources, because of the length of the work and the amount of time he spent on its composition. In addition to Livy, Biondo read and used almost all the classical Latin historians: Caesar, Tacitus, Sallust, Suetonius, and many of the later ones, especially Orosius.[48] He seized any chance to consult old documents, and his work in the Curia gave him the opportunity to read and incorporate the sources in the papal archives. This wealth of sources meant that Biondo often found contradictions and omissions; his dealings with them offered an interesting insight into his approach to the past. He casually condemns the most authoritative historians, like Procopius, because other authors closer to the events tell a different story. He lists the inconsistencies of his sources and refuses to reach a conclusion that cannot be proved: for example, who was pope when Emperor Otto II died. He discusses critically the negligence of an ancient copyist whose carelessness resulted in confusion between Popes Gregory II and III and in the misdating of a whole series of

45. Bk. vii, chap. xxvi; he was writing the history of the sixth century.
46. Third decade, bk. i.
47. Opening of bk. xiii.
48. He worked with more than fifty sources, including classical authors, medieval chronicles, papal privileges and registers, and archaeological material. Among the ancient authors, he did not use Ammianus Marcellinus; for an explanation of this exclusion, in a work otherwise so ecumenical, see Rita Cappelletto, *Recuperi Ammianei da Biondo Flavio* (Rome: Edizioni di storia e letteratura, 1983).

events. He seems consistently to prefer the sources that were the closest to the event, either geographically or chronologically.

He does, however, trustingly follow stories about saints, prophets, and miracles: if the Lateran librarian, one of his sources, reports that Pope Leo III had had his tongue cut off but miraculously had regained his speech, Biondo uncritically reports this tale. In the same vein, he does not hesitate to claim that certain defeats were signs of divine displeasure, as when a sudden storm destroyed a whole fleet of two thousand boats belonging to the iconoclast emperor Constantine. Biondo does not doubt the veracity of such extraordinary happenings. Similarly, when confronted with too much information, Biondo sounds a retreat. The histories he consulted overflow with descriptions of Lothar's impiety toward his father. But because these sources offer numerous conflicting reasons for Lothar's betrayal, Biondo believes it is better to omit them altogether.

The *primus omnium ex recentioribus* (the first of all moderns) was very much a man of his time.[49] He read and probed his sources to find a self-evident truth that could be checked against the facts, but he simultaneously worked on the assumption that Christianity was God's gift to undeserving humans. He accepted people's failings, even if the people were popes, and wanted to show them how to improve, but he did not doubt the right of the papacy to guide Christendom. He saw the history of humanity in its passing glories and appalling downfalls throughout the centuries but was sure that Rome and Italy would continue to bear the light of civilization in the future, just as they had in the past.

APPENDIX: FLAVIO BIONDO, THE DECADES OF HISTORY SINCE THE FALL OF THE ROMANS[50]

This is from the last section of the work, but the section Biondo chose to write first. He felt that this story of the tangled events, alliances, and betrayals that had shaped contemporary Italy had an important place in the larger history of western Europe. In fact, he explicitly stated that he wanted to write it first, to ensure its completion even in the event of his untimely death, which

---

49. Onofrio Panvinio, *Centum Libros Antiquitates*, written in the mid–sixteenth century but published only in the nineteenth century by Angelo Mai in *Spicilegium Romanum* (Rome: Typis Collegii Urbani, 1839).

50. This passage is translated from the 1559 Basle edition, Flavio Biondo, *Historiarum ab inclinatione Romanorum Decades* (Basle: Froben, 1559), 563, 564, 565.

could take him before his great work was finished. This decade deals with contemporary events in which Biondo himself played a role, and describes historical figures whom he knew intimately.

[In the battles of the years 1435–36, Niccolò Piccinino—Filippo Maria Visconti of Milan's general in his war against the papacy, Florence, Venice, and Francesco Sforza—had conquered some villages and castles in Romagna, where the Malatesta, previously in the service of Venice, had gone over to Piccinino's side because of a shortage of provisions and men.]⁵¹

Still Filippo [Maria Visconti] was mainly interested in keeping them [the Romagnole villages] out of the war, since at that same time he had to fight the Roman pontiff and his allies, Venice, Florence, and [Francesco] Sforza.⁵² Thus he thought that it would be enough of an advantage if he attacked the undefended Florentine people with his own troops. The fact was that the only commander of the Florentine cavalry in the field was [Pietro Gianpaolo] Orsini, and although his character was not warlike, he was nonetheless eager to stop Filippo Maria and his general. It was believed, just as we stated earlier concerning Piccinino's departure from Lombardy, that he sought nothing greater than that Sforza would fear the devastation of the countryside around Florence and in the March of Ancona, and thus break off the expedition to Brescia he was preparing and that was growing larger by the day. He would return, they believed, south of the Po. But it hardly seemed likely that Filippo, knowing that Sforza was an able general whose great army was growing daily, would foolishly endanger his own defenses, deprive his own territory of aid, and give up the siege of Brescia, which was on the verge of conclusion, in order to create devastation, no matter how great, in enemy territory unless there was some prospect of a city's defection to him or of some other likely outcome affecting the enemy. This was the opinion of the pontiff, preoccupied with Church matters, and also of the Florentines, who for a long time had feared the actions of their exiles.⁵³

51. Filippo Maria Visconti, duke of Milan (1392–1447), died without legitimate heir. His illegitimate daughter Bianca Maria was married to Francesco Sforza, who eventually seized power in Milan. The Malatesta were the lords of Rimini and Pesaro on the Adriatic coast. They lost their lands in the second half of the fifteenth century to the papacy, Francesco Sforza of Milan, and the Republic of Venice.

52. Francesco Sforza (1401–66), together with Niccolò Piccinino and Francesco Carmagnola, was the most successful and famous captain, or condottiere. His family traditionally had lands and political ties in Romagna and the March of Ancona. He eventually married Filippo Maria's illegitimate natural daughter and seized power in Milan in 1450.

53. The situation in Florence in the 1430s was highly unstable. Cosimo de' Medici had been sent into exile by the Albizzi faction in 1433, only to return triumphantly in 1434. He

It now came to light that what previously had been mere conjecture was evidently true. The [secret] support of the cardinal Florentine had kindled these hopes and bold plans of the duke of Milan and of Piccinino. The cardinal Florentine is the same Giovanni Vitelleschi, who, as we discussed much earlier, was from one of the first families of the town of Corneto. He had been an apostolic notary before the pope made him the bishop of Recanati and appointed him to conduct the war against Giacomo Vico, prefect of Rome, and Antonio Colonna, prince of Salerno. It was this same man who was appointed governor of the March of Ancona and ruled that province with arrogance and greed; and it could be said that he handed it over to Francesco Sforza rather than lost it by force. It was this man who had been made patriarch of Alexandria, charged with restoring order in the kingdom of Naples, but he brought only deep misery to that province. As a reward for his capture of the prince of Taranto [Antonio Orsini] he had been made cardinal. But he deserted his army that was besieging the town of Veglie in Puglia and, with a few of his men, sailed away to Venice. He enjoyed the pope's favor to such an extent that although the virtues by which he was distinguished (namely diligence and an efficient and—when he put his mind to it—prudent administration of affairs) were far surpassed by his enormous vices, yet the pontiff was never willing to listen to anyone who pointed them out, since he thought (and said so to anyone who accused him) that these claims were due to jealousy and the intrigues of those ill disposed to him, rather than products of sound judgment. Almost all the members of the Curia hated him, either out of jealousy of his influence or because of his ambitions to gain the papal throne through fair means or foul. The cardinal Florentine was raised far above the customary power of the Roman Church of our age: he was lord of the best defended strongholds of the Papal State, Soriano nel Cimino, Castelnuovo di Porto, Civitavecchia, and Ostia. He had an army of four thousand knights and two thousand infantry. And although he professed absolute obedience to the pope, he did not behave accordingly. He was so carried away by his own madness, he thought that so long as Pope Eugenius survived, he could steer and govern Italy as he pleased and that he could then succeed him as pope. It is believed that this was at the root of the man's insanity.

Vitelleschi initially hated the Venetians ardently because he had learned that the republic had once urged the pope not to associate with him because

---

then exiled his opponents. The fear of exiled political factions was always a real threat in Florence.

he was unworthy of friendship. And he hated the Florentines (who had supported him as his influence grew with the pope) because he had made enemies of them by extorting twenty thousand golden coins from them and by attacking Foligno. These matters seemed minor to Vitelleschi, who hated the two republics even more fiercely because they were allied with Sforza, toward whom he harbored a great enmity due to his defeat at Piceno. Hence, although he knew that, after the defeat received at his hands at Bologna and in Romagna, the pontiff considered Piccinino a bitter enemy, it is alleged that the latter had an understanding with the cardinal Florentine and that he had entered into a conspiracy against the two republics and Sforza. What we can say for certain is that, unknown to the pontiff, the cardinal Florentine engaged in clandestine communications with Piccinino through intermediaries. This is proved by letters exchanged between them that were intercepted by a Florentine magistrate at the city of Montepulciano [in southern Tuscany] and that were cloaked so skillfully in certain ciphers that no one could unriddle their concealed meanings.

The cardinal Florentine, after wintering with his army in Rome, decided to visit the magnificent palace he had built for himself in Corneto. On the first of April he informed the prefect of Castel Sant'Angelo that the next day he was going to cross Hadrian's Bridge and lead his army into Tuscany.[54] He was moving in support, since there were rumors that Piccinino was preparing to invade the Church's land there. The prefect was to come out to meet him, so that he could inform him as to the measures necessary for this purpose. Now, the prefect, a Paduan named Antonio Rido, did as he had arranged on the previous day with his close friend the patriarch of Aquileia, and met him on arrival, alone and unarmed, at the foot of the bridge. After greetings had been cordially exchanged on each side, and after he had spoken at length about the troops who were to guard the castle and the provision of military supplies to the cardinal, as [Vitelleschi] sat on his horse, the prefect walked alongside him, matching his steps to those of the slowly moving horse and keeping close to him, his hands touching the bridle, as if to ensure that the guards who preceded and followed him should not overhear him as he spoke. The conversation continued until they reached the last piling of the bridge, and just as the cardinal was preparing to turn left to go out by the brazen

54. Castel Sant'Angelo, the former mausoleum of the Roman emperor Hadrian (124–38 C.E.), changed its name in the seventh century, when Pope Boniface IV dedicated it to Sanctus Angelus inter Nubes. From 933 the castle was used by the party in charge of Rome to control the people. From the end of the fourteenth century it was held almost continually by the popes.

gate that leads to the suburbs of the Vatican, a portcullis, which for that purpose the prefect had surreptitiously hung above it, was suddenly released,
closing the gate. At the same moment, a chain that spanned the middle of
the bridge, set in a groove carved for that express purpose, and that they
had covered over with dust lest it be seen by those who passed over it, was
raised to a height of four cubits by weights hanging under the arch. These
the guards on the castle released by a rope attached to them, so that as they
plunged downward, they simultaneously raised the chain and stretched it
tight. "You are my prisoner!" cried the prefect, and held fast to the bridle.

The cardinal let out a roar. Drawing the sword strapped to his side and
spurring on his horse, he attempted to break free of the prefect's hands. Then
suddenly soldiers lying in wait appeared, who struck him with their hal-
berds, one on the neck, another on his sword arm as he raised it to strike,
the rest on either side. They set upon him, attacking him in a disorganized
mass, each aiming at a different part. The horse followed the lead of the
prefect as he tugged it, and the cardinal, wounded on the neck close by the
ear and on his right knee, was dragged into that enclosure in the fortifications whose walls bear inscriptions of the emperor Hadrian cut in marble
in enormous letters. The prefect calmed the tumult that the troops ahead
had begun to raise once they realized what had happened. He explained to
them that the deed had been carried out at the pontiff's order and displayed
from the walls the decrees that authorized it. Shortly after that, in an effort
to console the cardinal, who had had his wounds bound up and was lying
on an ornate litter, he told him to be of good cheer, predicting that he would
be released and could carry on his life—no longer under arms, to be sure,
but in retirement at the papal court. The cardinal, in words drawn (as it
seemed to those who saw it) from the very depths of his heart, replied in a
hoarse and constricted voice that it was not customary for those whose
greatness did not shrink from violence to be released when captured.[55]

News of this event swiftly spread through all of Italy, and since it was
clear to everyone that Piccinino had embarked on his expedition in expectation of the cardinal's support, it was generally assumed that he would
return to Lombardy to face Sforza by the same route by which he had come.
Instead, he marched on and assisted in the capture by Guidantonio [Man-
fredi], lord of Faenza, of certain fortified castles that the Florentines held
across the Apennines [in Romagna]—Rocca San Casciano, Portico, Monte-
vecchio, Tredozio, Oriola di Roncofreddo, and Modigliana. He then led his

---

55. Vitelleschi died the next day, April 2.

army to the Apennines, which were covered everywhere in deep snow, and since those places by which he had intended to cross were inaccessible, he continued his march.

In the meantime the Florentines were fully occupied with the recruiting of mercenaries. Foreigners were arriving from all places, and still the Florentines did not think there were enough of them, so they also recruited among their own subjects, paid them, and incorporated them among the veterans. Also, the Florentines pleaded with Sforza to support them and to send them some soldiers so that they could better defend themselves; likewise they sent urgent pleas to the pope to summon the army accustomed to fight for the cardinal Florentine. For although the approach of Piccinino's well-equipped enemy terrified them and they had never previously been so unprepared, they feared still more greatly the exiles [from the Albizzi faction] whom he brought with him.

Then the pope, fearing for himself and his cardinals (since it was clear that they, as much as the Florentines, were Piccinino's target), did what he had never previously been convinced to do, no matter what reverses he had suffered at the hands of Filippo and Piccinino: he made a treaty with his military allies. Each promised to make common cause in war and peace everywhere outside Lombardy and to defray a third of the expenses for the pope's four thousand cavalry and two thousand foot soldiers. Luigi [Scarampo], the patriarch of Aquileia, was deputed to lead the troops to Florentine territory and dispatched to Rome in place of the captured cardinal Florentine.[56] With him as their leader, on the day following the cardinal's death, the troops moved out from the winter quarters they had been occupying in Latium and on the outskirts of the city.

Piccinino, in order to cross the Apennines, was busying himself in all the places that lie between the valleys of the Savio and of the Lamone Rivers and the tops of the valleys.[57] Meanwhile, the Florentines placed Nicola Pisano, Sforza's former lieutenant (who happened to have arrived in Florence without a commission) at the head of the mercenary force. They appointed Bartolomeo Orlandino, a citizen of knightly rank, leader of the Tuscan recruits. Pisano thereupon crossed the Apennines and, falling upon Piccinino, who was then besieging the castle of Premilcuore, dislodged him, inflicting no

56. Ludovico Trevisan (1401–65), also known, from the seventeenth century, as Ludovico or Alvise Scarampi. Before his election he had been the doctor of Cardinal Condulmer. When he became pope, Trevisan made an impressive career leading the papal armies more than once, becoming patriarch of Aquileia and, in 1440, cardinal of San Lorenzo in Damaso.
57. Valleys leading into Tuscany from Cesena and the Romagna.

small losses on him in the process. The following day he repelled Piccinino's attempt to climb the hills leading to the pass of San Benedetto, which is an easier route than the others into Tuscany. At that point Piccinino, aiming to make the crossing at a distance from an enemy whose prowess he had experienced on the Benaco, made his way to the Lamone valley.

Book I of the Third Decade[58]

At this point, I was happy and elated to have recovered and brought to light in twenty books one thousand years of history, which is now no longer concealed and buried. I thought that when I put in order a certain sequence of events, I could proceed more easily to narrate the notable history of our times, but numerous issues came up that none of those who had written during more fortunate centuries had taken into account. Although up to that time I had labored to clarify various and obscure traditions, I was now compelled to consider the properties of words and the Latin language itself.

For in past times profound changes were made in the public administration of Italian provinces and cities, in private life, but even more in the way wars were fought. Hence, those [expressions] that came very easily and were used daily by the antique writers proved to be largely useless for us.[59] And yet if we are bound by the rules of eloquence, we cannot abandon them. For truly a desire for the eloquence of those happier times has been rekindled in our own time after being abandoned for many centuries. Our contemporaries desire the eloquence and the style of Livy, Julius Caesar, Sallust, Curtius, Tacitus, Suetonius, and Justin even if little remains to our days of Livy's and Sallust's works.

One should actually consider calmly how rarely in these past thousand years anybody has written Latin, much less with elegance. In fact none of these written remains should be called history, nor has anyone desired to write such a thing. So at the present time, we alone must take up the burden such that elegant Latin can be preserved free of the barbarity and utter impropriety of modern words. Of course, there will be times when circumlocutions might help, but if one must understand singular events that really are unique, such a change in meaning of words would take place that if I attempted to explain the event with ancient words, I myself would not understand what I had written when I reread my own words. If, on the other hand, I were to write in our contemporary style, then the prose would come

58. Biondo, *Decades*, 293–94.
59. The Latin shifts from the first-person singular to the first-person plural throughout the passage.

out distorted and move readers to nausea and anger. Here are a few examples from the many I could mention. What should we call him who leads in war, whether he manages his own or mercenary troops? If in the ancient manner I call him *imperator* [emperor], I would put him in the place we have given to Caesar.[60] Then again, were I to call him "captain," I would need to add "general," to distinguish him from all the other captains that command other troops, towns, and fortresses. Again, if I were to call him *duce,* I would create uncertainty as to his position and could not distinguish him from the many who are today the lords of provinces or cities.[61] Who can read without annoyance about the same combatant with two names, or the absurd substitution of the names of saints or hills they now have for the names of castles, fortresses, and cities? For truly we do not believe it is possible that anyone can compose an elegant speech if talking of Pietro Giovanni, Paolo Orsini, Gianfrancesco Gonzaga, or of a captain general, of a hill called Santa Maria in Giorgio, a fortification named San Giovanni in Persiceto, or things like that.[62] There would be too many absurdities when writing of a troop review, of construction of fortresses, of assaults and battles. In fact, nobody asks youths to take oaths anymore or distributes the army in legions, cohorts, and maniples.[63] They adopt these words as a form of ornate writing to attract the reader through examples of virtues by using words drawn from the poets. No one fortifies a single point any more, but rather they spread troops in villages and under tents. They do not fortify with palisades and trenches, so that in a conflict, if an enemy does break through, hoping to decide the fight, they can flee and re-form themselves a short distance away. In assaults on fortresses, moreover, our contemporaries are no less able than our ancestors. Therefore, the new devices created by

60 *Imperatore* is the ablative of *imperator,* "emperor." However, the passage makes sense only in Latin, where it plays on the different meanings of the same word. In the time of the Roman republic, the work indicated the victorious general (or one who has the power of command); in Biondo's time, it was the title of the Holy Roman Emperor.

61 Again, the confusion is understandable only in Latin: the *dux* was a leader, and the word was prevalently used by Cicero to mean a military commander. During the Middle Ages, the position of *dux* had evolved to fill a leadership that was both military and civil. The term is the Latin root both of the word "duke" and on the title of the Venetian leader, the doge. Eventually, the progressive autonomy of some of these "dukes" had allowed them to create small states. In Biondo's times, Federico da Montefeltro, duke of Urbino, was repeatedly at the head of different Italian armies. Hence, he happened to be both a duke and a *dux,* but this accident did not seem to have made an impression on any of his contemporaries, who were presumably less etymologically minded than Biondo.

62 These are examples of some modern names that Biondo had to use when writing about his own times.

63 Names of different units of infantry in the Roman army.

men should get new names. Readers would be offended if they did not read about *arietem, fallaricam,* scorpions, and *fundas* [in an account of a battle], and they would even think that there had been no assault or a completely insignificant one.[64] Those who would read carefully present-day accounts will be pleased by the contrast between the inventiveness and energy of our contemporaries and the expertise and bravery of our ancestors. Although our contemporaries dig tunnels, divert watercourses, create parapets, wickerworks, mantelets, siege shelters, towers, and castles, for these and others we use words we share with the ancients. And if we find that the name has changed, we describe it. But we call "bombard" the new device that the Germans supplied to the Venetians, who used it against the Genoese in the War of Chioggia. Writers tolerated with equanimity the clumsiness of the word because of its great utility.[65] Who in fact would not read willingly, and admire eagerly, an instrument from molten bronze or iron, long like a piece of cane, that could propel into the air stones weighing six or seven hundred pounds just by the pressure caused by a fire of sulfurous powders and vapors inside? These instruments can smash walls and knock down the most solid constructions with less effort than a battering ram. It can be operated by a single workman, assisted by two servants, behind a shield protecting them against the enemy missiles.

Certainly the use of this device was not known in the ancient world. It suffices to read Julius Caesar and Sallust very diligently, or Vegetius and Frontinus, who wrote four centuries after them, to find nothing but leather straps for hurling stones, military engines to take out stones, catapults, staff-slings, and war machines to throw stones. These weapons threw both small and large stones from wooden bases, or by means of a wooden arm constructed by craftsmen and hitched to the ground with ropes, as we can still see from the images of them, shown in the triumphal marble bas-reliefs that are all around the town.

Indeed we might read that Marcus Regulus carried to Rome the skin of a great serpent that measured 120 feet. The snake had been killed not far from Bragada [in Portugal] when its spine was broken by a wall stone shot from a siege engine that loosened the joints of the animal's body. It has also been written that, when they were close to Marseilles, Caesar's soldiers used

64 *Arietem* was the battering ram; *fallaricam* was an engine to throw stones that had three-foot-long iron extremities; *fundas* were slingshots. For the scorpion, see the following paragraphs.

65 Apparently it was very well tolerated. The "new" Latin word "bombard" was the immediate source of the term in English, Italian, and French.

such big siege engines to throw stones that as a result the javelins themselves became misshapen. Although the variety of thrown objects was so great, people who read history could easily understand everything that we mentioned earlier except the slingstone. As a consequence, I think that in our time it has turned out that the kind of catapult the ancients called a scorpion misuse by posterity now calls a ballista, [which properly refers to] an engine to throw stones. On the contrary, the name "scorpion" ought to be saved for this machine, because the bow in its form recalls Scorpio's claws, the spring is like the wound up length of the body, and the hook hanging from the spring is like the scorpion's twisted tail. Yet, because this one-thousand-year-old misapplication continues, we persist in calling the scorpion a ballista.

On the other hand, what elegant prose might we bestow on our contemporary warfare that [truly] resembles adolescent games? That in which no order is maintained cannot be described using the vocabulary customary to the ancients. For [today the soldiers only] fight after having been given the sign for the battle to start: the heads of their spears are not arranged in order, but the fighting is scattered among clots of three or four soldiers in a few places. The men watch [to see] which army seems likely to win; then [those on losing side] run away fast, while the winners are satisfied that they managed to repel the enemy, and proceed to return to their own country. If victory ensues, [the soldiers] seize the horses and the baggage as plunder of the unbroken enemy. Even if there is a confrontation with a large gathering of forces, we see that great armies are routed or captured without any bloodshed, or perhaps with just one out of every one thousand men being killed.[66]

---

66 Compare this passage with later reflection on fifteenth-century warfare: "But were they playing at war, as Machiavelli suggested, too concerned about conserving their limited resources and too interested in easy loot to risk serious battles?" Michael Mallet, "The Condottiere," in *Renaissance Characters*, ed. Eugenio Garin (Chicago and London: University of Chicago Press, 1991), 39.

BIBLIOGRAPHY

Ackroyd, Peter. *London: The Biography.* New York: Nan A. Talese, 2000.

Albanese, Gabriella. "Per la storia della fondazione del genere novella tra volgare e latino, edizioni di testi e problemi critici." *Medioevo e Rinascimento*, n.s., 9 (1998): 263–84.

Albertini, Francesco. *Opusculum de mirabilibus novae & veteris urbis Romae.* In *Five Early Guides to Rome and Florence*, edited by Peter Murray. Farnborough: Gregg, 1972.

Albertus de Bezanis. *Alberti de Bezanis abbatis S. Laurentii Cremonensis Cronica pontificum et imperatorum.* In *MGH: Scriptores rerum Germanicarum in usum scholarum separatim editi,* [3,] edited by Oswald Holder-Egger. Hanover and Leipzig: Hahn, 1908.

Alexandri Telesini Abbatis Ystoria Rogerii Regis Sicilie Calabrie atque Apulie. Edited by Ludovica de Nava. Commentary by Dione Clementi. Fonti per la storia d'Italia, 112. Rome: Istituto storico italiano per il Medio Evo, 1991.

Amari, Michele, comp. *Bibliotheca Arabo-Sicula.* 2 vols. Turin: E. Loescher, 1880–81.

Andenna, Giancarlo. "Il concetto geografico-politico di Lombardia nel Medioevo." In *Comuni e signorie nell'Italia settentrionale: La Lombardia*, edited by Giancarlo Andenna et al., UTET: Storia d'Italia, 6:3–20. Turin: UTET, 1998.

———. *Storia della Lombardia medievale.* Turin: UTET, 1999.

Andenna, Giancarlo, and Renata Salvarani, eds. *Deus non voluit: I lombardi alla prima crociata, 1100–1101; Dal mito alla ricostruzione della realtà.* Milan: Vita e pensiero università, 2003.

Andreolli, Bruno, et al., eds. *Repertorio della cronachistica emiliano-romagnola (secc. IX–XV).* Nuovi studi storici, 11. Rome: Istituto storico italiano per il Medio Evo, 1991.

Annales Bergomates. Edited by Philipp Jaffé. In *MGH: Scriptores*, 18:809–10. Hanover: Hahn, 1863.

Annales Brixienses. Edited by Ludwig Bethmann. In *MGH: Scriptores*, 18:811–20. Hanover: Hahn, 1863.

Annales Cremonenses. Edited by Oswald Holder-Egger. In *MGH: Scriptores*, 31:1–21. Hanover: Hahn, 1903.

Annales et Notae Parmenses et Ferrarienses. Edited by Philipp Jaffé. In *MGH: Scriptores*, 18:660–799. Hanover: Hahn, 1863.

Annales Mantuani. Edited by Philipp Jaffé. In *MGH: Scriptores,* 19:19–31. Hanover: Hahn, 1866.

Annales Mediolanenses minores. Edited by Philipp Jaffé. In *MGH: Scriptores*, 18:383–402. Hanover: Hahn, 1863.

Annales Mediolanensis. RIS, 16. Milan: Società Palatina, 1730.

Annales Placentini (Annales Gibellini). Edited by Philipp Jaffé. In *MGH: Scriptores,* 18:457–581. Hanover: Hahn, 1863.

Annali genovesi di Caffaro e dei suoi continuatori. Translated by Giovanni Monleone. Vol. 8, *Jacopo Doria.* Genoa: Municipio di Genova, 1930.

Anonimo Cumano. *La guerra dei milanesi contro Como (1118-1127).* Translated by Enrico Besta. Milan: A. Giuffrè, 1985.

Anonymus Novocomensis, Cumanus sive Poema de bello et excidio urbis Comensis (1118-1127). RIS, 5. Milan, 1724.

Aquilecchia, Giovanni. "Dante and the Florentine Chroniclers." *Bulletin of the John Rylands Library* 48 (1965-66): 30-55.

Arnaldi, Girolamo. "Andrea Dandolo doge-cronista." In *La storiografia veneziana,* 127-268.

———. "Annali, cronache, storie." In *Lo spazio letterario del Medioevo,* sect. 1, *Il Medioevo latino,* edited by Guglielmo Cavallo, Claudio Leonardi, and Enrico Menestò, vol. 1, *La produzione del testo,* pt. 2, 463-513. Rome: Salerno, 1993.

———. "Cronache con documenti, cronache 'autentiche' e pubblica storiografia." In *Fonti medioevali e problematica storiografica,* 1: 351-74. Rome: Istituto storico italiano per il Medio Evo, 1976. (Reprinted in *Storici e storiografia del Medioevo italiano,* edited by Gabriele Zanella, 111-37. Bologna: Pàtron editore, 1984.)

———. "Il notai-cronista e le cronache cittadine in Italia." In *La storia del diritto nel quadro delle scienze storiche,* 293-309. Florence: Leo S. Olschki, 1966.

———. *Studi sui cronisti della Marca trevigiana nell'età di Ezzelino da Romano.* Istituto storico italiano per il Medio Evo: Studi storici, 48-50. Rome: Istituto Palazzo Borromini, 1963.

Azario, Pietro. *Liber Gestorum in Lombardia. RIS,* n.s., 16, pt. 4. Edited by Francesco Cognasso. Bologna: Nicola Zanichelli, 1925-39.

Baldassarri, Stefano Ugo, and Arielle Saiber, eds. *Images of Quattrocento Florence.* New Haven and London: Yale University Press, 2000.

Banti, Ottavio, and Maria Laura Testi Cristiani. *Le illustrazioni delle Croniche nel codice lucchese.* Accademia lucchese di scienze, lettere, arti: Studi e testi, 10. Genoa: Silvio Basile editore, 1978.

Baron, Hans. *The Crisis of the Early Italian Renaissance: Civic Humanism and Republican Liberty in an Age of Classicism and Tyranny.* Rev. ed. Princeton: Princeton University Press, 1966.

Bejczy, István. *Erasmus and the Middle Ages: The Historical Consciousness of a Christian Humanist.* Leiden and Boston: Brill, 2001.

Belgrano, Luigi Tommaso, and Cesare Imperiale di Sant'Angelo, eds. *Annali genovesi di Caffaro e de' suoi continuatori dal MXCIX al MCCXCIII.* Fonti per la storia d'Italia, 11-14bis. 5 vols. Rome: Tipografia del Regio istituto sordomuti, 1890-1929.

Bentley, Jerry H. *Politics and Culture in Renaissance Naples.* Princeton: Princeton University Press, 1987.

Bierce, Ambrose. *The Collected Works of Ambrose Bierce.* Vol. 7. New York and Washington, D.C.: Neale Publishing Company, 1911.

Biglia, Andrea. "In exequiis Iohannes Galeatii Vicecomitis ducis Mediolani laudatio funerea." *RIS,* 19:9-158. Milan: Società Palatina, 1731.

Biondo, Flavio. *Historiarum ab inclinatione Romanorum Decades.* Basle: Froben, 1559.

———. *Scritti inediti e rari di Biondo Flavio.* Edited by Bartolomeo Nogara. Studi e testi, 48. Rome: Tipografia poliglotta vaticana, 1927.

Black, Jane W. "The Limits of Ducal Authority: A Fifteenth-Century Treatise on the Visconti and Their Subject Cities." In *Florence and Italy: Renaissance Studies in Honour of Nicolai Rubinstein*, edited by Peter Denley and Caroline Elam, 149–60. London: Westfield College, 1988.

Bongi, Salvatore. *Inventario del R. Archivio di Stato in Lucca*. 4 vols. Lucca: Tipografia Giusti, 1892.

Bonvesin de la Riva. "De magnalibus urbis Mediolani." Edited by Francesco Novati. *Bullettino dell'Istituto storico italiano per il Medio Evo* 20 (1898): 61–176.

———. *Le meraviglie di Milano*. Translated by Giuseppe Pontiggia. Milan: Bompiani, 1974.

Bordone, Renato. "L'età dei comuni." In *Comuni e signorie nell'Italia settentrionale: La Lombardia*, edited by Giancarlo Andenna et al., UTET: Storia d'Italia, 7:327–84. Turin: UTET, 1998.

———. *Memoria del tempo e comportamento cittadino nel Medioevo italiano*. Turin: Scriptorium, 1997.

Bornstein, Daniel. *The Bianchi of 1399: Popular Devotion in Late Medieval Italy*. Ithaca: Cornell University Press, 1993.

Brown, Horatio. *Studies in the History of Venice*. 2 vols. New York: E. P. Dutton & Co., 1907.

Brown, Thomas S. "The Political Use of the Past in Norman Sicily." In *The Perception of the Past in Twelfth-Century Europe*, edited by Paul Magdalino, 191–210. London and Rio Grande, Ohio: Hambledon Press, 1992.

Brucker, Gene. *The Civic World of Early Renaissance Florence*. Princeton: Princeton University Press, 1977.

———. "The Ghibelline Trial of Matteo Villani." *Medievalia et Humanistica* 13 (1960): 48–55.

Bruni, Leonardo. "The Dialogues." In *The Humanism of Leonardo Bruni: Selected Texts*. Translated by Gordon Griffiths, James Hankins, and David Thompson, 63–84. Binghamton, N.Y.: Renaissance Society of America, 1987.

———. *Epistolarum libri VIII*. Edited by Lorenzo Mehus. Florence: Paperini, 1741.

———. *Historiarum florentini populi libri XII*. Edited by Emilio Santini. *RIS*, n.s., 19, pt. 3. Città di Castello: S. Lapi, 1914–26.

———. *History of the Florentine People*. Vol. 1. Edited and translated by James Hankins. Cambridge, Mass.: Harvard University Press, 2001.

———. *Panegyric to the City of Florence*. Translated by Benjamin G. Kohl. In *The Earthly Republic*, edited by Benjamin G. Kohl and Ronald G. Witt, 135–75. Philadelphia: University of Pennsylvania Press, 1978.

Bueno de Mesquita, Daniel M. *Giangaleazzo Visconti*. Cambridge: Cambridge University Press, 1941.

Burr, David. *The Spiritual Franciscans: From Protest to Persecution in the Century After Saint Francis*. University Park: Pennsylvania State University Press, 2001.

Cabrini, Anna Maria. *Un'idea di Firenze: Da Villani a Guicciardini*. Rome: Bulzoni, 2001.

Caenegem, R. C. van. *Guide to the Sources of Medieval History*. Amsterdam: North-Holland Publishing Company, 1978.

Caferro, William. *Mercenary Companies and the Decline of Siena*. Baltimore and London: Johns Hopkins University Press, 1998.

Cameron, Averil. "Remaking the Past." In *Interpreting Late Antiquity*, edited by Glenn W. Bowersock, Peter Brown, and Oleg Grabar, 1–20. Cambridge, Mass.: Harvard University Press, 2001.

Campi, Antonio. *Cremona fedelissima città*. Cremona, 1585.

Canning, Joseph. *The Political Thought of Baldus de Ubaldis*. Cambridge: Cambridge University Press, 1987.

Capo, Lidia. Pts. 4–7 of "I cronisti di Venezia e della Marca Trevigiana nel secolo XIV." By Girolamo Arnaldi and Lidia Capo. In *Storia della cultura veneta*, vol. 2, *Il Trecento*, 290–337. Vicenza: Neri Pozza, 1976.

Cappelletto, Rita. *Recuperi Ammianei da Biondo Flavio*. Rome: Edizioni di storia e letteratura, 1983.

Cardini, Franco. *Il Barbarossa: Vita, trionfi e illusioni di Federico imperatore*. Milan: A. Mondadori, 1985.

Carile, Antonio. "Aspetti della cronachistica veneziana nei secoli XIII e XIV." In *La storiografia veneziana*, 75–126.

Le carte cremonesi dei secoli VIII–XII. Edited by Ettore Falconi. 4 vols. Cremona: Biblioteca statale di Cremona, 1979–88.

Castner, Catherine J. "Direct Observation and Biondo Flavio's Additions to *Italia Illustrata*: The Case of Ocriculum." *Medievalia et Humanistica*, n.s., 25 (1998): 93–108.

Ceriotti, Giancarlo. "Interpretazione storica di Fra Jacopo Bussolaro." *Bollettino della Società pavese di storia patria* 24 (1972): 3–34.

Cermenate, Giovanni. *Historia Iohannis de Cermenate, Notarii Mediolanensis*. Edited by Luigi Alberto Ferrai. Rome: Forzani, 1889.

Cherubini, Giovanni. *Signori, contadini, borghesi: Ricerche sulla società italiana del basso Medioevo*. Florence: La nuova Italia, 1974.

Chiesa, Paolo, ed. *Le cronache medievali di Milano*. Milan: Vita e pensiero, 2001.

Chronicon Marchiae Tarvisinae et Lombardiae. Edited by L. A. Botteghi. *RIS*, 8, pt. 3. Città di Castello: S. Lapi, 1916.

Cicero. *De oratore*. Translated by E. W. Sutton and H. Rackham. Cambridge, Mass.: Harvard University Press, 1988.

Cielo, Luigi R. *L'abbaziale normanna di S. Salvatore de Telesia*. Naples: Edizioni scientifiche italiane, 1995.

Civiltà comunale: Libro, scrittura, documento. Atti della Società ligure di storia patria, n.s., 29 (103), fasc. 2. Genoa: Società ligure di storia patria, 1989.

Clementi, Dione R. "Alexandrini Telesini 'Ystoria Serenissimi Rogerii Primi Regis Siciliae,' Lib. IV.6–10. (Twelfth-Century Political Propaganda)." *Bullettino dell'Istituto storico italiano per il Medioevo* 77 (1965): 105–26.

Cochrane, Eric. *Historians and Historiography in the Italian Renaissance*. Chicago: University of Chicago Press, 1981.

Codice diplomatico verginiano. Edited by Placido Mario Tropeano et al. 11 vols. Montevergine: Edizioni Padri Benedettini, 1977–98.

Coleman, Edward. "Cities and Communes." In *Italy in the Central Middle Ages: 1000–1300*, edited by David Abulafia, The Shorter Oxford History of Italy, 2:27–57. Oxford: Oxford University Press, 2003.

———. "The Italian Communes: Recent Work and Current Trends." *Journal of Medieval History* 25 (1991): 375–81.

Coleman, Janet. *Ancient and Medieval Memories.* Cambridge: Cambridge University Press, 1992.

Collodo, Silvana. *Una società in trasformazione: Padova tra XI e XV secolo.* Padua: Editore Antenore, 1990.

Conversini da Ravenna, Giovanni. *De primo eius introitu ad aulam.* In *Two Court Treatises,* edited and translated by Benjamin G. Kohl and James Day, 22–83. Munich: Wilhelm Fink Verlag, 1987.

———. *Dragmalogia de Eligibili Vite Genere.* Edited and translated by Helen Lanneau Eaker, introduction and notes by Benjamin G. Kohl. Lewisburg, Pa.: Bucknell University Press, 1980.

Cortese, Libia, and Dino Cortese, eds. *Giovanni Conversini di Ravenna, 1343–1408: L'origine della famiglia di Carrara e il racconto del suo primo impiego a corte.* Padua: Centro studi Antoniano, 1980.

Cortesi, Paolo. *De cardinalatu.* Castro Cortesiano: Symeon Nicolai Nardi senensis, alias Rufus Calchographus imprimebat, 1510.

Cortusi, Guglielmo. *Chronica de novitatibus Padue et Lombardie.* Edited by Beniamino Pagnin. *RIS,* n.s., 12, pt. 5. Bologna: Zanichelli, 1941.

Coulton, G. G. *From St. Francis to Dante.* 2nd ed. Introduction by Edward Peters. Philadelphia: University of Pennsylvania Press, 1972.

Cracco, Giorgio. "Il pensiero storico di fronte ai problemi del comune veneziano." In *La storiografia veneziana,* 45–74.

Crema 1185: Una contrasta autonomia politica e territoriale. Crema: Biblioteca comunale di Crema, 1988.

Dale, Sharon. "Contra damnationis filios: The Visconti in Fourteenth-Century Papal Diplomacy." *Journal of Medieval History* 33 (2007): 1–32.

Daniel, E. Randolph. "The Double Procession of the Holy Spirit in Joachim of Fiore's Understanding of History." *Speculum* 55 (1980): 469–83.

Davis, Charles T. "Topographical and Historical Propaganda in Early Florentine Chronicles and in Villani." *Medioevo e Rinascimento* 2 (1988): 35–51.

Del Monte, Alberto. "La storiografia fiorentina dei secoli XII e XIII." *Bullettino dell'Istituto storico italiano per il Medio Evo* 62 (1950): 175–282.

Dotson, John E., ed. and trans. *Merchant Culture in Fourteenth-Century Venice: The Zibaldone da Canal.* Binghamton, N.Y.: Medieval and Renaissance Texts and Studies, 1994.

———. "Naval Strategy in the First Genoese-Venetian War, 1257–1270." *American Neptune* 46 (1986): 84–90.

———. "Venice, Genoa, and Control of the Seas in the Thirteenth and Fourteenth Centuries." In *War at Sea in the Middle Ages and the Renaissance,* edited by John B. Hattendorf and Richard Unger, 119–35. Woodbridge, Suffolk, and Rochester, N.Y.: Boydell Press, 2003.

Dykmans, Marc, ed. *Les sermons de Jean XXII sur la vision béatifique.* Miscellanea Historiae Pontificiae, 34. Rome: Gregorian University Press, 1973.

Epstein, Steven A. *Genoa and the Genoese, 958–1528.* Chapel Hill and London: University of North Carolina Press, 1996.

Esposito, Anna. "La minor parte di questo popolo sono i romani." In *Effetto Roma: Romababilonia,* 41–60. Rome: Bulzoni, 1993.

Fabris, Giovanni. *Cronache e cronisti padovani.* Padua: Rebellato Editore, 1977.

Face, Richard D. "Secular History in Twelfth-Century Italy: Caffaro of Genoa." *Journal of Medieval History* 6, no. 2 (1980): 169–84.

Falcone di Benevento. *Chronicon Beneventanum*. Edited by Edoardo D'Angelo. Florence: SISMEL edizioni del Galluzzo, 1998.

Fasoli, Gina. "I fondamenti della storiografia veneziana." In *La storiografia veneziana*, 11–44.

Fentress, James, and Chris Wickham. *Social Memory*. Oxford and Cambridge, Mass.: Blackwell, 1992.

Ferrai, Luigi Alberto. "Gli annali mediolanensis e i cronisti Lombardi." *Archivio storico lombardo* 7 (1890): 277–313.

———. "Le cronache de Galvano Fiamma e le fonti della *Galvagnana*." *Bullettino dell'Istituto storico italiano* 10 (1891): 93–128.

Fiamma, Galvano. *Opusculum de rebus gestis ab Azone, Luchino et Iohanne vicecomitibus ab a. 1328 ad a. 1342. RIS*, n.s., 12, pt. 4. Edited by Carlo Castiglioni. Bologna: Nicola Zanichelli, 1938.

Finucane, Ronald C. *Miracles and Pilgrims: Popular Beliefs in Medieval England*. London: J. M. Dent, 1977.

Fissore, Gian Giacomo. "Alle origini del documento comunale: Rapporti fra i notai e l'istituzione." In *Civiltà comunale: Libro, scrittura, documento*, 99–128.

Fubini, Riccardo. "All'uscita dalla scolastica medievale: Salutati, Bruni, e i *Dialogi ad Petrum Histrum*." *Archivio storico italiano* 150 (1992): 1065–1103.

———. "Biondo Flavio." In *Dizionario biografico degli italiani*, 10:536–59. Rome: Istituto dell'enciclopedia italiana, 1968.

———. "Cultura umanistica e tradizione cittadina nella storiografia fiorentina del '400." In *La storiografia umanistica*, 1, pt. 1, 399–443. Messina: Sicania, 1992.

———. *Italia quattrocentesca*. Milan: Franco Angeli, 1994.

———. "Osservazioni sugli *Historiarum florentini populi libri XII* di Leonardo Bruni." In *Studi di storia medievale e moderna per Ernesto Sestan*, 1:403–48. Florence: Leo S. Olschki, 1980.

———. "La rivendicazione di Firenze della sovranità statale e il contributo delle *Historiae* di Leonardo Bruni." In *Leonardo Bruni cancelliere della Repubblica di Firenze*, edited by Paolo Viti, 29–60. Florence: Leo S. Olschki, 1990.

Fueter, Eduard. *Storia della storiografia moderna*. Translated by Altiero Spinelli. Milan: Ricciardi, 1970.

Gargan, Luciano. "Il preumanesimo a Vicenza, Treviso, e Venezia." In *Storia della cultura veneta*, vol. 2, *Il Trecento*, 142–70. Vicenza: Neri Pozza, 1976.

Garin, Eugenio. *Ritratti di umanisti*. Florence: Sansoni, 1967.

Gatto, Ludovico. "Il sentimento cittadino nella 'Cronica' di Salimbene." In *La coscienza cittadina nei comuni italiani del Duecento*, Convegno del Centro di studi sulla spiritualità medievale, 11:365–94. Todi: Accademia Tudertina, 1972.

Gentili, Bruno, and Giovanni Cerri. *History and Biography in Ancient Thought*. Amsterdam: J. C. Gieben, 1988.

Gesta magnifica domus carrariensis. Edited by Roberto Cessi. *RIS*, n.s., 17, pt. 1, vol. 2. Bologna: Zanichelli, 1942–48.

Giardina, Andrea, and André Vauchez. *Il mito di Roma: Da Carlo Magno a Mussolini*. Rome: Editori Laterza, 2000.

Gibbon, Edward. *The History of the Decline and Fall of the Roman Empire*. London: Printed for W. Strahan and T. Cadell, 1776–88.

Gilbert, Felix. "Biondo, Sabellico, and the Beginnings of Venetian Official Historiography." In *Florilegium Historiale: Essays Presented to Wallace K. Ferguson*, edited by John Gordon Rowe and W. H. Stockdale, 275–93. Toronto: University of Toronto Press, 1971.

———. *Machiavelli and Guicciardini: Politics and History in Sixteenth-Century Florence*. Princeton: Princeton University Press, 1965.

Giovanni Sercambi e il suo tempo. Lucca: Biblioteca statale and Archivio arcivescovile, 1991.

Given-Wilson, Chris. *The Chronicle of Adam Usk, 1377–1421*. Oxford: Clarendon Press, 1997.

———. *Chronicles: The Writing of History in Medieval England*. London and New York: Hambledon, 2004.

Goetz, Hans-Werner. *Geschichtsschreibung und Geschichtsbewusstsein im hohen Mittelalter*. Berlin: Akademie Verlag, 1999.

Gorni, G. "Il 'Liber Pergaminis' di Mosé di Brolo." *Studi medievali*, 3rd ser., 11 (1970): 407–39.

Grant, Lindy. *Abbot Suger of St. Denis: Church and State in Early Twelfth-Century France*. London and New York: Longman, 1998.

Green, Louis. *Castruccio Castracani: A Study on the Origins and Character of a Fourteenth-Century Italian Despotism*. Oxford and New York: Clarendon Press and Oxford University Press, 1985.

———. *Chronicle into History: An Essay on the Interpretation of History in Florentine Fourteenth-Century Chronicles*. Cambridge: Cambridge University Press, 1972.

———. "Galvano Fiamma, Azzo Visconti, and the Revival of the Classical Theory of Magnificence." *Journal of the Warburg and Courtauld Institutes* 53 (1990): 98–113.

Grubb, James. "Memory and Identity: Why Venetians Didn't Keep Ricordanze." *Renaissance Studies* 8 (1994): 375–87.

Guenée, Bernard. *Histoire et culture historique dans l'Occident médiéval*. Paris: Aubier Montaigne, 1980.

Hay, Denys. *Annalists and Historians: Western Historiography from the Eighth to the Fifteenth Century*. London: Methuen, 1977.

———. "Flavio Biondo and the Middle Ages." *Proceedings of the British Academy* 45 (1959): 97–128.

Heninger, S. K. *Touches of Sweet Harmony: Pythagorean Cosmology and Renaissance Poetics*. San Marino, Calif.: Huntington Library, 1974.

Hoffmann, Hartmut. "Hugo Falcandus und Romuald von Salerno." *Deutsches Archiv für Erforschung des Mittelalters* 23 (1967): 117–70.

———. "Langobarden, Normannen, Päpste: Zur Legitimationsproblem in Unteritalien." *Quellen und Forschungen aus italienischen Archiven und Bibliotheken* 58 (1978): 137–80.

Hood, Gwenyth E. "Falcandus and Fulcaudus, 'Epistola ad Petrum, Liber de Regno Sicilie': Literary Form and Author's Identity." *Studia medievali*, 3rd ser., 49 (1999): 1–41.

Hörnqvist, Mikael. "The Two Myths of Civic Humanism." In *Renaissance Civic*

Humanism, edited by James Hankins, 105–42. Cambridge: Cambridge University Press, 2000.

Houben, Hubert. *Roger II of Sicily: A Ruler Between East and West.* Translated by Graham A. Loud and Diane B. Milburn. Cambridge: Cambridge University Press, 2002.

Hugo Falcandus. *La historia o Liber de Regno Sicilie e la Epistola ad Petrum Panormitane Ecclesie Thesaurarium di Ugo Falcando.* Edited by Giovanni Battista Siragusa. Fonti per la storia d'Italia, 22. Rome: Istituto storico italiano per il Medio Evo, 1897.

———. *The History of the Tyrants of Sicily by "Hugo Falcandus," 1154–69.* Translated by Graham A. Loud and Thomas E. J. Wiedemann. Manchester: Manchester University Press, 1998.

Hyde, John Kenneth. "Guglielmo Cortusi." In *Dizionario biografico degli italiani,* 29:806–7. Rome: Istituto dell'enciclopedia italiana, 1983.

———. "Italian Social Chronicles in the Middle Ages." *Bulletin of the John Rylands Library* 49 (1966): 107–32.

———. *Literacy and Its Uses: Studies on Late Medieval Italy.* Edited by Daniel Waley. Manchester: Manchester University Press, 1993.

———. *Padua in the Age of Dante.* Manchester: Manchester University Press, 1966.

Ianziti, Gary. *Humanistic Historiography Under the Sforzas: Politics and Propaganda in Fifteenth-Century Milan.* Oxford: Oxford University Press, 1988.

Ignoti Monachi Cisterciensis S. Mariae de Ferraria Chronica et Ryccardi de Sancto Germano Chronica priora. Edited by Augusto Gaudenzi. Naples: F. Giannini, 1888.

Jamison, Evelyn M., ed. *Catalogus Baronum.* Rome: British School at Rome, 1972.

Jorga, Nicolae. *Notes et extraits pour servir à l'histoire des croisades au xve siècle.* 3 vols. Paris: E. Leroux, 1899–1902.

Kelley, Donald R. *Faces of History: Historical Inquiry from Herodotus to Herder.* New Haven and London: Yale University Press, 1998.

———. "Humanism and History." In *Renaissance Humanism: Foundations, Forms, and Legacy,* edited by Albert Rabil Jr., vol. 3, *Humanism and the Disciplines,* 236–70. Philadelphia: University of Pennsylvania Press, 1988.

Kohl, Benjamin G. "Giovanni Conversini da Ravenna." In *Dizionario biografico degli italiani,* 28:574–78. Rome: Istituto dell'enciclopedia italiana, 1983.

———. *Padua Under the Carrara, 1318–1405.* Baltimore and London: Johns Hopkins University Press, 1998.

———. "Petrarch's Preface to *De Viris Illustribus.*" *History and Theory* 13 (1974): 132–44.

———. "Valerius Maximus in the Fourteenth Century: The Commentary of Giovanni Conversini da Ravenna." In *Acta Conventus Neo-latini Hafniensis,* edited by Rhoda Schnur et al., 537–46. Binghamton, N.Y.: Medieval and Renaissance Texts and Studies, 1994.

———. "The Works of Giovanni di Conversino da Ravenna: A Catalogue of Manuscripts and Editions." *Traditio* 31 (1975): 349–67.

Krautheimer, Richard. *Rome, Profile of a City (312–1308).* Princeton: Princeton University Press, 1980.

LaCapra, Dominick. "Rethinking Intellectual History and Reading Texts." *History and Theory* 19 (1980): 245–76.

Lanzillotta, Maria Accame. *Contributi sui "Mirabilia Urbis Romae."* Genoa: D.AR.FI.CL.ET, Dipartimento di archeologia, filologia classica e loro tradizioni "Francesco della Corte," 1996.

Lee, Egmont. "Foreigners in Quattrocento Rome." *Renaissance and Reformation*, n.s., 7 (1983): 135–46.

Lefèvre-Pontalis, Germain, and León Dorez, eds. *Chronique d'Antonio Morosini: Extraits relatifs à l'histoire de France.* 4 vols. Paris: Librairie Renouard, 1898–1902.

Little, Lester K. "Salimbene." In *Dictionary of the Middle Ages,* edited by Joseph R. Strayer. New York: Scribner, 1982–89.

Loud, Graham A. *The Age of Robert Guiscard: Southern Italy and the Norman Conquest.* Harlow, Essex, and New York: Longman, 2000.

———. *Conquerors and Churchmen in Norman Italy.* Aldershot: Ashgate, 1999.

———. "Continuity and Change in Norman Italy: The Campania During the Eleventh and Twelfth Centuries." *Journal of Medieval History* 22 (1996): 313–43.

———. "The Genesis and Context of the Chronicle of Falco of Benevento." In *Anglo-Norman Studies, xv: Proceedings of the Battle Conference, 1992,* edited by Marjorie Chibnall, 177–98. Woodbridge: Boydell Press, 1993.

———. *Montecassino and Benevento in the Middle Ages: Essays in South Italian Church History.* Aldershot: Ashgate, 2000.

———. "William the Bad or William the Unlucky? Kingship in Sicily, 1154–1166." *Haskins Society Journal* 8 (1999, for 1996): 99–113.

Luzzati, Michele. *Giovanni Villani e la compagnia dei Buonaccorsi.* Rome: Istituto dell'enciclopedia italiana, 1971.

Madden, Thomas. *Enrico Dandolo and the Rise of Venice.* Baltimore and London: Johns Hopkins University Press, 2002.

Magenta, Carlo. *I Visconti e gli Sforza nel Castello di Pavia.* 2 vols. Milan: Hoepli, 1883.

Mai, Angelo. *Spicilegium Romanum.* Rome: Typis Collegii Urbani, 1839.

Maire-Vigueur, Jean Claude, ed. *I podestà dell'Italia comunale,* pt. 1, *Reclutamento e circolazione degli ufficiali forestieri (fine XII secolo–metà XIV secolo).* Rome: Istituto storico italiano per il Medio Evo, 2000.

Mallet, Michael. "The Condottiere." In *Renaissance Characters,* edited by Eugenio Garin, 23–45. Chicago and London: University of Chicago Press, 1991.

Marchente, Carmela. *Ricerche intorno al "De principibus Carrariensibus et gestis eorum liber" attribuito al Pier Paolo Vergerio.* Padua: CEDAM, 1946.

Matthew, Donald J. A. "Maio of Bari's Commentary on the Lord's Prayer." In *Intellectual Life in the Middle Ages: Essays Presented to Margaret Gibson,* edited by Lesley Smith and Benedicta Ward, 119–44. London and Rio Grande, Ohio: Hambledon, 1992.

Maurisio, Gerardo. *Chronica dominorum Ecelini et Alberici.* Edited by Giovanni Soranzo. *RIS,* 8, pt. 4. Città di Castello: S. Lapi, 1914.

McCormick, Michael. *Les annales du haut Moyen Âge.* Typologie des sources du Moyen Âge occidental, 14. Turnhout: Brepols, 1975.

McGinn, Bernard. *The Calabrian Abbot: Joachim of Fiore in the History of Western Thought.* New York: Macmillan, 1985.

McManamon, John M., S.J. *Pierpaolo Vergerio the Elder: The Humanist as Orator.* Medieval and Renaissance Texts and Studies, 163. Tempe, Ariz.: Medieval and Renaissance Studies, 1996.

Meek, Christine. *Lucca, 1369–1400: Politics and Society in an Early Renaissance City-State.* Oxford and New York: Oxford University Press, 1978.

———. "Il tempo di Giovanni Sercambi." In *Giovanni Sercambi e il suo tempo*, 1–30.

Meiss, Millard. *Painting in Florence and Siena After the Black Death.* New York: Harper, 1964.

Miglio, Massimo. *Storiografia pontificia del Quattrocento.* Bologna: Patròn, 1975.

Mollat, G[uillaume]. *The Popes at Avignon, 1305–1378.* Translated by Janet Love from the 9th French ed. London: Thomas Nelson & Sons, 1963.

Momigliano, Arnaldo. *Essays in Ancient and Modern Historiography.* Oxford: Blackwell, 1977.

Moorman, John R. H. *A History of the Franciscan Order from Its Origins to the Year 1517.* Oxford: Clarendon Press, 1968.

Morigia, Buonincontro. *Chronicon Modoetiense. RIS*, 12: cols. 1061–184. Milan: Società Palatina, 1728.

Morosini, Giovanni. *The Morosini Codex.* Edited and translated by Michele Pietro Ghezzo, John R. Melville-Jones, and Andrea Rizzi. Vols. 1–2. Padua: Uni-Press, 1999–2001.

Moskowitz, Anita Fiderer. *Italian Gothic Sculpture, c. 1250–c. 1400.* Cambridge: Cambridge University Press, 2001.

Muffel, Nikolaus. *Descrizione della città di Roma nel 1452.* With Italian translation and commentary by Gerhard Wiedmann. Bologna: Pàtron, 1999.

Muratori, Ludovico. *Annali d'Italia, dal principio dell'era volgare sino all'anno 1500.* Rome: Appresso gli eredi Barbiellini mercanti di libri, 1744–49.

Murray, Peter. *Five Early Guides to Rome and Florence.* Farnborough, Hampshire: Gregg, 1972.

Mussis, Johanne de. *Chronicon Placentinum. RIS*, 16. Milan: Società Palatina, 1730.

Najemy, John. "*Arti* and *Ordini* in Machiavelli's *Istorie Fiorentine*." In *Essays Presented to Myron P. Gilmore*, edited by Sergio Bertelli and Gloria Ramakus, 1:161–91. Florence: La nuova Italia, 1978.

Nardella, Cristina. *Il fascino di Roma nel Medioevo: Le "Meraviglie di Roma" di maestro Gregorio.* Rome: Viella, 1997.

Nelli, Sergio, and Maria Trapani. "Giovanni Sercambi: Documenti e fatti della vita familiare e sociale." In *Giovanni Sercambi e il suo tempo*, 33–100.

Nicholson, Peter. "The Two Versions of Sercambi's *Novelle*." *Italica* 53 (1976): 201–13.

Nissen, Christopher. Review of Giovanni Sercambi's *Novelle*, edited by Giovanni Sinicropi (1995). *Italica* 74 (1997): 423–25.

Nuti, Giovanni. "Iacopo Doria." In *Dizionario biografico degli italiani*, 41:391–96. Rome: Istituto dell'enciclopedia italiana, 1992.

Offler, Hilary S. "Empire and Papacy: The Last Struggle." *Transactions of the Royal Historical Society*, 5th ser., 6 (1956): 21–47.

Orderic Vitalis. *The Ecclesiastical History of Orderic Vitalis.* Edited by Marjorie Chibnall. 6 vols. Oxford: Clarendon Press, 1969–81.

Orosius, Paulus. *The Seven Books of History Against the Pagans*. Translated by Roy J. Deferrari. Washington, D.C.: Catholic University of America Press, 1964.

Ortalli, Gherardo. "Cronache e documentazione." In *Civiltà comunale: Libro, scrittura, documento*, 507–39.

Ottonis Morenae et continuatorum historia Frederici I. Edited by Ferdinand Güterbock. In *MGH: Scriptores rerum Germanicarum in usum scholarum*, n.s., 7. Berlin: Weidmann, 1930.

Pagden, Anthony. "Rethinking the Linguistic Turn: Current Anxieties in Intellectual History." *Journal of the History of Ideas* 49 (1988): 519–29.

Paoli, Marco. "I codici." In *Giovanni Sercambi e il suo tempo*, 193–240.

Partner, Peter. *The Lands of St. Peter*. Berkeley and Los Angeles: University of California Press, 1972.

Patavino, Rolandino. *Cronica in factis et circa facta Marchie Trivixane*. Edited by Antonio Bonardi. *RIS*, 8, pt. 1. Città di Castello: S. Lapi, 1906.

Patrologiae cursus completus: Series Latina (PL). Edited by J.-P. Migne. Paris, 1844–91.

Petti Balbi, Giovanna. "Caffaro." In *Dizionario biografico degli italiani*, 16:256–60. Rome: Istituto dell'enciclopedia italiana, 1973.

———. *Caffaro e la chronachista Genovese*. Genoa: Tilgher, 1982.

Phillips, Mark S. "Machiavelli, Guicciardini, and the Tradition of Vernacular Historiography in Florence." *American Historical Review* 84 (1979): 86–105.

Piccolomini, Enea Silvio (Pope Pius II). *Commentarii rerum memorabilium*. Edited by Luigi Totaro. 2 vols. Milan: Adelphi, 1984.

Plaissance, Michel. "Les rapports ville-campagne dans les nouvelles de Sacchetti, Sercambi et Sermini." In *Culture et société en Italie du Moyen-Âge à la Renaissance: Hommage à André Rochon*, Centre interuniversitaire de recherche sur la Renaissance italienne, 13:61–67. Paris: Université de la Sorbonne nouvelle, 1985.

Polybius. *The Histories*. Translated by W. R. Paton. 6 vols. Cambridge, Mass.: Harvard University Press, 1922–27.

Popolo e stato in Italia nell'età di Federico Barbarossa: Alessandria e la lega lombarda. Turin: Deputazione subalpina di storia patria, 1970.

Porta, Giuseppe. "La costruzione della storia in Giovanni Villani." In *Il senso della storia nella cultura medievale italiana (1100–1350)*, 125–38. Pistoia: Centro italiano di studi di storia e d'arte, 1995.

———. "Giovanni Villani storico e scrittore." In *I racconti di Clio: Tecniche narrative della storiografia*, 147–56. Pisa: Nistri-Lischi, 1989.

Possenti, Furio. *La poesia nelle croniche di Giovanni Sercambi*. Accademia lucchese di scienze, lettere ed arti: Studi e testi, 8. Lucca, 1974.

Ragone, Franca. "Le 'croniche' di Giovanni Sercambi: Composizione e struttura dei prologhi." *Annali dell'Istituto italiano per gli studi storici* 9 (1985–86): 5–34.

Reeves, Marjorie. "Joachimist Expectations in the Order of Augustinian Hermits." *Recherches de théologie ancienne et médiévale* 25 (1958): 111–41.

Reichenmiller, M. "Bisher unbekannte Traumerzählungen Alexanders von Telese." *Deutsches Archiv für Erforschung des Mittelalters* 19 (1963): 339–52.

Repertorium Fontium Historiae Medii Aevi. Vol. 2. Rome: Istituto storico italiano per il Medio Evo, 1967.

Robey, David. "P. P. Vergerio the Elder: Republicanism and Civic Values in the Work of an Early Humanist." *Past and Present* 58 (1973): 3–37.

Robinson, Ian S. *The Papacy, 1073–1198: Continuity and Innovation.* Cambridge: Cambridge University Press, 1990.

Rogerii II Regis Diplomata Latina. Edited by Carl-Richard Brühl. Codex Diplomaticus Regni Sicilae, 2:1. Cologne: Böhlau, 1987.

Romano, Giacinto. "Eremitani e canonici regolari in Pavia nel secolo XI e loro attinenze con la storia cittadina." *Archivio storico lombardo* 4 (1895): 5–42.

Romualdi Salernitani Chronicon. Edited by Carlo Alberto Garufi. *RIS,* n.s., 7, pt. 1. Città di Castello: Stamperia S. Lapi, 1935.

Rösch, Gerhard. "The Serrata of the Grand Council and Venetian Society, 1286–1323." In *Venice Reconsidered: The History and Civilization of an Italian City-State, 1297–1797,* edited by Dennis Romano and John Martin, 67–88. Baltimore and London: Johns Hopkins University Press, 2000.

Rovere, Antonella. "I 'libri iurium' dell'Italia comunale." In *Civiltà comunale: Libro, scrittura, documento,* 157–99.

Rubinstein, Nicolai. "The Beginnings of Political Thought in Florence." *Journal of the Warburg and Courtauld Institutes* 5 (1942): 198–227.

Sabbadini, Remigio. *Giovanni da Ravenna, figura insigne d'umanista (1343–1408).* Como: Tipografia editrice Ostinelli, 1924.

Salimbene de Adam. *The Chronicle of Salimbene de Adam.* Translated by Joseph L. Baird, Giuseppe Baglivi, and John Robert Kane. Medieval and Renaissance Texts and Studies, 40. Binghamton, N.Y.: Medieval and Renaissance Texts and Studies, 1986.

———. *Cronica.* Edited by Giuseppe Scalia. 2 vols. Scrittori d'Italia, nos. 232–33. Bari: Laterza, 1966.

———. *Cronica a. 1168–1287.* Edited by Giuseppe Scalia. Corpus Christianorum, Continuatio Mediaevalis, 75. 2 vols. Turnhout: Brepols, 1998–99.

Salwa, Piotr. "Retorica e politica—croniche e novelle di Giovanni Sercambi, lucchese." In *Renaissance Studies in Honor of Craig Hugh Smyth,* edited by Andrew Morrogh, 1:465–79. Florence: Giunti Barbèra, 1985.

Santini, Emilio. "La fortuna della storia fiorentina di L. Bruni." *Studi storici* 20 (1911): 177–95.

Scavo, Rosanna. *Storia della storiografia: Dalle cronache comunali all'illuminismo.* Bari: Archivio di stato, 1998.

Schmeidler, Bernhard, ed. *Die Annalen des Tholomeus von Lucca in doppelter Fassung, nebst Teilen der Gesta Florentinorum und Gesta Lucanorum.* In *MGH: Scriptores rerum germanicarum,* n.s., 8. Berlin: Weidmannsche Buchhandlung, 1955.

Sercambi, Giovanni. *Le croniche di Giovanni Sercambi, lucchese.* Edited by Salvatore Bongi. Istituto storico italiano: Fonti per la storia d'Italia, 19–21. Lucca: Tipografia Giusti, 1892.

———. *Novelle.* Edited by Giovanni Sinicropi. 2 vols. Bari: Laterza, 1972.

———. *Novelle.* Edited by Giovanni Sinicropi. 2 vols. Florence: Le lettere, 1995.

———. *Il novelliere.* Edited by Luciano Rossi. 3 vols. Rome: Salerno editrice, 1974.

Settia, Aldo A. *Comuni in guerra: Armi ed eserciti nell'Italia delle città.* Bologna: CLUEB, 1993.

Sicardi Episcopi Cremonensi Cronica. Edited by Oswald Holder-Egger. In *MGH: Scriptores*, 31:22–183. Hanover: Hahn, 1903.

Sinicropi, Giovanni. "Giovanni Sercambi, *Nota ai Guinigi*, testo critico, introduzione e note." *Momus* 3–4 (1995): 7–45.

Skinner, Quentin. *The Foundations of Modern Political Thought*. Vol 1, *The Renaissance*. Cambridge and New York: Cambridge University Press, 1978.

Smalley, Beryl. *Historians in the Middle Ages*. London: Thames & Hudson; New York: Charles Scribner's Sons, 1974.

Southern, Richard. "Aspects of the European Tradition of Historical Writing." *Transactions of the Royal Historical Society*, 5th ser., 20 (1970): 173–96; 21 (1971): 159–79; 22 (1972): 159–79.

Spiegel, Gabrielle. *The Past as Text: The Theory and Practice of Medieval Historiography*. Baltimore: Johns Hopkins University Press, 1997.

Stinger, Charles L. "Roman Humanist Images of Rome." In *Roma capitale (1447–1527)*, edited by Sergio Gensini, 17–38. San Miniato: Pacini, 1994.

La storiografia veneziana fino al secolo XVI: Aspetti e problemi. Edited by Agostino Pertusi. Florence: L. S. Olschki, 1970.

Stroll, Mary. *The Jewish Pope: Ideology and Politics in the Papal Schism of 1130*. Leiden: E. J. Brill, 1987.

Struever, Nancy S. "The Study of Language and the Study of History." *Journal of Interdisciplinary History* 4 (1974): 401–15.

Supplementum Annalium Cremonensium. Edited by Oswald Holder-Egger. In *MGH: Scriptores*, 31:184–88. Hanover: Hahn, 1903.

Tacchini, Gualtiero. *San Lanfranco Beccari: Vescovo di Pavia, 1180–1198*. Pavia: Giovane Artigiano, 1998.

Takayama, Hiroshi. *The Administration of the Norman Kingdom of Sicily*. Leiden: E. J. Brill, 1993.

Tori, Giorgio. "Profilo di una carriera politica." In *Giovanni Sercambi e il suo tempo*, 101–34.

Travaini, Lucia. *La monetazione nell'Italia normanna*. Rome: Istituto italiano per il Medio Evo, 1995.

Ullman, Berthold L. "Leonardo Bruni and Humanistic Historiography." In *Studies in the Italian Renaissance*, 2nd ed., 321–43. Rome: Edizioni di storia e letteratura, 1973. (Originally published in *Medievalia et Humanistica* 4 [1946]: 45–61.)

Die Urkunden Friedrichs I. Edited by Heinrich Appelt et al. In *MGH: Die Urkunden der deutschen Könige und Kaiser*, 10, pts. 1–5. Hanover: Hahn, 1975–90.

Die Urkunden und Briefe der Markgräfin Mathilde von Tuszien. In *MGH: Laienfürsten- und Dynastenurkunden der Kaiserzeit*, 2, edited by Elke Goetz and Werner Goetz. Hannover: Hahnsche, 1998.

Varanini, Gian Maria. "Propaganda dei regimi signorili: Le esperienze venete del Trecento." In *Le forme della propaganda politica nel Due e nel Trecento*, edited by Paolo Cammarosano, 313–43. Rome: École française de Rome, 1994.

Vasoli, Cesare. "Leonardo Bruni." In *Dizionario biografico degli italiani*, 14:621–23. Rome: Istituto dell'enciclopedia italiana, 1972.

Vergerio, Pier Paolo. *De principibus Carrariensibus et gestis eorum liber*. Edited by Attilo Gnesotto. *Atti e memorie della R. Accademia di scienze, lettere ed arti in Padova* 41 (1924–25): 327–475. (Reprinted, with Italian translation and commentary, as *Liber de principibus Carrariensibus et gestis eorum incipit feliciter.* Fasano, Brindisi: Schena, 1997.)

Vignati, Cesare. *Storia diplomatica della lega lombarda.* Milan: P. Agnelli, 1866.

Villani, Giovanni. *Nuova cronica.* Edited by Giuseppe Porta. 3 vols. Parma: Fondazione Pietro Bembo, 1990–91.

Villani, Matteo. *Cronica con la continuazione di Filippo Villani.* Edited by Giuseppe Porta. 2 vols. Parma: Fondazione Pietro Bembo, 1995.

Visceglia, Maria Antonietta. *La città rituale.* Rome: Viella, 2002.

Volpe, Gioacchino. *Studi sulle istituzioni comunali a Pisa: Città e contado, consoli e podestà, secoli XII–XIII.* New ed. Introduction by Cinzio Violante. Florence: G. C. Sansoni, 1970.

Voltmer, Ernst. *Il carroccio.* Turin: Einaudi, 1994.

Walsh, P. G. *Livy: His Historical Aims and Methods.* Cambridge: Cambridge University Press, 1970.

White, Hayden V. *The Content of the Form: Narrative Discourse and Historical Representation.* Baltimore: Johns Hopkins University Press, 1987.

———. *Metahistory: The Historical Imagination in Nineteenth-Century Europe.* Baltimore: Johns Hopkins University Press, 1973.

Wickham, Chris J. *Land and Power: Studies in Italian and European Social History, 400–1200.* London: British School at Rome, 1994.

Wilcox, Donald J. *The Development of Florentine Humanist Historiography in the Fifteenth Century.* Cambridge, Mass.: Harvard University Press, 1969.

Witt, Ronald G. *Hercules at the Crossroads: The Life, Works, and Thought of Coluccio Salutati.* Durham, N.C.: Duke University Press, 1983.

———. *"In the Footsteps of the Ancients": The Origins of Humanism from Lovato to Bruni.* Leiden: Brill, 2000.

Zabbia, Marino. *I notai e la cronachistica cittadina italiana nel Trecento.* Istituto storico italiano per il Medio Evo: Nuovi studi storici, 49. Rome: Istituto Palazzo Borromini, 1999.

Zanella, Gabriele. *Storici e storiografia del Medioevo italiano.* Bologna: Pàtron editore, 1984.

Ziese, Jürgen. *Wibert von Ravenna: Der Gegenpapst Clemens III. (1084–1100).* Stuttgart: A. Hiersemann, 1982.

CONTRIBUTORS

Edward Coleman is Lecturer in the School of History and Archives, University College Dublin. His research interests are focused principally on the political and social history of the north Italian city-communes in the twelfth and thirteenth centuries; in particular, such topics as power and authority, representation, civic identity, and historical writing. His recent publications include "Representative Assemblies in Communal Italy," in P. S. Barnwell and M. Mostert, eds., *Political Assemblies in the Earlier Middle Ages* (Turnhout, 2003); "Sicard of Cremona as Legate of Innocent III in Lombardy," in A. Sommerlechner, ed., *Innocenzo III. Urbs et Orbis*, 2 vols. (Rome, 2003); and "Cities and Communes," in D. Abulafia, ed., *Italy in the Central Middle Ages*, The Shorter Oxford History of Italy, vol. 2 (Oxford, 2004). He is currently completing a monographic study of the city of Cremona in the Communal period and co-editing a volume of essays on the subject of "Travel and Movement in Medieval and Renaissance Italy."

Paula C. Clarke is Associate Professor of History at McGill University. She has published various studies on fifteenth-century Italy, including *The Soderini and the Medici: Power and Patronage in 15th-century Florence* (Oxford, 1991), and, in collaboration with Elisabetta Barile and Giorgia Nordio, *Cittadini veneziani del Quattrocento: I due Giovanni Marcanova, il mercante e l'umanista* (Venice, 2006).

Sharon Dale is Associate Professor of Art History at the Behrend College of the Pennsylvania State University at Erie. Her research interests center on the intersection of cultural and political history in Late Medieval Italy. Her publications include "Contra Damnationis Filios: The Visconti in Fourteenth-Century Papal Diplomacy," *Journal of Medieval History* 33 (2007); "Baldo degli Ubaldi and the Infeudation of Biscina: The Original Bulls Rediscovered," in Carla Frova, Maria Grazia Nico Ottaviani, and Stefania Zucchini, *VI centenario della morte di Baldo degli Ubaldo 1400–2000* (Perugia: Università degli Studi, 2005); and "To the Victors Goes the Hagiography: The Frescoes at Montesiepi and the Vitae Galgani," *Cîteaux, commentarii cistercienses* 48 (1997). She is presently completing a book on Visconti Lombardy.

John Dotson is Professor Emeritus of History at Southern Illinois University in Carbondale. He specializes in the maritime and naval history and the social history of business of Medieval and Renaissance Genoa and Venice. He has edited and translated two volumes of documents: *Merchant Culture in Fourteenth Century Venice: The Zibaldone da Canal* (1994) and *Christopher Columbus and His Family: The Genoese and Ligurian Documents* (Aldo Agosto, Textual Editor, 1998). He has also written numerous articles and chapters on maritime, naval, and business history. He is presently working on Italian sea power in the Medieval Mediterranean.

Gary Ianziti is Associate Professor of History in the School of Humanities and Human Services Queensland University of Technology. A specialist in Renaissance historiography, he is author of *Humanistic Historiography under the Sforzas: Politics and Propaganda in Fifteenth Century Milan;* "A Life in Politics: Leonardo Bruni's Cicero," *Journal of the History of Ideas* 61 (2000); "Storici, mandanti, materiali nella Milano sforzesca, 1450–1480," in *Il principe e la storia;* and "Historiography and its Discontents: The Windshuttle Gambit," *History Australia* 2 (2005).

Benjamin G. Kohl is Professor Emeritus of History at Vassar College, Poughkeepsie, New York, where he taught Medieval and early modern history from 1966 to 2001. Among his recent publications are *Padua under the Carrara, 1318–1405* (1998); *Culture and Politics in Early Renaissance Padua* (2001); and *The Records of the Venetian Senate on Disk, 1335–1400* (2001). He is currently at work with a team of scholars funded by the Delmas Foundation on an electronic data bank of the noble officeholders of Venice in the later Middle Ages, entitled *Rulers of Venice, 1332–1524,* and scheduled for publication in 2008.

Alison Williams Lewin is Associate Professor of History at Saint Joseph's University in Philadelphia, addressing in her courses questions of political legitimacy and cultural manifestations of power. Her first book, *Negotiating Survival: Florence and the Great Schism, 1378–1417,* led her to the chronicle of Bindino da Travale and the works of other contemporary chroniclers. She has completed a translation of Bindino's chronicle and is beginning a new project, *Perceptions and Realities of Aging in the Italian Renaissance.*

Graham A. Loud is Professor of Medieval Italian History at the University of Leeds, where he has taught since 1978. His principal field of research is on the history of southern Italy and Sicily from the tenth to the thirteenth centuries, and especially its ecclesiastical and social history. Among his books are *Church and Society in the Norman Principality of Capua, 1058–1197* (1985); *The Age of Robert Guiscard. Southern Italy and the Norman Conquest* (2000); and English translations of the "History of the Tyrants of Sicily" by the so-called Hugo Falcandus (1998, with Thomas Wiedemann) and the "History of the Normans" by Amatus of Montecassino (2004, with Prescott Dunbar). His newest book, *The Latin Church in Norman Italy*, was published by Cambridge University Press in the autumn of 2007.

John R. Melville-Jones, Professor of Classics and Ancient History, University of Western Australia, is a numismatist and Byzantinist with a special interest in the relationship between Byzantium and Venice. His publications include a two-volume work on Ancient Greek coinage, *Testimonia Numaria*, 1993 and 2007, and a two-volume collection of accounts of the Venetian occupation of Thessalonica entitled *Venice and Thessalonica 1423–1430* (2002 and 2006). He has been working for some years to publish the largest surviving Venetian chronicle, the *Cronaca Morosini*, which is the main focus of the chapter written by him for this volume.

Duane J. Osheim is Professor of History at the University of Virginia whose research interests have concentrated on late Medieval social and institutional history. He is author or editor of *An Italian Lordship, the Bishopric of Lucca in the Late Middle Ages* and *An Italian Monastery and its Social World: San Michele di Guamo*. He is presently at work on rumors of plague in Renaissance Italy.

Nicoletta Pellegrino is a Ph.D. candidate in the Department of History at New York University with a special interest in the Renaissance Italian Church. She has written "Tutti gli uomini del papa: le istruzioni di Ercole Gonzaga al nipote," in Laura Fortini, ed., *Un'idea di Roma: Società, arte e cultura tra Umanesimo e Rinascimento* (Roma: Roma nel Rinascimento, 1993) and "Nascita di una 'burocrazia': Il cardinale nella trattatistica del XVI secolo," in Cesare Mozzarelli, ed., *"Familia" del principe e famiglia aristocratica* (Roma: Bulzoni, 1988).

INDɛX

Page numbers in *italics* refer to translated excerpts.

LaVergne, TN USA
02 June 2010
184614LV00001B/205/P